**C**HRIS CARTER CLAIMS that *The Night Stalker* inspired his series, but what were the real origins? What shows come far closer to the spirit of *The X-Files*?

**H**OW SIMILAR ARE Duchovny and Anderson to the characters they play?

**W**HY DID DUCHOVNY'S relationship with Perrey Reeves, the woman who supported him through his years as a struggling young actor, end up on the rocks?

*If this discovery is confirmed, it will surely be one of the most stunning insights into our universe that science has ever uncovered. Its implications are as far-reaching and awe-inspiring as can be imagined. I am determined the American space program will put its full intellectual power and technological prowess behind the search for further evidence of life on Mars.*

—President Clinton, 1996

# THE UNAUTHORIZED
# GUIDE TO THE
# X-FILES™

## HAL SCHUSTER

PRIMA PUBLISHING

*The X-Files* is a trademark of Twentieth Century Fox.

This book was not prepared, approved, licensed, or endorsed by any entity involved in creating or producing the *X-Files* television series.

Photographs on pages 5, 11, 57, and 65 printed with permission of AP/Wide World Photos.

PRIMA PUBLISHING and colophon are registered trademarks of Prima Communications, Inc.

Library of Congress Cataloging-in-Publication Data on File
ISBN 0-7615-0845-7

97 98 99 00 01 GG 10 9 8 7 6 5 4 3 2 1
Printed in the United States of America

HOW TO ORDER:

Single copies may be ordered from Prima Publishing, P.O. Box 1260BK, Rocklin, CA 95677; telephone (916) 632-4400. Quantity discounts are also available. On your letterhead, include information concerning the intended use of the books and the number of books you wish to purchase.

Visit us online at http://www.primapublishing.com

# CONTENTS

ACKNOWLEDGMENTS    VIII

PREFACE    IX

### PART I

## THE MAKING OF THE X-FILES    1

*How did an ex-surfer create such a popular series?*
*What crises were faced and solved along the way?*
*The background and history of the series revealing the creative and*
*acting talent, explaining the origins of the series, and showing how*
*critics, the industry, and viewers reacted. Plus a surprising look*
*at the real origins of* The X-Files.

1. The Man Behind The X-Files: Creator Chris Carter    3

2. Opening the Files: Creating and Producing the Series    8

3. Year One    20

4. Year Two    26

5. Year Three    34

6. Year Four    39

7. Children of The X-Files    41

8. Precursors to The X-Files    47

## PART II

# THE CAST OF THE X-FILES 51

*Why did David Duchovny and Gillian Anderson accept their roles in
The X-Files after swearing never to do series television?
Revealing biographies of Duchovny and Anderson, an in-depth look at the
characters they play, and biographies of the supporting cast and characters.*

9.  Gillian Anderson    53
10. Special Agent Dana Katherine Scully    60
11. David Duchovny    62
12. Special Agent Fox William Mulder    72
13. The Other Players    75

## PART III

# EPISODE GUIDE 83

*How many mistakes appear in an average episode of The X-Files?
What in-jokes were included to keep the viewers attentive?
And how do all the conspiracies fit together?
A guide to the episodes and a look at how each show ties into the overall
mythos. SNAFUS, in-jokes, and interesting facts about each episode
revealed. Plus a special look at the conspiracies.*

14. Season One    85
15. Season Two    95
16. Season Three    108
17. Season Four    120
18. Conspiracy    123

## PART IV

# THE WORLD OF THE X-FILES 127

*How can you help search for the truth?
The world of X-Philes fandom.*

19. The X-Philes    129
20. Novels, Comics, and More    133
21. The X-Files Jokebook    140

## PART V
# APPENDIXES 143

A. The Federal Bureau of Investigation 145

B. Real-Life X-Files and the Organizations That Investigate Them 158

C. For Further Sleuthing 198

D. Addresses 217


BIBLIOGRAPHY 219

INDEX 222

# ACKNOWLEDGMENTS

Thanks to Somjitra and Noom, David and Mark, Peter and Lori, Paul and Sarah, Benjawan and Craig, Michael and Michelle, and Paula and Jennifer. Netpicking thanks to Kymberlee Ricke. Additional thanks to Bill Van Heerden, Paula Vitaris, Pat Gonzales, Brian Lowry, Mark Owen, Bob Potter, Shadow, Alex, Boz, Nic Hibberd, Steven Herod, Ronald de Graaf, Rhea Tla Virginia, Rhea Merana, the Nussbaum Family, Anthony, Elias, Katrina McDonnell, Luke, Alexander Lum, Scott Lindsay, Barney O'Borg, Mark Ottow, the Weasel, Grace, the digit, Michael Ahern and Ralph Baldino, Ryan Bloom, Darren Terry, Paula Vitaris, Rydeen Alley, Tony J. Boatright, Jen Grady, Jesse Dubus, John Donald, Brian Lentz, Collin Magennnis, Robert Green, Deanna and Craig, Jeannine F. Delwiche, Velvet, Ronnie Chen, Patrick Lee, Dana D., Luke E, Ronnie Chen, Liz Kyonka, Lawrence Sufrin, Bob Shier, Debrah, Geoffrey Funnell, Joe Gottman Bill Cobb, Karla Jameson, Rutger van Bergen, Antje Reinecke, Mary Israel, Constantine Rye, Gary Villa, Dave Winter, Cristina, Greg Barnes, Danny Nicholson, Melanie Oh, Stephan Roy, Wanda Beers, Paul Rydeen, Paul Rydeen, Stephanie, Richard Burr, Andrew Chong, Rod Oto, Martine, Leikin Sky, Henry Lee, Jo Holloway, Constantine Rye, Jeff Crigger, Jonathan Amiran, Dan Amrich, Lisa, Paul Rydeen, John Donald, Frederic Le Garrec, Karla Jameson, Terra Colwell, Jason, Simon Beale, Nathan Morris, Rachel Hull, and Kathleen Jenkins.

And special thanks to Cliff Chen (Keeper of the X-Files Episode Guide) and Pat Gonzales (Keeper of the X-Files FAQ).

# PREFACE:
## "NOTHING IS AS IT SEEMS"

*When I was seventeen, I witnessed something so diabolical it could only have come from outer space or Washington, D.C. I was working as a ranch hand in Wyoming after my family had decided (with my grudging concurrence) that for that particular summer I should be someone else's problem. It was early September, and we had trucked our horses to a trailhead leading to a high alpine meadow surrounded on three sides by the sheer ridges of the Wind River Range. The meadow was accessible only by a single steep and narrow trail. Our plan was to herd a small number of cattle back down the trail to a lower pasture before the first frost.*

*About fifty yards from the bare spot was a cow lying on her side, apparently dead. The foreman approached, straightened visibly and slowly walked around the carcass as he fidgeted with his ear. Without looking up, he said, "This cow's been mutilated."*

*State law required that all cow mutilations be reported and investigated. Here's what they found: The cow had been completely drained of blood. Its udder and reproductive organs had all been removed and the wounds cauterized. An incision had been made along the snout, removing the upper lip, tongue and one eye with an instrument so sharp that the hair along the cut had not been disturbed. These cuts, too, were cauterized. There was no blood or footprints on the muddy ground, nor any visible mortal wound, only a mysterious inch-long incision across the animal's windpipe.*

*I learned later that while no mutilations had been reported in that area in some years, mutilations had occurred in the three adjoining counties at about the same time that our cow met her end. The mystery was never solved, and the ranch never suffered another like it. Among the local folks familiar with this periodic phenomenon, the consensus held that it was either the work of UFOs or the government. "Who else," they said, "would do something this weird or this dumb?"*

—FROM AN EDITORIAL IN *George* MAGAZINE, DECEMBER 1996

Critics have complained because of the supposed unreality of FBI agents Mulder and Scully tracking extraterrestrial intelligences loose upon our world in *The X-Files*. Despite reports of abductions and cattle mutilations by visiting extraterrestrials, they insist that since we are the only intelligent life, indeed the *only* life, in our universe, such stories border on the ridiculous. Now the shoe may be on the other foot. The biggest story in the history of humankind, rivaling the flood, the entering of the Covenant, and the births of Mohammad, Jesus, and Buddha, broke even as I wrote this book about the fictional, if wildly popular, television series.

Yes, these are strong words, but they are not mine alone. President Clinton said, "If this discovery is confirmed it will surely be one of the most stunning insights into our universe that science has ever uncovered. Its implications are as far-reaching and awe-inspiring as can be imagined." While Louis Friedman, executive director of the Planetary Society, insisted, "This changes our view of ourselves, it changes our view of the universe." Richard Erlich, a careful Miami University scholar and not a public figure of any kind, added, "It represents both our greatest hope that we are not alone and our worst fear that, when we finally meet our neighbours, they will destroy us."

A personal intellectual hero of mine, normally skeptical Carl Sagan, the late Cornell University scientist who wrote the "Life" entry in the *Encyclopaedia Britannica*, told Reuters, "If the results are verified, it is a turning point in human history, suggesting that life exists not on just two planets in one paltry solar system, but throughout this magnificent universe."

Even as I wrote about *The X-Files*, the wall between reality and fiction crumbled. While we still lack proof of intelligent life on other worlds, we now have proof that we are not alone in the universe. The barrier between lower life-forms and sentient life is far easier to believe than that between inorganic matter and life. In fact, many scientists have said that once life emerges, it will inevitably evolve toward more complex systems, ultimately resulting in intelligent, tool-building, perhaps spaceship-building, intelligences. Suddenly *The X-Files* seems far closer to reality.

For me it began on August 7, 1996, when I scanned the Reuters News Service headlines. Lodged between the usual international crises, I found the unexpected: "Life on Mars? No Surprise, Scientists Say." Yet it had been a surprise the day before. Few would have agreed with that statement before the reality arrived, despite protestations afterward. Even now, many scientists hedge their bets.

The Reuters story went on to report, "They say discoveries of hardy bacteria in underwater volcanoes, miles below the Earth's surface and in oil wells, make it clear that life can arise and survive in extreme conditions. NASA scientists were expected to announce they had found the fossilized remains of organisms resembling bacteria in a meteorite that fell to earth in the Antarctic 13,000 years ago."

The Associated Press offered a similar story that same day, reporting, "Earthlings have yearned for centuries to find life on Mars. Now, a NASA study provides the first serious evidence of past microbes on the red planet. Researchers at the National Aeronautics and Space Administration and three universities claimed today to have found in a rock from Mars organic compounds that they say were deposited by primitive life forms before the rock was blasted into space and sent on a fifteen-million-year voyage to Earth."

The news emerged from a study conducted by David McKay and Everett K. Gibson, Jr., of NASA's Johnson Space Center in Houston; Kathie L. Thomas-

Keprta of Lockheed Martin, a NASA contractor in Houston; Hojatollah Vali of McGill University in Montreal; Christopher S. Romanek of the University of Georgia laboratory in Aiken, S.C.; and Simon J. Clemett, Xavier D.F. Chillier, Claude R. Maechlin, and Richard N. Zare of Stanford University. They had not planned to release the findings yet, but a news conference was held after the results were leaked to the press.

McKay announced, "We believe we have found quite reasonable evidence of past life on Mars. The simplest explanation is that they are the remains of early Martian life."

The next day, August 8, 1996, Reuters offered the story, "NASA Says Mars Findings to Spur New Mission." The story began, "The first potentially historic evidence of extraterrestrial life—possible microscopic life-forms from Mars—will likely spur 'a worldwide mission' to explore the red planet, the head of the U.S. space agency said Wednesday. 'I think we may have to accelerate some activities,' NASA chief Dan Goldin said at a packed news briefing. Goldin added, 'I believe it will be a worldwide mission.'" As he spoke, he displayed a golf-ball-sized chunk of the meteorite cradled in midnight blue velvet and contained in a clear plastic case labeled ALH84001.

Reuters went on to report that President Clinton said U.S. scientific prowess would be poured into follow-up investigations of possible life on Mars, including an aggressive unmanned space-probe program and a bipartisan White House summit on future U.S. space policy.

The research team had found four key pieces of evidence in their little space ball: the meteorite came from Mars and contains carbonate chemicals that could harbor life; the rock's mineralogy is biological in origin; the space ball contains organic material; and photos show microscopic fossils. Even Mulder couldn't have hoped for anything more.

NASA's Johnson Space Center in Houston got part of a 4.1-pound meteorite in August 1994. A National Science Foundation group had found it in Antarctica in 1984. Chemical analysis compared it with information gathered by the Viking missions to Mars in the 1970s. They learned that the spaceball was 3.6 billion years old—give or take a few weeks—and the oldest of twelve known Martian meteorites on Earth. It is the only one to yield evidence of life. This would satisfy Scully's scientific inclinations.

The meteorite, now known as Allan Hills 84001 because of where it was found, is believed to have been knocked into space by an asteroid collision on Mars sixteen million years ago.

A high-resolution electron microscope and laser mass spectrometer revealed golden-colored specks of organic material and microscopic fossilized worms one hundred times smaller than the oldest fossils, also worm-like, ever found on Earth. Since the organic matter and fossils were found deep inside the meteorite, rather than near the surface, the research team discounted any possibility that the material formed after the meteorite landed on Earth. The organic matter, polycyclic aromatic hydrocarbons (or PAHs), are mineral compounds associated with microscopic organisms. Team member Thomas-Keprta announced, "The simplest explanation is that these are products of microorganisms on Mars."

McKay showed extremely high-resolution photographs of the alleged fossils, which looked like tiny worms on the rock surface. The oldest Earth fossils, microscopic worms found in Australia, are 3.4 billion years old, while these from Mars are 3.6 billion years old.

Before holding the news conference, the team submitted its findings to a strict peer review required for publication in the journal *Science*. It was word of this article that leaked, alerting the press

Team leader and geochemist McKay then told *USA Today*, "For the first six months, we didn't find anything exciting. Then we started using new tools, things that didn't even exist five years ago. And about a year ago was when we got really excited. I've spent many nights in the laboratory looking at this rock because I was too excited to go home." NASA Houston Center geochemist Everett Gibson, a mission science adviser for the Apollo 14 moon landing, added, "One evening I was on the electron microscope, it was just Dave and me, and we asked, 'Is this for real?' It is the most exciting thing I've ever done. The excitement for me even beats Apollo, and that's hard to do."

After the scientists spoke, Clinton added his commitment, "I am determined that the American space program will put its full intellectual power and technological prowess behind the search for further evidence of life on Mars."

Reaction to the discovery of alien life has been mixed. While most scientists accept the finding, some are withholding judgment or even criticizing the investigative team's announcement. Religious leaders are equally divided. Reverend Frank Cook, pastor of Northwest Baptist Church in Denver, told the *Rocky Mountain*

*News*, "If there was intelligent life on other planets, which would eventually affect us, we would find evidence in scripture. But there is none." But Reverend John Anderson, rector of the nearby Cathedral of the Immaculate Conception, also in Denver, disagreed, telling the same paper, "There could be a parallel existence. Perhaps God has a whole new creation someplace, another Garden of Eden where they're still romping around, free of original sin. Nothing precludes that."

Frederick Greenspahn, a professor of religious and Judaic studies at the University of Denver told the *News* that if God made humankind in his image, even fantastic-looking beings could fit the mold, since the phrase doesn't refer to a specific physical resemblance, and Regis University professor Dave Thomas added, "This news implies there's a kind of magnificence and variety in creation. For instance, we say there's one type of human being divided into women and men. But there may be other varieties. To me that's why we've had the teaching about angels—because there's a lot more out there than just us."

The Koran predicts finding life on other worlds, said Mohamed Jodeh, president of the Colorado Muslim Society. It encourages Muslims to seek other planets "to see the glory of the kingdom." Simon Luna of the Karma Dzong Meditation center in Boulder said that Buddhists could accept reincarnation with extraplanetary species, "It's not beyond the realm of possibility."

Science fiction authors are more enthusiastic. Many had long predicted that such evidence would come to light. Award-winning author Greg Bear, son-in-law of longtime science fiction author Poul Anderson, told Reuters, "The biologists will just throw their hands up in the air at first. It's the duty of science fiction writers to sit down and think up a hundred highly improbable possibilities that make fascinating material. This is very exciting stuff and every culture needs exciting stuff to keep it pumped up. We need something like this to knock us upside the head and make us realize what's going on out there."

Kim Stanley Robinson, author of a trilogy about the colonization of Mars, added, "This is so suggestive that really, we've got to go there and take a look. They've found thermal vents on the bottom of the Pacific with bacteria living on nothing but water, heat, and sulfur. There's obviously been lots of volcanic activity on Mars. If any of that is still happening, so that there's heat creating sort-of-underground hot springs, there could be living bacteria still on Mars."

But Goldin has cautioned against too much speculation, saying, "NASA has made a startling discovery that points to the possibility that a primitive form of microscopic life may have existed on Mars more than three billion years ago. I want everybody to know that we are not talking about 'little green men.' These are extremely small, single-celled structures that somewhat resemble bacteria on Earth. There is no evidence or suggestion that any higher life-form ever existed on Mars." So we still haven't proven Mulder's case, but we have come many steps closer.

Even odder possibilities than those Mulder postulates exist. In 1976, Chandra Wickramasinghe and Sir Fred Hoyle, mathematics and astronomy professors at the University of Cardiff, proposed that life could have been brought to Earth from outside its solar system on comets. Their theory was met with the skepticism of an unbelieving scientific world. Now astronomers believe comets carry amino acids and proteins, components of all living beings. Others note that rocks knocked into space from Earth, the moon, Mars, and other planets by collisions with meteors or asteroids eventually land on other planets. Christian de Duve of Brussels' Saint Luc Hospital, who wrote *Vital Dust*, a book about the origins of life in the universe, told Reuters, "We cannot exclude the possibility that life came to this planet from Mars or that life came from our planet to Mars by way of some meteorites that carried some very hardy bacteria." Paul Davies of the University of Adelaide added, "Inside rocks, bacteria might remain viable as spores for millions of years. It is possible Mars was seeded with life from the Earth, or the Earth from Mars."

This primitive bacteria could have been carried by meteorites across the Earth's own Milky Way galaxy, pointing to recent findings that microbes have survived dormant and encased in amber for millions of years. Perhaps Stanford University's Richard Zare summed it up best. Echoing a decades-old statement by author Ray Bradbury, he noted the possibility that life on Earth might have been "seeded" by a meteorite crashing in from Mars and added, "Who is to say that we are not all Martians?"

This all offered me quite a bit to absorb while writing this book. I hope you enjoy it while also taking the time to ponder the possibilities. Truth can indeed be stranger than fiction.

—Hal Schuster
*Bangkok and Berkeley*

# PART I

# THE MAKING OF *THE X-FILES*
## "THE TRUTH IS OUT THERE"

# CHAPTER 1

# THE MAN BEHIND *THE X-FILES*: CREATOR CHRIS CARTER

Christopher Carter, the California-bred son of a construction worker, revolutionized television with the creation of *The X-Files*. The beach-bum-turned-workaholic now refuses to delegate authority and prefers to do everything himself while heading two television series with a possible third one on the way. Chris Carter is more surf-dude than computer-nerd. David Duchovny described him to *The X-Files* magazine as "very California—handsome, blue eyes, long blond surfer hair, tan, athletic . . . a little like Vitas Gerulaitis, or the porn star Randy West."

The creator of television's most terrifying series grew up in Bellflower, a painfully normal blue collar suburb of Los Angeles, the son of William, a construction worker, and Catherine, a housewife, now deceased. He pitched little league and high school baseball, then discovered surfing when he was twelve. His younger brother, Craig, told *People*, "He was really passionate about it."

Carter began working part-time as a potter when he was nineteen, while majoring in journalism at California State University at Long Beach. He graduated in 1979, and started writing for *Surfing* magazine in San Clemente. During a 1995 interview on CBC Radio's *The Gabereau Show*, Carter admitted, "It was a way to postpone growing up. I ended up working for them for thirteen years. I was listed as senior editor at the ripe age of twenty-eight. I went around the world, surfing, and I got to write. I wrote constantly. I learned how to run a business. I did many other things, too. I was a production potter during those times also. I made hundreds of thousands of pieces of pottery at the potter's wheel. It was wonderful, repetitious. It was a Zen thing, when you make a lot of things over and over."

He told *Sci-Fi Entertainment*, "I was hired because I was a journalism major in college and had been a surfer all my life. Traveling around the world and surfing, I had one of the best prolonged adolescence a young man could want. It allowed me a lot of freedom to write, develop a voice, read, and see the world . . . and surf, of course." He even lived for a year in Brisbane, Australia, traveling the Gold Coast to ride the waves.

Sam George, the editor of *Surfer*, later said, "We used to spend a lot of time in the water philosophizing. You wouldn't have thought he'd start some show about a renegade FBI agent and space aliens. There's something going on in the back of his head."

So what did prompt Chris Carter to write the *X-Files*? See *Chapter 8: Precursors to The X-Files* to get all the details!

And, no, that "something" wouldn't be drugs. Although Carter experimented with recreational drugs, he wasn't heavily into it. "I was never a big druggie," he told *Rolling Stone*. "But I was a surfer, so I was around it. There are certain sacraments and rituals that had to be conducted. I did do a Native American Church peyote ritual with the Navajos in New Mexico."

Nor was he a science fiction fan, although he did enjoy science fiction television, such as the *Twilight Zone*, *The Outer Limits*, *Night Gallery*, and especially, *Night Stalker*. In 1995, he told C|net, "I was never a science fiction fan. I spoke to a Mensa group, and they were very upset that I'd never seen an episode of *Star Trek*. It's never interested me. I'm interested in personal experiences that could affect me in this place and time." He explained to *People*, "The main misperception of me is that I'm some kind of sci-fi maven. People would be surprised to learn that I'm really the guy next door, not a paranoid, kook or crank . . . I have no reason to believe in paranormal phenomena."

So what did prompt him to write *The X-Files*? He told the Sydney *Morning Herald*, "I just loved scary movies, good scary stories, good mysteries and . . . political thrillers, *Parallax View*, *All the President's Men*, *Three Days of the Condor*. [I] loved those kind of movies. We live in fear every day. We live in denial. If you can find the elements of everyday life that scare us and bring them into play, embellish or find new ways to look at the world, then you have naturally scary situations."

## TELEVISION BEFORE *THE X-FILES*

Although Carter majored in journalism and wrote factual articles for *Surfer* magazine for thirteen years, his interest in dramatic writing didn't develop until he met Dori Pearson in 1983. They began dating, and Pearson encouraged him to finish his first movie script. Though that script didn't go anywhere, their relationship did, and they were married in 1987. Pearson is currently working on a novel, and the couple now live in a three-bedroom, Pacific Palisades, California, home.

In 1985, Carter's second television script caught the notice of Jeffrey Katzenberg, boy genius of Disney's film division and Pearson's boss at the time. Katzenberg brought him in to write for television and produce several television movies, including the television pilot *Cameo by Night* for NBC and *The Nanny* for the Disney Channel. Softball pal Brandon Tartikoff convinced Carter to take a leave of absence from Disney to coproduce the second season of the NBC comedy *Rags to Riches*, starring Joe Bologna. He returned to Disney in 1989 to create and executive-produce *Brand New Life*, a recurring comedy series that ran as part of a rotating schedule on Disney's Sunday night lineup. Carter then signed a 1992 exclusive deal with Twentieth Television (now Twentieth Century Fox Television) to create and develop television projects. When

asked by Twentieth president Peter Roth to describe the type of show he wanted to create, Carter's response was immediate: "I want to make a show that will scare people the way *Night Stalker* scared me when I was a teenager."

## BIRTH OF *THE X-FILES*

Carter admits that *The X-Files* was not the culmination of a lifelong dream to tell the world weird tales about government conspiracies and alien abductions. It arose from a desire to tell "good, smart stories rooted in a speculative science—to do the scariest, smartest show possible."

When creating a television series, Carter told *Reel West* magazine, "You have to create a situation that you like and from which stories can spring. Some ideas just seem like a TV show, in that you can go somewhere with it week after week. This show felt like that to me. I felt that there would be a long life for it if we kept the quality and told good, interesting tales. It takes place in what I call the realm of extreme possibility. I sent out orders to the staff and myself that it has to be believable. It has to have a kernel of scientific basis. From there you can speculate and go far out. The show is only as scary as it is real. Some of the shows seem very real, some of them have the most impressionistic element of the unknown. That's what *Outer Limits* and *Twilight Zone* did so well."

Of course, the hardest part of creating any television series is coming up with the original concept. In this case, Carter had a clear vision: he pitched a scary show inspired by his old favorite *Kolchak: The Night Stalker*. This 1973 series was produced by Dan Curtis, and it featured an investigative reporter, played by Darren McGavin, who tracked down vampires and werewolves. *The Night Stalker* shook him up as an adolescent, inspiring thoughts that there might indeed be a twilight world of bloodsucking creatures.

Loving and missing the original series, Carter worked to develop a story in the same vein, but, as he told the U.K.'s *The X-Files* magazine, "without the built-in problems—we couldn't do monster-of-the-week or vampire-of-the-week." Carter did not want to copy *The Night Stalker*, but to capture its spirit. (In homage to the show, Carter tried to cast Darren McGavin, the actor who played the lead character of

Kolchak, as Fox Mulder's father, but there were too many scheduling conflicts.) It was during this period that Carter had a fateful dinner with a Yale psychology professor and researcher—who just happened to have been a consultant on Dan Curtis's *Intruders*, a 1992 drama about UFO abductions. Carter said, "he told me that 3 percent of the public believed in this syndrome. I was astounded. I realized there was a topicality to this theme of the unknown, and *X-Files* grew out of that fascination."

"ROUND ABOUT THE ACCREDITED AND orderly facts of every science there ever floats a sort of dust-cloud of exceptional observations, of occurrences minute and irregular and seldom met with, which it always proves more easy to ignore than to attend to . . . Anyone will renovate his science who will steadily look after the irregular phenomena, and when science is renewed, its new formulas often have more of the voice of the exceptions in them than of what were supposed to be the rules."

—WILLIAM JAMES

Carter's other influence was a book by Harvard psychiatrist John Mack, *Abduction: Human Encounters with Aliens*. In the book, Mack, a respected academic, uses scientific rigor to assess people who claim to be victims of alien abductions, and he finds truth in some of the stories. Carter told *Omni*, "I read this and I thought what a wonderful entry into the exploration of the paranormal. I'm interested in exploring other realms, those that deal with the psychic world, weird science, paranormal matters that question our beliefs . . . not just what's up in the heavens but also what dwells within."

Though Carter decided that in his new show the lead characters would track biological anomalies, chemical anomalies, twists on genetic engineering, and fanciful tales of alien landings, he didn't want his *X-Files* to become a traditional horror series. He wanted shows based in science, like *Coma* or *The Andromeda Strain*, that posed provocative, "what if" scenarios. He told the San Francisco *Chronicle*, "It's the idea that shakes up you and your beliefs, not some hideous Frankenstein monster or a hand clasping the heroine's shoulder."

The idea of focusing the show around the work of FBI agents was influenced by the success of *The Silence of the Lambs*, and from the beginning Carter wanted two leads, one male, one female, and to flip their gender stereotypes—so that Fox Mulder, the male, would be the believer, the intuitive one, and Dana Scully, the female, would be the skeptic and the scientist. It was also important that Scully be Mulder's equal in rank, intelligence, and ability because in real life the FBI is a boy's club, and Carter didn't want her to take a back seat. The female lead, Dana Scully, was modeled closely after Jodie Foster's role in *Lambs*.

All of these influences combined to lead Carter into creating his new concept for a television pilot. Many other factors also added to the mix, not the least of which was an intangible feel for the material. He told the Australia's *Sunday Telegraph*, "You develop an

*Chris Carter on the set.*

instinct for what works and what doesn't; how a scene will play, how it fits into the story, how an actor will respond to certain work, how he'll deliver certain lines. Once you develop a feel for all these things, if you've got the drama gene, you exercise it in such a way that you start to build muscle in ways and in places that you didn't know you had before. The experience is rewarding on so many levels."

While Carter reaches for realism in his stories, he doesn't turn to experts for help. He told *Omni*, "We generally don't use consultants. There is no real Deep Throat. All of our research is done from diverse materials, wherever we can find it. But I have to say that we take the information, but don't use it in any kind of literal or verbatim way. We use it as a jumping-off point. I did consult with a virologist to make sure that the genetic science in the last show of the first season was correct. Beyond that we do it all ourselves."

Filming for Carter's new *X-Files* finally began in March 1993. Even Dori, his wife, was surprised at the bent her husband's mind had taken, saying, "I didn't know those stories existed in his head."

Carter knew instantly that David Duchovny was the right actor to play Fox Mulder, and he fought hard for Gillian Anderson as Dana Scully. Carter even tried to cast Darren McGavin, the actor who played Kolchak in *The Night Stalker*, in the role of Fox Mulder's father—as an homage to that show—but there were too many scheduling conflicts. Such inside jokes have become well-known *X-Files* lore: Mulder is actually the maiden name of Carter's mother, and Scully was named for Los Angeles Dodgers announcer Vin Scully, whom Carter used to listen to as a kid. And if you notice it's often 11:21 when Mulder calls Scully in the middle of the night, that's no accident: that's also the day Carter's wife was born.

## DO YOU BELIEVE?

But one of the most persistent questions remains, How much does the creator of the *X-Files* actually believe? He admitted to *Omni*, "I've never had a personal experience with the paranormal. I've never seen a UFO. I've never been contacted by anything or anyone. My personal opinion? Well, I should preface this by saying that I'm a natural skeptic. My tendency is to discount most of the stuff because my personal experience doesn't include it. [Scully and Mulder] are the equal parts of my desire to believe in something and my inability to believe in something. My skepticism and my faith. And the writing of the characters and the voices came very easily to me. I want, like a lot of people do, to have the experience of witnessing a paranormal phenomenon. At the same time I want not to accept it, but to question it. I think those characters and those voices came out of that duality."

Carter says that faith comes to him with difficulty. He sees himself as a nonreligious person seeking a religious experience, as someone who wants to believe. "Some things I find intriguing," he told *Sci-Fi Entertainment*. "We read enough in the news to know the government keeps things from us every day, but I tend to think that the government runs out of chaos, and organization of thought or of systems inside the government is a joke. That's why I find most conspiracy theories difficult to believe. Do I think that Bob Lazar [a scientist who claims to have worked on alien technology in Area 51] is telling the truth? I have no reason to believe him; I have no reason to disbelieve him."

Carter respects the legions who believe in the strange and supernatural, telling the *Los Angeles Times*, "Most of the people who believe in these phenomena are sane, credible, normal everyday folk, who believe that it happened to them. You have no reason to doubt them. When I'm standing around on location, somebody will inevitably come up and say, 'Can I tell you my story?' We get lots and lots of fan mail. I'm a natural skeptic, but it has chipped away at my own skepticism about these things. There's a large segment of people who believe literally in a lot of stuff we're doing. Then there's a large subgroup who believes figuratively—it's possible, what we're doing. If there is not a literal six-foot fluke worm, at least the possibility of it exists. So there is the literal group and the figurative group, but they're both believers."

The number of believers has come as a surprise to Carter. He told *Sci-Fi Entertainment*, "Now that Russia is no longer our very recognizable enemy, we suddenly need to find other enemies and other sources of discontent. That's when we start looking to the skies. . . ."

But no matter what he does or does not believe, Carter doesn't intend to deliver a pointed political message. He wants the stories to be provocative, not didactic—to question and theorize without giving pat, glib answers. What brings the believer Mulder and the skeptic Scully together is their search for truth, and it's this search that energizes the show.

Carter told the Sydney *Morning Herald* that after creating a show, "You hope you get an order for your pilot. . . . You hope the pilot gets picked up for a series and you hope the series gets picked up for another [year]. . . . I call it taking the pig to the fair. You want to make it to the final judging with the viewing public. You want them to like it."

## TAKING IT IN

Carter is pleased with the way the show has developed in its first four seasons. He takes satisfaction not only in how close *The X-Files* is to his original vision but in how the show has gotten better while maintaining its distinctive character and tone.

But the show's phenomenal success has definitely been a surprise. He told CBC Radio's *The Gabereau Show*, "You can imagine what it's like for me to have been sitting there playing ball with my dog, barefoot in surf trunks, and all of a sudden, it's become as popular as it has. Nothing prepares you for it. For me, it's been a dream, and I hope no one pinches me. I've become so focused on what I do that my life has only become more narrow as a result of this success. I do the same thing every day. I have not succumbed to the perceived glamours of Hollywood. Professionally, certainly I'm more considered now as a person who has put a successful TV show on the air. Personally, I have much less time to go surfing. The day I swan around in expensive suits is the day I hope someone puts a bullet in my head. I don't see it happening."

And yet, as he admitted to the Houston *Chronicle*, "I'm still motivated by fear of failure. Who knows if I'll ever do anything this successful again? I always tell people this is a business of failure. To actually get something on the air is a huge success in network television. To get something on that lasts a year is an enormous feat. To get something this big is . . . I don't know. It could be once in a lifetime. . . . It's the hardest work I've ever done. I can't imagine working any harder in my life. It's all I do. I owe it to David and Gillian. They're giving up so much of their lives."

Others recognize his success. Not only has his series received several Golden Globe Awards and recognition in the Emmys, but John Matoian, the president of the Fox Entertainment Group, and thus Carter's ultimate boss, told *Rolling Stone*, "Chris is a perfectionist and his own worst critic, which is great for me."

# CHAPTER 2

# OPENING THE FILES: CREATING AND PRODUCING THE SERIES

## PITCHING THE SERIES

Before *The X-Files*, a documentary series about UFO encounters called *Sightings*, which was produced by an outside company, held down the Friday night time slot. According to independent producer Henry Winkler, Fox preferred to produce their own shows, and they asked Chris Carter to come up with a new series to replace *Sightings*.

Carter gladly accepted the challenge, since he hadn't produced a series before, but he realized it would be risky. He was comfortable as a writer, but developing and pitching an original TV show raised the stakes on his career. He told *Producer* magazine, "It was like fishing in a barrel, but I was writing other people's idea. And I decided to stake my own claim and not be a writer for hire."

Carter knew he needed a clear concept that would not be diluted in the production and editing process, and perhaps one of his greatest successes has been defending his unique vision from nervous executives who would have made it more mainstream. Good episodic television must have a specific voice, which often comes almost exclusively from the executive producer. As his ideas coalesced, his instincts told him he had a good basis for an ongoing series, but he has also admitted that he didn't have a clear philosophy guiding the show. He just wanted "the scariest, smartest show possible."

The Fox executives weren't confident that Carter's new FBI agents in search of witches, mutants, and extraterrestrials would attract an audience. Bob Greenblatt, Fox's senior vice president of drama development, later admitted to the *Los Angeles Times*, "Chris pitched the show to me originally, and I was concerned nobody would buy it because it's so far out there."

In an online interview on Delphi, Carter said, "You always prepare to have your idea, your pilot, your project get nuked somewhere along the way. To get on the air is rare. To have the kind of response we've had is absolutely mind-boggling. I pitched it to Fox. They reluctantly bought the idea, but it took two pitch meetings to convince them that we had something worth proceeding on."

After the network spurned his first pitch, Carter fleshed out his concept for *The X-Files* and tried again. As Carter said on KROQ, an L.A. radio station, "They didn't know what it was, and then I went back with a guy named Peter Roth, and we were able to sell it to them." On the Martin-Molloy radio show in Australia, he said, "Whether they bought it to get rid of me or because they actually liked it, I'm not sure. But they bought it the second time."

Fox first ordered a pilot. Once they'd seen that, they ordered thirteen shows, and eventually twenty-two shows—a whole season's worth. Now that he had the green light, would people watch?

## AMERICA IS READY TO BELIEVE

*The X-Files* is an enticing stew of many genres: science fiction, mystery, drama, horror, and police procedural. And each show serves this up with psychological sophistication and humor, avoiding, for the most part, formulaic convention. Its two main characters, Mulder and Scully, are played by two likable, attractive actors, and their roles offer two clear, contrasting points of view. It's solid television, but it's also "out there"—full of UFOs, aliens, and dark conspiracies—and Carter was gambling that people wouldn't be turned off. As it turns out, the show seems to have touched a hidden wellspring of anxiety and belief.

The signs were there. Not only had *Sightings* and other supposedly nonfiction documentaries paved the way, but a number of more credible books had also already appeared. Harmony Press had released *The Fringes of Reason* in 1989, five years before *The X-Files*. This could have almost been a handbook for Scully and Mulder: it looked at channeling, psychic powers, crystals, perceptual motion, weird phenomena, bigfoot, shamanism, UFOs, conspiracies theories, reincarnation, spontaneous human combustion, Atlantis, and alien abductions. The book's editor and contributing writer, Ted Schultz, now a graduate student in evolutionary biology at Cornell University, told *Omni*, "I don't believe in the paranormal, but I think there's an entirely different dimension of the mind that we're only beginning to understand." Jay Kinney, the publisher and editor-in-chief of *Gnosis* magazine, helped put *The Fringes of Reason* together. Kinney added, "In our materialist, scientifically based society where people are only willing to believe something they are able to prove with hard scientific fact, UFOs are something like a tantalizing reminder that the universe is bigger than our day-to-day philosophies allow for. In that sense, UFOs give an opening for people's spiritual urges. Carl Jung viewed UFOs as a sort of eruption of archetypes out of the collective unconscious."

Patrick Harpur, who wrote *Daimonic Reality*, insists that paranormal phenomena, such as bigfoot, UFOs, fairies, visions of the Virgin Mary, and contacts with aliens, arise from the same source. They are outcroppings of life between the physical and some high spiritual, other reality. They are entities whose existence isn't quite on the same plane as ours. UFO researchers John Keel and Jacques Vallee have similar theories.

Even skeptics love the show. Barry Karr, the executive director of *The Skeptical Inquirer*, a magazine that debunks various hoaxes and other supposedly paranormal phenomenon, said, "I enjoy the show. It's fiction; it's labeled as fiction. Our culture loves horror stories, and this series is entertaining. There are a lot of TV programs these days coming across as true documentaries. TV has gone crazy on the paranormal bandwagon. *Encounters. Unsolved Mysteries. Sightings.* They label them as true. *X-Files*, though, is a good show."

Perhaps *The X-Files* is more real than most realize. Carter told the Martin-Molloy radio show in Australia, "I've had contact with a lot of former intelligence agents, who come to me and say, 'So who's your inside source?' And I'll say, 'What do you mean?' And they'll say, 'Well, you don't know how close you are.'" Officially, however, the FBI denies that they keep anything like the X-Files, nor do they admit to assigning FBI agents to investigate paranormal phenomena.

*The X-Files* cast and crew once took a tour of the real FBI headquarters under the guidance of special agent John Kundts. Kundts later told *Details*, "The stories that are presented on TV are fictitious, and we offer no technical assistance because we can't. They are not true stories, you know. . . . Unless a UFO was somehow violating the laws or security interests of the United States, then the FBI per se would not have a legal basis to get into that arena. The Department of Defense used to have an organization that looked into these, called Project Blue Book. The purpose of that office was to look into sightings, and what they were on a scientific basis."

"I don't think that you ever know the truth," Carter said on the Sci Fi Channel. "There is no truth. The truth is a hundred, a thousand, a million different things. The truth is like Rashomon. For every person, there's a different truth."

## HIRING THE CREATIVE TEAM

Chris Carter serves as executive producer for *The X-Files*. Before launching his series, he had to choose a creative team, including writers, to breathe life into his vision. Ultimately, R. W. Goodwin and Howard Gordon became coexecutive producers, and Paul Rabwin the coproducer. Rob Bowman, Kim Manners, and Joseph Patrick Finn are producers. Story editors are Frank Spotnitz, Darin Morgan, and Jeff Vlaming. Vince Gilligan is creative consultant.

Howard Gordon and R. W. Goodwin have been with *The X-Files* since its inception. Carter was aware of their work when he planned the series. They became involved in the daily operation of the set with season four, when David Nutter, a veteran of *The X-Files'* early years, began to help Carter supervise *Millennium*.

Gordon works seven days a week. He served as supervising producer during the show's first and second seasons, while writing fourteen episodes. Gordon moved to Los Angeles with his writing partner, Alex Gansa, to write for television after graduating from Princeton University in 1984. They first worked freelance for the ABC series *Spenser for Hire*. The team then joined the Emmy-nominated *Beauty and the Beast* as staff writers, and later as producers. Gordon and Gansa also had a two-year deal with Witt-Thomas Productions, and they produced pilots. One of their pilots, *Country Estates*, caught the attention of Carter, who hired them both as supervising producers and writers for *The X-Files*. Gansa later departed to pursue independent projects. Carter told Delphi, "Without them, *The X-Files* wouldn't be the show it is."

**"I KNOW THAT MOST MEN, INCLUDING** those at ease with problems of the greatest complexity, can seldom accept even the simplest and most obvious truth if it be such as would oblige them to admit the falsity of conclusions which they have delighted in explaining to colleagues, which they have proudly taught to others, and which they have woven, thread by thread, into the fabric of their lives."
—TOLSTOY

Before *The X-Files*, R. W. Goodwin was coexecutive producer for the third and fourth season of the ABC series *Life Goes On*. He had begun his career as a writer for Paramount and a studio executive. He developed the script that became the first *Star Trek* feature film, *Star Trek: The Motion Picture*. He also produced the feature film *Inside Moves*, starring John Savage and David Morse. Goodwin's producer credits for television movies include NBC's *Born Too Soon* and *Living a Lie* and ABC's *California Girls*. He also produced and wrote for the television series *Hooperman* and *Mancuso FBI*.

Rob Bowman is a producer for *The X-Files*. He previously served as a director for the film *Airborne* (1993) and for the TV series *Star Trek: The Next Gener-*

*ation*, *Dark Shadows*, and *The Adventures of Brisco County Jr.* Bowman told Cinescape, "*X-Files* opened on Fox, which already likes to try different things. We were never intended to be anything except something dark, mysterious, and fun. I don't think we ever expected to be as popular as *Melrose Place* or any of the shows like that. If that was the original goal, we wouldn't have the shows we have. It's everything that's really fun about storytelling and it's about as advanced or risky as you could find in television."

Carter told a Delphi online audience in 1993, "We strive very hard to make the show look like it does. Two key people bring us that look: John Bartley and Graeme Murray. Our two secret weapons." Graeme Murray is the production designer, and Australian John Bartley was the director of photography for the first three seasons. (Jon Joffin has taken over as director of photography for the fourth season.) As he told America Online, Paul Rabwin credits Bartley with giving the show "a dark, rich feel . . . not too bright . . . eerie. Colors are pastel and desaturated. The sound complements the dark tone. The show is a dark sort of series. We don't have bright colors very often. I like it that way, sort of creepy." Carter told *Producer* magazine that Bartley's "painterly in the way he gives us our mood, and our mood is what the show is about." Bartley previously worked on the film *Beyond the Stars* (1989) and the television movies *Sky High* (1990) and *Beyond Betrayal* (1994). Bartley has long been involved in TV and theater, and he worked as a gaffer on many commercials and music videos after moving to Canada from Australia. He first met Morgan and Wong while working as director of photography on *The Commish*.

Bartley received some *X-Files* scripts only days in advance, and they shoot much of the action on location in Vancouver, where the weather—gray and rainy one moment, bright and sunny the next—makes matching shots challenging. Bartley has said, "Every episode is like a mini-movie, with the difference that you only get eight days to shoot it." He used an Arriflex 35mm camera on 5293 and 5298 film stock.

David Nutter and Jerrold Freedman also serve as cinematographers for *The X-Files*. Nutter also worked on the films *Cease Fire* (1985), *Trancers 4: Jack of Swords* (1994), and *Trancers 5: Sudden Death* (1995). He is now a producer for Carter's *Millennium* TV series. Freedman has a long list of credits to his name, including the films *Kansas City Bomber* (1972) and *Borderline* (1980) and the television films *A Cold Night's Death* (1972), *Blood Sport* (1973), *The Last Angry Man* (1974), *Lawman Without a Gun* (1977), *This Man Stands Alone* (1979), *The Streets of L.A.* (1979), *Some Kind of Miracle* (1979), *The Boy Who Drank Too Much* (1980), *Victims* (1982), *Legs* (1983), *The Seduction of Gina* (1984), *Best Kept Secrets* (1984), *Seduced* (1985), *Thompson's Last Run* (1986), *Native Son* (1986), *Family Sins* (1987), *Unholy Matrimony* (1988), *Night Walk* (1989), *The Comeback* (1989), *Good Night, Sweet Wife: A Murder in Boston* (1990), *Condition: Critical* (1992), and *The O.J. Simpson Story* (1995), as Alan Smithee. He also wrote A *Cold Night's Death* and *Borderline*.

*The X-Files* relies on a regular staff of writers. Carter told the *New York Times*, "On this show, we've never used an idea that came from the outside. [Freelance writers] don't understand that the main characters, and the relationships between them, drive the story from the inside."

That doesn't mean the show is closed to outside writers—they will accept spec scripts from agents—but it is very difficult, as Darin Morgan elaborated to the IRC Chat on Internet, "It is so hard to have a spec script work because there are so many political things that go on in a show every year that someone outside the staff doesn't know about."

Important staff writers include Morgan and Wong, who write episodes as well as produce, Gordon, Carter, Gilligan, Kim Newton, John Shiban, Frank Spotnitz, and Jeff Vlaming. According to Morgan, Twentieth Television worked with Carter to put together the initial writing team, but that Carter "has chosen everyone who has come aboard since." Morgan said he doesn't see himself as a writer but rather as "a guy who puts a TV show down on paper."

Gordon told the *New York Times*, "Somebody told me very early on that the idea of episodic television is to give the audience the pilot episode again and again and again. Which isn't necessarily true, but it's not entirely wrong either. What is absolutely true is that any good series has a specific voice. And I think that voice is almost exclusively the domain of the executive producer. In this case, the voice is Chris. As a staff writer you're not being called upon to be the great creative person. You're being called upon to understand the characters and their voices and put them through paces."

Kim Newton graduated from Southwest Texas State University in 1988 with a B.A. in Journalism. He

then became a copywriter in Dallas before relocating to Los Angeles in 1991 and becoming a screenwriter. He has worked as production assistant on *Picket Fences*, and done story research for *Picket Fences* and *Chicago Hope*. His first script was produced by *Chicago Hope*.

John Shiban received his B.A. in English literature from UCLA and an M.F.A. in screenwriting from the American Film Institute. While at AFI, Shiban was awarded the Mary Pickford Scholarship for writing and was the Institute's candidate for Paramount fellowship his senior year. He also worked as a software engineer for Unisys Corporation.

Story editors include Frank Spotnitz, Jeff Vlaming, and Darin Morgan. Morgan also performed on "The Host" as the evil flukeworm-man.

Spotnitz graduated from the American Film Institute in 1991 with a master's degree in screenwriting. He started his career working as a newspaper and magazine writer, spending three years with the United Press International in New York and serving as a correspondent for Associated Press in Paris. He was with *Enter-*

*Special Agents Fox Mulder and Dana Scully.*

*tainment Weekly* for three years. He has also written for *Rolling Stone* and *American Film*, and he wrote and directed the documentary *John Fante: A Life*. Vlaming grew up in Minneapolis, where he began his career as an advertising art director. Later he became a staff writer on the award-winning television series *Northern Exposure*, worked for USA network's *Weird Science*, and wrote episodes of *Due South*, *The Adventures of Brisco County Jr.*, and MTV's *Catwalk*.

Juilliard-trained Mark Snow serves as composer for *The X-Files*. Coexecutive producer Paul Rabwin told an America Online audience, "The chemistry of Mark Snow's work on the Synclavier and Chris Carter's vision was magical. I can't imagine anyone else doing better."

Snow has played oboe with a symphony orchestra and is a veteran of the New York Rock and Roll Ensemble. He moved to Los Angeles and began scoring for television movies. Snow uses a Synclavier-repository of sampled sounds and a Macintosh computer to create the music for the show. He puts in long hours to make the unusual show work. Although most hour-long TV shows have ten to fifteen minutes of music, *The X-Files* has thirty to thirty-five minutes. Each episode takes Snow five or six days to score. He works closely with Carter and Rabwin, the producer in charge of post production. Snow plays a similar role for Carter's *Millennium*. Snow's other TV work includes *T.J. Hooker*, *Falcon Crest*, *Hart to Hart*, and *Starsky and Hutch*. His film credits include *Dead Badge* (1995), *Mob Justice* (1995), *Caroline at Midnight* (1994), *A Place for Annie* (1994), *Playmaker* (1994), *Dolly Dearest* (1992), *Jake Speed* (1986), *High Risk* (1981), *Something Short of Paradise* (1979), and *Skateboard* (1977). He has also scored dozens of TV movies, beginning in 1982.

## HIRING THE ACTORS

*The X-Files* would never have achieved the success it has without the talent and charisma of its lead actors.

---

### *The Night Stalker:* The Inspiration Behind *The X-Files*

"Kolchak really isn't a pure horror show, although it deals with man-killing monsters and creatures every week. The simple fact is you can't do a legitimate 'horror show' on network time, as the sponsors don't want to scare people out of their pants. So we decided to titillate, not terrify, to have fun with it."
—Darren McGavin on
Kolchak: The Night Stalker

*The Night Stalker*, Chris Carter's childhood favorite television series, inspired him in creating *The X-Files*. Carl Kolchak, played by Darren McGavin, works as a reporter for the Independent News Service in Chicago. Carl knows the truth is out there, no matter how unlikely that truth may be. His quests lead him to vampires, Indian spirits, werewolves, goddesses, robots, zombies, and extraterrestrial invaders. His skeptical editor, Tony Vincenzo, played by Simon Oakland, rarely fully believes him. Of odd interest was an actress on the series with the notable name Diana Muldaur.

#### KOLCHAK: THE NIGHT STALKER

1974–1975

**Cast:** John Fiedler (Gordy Spangler), Jack Grinnage (Ron Updyke), Ruth McDevitt (Emily Cowles), Darren McGavin (Carl Kolchak), Simon Oakland (Tony Vincenzo), and Carol Ann Susi (Monique Marmelstein)

**Executive Producer:** Darren McGavin

**Producer:** Paul Playdon and Cy Chermak

**Creator:** Jeff Rice

**Story Consultant:** David Chase

**Music:** Gil Melle

#### DARREN MCGAVIN

"This guy, I've got him in my mind, see, he's fired from the New York Journal in 1955. That day, the day he was fired, he was wearing a seersucker suit, a black string tie and a white shirt with a button-down collar. So, he's still wearing 'em. He hasn't bought a suit of clothes since he was fired. . . . The truth of the matter is I love Kolchak. He's terrific.

What he's saying to the world is beautiful—the heck with you, brother, I'll get my story anyway. He's a man in a million."
—Darren McGavin on the
character he portrayed, Carl Kolchak

Blustery and hammy Darren McGavin—born on May 7, 1922, in San Joaquin, California—saved many otherwise dismal films. His best work appeared in *The Natural*, alongside Robert Redford, and as the first actor to portray Steve Austin's superior for *The Six Million Dollar Man*. McGavin not only starred in *The Night Stalker*, but also coproduced the series.

#### SIMON OAKLAND

Simon Oakland—who was born in 1922 in New York City and died in 1983—brought Tony Vincenzo, Kolchak's doubting editor, to life. He added his special touch to a number of important films, including *Psycho*, *The Sand Pebbles*, *West Side Story*, and *Bullit*.

Though the actors seem perfect in their roles now, they were, in TV terms, relative unknowns when it came time to cast the pilot, and these days studio executives are terrified of putting out shows lacking in star power. Several television executives told *Variety* that they would not produce any new shows unless they could sign top film stars to them. Just look at who headlines on the big networks—Ted Danson, Mary Steenburgen, Michael J. Fox, and Rosie O'Donnell. Fox' position as a minor network allowed it a freedom the larger networks lack. Carter took advantage of that, deliberately bucking the network trend, and he still avoids using the many superstars who beg to guest star in a show they have grown to love.

Carter knew he wanted the lead characters to be opposites, since their opposing viewpoints would make for interesting storytelling. And, as James Wolcott said in *The New Yorker*, "Their partnership achieves a rare parity between the sexes." But knowing what he wanted and finding the right actors were two very different things.

Carter told the *Times Mirror*, "Much of the show's success is because of the relationship between Mulder and Scully. It seems so easy now, but I remember of course that when you go through the casting process it is tedious finding the right people for the roles. David is a star, and he had already done a considerable amount, so it was easy to see his quality. Gillian had done relatively little work, and it was harder to convince the people whose money I was spending that she was Dana Scully, but ultimately they believed that I knew what I was doing. She has, first of all, a tremendous acting ability. Secondly, she has an intensity both as a person and an actress which really serves that character well. I believed her in the role."

Anderson was out of work and living in Los Angeles at the time they began auditioning for *The X-Files*. She had never appeared on television and did not want to work in television, but she had been unemployed for a year and decided to go for it. She told *Wrapped in Plastic* magazine, "It was an audition like any other audition. I went and did my thing, and they called me back, and then called me back again, and I went to network. It was just one of those things. I think they had initially auditioned many people, but they were pretty intent on casting David. In the actual network audition, there were many, many women left, and David and one other man. And David got cast the first day of the network auditions, and I was there and read with him. But I think the network was still pretty freaked out at the possibility of casting somebody with as little background as I had, so they flew in some more girls from New York, and I had to sit in the hallway with more girls from New York and go in again and read with him. It was pretty hair raising."

At the time, Anderson felt that television represented a step down and a sellout, and she wanted her future to be as a stage actress. However, she believed television was changing. She told the *Sydney Morning Herald*, "It was one of the first television scripts I had taken a look at. The relationship between Mulder and Scully was compelling. Their intellectual repartee, the dynamic tension between them. The idea was brilliant. I was ignorant about television. I didn't know what a pilot was, what going to network was, and what auditioning for network was. I didn't know and I didn't care up until then. I was excited when I got the role. I assumed that I would be shooting the three weeks of the pilot. I didn't know what it meant to be picked up or that things had seasons."

## "IF A MAN IS IN TOO BIG A HURRY TO give up an error, he is liable to give up some truth with it." —WILBUR WRIGHT, 1902

When she arrived at the audition, Carter said in *Entertainment Weekly*, "She came in looking a little disheveled, a little grungier than I'd imagined Scully, but you can't miss those classic features. And she had a seriousness, a believability as a scientist."

In fact, Anderson didn't have any money at the time and had to borrow a suit, which was too big. She walked into the first audition looking more than a little "frumpy." She told Australia's *TV Week* magazine that she never thought she would get the job. The TV executives "were looking for someone leggier, and with a bigger chest." She told *Rolling Stone*, "During auditions, the network kept asking me to wear something smaller and more form fitting, and higher heels."

Carter told *US* magazine, "The network wasn't sure how Gillian would look in a bathing suit. They didn't really know what the show was."

The network execs argued heavily to cast an established TV actress. Carter trusted his instincts and held his ground. He told *Producer* magazine, "I stood up in a room full of people and said that I wanted this person and nobody else. I thought later that I'd laid my whole career on the line."

A grateful Anderson recalled to the *Sydney Morning Herald*, "There was something in my performance that [Carter] saw and said, 'This is the character that I wrote.' I don't know exactly what that was. There is a seriousness about me, sometimes to a fault, that helped me get the role. The character rarely cracks a smile. She is singlemindedly dedicated to her work. Maybe that came across in the audition." Carter told *People*, Anderson "has an intensity that makes her perfect as Scully."

Casting David Duchovny was a lot easier, even though he, like Anderson, had had no plans for a career in television. Duchovny had just finished working on the film *Kalifornia* when his agent gave him the pilot to read. Both coexecutive producers Paul Rabwin and Glen Morgan had recalled Duchovny's work on *Twin Peaks* and *Red Shoes Diaries*, and Twentieth Television casting vice-president Randy Stone had thought Duchovny would be a star even before he was cast in *Kalifornia*. They all wanted him for their new series. But Duchovny only wanted to do films. Duchovny told the *Los Angeles Times*, "I read it, and I thought, 'A, it's a really good pilot. B, it's about extraterrestrials—it's never gonna go. Who cares about this crap?' Even if it did go, I thought, 'Yeah, it'll go six episodes, but, after six, how many shows can you do about extraterrestrials?'"

"David read for the part and was perfect," Carter told *Who* magazine. "We were obligated to give the network a choice of at least two actors, but we knew David was it from the start. He was just very, very right for the role."

Even though Carter told a Delphi online audience that he "loved both David and Gillian from the start," he also admitted that "the chemistry between them is just pure luck." That kind of luck seems to have blessed *The X-Files* in many ways.

## PRODUCTION

The process of creating a television series is complicated and intense, especially when the series requires the high production values and special effects of an hour-long show devoted to alien abductions and genetic monsters. Given the limited production schedule, Carter said his *X-Files* cowriters must know what occurs in every frame while they are writing. He elaborated to *ReelWest* magazine, "A really good writer thinks like a prop man and a set decorator and all the department heads when he is writing the script, so that it is easier to communicate what is needed when he sits down with them to go over the script. That doesn't mean that I, as a producer, dictate to them what they should be doing. But as the writer, I have made a choice of the way I think the script should be carried out. They then tell me, as experts on their particular areas, how they think the scene should be handled. Because I've made a choice, I can vary from that choice. I can be flexible if I believe that being flexible would make the scene better."

Though directors change from episode to episode, they all try to maintain a consistent feel and tone—a creepy tone, that is. Michael Lange, who directed the Salamander Man episode, told *Entertainment Weekly*, "They encourage cinematic stuff. Instead of shooting at a normal eye level as the Salamander man takes the gun, I tilt up, and now I'm shooting up his nose almost, and it was kind of like very disorienting. The show's got a certain ennui that appeals to me, the film noiry movies of the '40s look, an undercurrent of tension and anxiety 'cause of all the weird things going on."

Episodes involving the paranormal can create problems not found in other television series, requiring special effects that strain tight budgets. But even if Carter had unlimited funds, he still would prefer to keep special effects to a minimum, since he believes the effects should never eclipse the story. Special effects are time-consuming as well. In the pilot, the story called for a whirling vortex of leaves, and they wanted real leaves whipping around in a whirlwind. To create the effect, they had to merge real leaves with digital leaves by using a special light rig that took eight hours to construct.

The weather also causes problems. *The X-Files* does most of its filming on location in Vancouver, where the weather can be very unpredictable. It can sometimes rain for days at a time, except during shooting when they want it to. The pilot called for a graveyard scene in the pouring rain, but the weather wouldn't cooperate, so they had to turn on the "rain birds." The actors had trouble with their lines because they were freezing; they were so cold they couldn't speak afterward. That same night several crew members fell into empty graves in the darkness and had to be carted off to the hospital.

*The X-Files* scripts are prepared weeks in advance. Days of preproduction go into preparing each episode for actual shooting. Carter said most of his time in Vancouver is consumed with supervising preproduction, scouting locations, and making sure the crew has what it needs to work quickly and efficiently. The series, with its extensive use of lower mainland and now interior locations, and its complicated camera setups, is one of the most demanding productions in series television. Writing producers fly up from Los Angeles for the last two days prior to shooting. The cast and crew (most of them Canadian) work on the shoot for twelve hour days, seven days a week, for an average eight days per episode. The raw footage is shipped to Los Angeles for one to three weeks of postproduction work by a team of about fifty. Twenty-two episodes are shot each year between mid-July and early May.

In terms of budget, the show falls about the middle range for an average one-hour prime-time drama. It was budgeted at $1.1 million per episode for the first season, $1.2 million the second year, and a bit more than that in season three, owing in part to salary increases (the stars have sweetened three-year deals, in recognition of the show's success).

On America Online, coproducer Paul Rabwin said, "I supervise the editing, work with the special effects producer, Mat Beck, supervise the color and all of the sound. When props have to be found in L.A., I'll do that, too! Occasionally I do some casting but I depend on the other producers to do a lot of that."

Writer Morgan expanded, "We're in L.A. They're in Vancouver. They call if there's a problem, but not as much rewriting goes on as with other shows. We go to Canada for a couple days at the end of preproduction. The set works, on average, fourteen to sixteen hours per day. They think we just sit around, but we put in twelve-hour days also. We actually don't spend much time on set. The things we want are established before we shoot."

Carter told *Entertainment Weekly* OnLine, "It is physically impossible to produce shows faster than we do. You have to have reruns in order for us to catch up. As it is we do twenty-five episodes a season, three more than most shows." He said on CBC Radio's *The Gabereau Show* that he's always working on five shows at once. He writes a show, preps a show to shoot,

shoots a show, edits a show, and puts the music and sound in a show, all at the same time. He even directed an episode, telling a Delphi online audience, "I've spent so much time whispering in directors' ears, it was nice to take the reins, but it was also very hard. Trying to get the best work possible in eight twelve-hour days."

Roughly one hundred full-time crew members work on *The X-Files* in Vancouver, with twenty to thirty more involved at any given time depending on what's required, such as set construction. The series uses North Shore Studios in west Vancouver, back-dropped by a snow-brushed mountain range (including the infamous skiers haven, Grouse Mountain).

## "IT'S LIKE RELIGION. HERESY IS THOUGHT

of as a bad thing, whereas in science it should be just the opposite." —T. GOLD

Carter has given two different reasons why the show began production in Vancouver. He told CBC Radio's *The Gabereau Show*, "Fox wanted to come up here because you get a good return on your money, which appealed to me, too, because I get to put more money up on screen." But he told *Entertainment Weekly's* OnLine audience, "I chose Vancouver originally for the great forests. We needed a good forest for the pilot. We came back because I love the city and because it works well for the kind of stories we tell. It has a great quality of light, too."

Both reasons no doubt play a part, but the feel of the location is probably the most important factor. Carter has also said that the rain in Vancouver gives the series a gray moodiness, and that the show loses this eerie quality in the sun. Originally, the creative team made a mighty effort to produce the pilot in the Los Angeles area, but they couldn't come up with an appropriate forest. Vancouver proved to be the ticket for the pilot, and it has since proven to be a chameleon city, providing a wealth of locations that can double for almost anywhere in the United States.

Coexecutive producer R. W. Goodwin told the *Seattle Times*, "Each episode is like a whole different movie. We have to scout locations, build new sets, cast the characters." There are only four permanent sets: Mulder's apartment and office, Mulder's boss's office, and a multistory prison block. The rest are built anew each time. The Gastown Post & Transfer in Vancouver handles the film processing and telecine transfer. The show is off-lined on an Avid Media Composer and onlined at Encore Video in Los Angeles.

Todd Pittson, the show's location manager, said that *The X-Files* is the only show that he has ever worked on where the writers ask for locations before the script is completed, and that allows him to be a part of the creative process. "I'm always talking to the writers, and as soon as they get a script idea, we discuss it," he told *ReelWest* magazine. "There was this one time where one of the writers told me he had this idea to use a mansion, and I told him not to do it because mansions are a big problem right now. They've been overused. I asked him what the story point was and if we couldn't use something that would be more visual to work with, because we don't want to be hackneyed

---

## Kolchak: The Night Stalker Episode Guide

### THE RIPPER

**Guest Cast:** Beatrice Colen and Ruth McDevitt
**Writer:** Rudolph Borchert
**Director:** Allen Baron

The original Jack the Ripper stalks Chicago. Kolchak tracks him to his lair.

### THE ZOMBIE

**Guest Cast:** Joe Sirola, Charles Aidman, Val Bisoglio, Earl Faison, Antonio Fargas, Pat J. O'Malley, Scatman Crothers, and John Fiedler
**Writer:** David Chase
**Story:** Zekial Markel
**Director:** Alex Grasshoff

A black zombie hunts the Chicago mob. Haitian magic plagues Chicago. Kolchak confronts the walking dead.

### U.F.O.

**Guest Cast:** James Gregory, Mary Wickes, Will Patten, Maureen Arthur, John Fiedler, Phil Leeds, Fritz Feld, and Rudy Challenger
**Writer:** Rudolph Borchert
**Director:** Allen Baron

Something sucks the bone marrow from zoo animals. The planetarium is filled with tarlike goo, invisible menaces, and the killer's alien spaceship.

### THE VAMPIRE

**Guest Cast:** William Daniels, Jan Murray, Kathleen Nolan, Suzanne Charny, John Doucette, Larry Storch, and Milt Kamen

**Writer:** David Chase
**Director:** Don Weis

This sequel to the pilot offers a beautiful prostitute-turned-vampire stalking the streets of L.A.

### THE WEREWOLF

**Guest Cast:** Eric Braedan, Henry Jones, Bob Hastings, Dick Gautier, Nita Talbot, Jackie Russell, Lewis Charles, Barry Cahill, Dort Clark, and Heath Jobes
**Writers:** David Chase, Paul Playdon
**Director:** Don Weis

A werewolf terrifies the passengers of a cruise ship.

### FIRE-FALL

**Guest Cast:** Fred Beir, Philip Carey, and Madlyn Rhue
**Writer:** Bill S. Ballinger
**Director:** Don Weis

A pyromaniac doppleganger sends Kolchak to the Church for help. (It was bundled with "The Energy Eaters" as the film *Crackle of Death*.)

### THE DEVIL'S PLATFORM

**Guest Cast:** Tom Skerritt, Ellen Weston, Julie Gregg, John Myhers, Jeanne Cooper, Bill Mims, Stanley Adams, and Robert Do Qui
**Writer:** Donn Mullally
**Director:** Allen Baron

Politician Tom Skerrit sells his soul to Satan for political advancement and the power to become a demonic canine.

### BAD MEDICINE

**Guest Cast:** Richard Kiel, Ramon Bieri, Alice Ghostley, Victor Jory, David Lewis, Marvin Kaplan, James Griffith, Dennis McCarthy, Morris Buchanan, Keith Walker, and Madilyn Clark
**Writer:** L. Ford Neale
**Director:** Alex Grasshoff

An American Indian spirit cursed to restore treasure stolen from the gods visits the rich of Chicago in the form of animal totems but fears the eye of the beholder. (Richard Kiel also appeared in "The Spanish Moss Murders.")

### THE SPANISH MOSS MURDERS

**Guest Cast:** Keenan Wynn, Severn Darden, Randy Boone, Richard Kiel, Johnny Silver, Ned Glass, Virgina Gregg, Brian Avery, Maurice Marsac, Elisabeth Brooks, and Donald Mantooth
**Writer:** Al Friedman
**Director:** Gordon Hessler

A sleep experiment subject looses Swamp Monsters. Kolchak tracks the fantasy creature through the sewers of Chicago. (Richard Kiel reappears.)

and use the same old stuff. Another time I suggested that we find a way to use [Vancouver's new hockey and basketball facility] GM Place. They had this big stadium without a roof, and it really made for a spooky look. But the great thing about this show is that people are always asking me 'How long have you been shooting here?' and I'll say 'From the beginning,' and they'll usually be really surprised because it doesn't look at all like Vancouver."

All series shooting is in a region known as "The Grid," the geographical zone in the lower mainland within which film crews work without travel penalties. Simon Fraser University in Burnaby became the FBI Headquarters in Washington, D.C. A mutant nested under one escalator of Vancouver's City Square Mall in "Tooms." Mutant insects ate hapless loggers in Lighthouse Park in West Vancouver for "Darkness Falls." Powertech Labs, Inc., of Surrey became a secret facility

---

### THE ENERGY EATER

**Guest Cast:** William Smith, Michael Strong, and John Alvin

**Writers:** Arthur Rowe, Rudolph Borchert

**Director:** Alex Grasshoff

An American Indian Bear Spirit kills with electricity. This time the authorities help Kolchak. (It was bundled with "Fire-fall" as the film *Crackle of Death*.)

### HORROR IN THE HEIGHTS

**Guest Cast:** Phil Silvers

**Writer:** Jimmy Sangster

**Director:** Michael T. Caffey

The flesh-eating Hindu Rakshasha demon kills Chicago's elderly Jews, assuming the form of trusted loved ones. (The cast is filled with classic Jewish character actors.)

### MR. R.I.N.G.

**Guest Cast:** Julie Adams and Corrine Michaels

**Writer:** L. Ford Neale

**Director:** Gene Levitt

Misunderstood android with a wax face kills his way through Chicago.

### THE PRIMAL SCREAM

**Guest Cast:** Pat Harrington, Katherine Woodville, and Lindsay Workman

**Writers:** Bill S. Ballinger, David Chase

**Director:** Robert Scheerer

Million-year-old Arctic cells rapidly reproduce into an ape-man in Chicago.

### THE TREVI COLLECTION

**Guest Cast:** Nina Foch and Lara Parker

**Writer:** Rudolph Borchert

**Director:** Don Weis

A Garment District mob, satanic mannequins, and a beautiful witch hinder Kolchak's investigation of the death of a fashion spy.

### CHOPPER

**Guest Cast:** Larry Linville, Jim Backus, and Sharon Farrell

**Writers:** Steve Fisher, David Chase

**Director:** Bruce Kessler

A headless spirit of a biker named "the Swordman" kills former rival gang members.

### DEMON IN LACE

**Guest Cast:** Andrew Prine and Keenan Wynn

**Writers:** Michael Kozoll

**Director:** Don Weis

An archaeology professor accidentally summons a succubus that inhabits recently deceased campus coeds, luring male students to their doom. (It was bundled with "Legacy of Terror" as the film *The Demon and the Mummy*.)

### LEGACY OF TERROR

**Guest Cast:** Ramon Bieri, Pippa Scott, Sorrell Booke, Victor Campos, and Erik Estrada

**Writer:** Arthur Rowe

**Director:** Don McDougall

An ancient Aztec mummy inhabits a ballpark, following a trail of victims with their hearts removed. (It was bundled with "Demon In Lace" as the film *The Demon and the Mummy*.)

### THE KNIGHTLY MURDERS

**Guest Cast:** John Dehner, Hans Conried, Robert Emhardt, and Jeff Donnell

**Writers:** Michael Kozoll, David Chase

**Director:** Vincent McEveety

The haunted armor of a twelfth-century knight objects to turning a museum into a nightclub.

### THE YOUTH KILLER

**Guest Cast:** Cathy Lee Crosby and Dwayne Hickman

**Writer:** Rudolph Borchert

**Director:** Don McDougall

A beautiful devotee of an ancient Greek goddess stalks the singles scene.

### THE SENTRY

**Guest Cast:** Kathie Browne and Tom Bosley

**Writers:** L. Ford Neale and John Huff

**Director:** Seymour Robbie

A bipedal lizard kills workers at a high-security underground complex when construction threatens her eggs.

in Mattawa, Washington, after feds spirited an "extraterrestrial biological entity" to the lab. Steveston Village, Richmond, served as Steveston, Maine, home to aliens, then it became Kenwood, Tennessee, when a faith healer battled forces of darkness. The shipyards of North Vancouver became the Maryland Waterfront where Mulder discovered evidence of a human/alien hybridizing project. Boundary Bay Airport, Ladner, filled in for Ellens Air Force Base, Idaho, when Mulder tried to catch the USAF test-flying a secret UFO-based craft. Ultimately, the serendipity of finding Vancouver in the first place has proven to be an important part of the success of the show.

## SPECIAL EFFECTS

*X-Files* creator Chris Carter deserves to feel proud of his show, and one of the things he's most pleased with has been their ability to create high-quality, but low-cost, special effects. He said to *ReelWest* magazine, "It's amazing what we've done. When we've set out to do something, we've done it. Rarely have we had to pull back. There was an elevator sequence in an episode. We couldn't do it the way we wanted to so we went another way. If you're a good producer and a smart writer, you'll find what isn't working and you'll change quickly and make yourself happy and do it for the money available. It's part of the dance. There's only so much money. Our special effects budget is very limited. Our show has really good and scary effects, but they serve the show rather than becoming the show."

Rabwin told an America Online audience, "We try to keep post-production effects around $30,000 per show, but we go over a lot. The practical effects on the set are a different matter. We do some CGI [computer generated images] on certain shows. We did a plane crashing into the trees in "Red Museum." Most of the space ships are CGI. Mat Beck is a great visual effects man."

Production designer Graeme Murray added, "I would love to have more time. It's the time really that I need, more than the money. You get to a stage where you need time, and no matter how much money you had you know it wouldn't be enough. It's not that we're working with [scriptwriters] who don't understand the difficulties. You give them what is written, but you have to get the essential part rather than the whole thing.

The emphasis of the show is on the 'look,' so that has to be interesting and unique every time out. So far nothing has been outside the realm of possibility, but it could go that way. We did a really good job last year of providing almost every thing that the scripts asked for. Now, naturally, the scripts are bigger and more ambitious and more complex. There is more being asked. But we're getting better, too, so we can keep up. We have to. The 'look' of the show is a major selling point, which is extremely satisfying to those of us who are involved in creating it."

If modern computer-driven tools aid the special effects artist, the expectations of today's television audiences keeps the work from becoming any easier. Dave Gauthier, special effects supervisor, says today's sophisticated audiences are extremely attentive to the way aliens are represented. "What is interesting about our effects is the idea of portraying other beings," he told *ReelWest* magazine. "It's not an ordinary show. Sure, we do pretty big effects; we had a huge fire in an episode last year, for instance, but we mostly try to make aliens who will be interesting to this very sophisticated audience of ours."

Gauthier continued, "We are trying to create things that don't exist, but sometimes, when we get a little carried away, we have to be reined back. It's part of the process. The most interesting thing we do is make people fly. We do a lot of flying. In most TV shows, you don't get much chance to do abduction scenes. Chris likes to see people being sucked up into space crafts. I think we all do, actually, and we create everything here as a group. We all bring ideas to the table, which makes the success of the show very satisfying."

Often objects are created entirely as computer graphics, such as the space ship in the "Deep Throat" episode in year one. A concert lighting rig fired off lights in different colors to form a triangle, so that real light rained down on Mulder, but the spaceship was digitally illustrated. The special effects crew usually work up their ideas on Macintosh Powerbooks before hiring a computer production house to create the effect.

Some hybrids of physical and digital effects also appear. Samantha's reflection in the window during her abduction in "Little Green Men" took an exterior image created during shooting, flopped it, and placed it faintly into the window space, working around a real shaft of light coming into the room.

The special effects make-up person, Toby Lindala, joined *The X-Files* team with the pilot episode. He was hired to do prosthetics for the first season and has stayed on. He created the famous worms for "Ice" by making body casts of the actors. Then he made fake skin realistic down to every fold and created a channel with monofilaments attached to a row of beads that could move and contract beneath the fake skin on command. The dog was actually a milk bottle tightly wrapped with fur; the first dog model, a gelatin-based prosthetic, had kept tearing. There were also digitally created worms, including the one that crawls into the dog. He built the Flukeman costume in ten days.

Lindala specializes in realism, which fits the reality-based, documentary style of *The X-Files*. He agrees with the producers that the visuals shouldn't become so involved they overwhelm the story, but he also notes that if the special effects become too graphic, they will be deleted by Standards and Practices, who have already deleted other ideas. Carter has called Lindala "one of the stars behind the camera." Lindala's crew includes Bill Terezakis, Adam Behr, Doug Morrow, Roy MacGregor, Robert Moon, Charlie Grant, and Brad Proctor.

Key make-up artist Fern Levin established a network of medical advisers and pathologists for *The X-Files*. Levin recalled two amusing incidents involving medical decisions, telling the *Seattle Times*, "I called up a hospital's burn unit once to ask what a severe burn should look like. The person there asked what type of burn it was. I told them it was a vampire burn. Another time I asked them what a burn from flying-saucer exhaust might look like."

The effects crew encounter all sorts of difficulties. For instance, one episode in year three, "Teso Dos Bichos," required Gillian Anderson to be attacked by a crazed feline, but it turned out that Anderson is allergic to cat fur. So the special effects crew created a dummy covered in rabbit fur. "It was the stupidest thing I've ever done," Anderson recalled to *TV Guide* of her three-hour struggle with the fake cat. "It was take after take of fighting and rolling around with this bunny-covered cat on my face. The fur was coming off, going up my nose, and sticking to my lipstick. That was the worst."

Anderson was also supposed to eat a live cricket in an episode about circus freaks, and the rumor was widely circulated that she did indeed eat it. But while she did put the insect in her mouth, she didn't actually swallow it. "I didn't even taste it," she said. "It was just kind of wriggling around in my mouth, and then I spit it out."

Paul Rabwin also notes that sometimes they don't do their own work, but they splice in a stock shot from another production. The series doesn't do many stunts, either, he says, due to the bad weather in Vancouver, which makes it difficult to shoot stunt scenes safely.

All in all, it's an amazing effort, and Carter told *Entertainment Weekly* OnLine, "*The X-Files* crew is great, but the work is hard. It's amazing that everyone gets along so well, but everyone really believes in the show."

# CHAPTER 3

# YEAR ONE

I finished the pilot on a Monday night, or early Tuesday morning," *The X-Files* creator Chris Carter said on CBC Radio's *The Gabereau Show*, "and at 8 A.M. that same morning, it was shown to the Fox executives, including Rupert Murdoch. Every smart executive before responding will turn and look to see what Rupert Murdoch's response is, but there was spontaneous applause. I wasn't there, but it was reported to me by 10 A.M. that morning. I had no idea what the response was going to be, but when they responded like that, I knew we were in contention to be a series. On Friday, they ordered thirteen episodes." The show premiered on Friday, September 10, 1993.

While the pilot turned out to be a little different, according to Carter, than the pilot script he originally wrote, he felt it worked extremely well setting up the characters and the ideas of the show. Pilot episodes differ from normal episodes in that they must tell a coherent story while simultaneously introducing unfamiliar characters and relationships quickly. Carter felt the pilot was a tremendous synthesis of all the parts.

In the pilot, we meet Special Agent Fox Mulder, played by David Duchovny. He's one of the FBI's greatest detectives, with a photographic memory and a background as a psychologist. He's helped profile many serial killers. However, Agent Mulder has taken a consuming interest in the X-Files—the FBI's "dead letter office," where unexplained and apparently unsolvable cases are filed, to be essentially forgotten. Nicknamed "Spooky" at the Academy, Mulder has had a fascination with the paranormal and extraterrestrial life ever since his sister disappeared when they were children. Mulder has come to believe that she was abducted by aliens.

Higher-ups at the bureau, apparently concerned about Mulder's obsession, decide to assign Agent Dr. Dana Katherine Scully to work with him. Scully, played by Gillian Anderson, quickly understands that her mission is to debunk Mulder's theories concerning the X-Files and get him to close up shop. Scully was recruited out of medical school and sees the FBI as a place to distinguish herself. She is, as a scientist, skeptical by nature, confident that logic and reason can explain what seems at first mysterious.

In episode one, Mulder is contacted by "Deep Throat," played by Jerry Hardin, a mysterious, influential government source willing to provide information. He initially warns Mulder not to investigate bizarre phenomena at Ellens Air Force Base, but most importantly he hints that Mulder is right to believe that there might be aliens hidden among the X-Files cases and that the government is playing some part in covering that up. Deep Throat continues to appear throughout the year, offering tantalizing clues and hints about the truth. As the year progresses, the scope of the government conspiracy begins to take shape, though its true nature is never revealed.

Another shadowy character who also makes occasional appearances over the course of the year, and seems to be deeply involved in the conspiracy and a member of a secret organization, is "Cigarette-Smoking Man," played by William B. Davis. This quiet but very powerful man has access to a secret vault in the Pentagon where alien specimens are recorded and kept.

In episode twelve, "Beyond the Sea," Agent Scully's father, Captain William Scully, played by Don S. Davis, dies. Margaret Scully, played by Sheila Larken, is Dana's widowed mother. Other family members also get introduced during the year. Melissa Scully, Dana's older sister, played by Melinda McGraw, is open to the metaphysical. William Mulder, played by Peter Donat, is Fox's divorced father; he may have once held a job under the Secretary of State, and he now lives in West Tisbury, Massachusetts. Mrs. Mulder, played by Rebecca Toolan, is Fox's mother, and she lives in Martha's Vineyard.

In episode sixteen, "E.B.E.," the Lone Gunmen, a trio of conspiracy nuts, are introduced, and they become recurring characters who occasionally work with Mulder. They are actually the three editors of *The Lone Gunman*, a paranoid publication devoted to exposing the hidden conspiracies of the U.S. government. Frohike, played by Tom Braidwood, is the most unkempt, with graying hair and glasses. Langly, played by Dean Haglund, has long blonde hair and glasses, while Byers, played by Bruce Harwood, has a mustache and beard and usually dresses in a suit.

It isn't until episode twenty, "Tooms," that we meet Mulder and Scully's boss, Assistant Director Walter S. Skinner, played by Mitch Pileggi. Skinner is one of the heads of the FBI, but he answers to a higher authority regarding the X-files. He is sympathetic to Mulder and is not happy with some of his job requirements. Section Chief Scott Blevins, played by Charles Cioffi, is the Head of the Office of Professional Responsibility, and he is the one who originally assigned Scully to the X-Files division to keep an eye on Mulder.

The first-season finale, "The Erlenmeyer Flask," ends with Deep Throat being murdered and the closing of the X-Files. Scully comes face to face with an alien, forcing her to finally relinquish some of her staunch skepticism. The episode closes with Mulder and Scully being reassigned. Carter believed that "The Erlenmeyer Flask" brought the series' first year full circle: closing down the X-Files left the show with an excellent cliffhanger, and it left the second season open to many new and interesting possibilities.

## REACTIONS

*The X-Files*' first season ranked 102 out of 118 series on the air, hardly a spectacular showing, even for the affiliate-starved Fox network. Carter told the *Sacramento Bee*, "I think we might have been overlooked at first. People are always looking for that big, explosive hit, but not a lot of people watched us at the beginning. And people don't always take Fox seriously. It's been the network of *Married . . . With Children*, *Studs*, and *90210*, and people have had to change their mind-set to accept something like *The X-Files*."

Despite low total viewer numbers, the series reached a lucrative demographic, and a strong fandom began to grow. Seventy-five hundred members immediately joined an official *The X-Files* fan club. The fans held their first convention, and twenty-three hundred people turned out. Twenty conventions were held within eight months, some of them attended by Carter, who began to call the fans "File-o-philes." The name didn't stick, though, and members of an Internet newsgroup chose "X-Philes," a name that seems to have become universally accepted.

X-Philes immediately invaded the online world of electronic communications, and online fandom grew to be the second largest of any TV series, surpassed only by Trekkers. Delphi is the official *X-Files* service, and the official World Wide Web page quickly received eight million hits. The Internet heats up Friday nights when as many as 150,000 hits occur before and after the show. There are dozens of private home pages, e-mail groups, and bulletin boards.

Carter used to read up to seventy pages of downloaded fan comments each night, and this has led the show's creators to play to their fan audience. Co-executive Producer Glen Morgan has said certain shows have been tailored to please online fans. Inside jokes are common: no number, name, or address goes into the show without forethought. Fans' names show up on passenger lists. Digital clocks flash 10:13, Carter's birthday, or 11:21, his wife's.

The actors are aware of the attention. Anderson told the *Sacramento Bee*, "I've been told that on one of the computer services there's something called the Gillian Anderson Testosterone Brigade. That just tickles me."

Carter told *Entertainment Weekly* that he's had some strange encounters of his own due to his series. He said, "Since the show started, people have sought me out. I was warned about nutcases but these are regular folks. A banker will tell about his experience with aliens. Pilots and flight attendants come up to me and claim to have seen UFOs. One friend told me, 'You don't know how accurate you are.' He broke down, telling me about his visitations. I've known this person for two years. I have no reason not to believe him."

He believes that what he encounters is only the tip of a huge iceberg, telling *Omni*, "Seeing those kinds of reactions makes one believe that there are things that are affecting people out there, whether they are real or imagined. There's too much evidence to dismiss it out of hand." Yet despite these X-Philes with very strong beliefs, only about half of the fans believe in the paranormal, a percentage not inconsistent with Gallup polls, which have consistently found that half of Americans believe in UFOs.

Carter believes the enormous traffic about *The X-Files* on the Internet and the attention given the show in science fiction fanzines helped put the show over with its core audience. He never expected fan clubs and T-shirts and all the other merchandise because the tone of his show is subdued, dark, and subtle, and Carter wants it to remain that way.

## "A LIE REPEATED OFTEN ENOUGH BECOMES the truth." —GOEBBLES

Fox executives were quick to jump on the bandwagon. Programming Chief Sandy Grushow told the *San Francisco Chronicle*, "*The X-Files* is a terrific show. *The X-Files* is a show people are really starting to talk about." Bob Greenblatt, Fox senior vice president of drama development, told the *Los Angeles Times*, "Now I hear from other writers and other networks, that everybody is trying to develop their own *X-Files*."

The series scored almost universally good notices. Magazines ranging from *Entertainment Weekly* to the Catholic journal *Commonweal* raved about *The X-Files*. Ray Richmond, of the *Los Angeles Daily News*, called it "one of the more intriguing new dramas of the fall season." *USA Today*'s Matt Touch wrote, "File this under your 'must see' heading: *The X-Files* just keeps getting better. And weirder. And scarier." The *Los Angeles Times* proclaimed the series "arguably the coolest drama on TV."

*Entertainment Weekly* reviewed *The X-Files* twice within four months. The first time, in the October 8, 1993, issue, they gave the new show a B+, saying, "I'm skeptical not only about the existence of UFOs and so-called paranormal activity but also about entertainment that dramatizes this stuff: hooey about hooey. Nonetheless, I'm hooked on *The X-Files*, a series about two fictional FBI agents who investigate fact-based, but nonetheless wacko, unearthliness every week. *The X-Files* is the most paranoid, subversive show on TV right now. There's marvelous tension between Anderson—who is dubious about these events—and

Duchovny, who has the haunted, imploring look of a true believer. Filled with florid dialogue and not-bad special effects, *X-Files* is a hoot about hooey." Then, in the January 21, 1994, issue, *Entertainment Weekly* added, "Unlike spook-TV predecessors such as *The Twilight Zone* or *The Outer Limits*, *X-Files* has no high-minded moral to teach, no winking irony to impart; all it wants to do is shake your faith in reality. The vintage program it's closest to in spirit is *Kolchak: The Night Stalker*, the 1974–75 oddity that starred Darren McGavin as a reporter who saw vampires and goblins where no one else did. But *The X-Files* is really its own creation; its scripts—most of them written by Carter—achieve a sort of hard-boiled eloquence. Carter, who's also the executive producer, elicits our heebie-jeebies by creating disturbing moods, and by extracting convincingly rattled performances from the actors."

*The X-Files* quickly became Britain's number one TV import. The U.K.'s *Times Mirror* reported, "*The X Files* has become the creepiest, scariest show on television. *The X Files* is now one of the most watched programs of the week." The series met with equal praise and enthusiasm in Australia. Australia's *Sun-Herald Now* announced the phenomenon, "In just one year *The X-Files* has established itself as the *Star Trek* of the nineties, inspiring a fervent obsession among those who call themselves X-Philes."

The professional community also recognized the production, writing, and acting quality of the new *X-Files*, granting the new series many awards and honors. *The X-Files* won the Emmy Awards for Outstanding Individual Achievement in Graphic Design and Title Sequences, and was a nominee for Outstanding Achievement in Main Title Theme Music. Carter won the Environmental Media Award for Outstanding Episodic Television (Drama) for writing the episode "Darkness Falls," and was a finalist for Best Writing at the New York Festival For Television Programming and Promotion for his episode "The Erlenmeyer Flask." James Wong and Glen Morgan were finalists for the same award for their episode "Beyond the Sea." The series also won the Parent's Choice Honors for Best Series and the Monitor Awards for Best Editing for James Coblentz's "Beyond the Sea" episode.

The acclaim came as a shock to ex-surfer Carter. He later told *Entertainment Weekly*, "I had no idea this could happen. I wrote this in my office in my surf trunks, playing with my dog. It never occurred to me that someday there'd be *X-Files* key chains."

## PROBLEMS

*The X-Files*, while becoming a blossoming cult hit, also suffered from its share of problems and crisis during its first year. There were creative problems as the show searched for its legs and actors struggled with their characters, and there were production problems, ranging from sexual harassment suits to lack of money.

The first season of *The X-Files* was focused on delivering entertaining stories and helping Mulder and Scully to become three-dimensional characters. Their exploits struck a chord with viewers, but Carter and company failed to create a coherent universe with a sense of unity and direction. *The X-Files* improved as the season progressed, but the writing remained weak and failed to pull together the elements into a coherent whole. Too often, the series lacked direction, unsure of what it wanted to be. Ideas were introduced and then forgotten as new information conflicted with previous episodes.

Duchovny felt uneasy with Mulder's underlying motivation, that every emotional moment seemed to link back to Mulder's sister being abducted by aliens. While that event was his character's foundation for interest in the supernatural, Duchovny believed Mulder had to become more complicated, that realism would be lost if everything in his character's life went back to one event.

Anderson had more mundane problems adjusting to the pacing of television work and getting used to the arcane dialogue her character used. She said that sometimes it was very hard to say the stuff and sound like she knew what she was talking about, since she didn't. There was always a level at which she felt lost as an actress, despite her early interest in biology. She also said that the lack of time to rehearse and the hectic pace of shooting left little time to make considered acting choices. She felt unsure of her work. She later told the *Sydney Morning Herald*, "During the first year, we were in a vacuum, getting used to the hours and the rhythm of television. It was hard to deal with the emotional ups and downs being away from home. That was getting in the way of success. We'd hear that the ratings were getting better, that there was a cult follow-ing, but I didn't have any frame of reference, so it didn't mean anything to me."

However, Anderson was happy that the characters were becoming positive role models for young kids. Despite the dark subject matter of the show, their characters were honest, hardworking, straightforward, dedicated, clean individuals.

Creating interesting stories remained an ongoing problem. Duchovny told the *Los Angeles Times*, "It's going to be hard to come up with really good stories every week. You can't be like a *Melrose Place*—you know, the guy's got a bad haircut, let's make an episode out of that. It's got to be a full-blown, movie-type story. So the pressure on the writers is immense." As a regular writer for *The X-Files*, Carter admitted that finding writers for the series was difficult.

Story editor Frank Spotnitz feared that either viewers wouldn't be able to figure out what the show's focus was or they would pigeonhole it too quickly. He said that at the beginning of the first season, people thought of *The X-Files* as a UFO series, but that after "Squeeze," they thought it was a monster show, then after "Ice," that it was a suspense thriller, and after "Erlenmeyer Flask," the first true government-paranoia show. People didn't know what to expect, although the "mythology" epi-sodes, those that dealt with the underlying government conspiracy, formed the core of the series. But people had pinned that down. The mythology arc had begun with the show's very first episode and progressed with consis-tency. The series did escape pigeonholing, without broadening into the kind of self-parody that many critics feel entrapped its spiritual forefather, *The Night Stalker*.

*The X-Files* also struggled with a tight budget, something shows on the bigger networks don't always have to worry about as much. However, *The X-Files* did well pulling off believable special effects, and the lack of funds and shooting time rarely forced the show to change shooting scenes after they were written. Carter told a Sci Fi Channel audience, "[Fox executives] have been extremely supportive from the beginning, even though there were some hard-fought battles and some really tedious arguments. There are always budgetary struggles, and those still exist. It's not like this big money's opened up and we can do whatever we want—far from that. There have been very few political problems, hierarchical, boss/worker problems. I think that's because we really set a tone. If you work hard, everyone else works hard, too."

There were some disagreements with the network over content, though. Apparently, executives weren't happy with "Beyond The Sea," the episode in which Scully's father dies. "The network didn't want to do that episode. There were hesitations and reservations about some of the plotting—but we stood our ground," Carter told *Sci-Fi Entertainment*. In addition, the end of "Deep Throat," the first episode after the pilot, had been a compromise with the network, who argued that there needed to be a more complete and satisfying closure, and this raised ongoing questions about how successful Mulder would be in convincing others of the conspiracy, alien invaders, and other aspects of the paranormal. The conflicting needs of resolution and continuing suspense created disagreements within the creative staff and between the creative staff and the network.

Carter said, "The idea of closure was still being forced on us. They wanted a summing up of the episode. It made the episode better. That motif of Scully doing a voice-over as she types became a running story crutch."

Carter told *Producer* magazine, "We try to scare the pants off of people. And we try to do it intelligently, in the realm of extreme possibilities. The ambiguous end is part of the beauty and mystery of the show, but there were big, big battles about this very issue in the beginning. In our very first episode, I had a rather heated argument [with the network] about 'wrapping the show up.' The executives wanted complete closure and explanation about what had happened. I argued that we can put things up for speculation, but we cannot draw hard conclusions."

Carter later reported that the executives who fought hard for a more traditional TV ending later changed their minds and are now behind him "100 percent." The "give and take" between the creative staff and the network executives remains of vital importance to the show. Carter continually tries to balance his instincts with other opposing points of view.

Judith A. Fairly, a former script coordinator for *The X-Files*, brought the series its saddest problem when she filed a sexual harassment suit against Carter and Howard Gordon, the show's coexecutive producer. Fairly alleges that the two men engaged in "continuous, pervasive and ongoing offensive and unwelcome sexual conduct" during her three-year tenure. Fairly also named Twentieth Century Fox Film Corp. and Twentieth Century Fox TV in the suit. Fox officials have called the suit "frivolous" and Carter said "this claim appears to be emblematic of a climate where disgruntled employees are manipulating the intent behind well-meaning laws for nothing more than undeserved personal financial gain."

## CHANGES

The first year saw the two lead actors fine-tuning their characters and establishing the rapport that would carry the series. Duchovny told *Starlog*, "There's more to this character than just a man with a mission, and each script attempts to draw out a bit more of his human side. Some weeks I'm happier than others at what personal sides of his character I get to bring in. Sometimes I think we forget that Mulder has a sense of humor and that we could be making him funnier than he is. I've noticed, as the season has progressed, that there has been an increase in his intensity. That's OK, but I'm already missing what he was like in some of the earlier episodes, when he was capable of going back and forth between moods much more easily."

After the first season, Anderson wanted the characters to become more emotionally involved in their cases, despite the need for detachment. Duchovny disagreed, as he told *The Prydonian Renegade*, "There's no way that two people could have the amount of experiences that we do if we were emotionally and personally involved in every case. So for every two that we are involved in personally, you have to have two where we're just detectives. We're just agents trying to solve a case who don't have anything at stake, personally."

He told *Starlog*, "From an actor's point of view, it's hard to be in search of the most important thing in the world every week. I've had to make gradations on how much these things really mean to Mulder. It all boils down to projecting bigger or lesser emotions. I've basically had to decide every week whether I'm up against the Holy Grail or the Shroud of Turin and then act accordingly."

The first season saw the two lead heroes develop a caring and sometimes flirtatious relationship, and many viewers wondered whether it would develop into a full-blown romantic relationship. Anderson told the *Washington Times*, "The show's not about that. We have a good rapport on film together. I think to tamper with something that's not broken is perhaps a mistake." At a January 14, 1994, press conference, Carter said, "The show is very plot-driven. . . . It's what I fought for from the beginning, which is, I didn't want this to be another *Moonlighting*. I didn't want . . . the relationship [between Mulder and Scully] to come before the cases."

While noting that the show suffered from a number of problems, and that some episodes failed to please him, Duchovny said he is satisfied with the overall quality of *The X-Files* during the first season. He told *The Prydonian Renegade*, "If we can turn out eighteen good ones, I think we're doing much better than anyone hoped for. It's not amazing that TV's as bad as it is, it's amazing that some of it is as good as it is. I know what it takes to do a good job. It's very difficult."

In looking ahead, Duchovny told *Starlog*, "I don't know where a second season will go. I'm not sure anybody knows at this point. The possibilities for this show are limitless; as limitless as the writers' imaginations. I guess we'll just have to see how limitless that ultimately is."

# CHAPTER 4

# YEAR TWO

The end of the first season whetted viewers' appetites for more while throwing the entire premise of the show into confusion. What was happening, and where was it going? Not only that, by the time shooting was to begin, Gillian Anderson was pregnant, and the writers would have to find some way to work around her condition. Fortunately, series creator Chris Carter had developed some clear ideas, and season two saw them developed in stunning fashion.

With Deep Throat dead and the X-Files closed down, the season opens with Scully reassigned to a teaching job at the academy and Mulder doing mundane details elsewhere. But Mulder, not surprisingly, refuses to abandon his quest. From her post at Quantico, Scully continues to help him; she even agrees that there is some merit to Mulder's theories. In that first episode, number twenty-five, "Little Green Men," the story of the abduction of Mulder's sister, Samantha, is told in flashback (though it somewhat contradicts the same story told in episode four, "Conduit").

In the first half dozen episodes, the government's conspiracy begins to unfold. In episode twenty-eight, "Sleepless," Mulder is approached by a new informant, known as "X" and played by Steven Williams. X is much less patient with Mulder than Deep Throat, though he plays the same role, feeding him clues about the alien cover-up. Mulder's method of requesting contact usually involves shining a light out of his apartment window in some unique way, in this case a masking tape "X."

In the same episode, Mulder gets a new partner, FBI agent Alex Krycek, who, we soon learn, is not all that he seems. In the following two-part story, "Duane Barry" and "Ascension," Scully is kidnapped and then eventually abducted by, possibly, aliens. Krycek is revealed to be working for the Cigarette-Smoking Man. By the episode's end, Mulder convinces his boss,

Assistant Director Skinner, of the intricate government conspiracy that swirls all around them, and Skinner decides to reopen the X-Files.

Then, in episode thirty-two, "One Breath," a comatose Scully mysteriously returns, but her blood reveals genetic tampering. Mulder confronts Cigarette-Smoking Man, who refuses to reveal any answers about what's going on. Later in the season, the two-parter, "Colony" and "End Game," episodes forty and forty-one, continue the arc. Mulder and Scully investigate the murder of a group of doctors and meet CIA agent Ambrose Chapel. The story takes a new twist when Mulder's sister, Samantha, returns. An alien Bounty Hunter then takes Scully prisoner, and Samantha reinforces Mulder's belief that there are aliens on earth. Mulder is forced to trade Samantha to the alien Bounty Hunter in exchange for Scully, but Samantha turns out to be one of many clones. As a consequence, Mulder discovers that his real sister is alive.

The second-season finale, "Anasazi," the first of a three-part story, begins as a Navajo youth finds an alien corpse in New Mexico just as a computer hacker downloads classified Defense Department information revealing government communications with extraterrestrials for the past fifty years. Mulder gets his hands on the tapes, and Mulder's father attempts to reveal his involvement in the central conspiracy to his son, but he gets killed. Mulder then finds a boxcar filled with alien corpses buried on the Navajo reservation—and becomes trapped inside as it is set on fire.

Just as he did with season one, Carter ended season two with a barnstorming cliffhanger that sent the story careening in new directions while seemingly jeopardizing the future of the series (were Mulder not to get out alive). Along the way, he and his team of writers had settled into a working formula for episodes and begun to create a cohesive if shadowy world that almost seemed to taunt viewers into figuring it out. Manipulative government powers moved just beyond the reach of the show's heroes, who were able to get just close enough to see snatches of the truth.

Carter insisted there were few rules to *The X-Files* story game, and no "bible," or written set of guidelines, for the show. "There was some resistance by the network to the closing of the X-Files, but I wanted to say, 'Look, anything can happen on this show, including shooting the main character and closing the X-Files.' You've got to take risks, or you're stuck.

"We tell smart, scary stories, but we will not stoop for the easy scare. We avoid the conventions of horror or science fiction for that scare. If you try to analyze and put a label on the stories we tell, you do yourself a disservice."

Carter told the *Houston Chronicle* the secret is to tell good stories but not reveal too much at once; this was the basis for the mythology episodes, which were the ones fans liked best. He said, "Those are the ones about the government conspiracy and what Mulder and Scully are not being told as they search for the truth. Am I putting ideas into people's heads? Other groups out there right now who've made big news are saying they don't trust the government. I don't want people to confuse what I'm saying with that political agenda. And it's weird—a lot of people contact me saying they are or were 'in the loop.' There's an enormous number of conspiracy theorists out there, and they're trying to get me to tell their story. I've not done that."

In its short life, *The X-Files* had transcended genre limitations, speaking to universal truths and contemplating the nature of secrecy and freedom in a democratic society. This was heady stuff for TV, and virtually unexplored territory for television fiction. In two seasons, not one show offered a Happy Ending. Mulder and Scully survived but made little progress in revealing the conspiracies or the paranormal to a skeptical world. The government conspirators almost always got away. Brutal betrayals seemed almost normal, and Mulder and Scully were in almost constant danger from fellow agents. And for the most part, the audience was left to fill in the blanks about what was actually going on. Conventional wisdom would have said such a story would never succeed on TV, but people flocked to the show—intrigued by a good mystery and by themes that were unexpressed anywhere else.

"A lot of the shows are based loosely on factual information," Gillian Anderson told CBC's RealTime online audience. "The writers read scientific information and formulate bits and pieces into stories. Some information is factual, but in order to make an episode playable on television, it's pulled and tugged here and there to make it entertaining."

Sometimes the writers would extrapolate from real events. In episode twenty-six, "The Host," a Russian freighter is carrying radioactive debris from the Chernobyl nuclear-plant disaster. In real life, people exposed to Chernobyl have exhibited mutations, and in the story a strange wormlike creature, the Flukeman, is the result. The first-season episode "Beyond the Sea" drew its inspiration from the fact that 70 percent of widows report seeing their husbands again in the year after they died. Another episode came about after the news reported that a woman had been rushed to an emergency room with crystallized blood, and that doctors had suffered from the fumes. A National Public Radio piece about three unrelated military suicides in Haiti inspired the episode "Fresh Bones," about a voodoo cult on a U.S. base, while a news clip about an Arizona woman who swore bats invaded her house while a UFO hovered outside led to an episode

> **"WHEN A DISTINGUISHED BUT ELDERLY** scientist states that something is possible, he is almost certainly right. When he states that something is impossible, he is very probably wrong." —ARTHUR C. CLARKE'S FIRST LAW

Carter noted that comments submitted by fault-finding fans put pressure on them to keep honest with their science, relying on accurate research. Many in the show's audience have a science background, watch very carefully, and love to "pick our nits." He told *Entertainment Weekly* OnLine, "We do most of our own research, though we have just recently gotten a dedicated researcher to start helping us with material. All the military stuff comes from military sources, though I've been slapped on the wrist lately for a few inaccuracies."

Rabwin told America Online that although they try for accuracy all the time, people must remember that

*The X-Files* is a dramatic TV show, and sometimes the requirements of drama win out over absolute accuracy.

Though it didn't wind up working out, David E. Kelley of *Picket Fences*, which is on CBS, proposed an idea that complicated their lives even further. He suggested the first-ever crossover plotline for shows on different networks. Writers for *Picket Fences* and *The X-Files* came up with similar stories that they planned to interweave. *The X-Files*'s "Red Museum" had the FBI investigating a farm where cows were reportedly being injected with alien DNA. The *Picket Fences* episode "Away in the Manger" had cows giving birth to human children. Kelley's concept was for Mulder to investigate, believing it would provide information on the "Red Museum" case. Though both episodes were produced, Mulder didn't appear on the CBS show. *X-Files* producer Bob Goodwin told *Cinescape*, "I spent days on the phone with a producer of *Picket Fences*. We spent days organizing our schedules. Then at the very last minute we found out that no one had told CBS, and they said, 'Forget it. We're having enough trouble on Friday nights without publicizing *The X-Files*.'"

Carter also carefully considered several guest roles during the season. Penn and Teller once asked to do a show, but to Carter's great shock, they didn't believe in the paranormal, and he declined their offer. Whoopi Goldberg asked, but they couldn't fit a date into her schedule. Carter isn't crazy about using guests, as he fears they will upstage his stories.

One guest star Carter has wanted desperately on his show is Darren McGavin, the actor who played Kolchak on *The Night Stalker*. Carter has said the series provided one of his main sources of inspiration for *The X-Files*, and he would like to pay homage to its star. Carter told *Entertainment Weekly* OnLine, "We've tried twice to get Mr. McGavin on the show. We'll keep trying, but his interest is iffy. Can't tell you why. I don't think he knew about the *X-Files* or the *NS* connection."

## REACTIONS

With the second season, *The X-Files* went from a basement-rated cult hit to a bona fide success. Its Nielsen numbers soared 45 percent in overall households, 62 percent in the key ages eighteen to forty-nine—the demographic group for which advertisers pay most—and 63 percent among adults twenty-six to fifty-four. Its second-season average was a respectable 9.0 rating (one ratings point equals 954,000 TV-viewing households). *The X-Files* had the most spectacular percentage gain of any prime-time series. Fox then aired *The X-Files* twice a week for a quick ratings fix during the November sweeps.

The series slowly creeped into pop culture popularity. A *New Yorker* essay called it this generation's *The Twilight Zone*. MGM called creator Chris Carter to see if he had any mugs or T-shirts to use as set dressing on its big-budget science-fiction movie *Species*. Carter told the Sci Fi Channel's Sci-Fi Buzz audience that the series had "gone beyond a cult status with the number of people who are watching it, but we're not in the top twenty each week."

Appearing on *The Late Late Show with Tom Snyder*, Duchovny said, "Some people's job is to see trends and to capitalize on them. I don't think there is a science fiction trend, or any other trend like that. I think *The X-Files* is a good show. Just making a show science fiction is not going to duplicate a success. Hopefully it will make us seem that much better. They'll say, 'That's like a faux *X-Files*.'"

The popularity of the show led to a deluge of licensing requests to produce *X-Files*-related merchandise. Carter told the *San Jose Mercury News*, "I don't want it to be overmarketed and I don't want it to be overcommercialized. This show has a subversive, anti-establishment quality that the commercialization and exploitation can work against. I'm not trying to slam J. C. Penney, but [that would be] sending the wrong message." Carter turned down a number of requests, including one to manufacture boxer shorts with images of Mulder and Scully.

A one-hour *Secrets of The X-Files* special aired on May 19, 1995, compiling clips chronicling the series' greatest moments. *People* named David Duchovny one of the world's fifty most beautiful people. *TV Guide* named the blue light that often bathes the show one of the fifty greatest things on television.

The crowning achievement for *The X-Files* was the award of the 1995 Golden Globe for Best Dramatic Series by the Foreign Press Association. *The X-Files* beat other quality drama shows such as *NYPD Blue*, *Picket Fences*, *ER*, and *Chicago Hope*. Carter said it was a complete surprise, but an honor for the show and good for crew morale.

He said when he called Vancouver to tell his cast and crew they were nominated for a Golden Globe, no one knew whether to believe him or not. He told a Sci Fi Channel audience, "We were all a little giddy. To be nominated was a big surprise. When they came to our category, I got a tightness across my chest. I had written my speech about ten minutes before I left the house, sitting in my underwear before I put my tux on, figuring I'd never have to read it. And then they announced that *The X-Files* had won. I got up on the stage and I looked down, and there's Elton John to the left of me and Diana Ross to the right of me, and the reality just slapped me in the face. It was a huge shock."

The series was also nominated for seven Emmy Awards, including Outstanding Drama Series, two editing awards, a writing award, and a cinematography award. The Television Critics Association nominated it for Best Drama Series. The Viewers for Quality Television also nominated it for Best Drama Series, and David Duchovny and Gillian Anderson both received nominations for Best Actor and Actress in a Drama Series. Among other award nominations for the second season, cinematographer John Bartley was nominated for an Outstanding Achievement Award by the American Society of Cinematographers for his work on "Duane Barry."

Carter told an *Entertainment Weekly* OnLine audience, "I think the publicity is good because it helps boost ratings. I don't think it will affect the subversive quality of the show. Increased ratings help loosen up money to do bigger and better stuff."

If Carter was pleased and amazed by his show's acceptance in the professional community, he was equally pleased with the growing band of devoted X-Philes. He told the *Houston Chronicle*, "It's astounding that there's this hardcore audience who have really taken those characters and this show and made it their own. It creates a little bit of responsibility. I actually felt as if I was working for these people."

The number of devotees continued to grow, and they ranged from super-fan Steven Spielberg, who's reportedly seen every episode, to real-life FBI agents. The most unexpected fan? "Tony Bennett," said an unhesitating Carter. "We were at the Golden Globes, and he approached David. It was kind of cool." Other fans include Whoopi Goldberg, Winona Ryder, Martin Short, Tom Petty, and Bruce Springsteen.

Kevin Humphreys, a "big fan" and a forensic scientist with the Oregon State Police Crime Lab, told *The Oregonian*, "I think everybody has that interest in the paranormal. I don't find *The X-Files* bizarre. At one time, people didn't know about ultraviolet light or infrared light, which are invisible to the naked eye. Maybe spirits or ghosts or hokish-pokish *Twilight Zone* kind of stuff can be explained scientifically some day."

Fan clubs and magazines as well as conventions aided the growth of the X-Philes, but nothing had the impact of the wired world of the Internet and other services. Carter told the *Houston Chronicle*, "I'm blessed. It's just a wonderful coincidence that *The X-Files* rose up when the Internet's popularity was just blooming. Here's an audience that's smart, computer-literate and computer-learned, and they like the show. They take advantage of this new tool, and so do I, to feel the pulse of my audience—every day, if there's time. Producers used to wait for fan mail. Now there's instant communication. I use it as a quality-control measure." He added before a CInet television audience, "*The X-Files* was a fluke, really. Here's this huge, growing thing in America and around the world, these computer on-line services and the Internet, and *The X-Files* just happened to come of age with those things, the perfect show at the perfect time with the perfect medium.

"I have a very strong idea as to how the show should progress and evolve, and so I listen to what people are saying, but I'm ahead of them because I know where the show is going. They can only react to what we show them. I take those things all to heart and incorporate them, but there are no ideas that I've taken off the Internet."

Carter is not a complete cheerleader for the Internet, however. He added, "for as much popularity as there is for the online services, to me it's a step backward in technology to the telegraph. I'm very interested to see how the technology develops and how I can use it creatively. I'm interested in real-time video. I'm very anxious to see how we leap into the future."

Anderson is aware of the on-line popularity of her character, but she doesn't involve herself in cyberspace. She told CBC's RealTime, "I don't participate [on the Internet] because it's very personal stuff, and in terms of the character, I don't want to be influenced too much by people's opinions. I have to stick very closely to how I feel the character needs to be portrayed."

Morgan believes that the America Online reactions are more important than the Nielsen ratings. He told an AOL online audience, "Opinions and comments of the online community to each other, not to us, have steered the direction of *The X-Files*. Around the time of episode twelve last year many people on AOL were saying Scully was a wet blanket. To counter this, we worked up 'Beyond the Sea.' Last year there wasn't a real season arc to the characters. We flew by the seat of our pants. This season, because of GA's pregnancy, we are a little bit more thought out about what to do with character."

Duchovny said, "I'm surprised at the popularity of the show and the success of the show so, therefore, I'm also surprised at the amount of fans. If I was to think about what kind of show it is and what kind of core fan base it has, it doesn't surprise me that they'd be fanatical in terms of like *Star Trek* fans or *Twin Peaks* fans or something like that. So, I think it's the kind of show that demands that kind of minute attention to detail and that kind of fanaticism, so that's not so surprising."

Anderson added, "I think we're all pretty surprised by the success of the show. I don't think any of us realized that it would grow as much as it has. I can't fathom how many people out there are watching or enjoying it."

"We were winging it so much of the first year and part of the second year," Carter told the *San Jose Mercury News*, "but I think we really found what makes [it] tick. With season three, we'll truly hit our stride."

## PROBLEMS

Writing and story development continued to be ongoing issues of concern, especially since two of the original writers decided to move on to other projects at the beginning of the season. However, perhaps the biggest problem was posed by Gillian Anderson's pregnancy.

Regarding the writing, Carter told a Sci Fi Channel audience, "I'd like to have every episode be a winner, so that we actually make the show better. I want to do twenty-four very, very scary episodes. I think that we had a really good year two, but there were probably three or four episodes that fell short of our expectations."

If anything, year two saw Carter get even more involved in every aspect of the show. Carter told the *Sydney Morning Herald*, "I don't think I've got the personality to really pull back. If I felt that the show was going to suffer in any way or was not going to be the show I thought it could be, I couldn't pull back. And right now I feel that this isn't just obsessing or a neurotic compulsion."

One major problem was the departure of writers Glen Morgan and James Wong, who left to produce their own pilot for Fox. Carter said, "I hate it. I think they're fabulous writers. I'm sure there are many talented writers out there, it's just that they know the show and they're good at what they do." Morgan told an IRC Chat audience, "Jim and I have the chance to do our own series. We love *The X-Files* and everything going on around it, but we're hungry and have to take our shot."

*The X-Files* creative staff and Fox executives continued to wrestle with the issue of closure. The series writers resisted wrapping up each episode with a neat little bow at the end—the show was too complicated. Not only would explaining take away from the mystery but there was no way to adequately explain the unexplainable, and their audience would see right through it. Carter told *Sci-Fi Entertainment*, "Closure seems to be a word that everyone throws around in TV drama. They want everything explained; they want the cuffs thrown on. They want somebody put in jail, and they want the morality tale. You can't do that with a show like this. It took [Fox] a while to come around. There have been many battles waged, and some are still going on, but we fight for what we believe in, and I'm not alone."

One reason the studio wanted "closure" and not continuing stories, Morgan told an America Online audience, was because that made it easier to sell the show in syndication. Fox also wanted logical jumping-on points for new viewers, rather than having them struggle by joining in the middle of a four-part episode.

Fox's broadcast standards also continued to force changes in show content. Morgan said during an IRC Chat, "They removed some kinky stuff that would have made it more erotic. Plus, too many people have an opinion on vampires. The network wanted us to do witches instead of demon worshipers, but the witches they wanted would be disrespectful to Wicca, so we kept it a bogus demon worship thing. It's weird that a network would be so uptight about not offending every other religion, but not Wicca. To be honest ABC was good about it when we worked there."

In "Irresistible," the villain was originally written as a necrophiliac. Standards and Practices wrote a one-line note saying, "Not approved for broadcast." Carter recalled that he changed some of the words in the script and made him a death fetishist. As soon as he became a collector of dead things, Fox removed the objection.

Keeping the show's cult flavor forced Carter into almost daily struggles with the network's censors. They fought over the episode "The Host," in which an intestinal fluke grew to immense size and escaped into a city sewer system, because it was too graphic. This time a note said, "You can't use this!" But Carter argued the scene was the heart of the episode and won. He also won most of the battles over the "circus freak" show, "Humbug," in which a slimy "twin" grew out of a man's body and a tattooed character ate just about anything, including the still-living killer.

Carter told the *Houston Chronicle*, "I'm not interested in gratuitous violence, but I do have to scare people, and I do have to gross them out sometimes."

Perhaps everyone could have anticipated the writing and creative struggles the show would face, but how they would work around or incorporate Gillian Anderson's pregnancy was a complete mystery and a tough challenge. As she told the *Sydney Morning Herald*, "The first season was about us finding our way, finding who these characters were, and adapting to life in Vancouver and fourteen-hour days. The second season was about coping with the pregnancy and post-pregnancy."

Anderson married freelance art director Clyde Klotz on January 1, 1993 and conceived on her wedding day. She told *Entertainment Weekly*, "It was intense, everyone was mad at me. It was pretty ballsy of me, after getting such a big break. I was afraid they were going to recast." Her husband told *US*, "We'd sit in silence and think, 'Oh, my God, what could the repercussions be?' I imagine that all kinds of worst-case scenarios were flashing through her head, but Gillian is not the type of person to verbalize them. She wouldn't want to tempt fate in that way."

Anderson said they never considered not having their child. She recalled to Australia's *TV Week*, "I knew the decision I had to make toward having a child, and I knew that I could also lose my job over it. I knew that if I didn't lose my job, I'd probably wish that I had, since I had to confront a lot of people about it. I knew

it would be rough, going through the term and having a child while working the kind of hours that we were working. But I got a lot of support from the cast and crew and friends and family, and it was something I knew that I needed to do, no matter what the outcome was."

## "IT IS THROUGH SCIENCE THAT WE PROVE,
### but through intuition that we discover."
#### —Jules-Henri Poincaré

Carter had a decision to make. Would he stick by his actress? He told the *Los Angeles Times*, "I had decided sometime after learning that she was pregnant to shoot around Gillian's pregnancy. Because the show is still in its infancy, I didn't think it would be a good thing to write her pregnancy into the show. There were all these rumors circulating that she was going to have an alien baby. Although I addressed every possible idea from a creative standpoint, that was never a serious plan."

Carter also considered making Scully a single mother, but he resisted domesticating the show. Instead her character fell into a stress-induced coma. Carter continued, "I have chosen not to make the show about the characters' lives. The show works best as two FBI agents investigating paranormal or unexplained phenomena, and that's what drives the show. If the stories don't drive the show, then we're working backward."

Instead, the producers wrote scenes with Anderson talking on the phone or sitting behind a computer, and the directors shot her from the bust up. Camera angles hid Anderson's condition with very high angles and trench coats; scripts called for less screen time for her character. When her condition became too obvious, the writers closed down the X-Files section, separating Mulder and Scully. When Anderson's due date approached, they filmed an episode, "Ascension," in which Scully is kidnapped. In one scene, Mulder even imagines aliens experimenting on Scully, inflating her belly like a balloon. The scene incorporates Anderson's eight-month bulge, her skin stretched tight and looking very much inflated.

Scully was written out of only one episode, "3." Anderson worked until two days before she gave birth, by Caesarean section, to a healthy baby girl, Piper, in

September 1994. Anderson remained in the hospital for six more days. She told the *Philadelphia Inquirer,* "My husband is German, and we were looking through his German yearbook. We came across that name. It just seemed to fit her personality and my belly so well. We knew right then that that was it."

The actress had to return to work by the time her daughter was ten days old because she was written into the next script. The producers didn't give her much choice in the matter. The first episode after she returned was easy. All she had to do was lie in bed in a coma. Anderson said on CBC's RealTime, "I was still blue from the Cesarean section. They didn't have to use much makeup. During some of it I slept. It was only a few days after I got out of the hospital, and it was an opportunity to get some rest." She told *SFX* magazine, "I actually fell asleep during the coma scenes. I'd just had Piper . . . I was in the hospital for six days, and then I was back to work four days later. It was nice only to have to play being in a coma, but they could have put another episode with me off in space in between."

Instead, the next episode required physically difficult running and jumping. Anderson had a stunt double to handle the more physical scenes. At the time, she told *USA Today*, "Much as I'd like to, my body is not back in the shape it was yet. Everything's a little off balance, not aligned yet. Even walking up and down stairs, my knees can go out a bit. They've been careful about not making things too strenuous."

The heroic work on the part of all involved led to good results. Anderson told CBC's RealTime online audience, "The show is doing very well. There was a lot of interest in Scully's disappearance, and they wanted to keep the duo working together. I wasn't expecting that I would go back that early. But I'm very glad to be back at work."

The X-Files were officially reopened by Mulder's boss, Skinner, in November 1994. Scully and Mulder returned to their regular working relationship in the episode that aired on November 18.

"It's working out just fine," she said on CBC Real-Time. "I'm blessed to be able to bring her on the set with me every day. She loves hanging around and being with the crew. She's got a big family over there and everybody plays with her. She makes everybody laugh." And she told *B.C. Woman*, "I have a fabulous nanny, and although I have to work ridiculous hours, one of the blessings of the show is having Piper on the set. In

fact, I'm still breast-feeding. Time spent on the script has decreased. I don't take it as seriously as I have taken it in the past. I'm not as obsessed as I was with it before. I'm still putting as much energy as I can into the show."

She's back to filming twelve hours a day, and, as she said on the *Sci-Fi Buzz* show of the Sci Fi Channel, "I have no time that is my own, it seems. The actors always have little trailers that they go to. This year the trailer has grown considerably, which is beneficial because I have a nanny and a baby on set with me, but I find myself wandering the streets because I can't go in there to get peace of mind." Still, despite fatigue, the actress is happy with her decision to have a child and return to work. She told the Associated Press, "I don't think that I could have been a full mother to [Piper] were I not feeding that part of my life."

Viewers were supportive, and ratings didn't suffer. The online fans have been enthusiastic about the birth, sending gifts and making charitable donations in Anderson's name. She appreciates the gifts and has telephoned some thank-you's via an assistant.

Anderson's determination not to disrupt her show while having her baby impressed everyone involved with *The X-Files* series. Howard Gordon, coexecutive producer for the third season, recalled that during his tenure on *Beauty and the Beast*, star Linda Hamilton had a similar pregnancy announcement that killed the show.

Carter told *Cinescape*, "I thought it was really a testament to both David and Gillian's dedication to us. David had to carry a tremendous amount of work because Gillian's work load was limited. But Gillian was such a trooper in that she wanted more work and worked right up until she couldn't anymore. Then she came back ten days after giving birth. Although her work in that episode, 'One Breath,' was minimal by design, she was such a trooper to come back so quickly."

Anderson's limited involvement brought attention to ancillary characters, fleshing out the *X-Files* universe, including "Cigarette-Smoking Man," Skinner, and "X," the most prominent addition to the second season. "The monster-of-the-week episodes are fun, but what makes the show really great are the extended stories, and I'm not sure if we would have discovered those otherwise. I think Gillian would agree," Duchovny told *US*.

## CHANGES

By the end of year two, Carter had succeeded in doing something extremely unusual: not only was he "a visionary," in the words of Fox network president John Matoian, but he had created a cult hit that had also scored high ratings and drew a large audience. But how popular could the cult show become before it lost the right to that label? By year end, the creative staff began to feel the pull of their popularity and the desire to play to a wider audience.

Anderson felt that if the show became more mainstream during the second year, it was because it had become more acceptable to believe in UFOs, and almost trendy to discuss frustration with the government, the government's secrecy, and cover-ups. Carter told the *San Jose Mercury News*, "This show has its feet firmly planted in the world of cult television. If it has become a popular show, that's because it's become a bigger cult show. I would sort of like to keep those roots intact."

During the second season, in order to deal with the heavy work load and make the production more efficient, directors began to serve as producers. David Nutter was employed in this dual role for half the second season, until he moved over to *Space: Above and Beyond*, a new Fox series. The role then fell to Bowman and Kim Manners, both of whom returned for the third season. Manners told *Cinescape*, "I think Chris Carter is starting a real smart trend here. He feels that directors make good producers, which is not how most people think of it." The second season also saw the introduction of new writers, including Sara Charno, Frank Spotnitz, and Darin Morgan, to help carry the burden.

The FBI became more cooperative during the second season. Carter told CBC Radio's *The Gabereau Show*, "When I was first researching, the FBI were reluctant to give me information. They gave me information, then cut me off. They didn't know who I was, or what I was doing. I didn't know this institution. A year goes by, and phone calls start coming from FBI agents who are secret fans, and we developed relationships. Finally they were able to coordinate an *X-Files* visit. I made notes. I have developed contacts since then, so if I need to know something, I've been able to get expert advice. Officially, they can't say that they endorse the show or that they are in any way connected

to the show. You go there and you realize that these people are protectors of the world."

Anderson recalled their red-carpet tour of the bureau on CBC's RealTime. "We visited the FBI at the beginning of this year, and they were very supportive. They let us know very clearly there were no such things as X-Files. They were pretty determined that we note that. We have a lot of fans in the FBI. We've never been warned."

There have been some episodes, however, when local law enforcement officials have persuaded them to change a story. The creators never know how close to fact they are.

Anderson saw her character changing over the course of the second year, becoming much more open to and accepting of Mulder's theories. However, the actress believes that even though Scully has seen a lot, she won't entirely abandon her skepticism, since her medical and scientific background will always guide her approach to new mysteries. The characters became much closer over the year; risking their lives for each other so often has created an intense unspoken bond. However, despite this inevitable closeness, the series seems predicated on them maintaining a professional, respectful relationship.

"Mulderisms" also became a big part of the show—Mulder has a certain way of releasing the pressure in a very tense situation with his humor. Carter says this comes from the actor, but everyone seems to have created a few of these witticisms. Morgan told an America Online audience that many Mulderisms and Scullyisms "belong to Chris Carter. Many are inside jokes Jim Wong and I are making to David Duchovny. David has many of his own."

Carter told a Sci Fi Channel audience, "There's a trick to doing this hour drama. It's finding the rhythms, knowing where to spend and expend energy, that's the real critical thing. And I feel that going into year three, I know how to do that. The challenges are always finding the great visual in which to anchor an episode, visual themes, visual tricks, computer-generated images, production images; how to contain an episode and make it doable in eight days is a real trick, too. We got a little ambitious a couple times last year and got ourselves into hot scheduling water. It wears on everybody. Those are the challenges, to figure out how to do a little movie in eight days for the money and make it as interesting as we possibly can."

# CHAPTER 5

# YEAR THREE

Much to no one's surprise, the third season begins with Mulder being saved from the burning boxcar and nursed back to health by the local Native Americans. The first two episodes of the season, "The Blessing Way" (episode fifty) and "Paper Clip" (episode fifty-one), complete the story begun with "Anasazi" at the end of the second season. These packed mythology episodes set the tone for the year, in which the specter of the secret government cabal becomes an increasing focus in many of the stories.

"The Blessing Way" introduces the Well-Manicured Man, another player in the mysterious organization that seems to be running everything. Mulder also finds out that his father and the Cigarette-Smoking Man are connected, and this hints at many possibilities. In "Paper Clip," Scully's sister, Melissa, is shot by Krycek, and the agent decides no one can be trusted. Skinner reveals that he is in possession of the hacker's tape of government files concerning extraterrestrials, and he tries to use this as leverage to help Mulder and Scully. Meanwhile, the two agents meet a former Nazi scientist, Victor Klemper, who tells them about a massive records storage facility in West Virginia that seems to be part of the government's secret alien experimentation program. They find information about both Samantha Mulder and Scully. Mulder sees a huge alien mothership, but Scully does not, although laughing aliens run past her at one point. Scully, still skeptical to the point of pathological denial, no longer seems to offer any credible alternatives to Mulder's theories.

In another two-part story, "Nisei" and "731" (episodes fifty-eight and fifty-nine) propel the arc another step as a videotape of an alien autopsy leads Mulder to a mysterious train car containing scientists experimenting on an alien. Scully tracks down the manufacturer of the implant found in her neck to a leper colony and discovers further evidence of medical experimentation in railroad cars. She also has a flashback about her abduction that suggests not aliens but one of these doctors was involved. Scully finally offers a possible plausible alternative to Mulder's aliens: the government is using the tales of alien abduction to cover up radiation experiments.

"Piper Maru" and "Apocrypha," episodes sixty-four and sixty-five, send Mulder and Scully to investigate a possible alien shipwreck. An old friend of Scully's father tells them of a previous naval salvage operation in the same location, when only 7 returned of 144 men sent to retrieve a supposed nuclear bomb. A black goop infests the only survivor of the modern salvage operation, then passes from person to person until entering Krycek, who apparently has been selling the secrets from the government tape he stole from Skinner. Krycek then trades the tape to Cigarette-Smoking Man for the location of the aliens' spacecraft. Mulder and Scully pursue Krycek to a missile silo in North Dakota, but are kicked out by Cigarette-Smoking Man after finding irradiated bodies.

Finally, the third season's cliffhanger, "Talitha Cumi" (episode seventy-three), leaves us with intimations that Mulder's mother and the Cigarette-Smoking Man have some kind of relationship. A renegade alien clone, Jeremiah Smith, seems bent on upsetting the grand master plan of Cigarette-Smoking Man, and Smith is pursued by the Bounty Hunter. While we are only somewhat closer to piecing together the mysterious alien plot, it seems clear that it will involve shocking revelations about Mulder and his parents' involvement.

The third season also added a new recurring character. Luis Cardinal, also known as "Hispanic Man," played by Lenno Britos, joined the series at the start of the third season. This man, in the employ of the Cigarette-Smoking Man, keeps questionable company.

At the end of the third season, Carter told *Cine-scape*, "I think the mythology of the episodes in the third season brought [the show] to an interesting point. We learned more about Cigarette-Smoking Man, what Mulder's past is. We know now that William Mulder had connections to these men. We know there's an international cabal of sorts, a syndicate that has spread the conspiracy beyond the borders of the U.S., and we see that there are probable alliances between people in the scientific community, who may be conducting a much larger conspiracy than what was once imagined. I would suggest to anyone who feels that he is now zeroing in on what we are doing, make sure you stay tuned for the opener of the fourth season."

Clearly, the emphasis of the series had shifted from the ambiguous relationship of the two leads, Scully and Mulder, the skeptic and the believer forced to combine efforts, to an emphasis on the "mythology" of government conspiracy and alien invasion. *The X-Files* began to lose its way; it offered fewer character and relationship-building shows and more "stand-alone" hours that pitted Mulder and Scully against the forces of the unexplained. Anderson told Australia's *TV Hits*, "There isn't room with everything that happens in each episode every week for them also to enter into our private lives. That would mean a whole twenty minutes, and there just isn't that time to do that."

> **"ONE COULD NOT BE A SUCCESSFUL** scientist without realizing that, in contrast to the popular conception supported by newspapers and mothers of scientists, a goodly number of scientists are not only narrow-minded and dull, but also just stupid."
>
> —J. D. WATSON

The increased emphasis on the government conspiracy, the all-pervasive paranoia that informs the show, may have been a response to the popularity of the series among devoted fans, particularly the online community, which is notorious for its obsession with conspiracy theories. Carter admitted to the *Vancouver Sun*, "I honestly can't say why people believe this. I think it has a lot to do with the global, political climate, the lack of a clear enemy and a certain amount of navel-gazing. But I think it also has to do with science. We are living in a world where technological and medical advancements are making quantum leaps. We don't quite know how to fathom those things, and it gives us a feeling that, in fact, we may not be in control."

Personally, Carter said in *Rolling Stone*, "I always dismiss conspiracy theories on the basis that the government seems incapable of conspiring to do much of anything. That's my feeling, too, about, like, JFK. Everything comes out in the end. But the idea that there are bad people out there working in dark and shadowy ways outside the system, I think, is very believable and real."

He also told *Rolling Stone*, "One survey by the Roper poll said there are 5 million people who believe they've been abducted by aliens. That's my fuel."

Anderson felt the show was on the right track. The actress told the Sydney *Morning Herald*, "The second season, for me, was about coping with the pregnancy and post pregnancy. Finally, this season feels like we're in it. Not only are we in it, but Scully is in it more than she was at the beginning. In the third season, they're side by side."

## REACTIONS

*The X-Files* not only attracted a large audience with its third season but continued to draw one very desired by advertisers. Fans were highly educated and middle class. *Electronic Engineering Times* reported that the series had a phenomenal popularity among technical and engineering professionals and related university students. A Rutgers University study showed that the audience mirrored the general Internet population—college-educated males between the ages of twenty-five and thirty-four (though many are in the thirty-five-to-fifty group). Their favorite show, besides *The X-Files*, was *Star Trek*. More than half held a bachelor's degree, and a third were graduate students or Ph.D.s.

With its third season, the small cult hit became the Fox network's top-rated show, and it joined the Nielsen Top-20.

The show continued to receive rave reviews in the press. One typically gushing account appeared in *Arcane: The Roleplaying Magazine* in April 1996: "Chris Carter's unstoppable machine has rewritten the book on stylish SF, with a show that thoughtfully, intelligently and with only the barest nod toward standard trappings of the genre, makes for the most subversive viewing this side of *The Simpsons*. Tapping into our fears, *The X-Files* deals not only with '90s nightmares such as alien abductions and corrupt governments, but more often the ecological, psychological and psycho-horrors we unleash upon ourselves. There are no easy fixes and very few rational answers or pat explanations."

Real-life tales of alien abductions began to receive more notice, and sometimes serious attention. John E. Mack, a Pulitzer Prize winner and professor of psychiatry at Harvard Medical School, said, "I've been a full-time psychiatrist for thirty-six years, and there's nothing in my experience that could account for what I am learning from these [abductee patients]." Mack said that though he's studied more than a hundred unrelated abduction cases, "the descriptions of their experiences are very consistent both sequentially and factually, down to minute details."

One sure sign of success was the number of imitations that began sprouting up on other networks, including *Dark Skies* and *The Burning Zone*. Even *Baywatch Nights* was turned into a kind of *The X-Files* clone. Carter told the *Vancouver Sun*, "I think David Hasselhoff said that he thought the problem with *The X-Files* is that we talk too much on it. Actually, I think that's the problem with *Baywatch*, too."

Even more than in its first two years, *The X-Files* was honored with industry awards and nominations in 1996. Every aspect of the show—from the writing to the cinematography to the sound to the acting—received praise from the professional community. The series has had far more success in this way than any *Star Trek* series ever had. Highlighting the awards (for a complete listing see chapter 16), *The X-Files* received five Emmys out of a total of eight nominations, and Gillian Anderson won the Screen Actor's Guild award for Best Actress in a Dramatic Series. Emmy awards included two for sound, one for writing, one for cinematography, and one for Outstanding Guest Actor (Peter Boyle in "Clyde Bruckman's Final Repose").

Anderson was also nominated for an Emmy, a Golden Globe, and a Quality Award as Best Actress, and David Duchovny was nominated for a Golden Globe, a Screen Actors Guild, and a Quality Award for Best Actor. The series itself received Best Drama nominations by the Emmys, the Producer's Guild, and the Quality Awards.

The cast and crew were certainly pleased with the wealth of awards and acknowledgments, even though there was one high-profile snub—Duchovny was not nominated for an Emmy, though his costar was. Carter told *Entertainment Weekly Fall Preview*, "I felt bad for David. I think the tendency is to see [Gillian and him] in competition with each other. You can't look at it that way, or you'll drive yourself crazy." Duchovny said it was "a confusing omission." For herself, Anderson doubted she would take home a statuette, saying, "I have a feeling that this is the Angela Lansbury award, but I will put something down on paper and place it under my left cheek and hopefully get to use it."

Carter remained pleased with the overall work on the show, with their success at maintaining the peculiar edge of their stories, despite pressure from the network and the show's increasing popularity. "There were stories they told us we wouldn't be able to tell," he told the *Sydney Morning Herald*. "We have pushed the limits. Every week there is a negotiation with the broadcast standards and practice wing of the network. It's extremely close to what I imagined. Of course, when I was sitting and writing the pilot, I never imagined episode seventy-three, which is where we'll be this year. No one who creates a show can look that far down the road. But I did, indeed, have an idea about how the Mulder and Scully relationship would progress, and how the stories would work. What is most surprising to me is the variety of stories we've told.

"We didn't set out to deliver a message. I still don't want that to be the purpose of the shows. I want to entertain, scare, and thrill. The motto of the show is 'the truth is out there.' I've always thought of it as a double entendre. The truth is out there to be found, and then it's so far out there that we'll never find it.

"I think that this [the third season] is the best year ever. The ratings reflect it. That has a lot to do with the directors. The first year is an important maturing process. You find what works, the pacing, the rhythms. All too often TV shows age rather than mature."

## PROBLEMS

In its third season, the series started to show the strain of pleasing its fans while appealing to a broader public. Perhaps the show's producers lost sight of why *The*

*X-Files* worked. The series turned self-referential. Mulder became a more normal hero, and *The X-Files* lost the eerie fatality that propelled it through its first two seasons. Scully no longer offered a plausible alternative to Mulder, and the emphasis shifted from the lead characters to a dazzling display of horrors.

Carter told *Entertainment Weekly Fall Preview*, "We've done vampires, we've done monsters. It becomes less obvious where the stories are." *The X-Files* had already offered a catalogue of gruesome bodily invasions: alien fetuses, implants, prehistoric insects, strands of extraterrestrial DNA fed into humans, cannibalism, and futuristic viruses. The show was beginning to repeat itself.

### "NOTHING IS TOO WONDERFUL TO BE TRUE

if it be consistent with the laws of nature."

—MICHAEL FARADAY

The *Orange County Register* summed up the dilemma nicely: How do you avoid the swelled head of self-referential X-cess when you've become a pop-culture buzz word? How to stay a cult when you're a craze? . . . You get back to *X-Files* basics, the fearsome potential for evil of the human mind."

But Carter didn't want the show to be confined to simply its government intrigues. Carter told *Cinescape*, "You can't have Mulder and Scully pursuing the conspiracy forever. Those episodes have to come along only occasionally in order to give the show its breadth, its life, and its longevity."

The government conspiracy to hide evidence of extraterrestrial contact and experiments involving human and alien DNA from the public was intended to be only one thematic arc among many. It grew to dominate the series. Carter told *Cinescape*, "From the beginning [of the show] the search for the truth about what the government may or may not know about the existence of extraterrestrials has been the backbone of the show. The other, stand-alone episodes are the search for other truths that may impact on the larger truths [involving the conspiracy] and those remain important. The audience has to be forgiving, and is— wonderfully so—because if we were just make this a mythology show, it wouldn't be as good a show as it is. It defies analysis, but whatever I've done works."

Gordon, who wrote "D.P.O.," the first stand-alone episode of the third season, added, "The third year really gave rise to the mythology episodes in a more concerted fashion. We started building a much more sustained narrative, a ladder that Chris describes as the scaffolding from which the rest of the series is hung. We don't have the isolated abduction stories anymore. The mythology shows have an emotional power that the stand-alones simply cannot have."

The search for ideas wasn't helped by the departure of story editor Darin Morgan, although it was aided by the return of Glen Morgan and James Wong, both of whom had left to pilot Fox's ill-fated *Space: Above and Beyond*. But on the whole, given the struggles of the first two seasons, the third season found the entire team hitting their stride, even if the work load hadn't gotten any easier.

Watching the episodes still provided a thrill to the series' creator, despite all of the problems involved in filming. Carter told the Sydney *Morning Herald*, "I think the biggest personal satisfaction for me is in seeing the final product. Everything else is done under such strict deadlines and time pressure that a lot of the enjoyment is just in finishing it."

## CHANGES

Perhaps the biggest change in the series' most successful season was simply the number of people watching. Carter told the *Atlanta Journal & Constitution*, "There's a sense that something has been found, pored over and looked at, and what was opened was a wonderful present, but it has now become everybody's present. The mainstream numbers that we get now, we've gained a certain popularity, and some of the people who found it early feel they're having to share it. I honestly think it's a lot of people listening to themselves talk. If anything, I think the show has gotten darker. It's still as subversive as it once was. I still think it's a cult show."

Still, for all the excitement, Carter felt an inevitable sense of loss, almost like seeing his child grow up and leave home for college. Carter talked to *Rolling Stone* about its commercialization, "If this becomes a show you can find at your local Kmart or Wal-Mart too easily, it's going to lose the thing that's made it special. *The X-Files* is coming out on videotape, and it's going to be in all those stores. It makes me a little sad. I'd like it better if you could only find them at a head shop in Van Nuys."

Duchovny wanted to see one change occur—he wanted Mulder to start having a personal life. This kind of change, however, is clearly heresy in some quarters. Duchovny told *Entertainment Weekly Fall Preview*, "I would like to expand into some kind of personal life, and an obvious way to do that is to have some kind of a love interest. But Chris gets scared and he puts it on my shoulders, like I'm a child asking him if I can go out with a girl. I've been asked that, and I bridle at that perception of myself—like I'm some kind of Frankenstein asking for a bride."

# CHAPTER 6

# YEAR FOUR

Year four was still in progress while this book was going to press, so it isn't possible to give a complete or adequate summation of episodes or story arc here. The year did begin with X seemingly killed; the U.N. operative Marita Covarrubias seems to be the likely successor. All we know for sure is: The Truth Is Out There.

One of the reasons we know this is that Fox launched the most expensive marketing campaign in the history of the network behind *The X-Files* and Chris Carter's new series, *Millennium*. The blitz included trailers for both shows in United Artists movie theaters, as well as a *Millennium* sneak preview on the big screen. For the first time, Fox won the weekly Nielsen ratings war among TV networks. Analysts credited the much-hyped debut of *Millennium*, the return of *The X-Files*, a Halloween marathon of *The Simpsons*, and above all, the World Series, which doubled the network's previous rating.

This result sent the three traditional networks, ABC, NBC, and CBS, into a state of shock and introspection. One outcome was the attempted cloning of *The X-Files* with such series as *Dark Skies*, *The Pretender*, and *Profiler*.

Carter's creation of *Millennium* allowed Fox to move *The X-Files* from Friday night to Sunday night, a move no one involved with the show appreciated. Carter had previously told *USA Today*, "I always felt that Friday was the scariest night of the week. There's no school or work the next day. People can stay up late and have a good scare." In March 1995, he told *Entertainment Weekly* OnLine, "I love our time slot. I think Friday night is the best night of the week to be scared. However, there are a limited number of viewers available on Fridays, which is why in the weekly accounting we end up in the middle of the pack. But I think we've been able to change some viewers' habits, keeping them home on Fridays. That's satisfying."

If Carter felt that the size of Friday night audiences limited the popularity of his series, he really disliked having his show aired on Sundays. "I wish it would've stayed where it is," Carter told *Entertainment Weekly Fall Preview*, repeating, "Friday is a good night to be scared."

Fox Entertainment president John Matoian admitted that Carter's own *Millennium* made the move possible, saying, "We would never have moved *X-Files* if we didn't have a worthy successor. We noticed that the three Sunday-night movies [on the other networks] had seen such a decline in the last five years that *X-Files* was a viable alternative."

> ## "A NEW SCIENTIFIC TRUTH DOES NOT
>
> triumph by convincing its opponents and making them see the light, but rather because its opponents eventually die and a new generation grows up that is familiar with it."
>
> —M. PLANCK

Anderson tried to make the best of a bad situation, telling the *Washington Times*, "Everyone I know who watches it says they tape it."

In one interesting *X-Files* development—that may or may not come about—film director Quentin Tarantino may direct an episode for season four. A Fox spokesman told *TV Guide* that Tarantino has approached them about directing, saying he's a "big fan." However, Tarantino refuses to join the Directors Guild of America, an industry union, before he works in television. The DGA granted Tarantino a waiver to direct an episode of *ER* in 1995, but they are reluctant to do so again. Tarantino shot *From Dusk Till Dawn* with an entirely nonunion crew. Guild attorneys are currently negotiating with Tarantino's agents at William Morris, DGA communications director Chuck Warn told *TV Guide*, saying, "We all think Quentin is a marvelous filmmaker, a great young talent, and all of us are looking forward to the day he joins Frank Capra, John Ford, Steven Spielberg, and all the other great directors who have been members of the Directors Guild." Alternatively, he may follow in the footsteps of Cecil B. DeMille and refuse to do the work if joining a union remains the requirement.

Perhaps the biggest event on *The X-Files* horizon is the upcoming feature film that's planned. Agents Mulder and Scully may finally hit the big screen. Carter told *USA Today*, "I have an idea for the movie, and I will make time to write the script." He said he will try to get it before the cameras after the fourth season wraps.

Duchovny said, "They're going to do it some time, so whatever. It's fine with me. Nobody else can do it. I'd like to see them take it a bit further than the TV show. Maybe Mulder will sleep with Scully; maybe we'll find his sister. Whatever it is, it has to be a big deal. Otherwise, it will just be like two episodes strung together."

Anderson added, "The show is really like a minifeature. It would be great to be able to take it to the extreme."

Unlike *Star Trek*, there are no plans to cancel *The X-Files* television show before the movie appears in theaters. Rather, the two will be seen together. Carter told the *Vancouver Sun*, "Whatever I do, I want to do it in such a way that it strengthens the show, not weakens it. The trick is to avoid doing something so big that you can't ever recover on the series. I want to make sure that when we do this *X-Files* feature that we don't just do it for the sake of doing it, but that we do it right."

Carter said the feature film would dovetail with the so-called "mythology episodes," which deal with alien invasion and government conspiracy.

In any case, all involved plan to continue *The X-Files* television show. Carter said that both series stars "renegotiated their contracts last year, so that's out of the way."

In regards to himself, Carter told *Cinescape*, "I can see where the allure is to do something new, but I wouldn't leave until the time is right. I don't imagine myself leaving *The X-Files* at all. I love working on it. But if the opportunity was right and I could hire the people I would want to hire, I could see producing something else."

Carter predicted to the *Sydney Morning Herald*, "I see it going for five years. Anything past that is great, but if it lasted any longer than seven, I would be surprised. It wouldn't be under my aegis."

# CHAPTER 7

# CHILDREN OF *THE X-FILES*

The popularity of Chris Carter's *The X-Files* created a demand for a companion series, and Carter was happy to try his hand at a second show. He created *Millennium*, and it premiered in its Friday-night slot with the highest debut Nielsen rating for any show in Fox history. Twenty-one percent of the viewing American public were tuned to *Millennium*'s first episode.

Fox took no chances, spending $10 million promoting the debut, flooding the media with promos, and even previewing the show in movie theaters across the country, sparking a *Millennium* mania that drew 17.1 million viewers to Fox for the Friday-night launch. It was, without a doubt, one of the most successful marketing campaigns in recent TV history. *Millennium* averaged an 8.9 rating and 16 share in households when Fox ordered nine more episodes, bringing the total season run to twenty-two episodes.

But Fox isn't alone. The other networks have taken notice of *The X-Files*'s success. Though CBS made one ill-fated attempt to cash in, it is NBC who has provided the strongest competition so far.

## MILLENNIUM

Bob Greenblatt, executive vice-president for development at Fox, told Futurenet's *SFX*, "The year 2000 has been written and prophesied about for hundreds of years as some magical number, and we're about to reach it."

Microsoft's prestigious online magazine *Slate* described *Millennium*, saying, "As its title implies, the show is rooted in fin de siècle anxiety—the sort of unease that compels its hero to move his family from a nasty Eastern city (Washington, D.C.) to somewhere that's green (the Pacific Northwest). *Millennium* makes *The X-Files* seem practically Capraesque. There's all that rain, plus signature Carter touches like flashlights piercing through fog as agents search a forest for freshly dug graves. The gore is laid on lavishly, and the evil transcends the individual nutcase."

*Science Fiction Weekly* reviewed *Millennium*, reporting, "*Millennium* is scarier than Executive Producer Chris Carter's *The X-Files*. While *The X-Files* is steeped in unexplained phenomena, *Millennium* comes from a much more real place. There are terrible people out there who do terrible things to other people. . . . As Carter has done with *The X-Files*, *Millennium* promises its own mythology (this time based on prophecy)."

The series centers on Frank Black (played by Lance Henriksen), a Seattle native who worked as a homicide detective before joining the FBI as a specialist in sexual homicide cases; he was known for catching a serial killer who ate his victims. Frank can enter the mind of criminals and experience what they see, think, and feel. That ability may have burned Frank out, causing rumors that he left the FBI under duress. Actually, after closing the case of a Minnesota serial killer, Frank began receiving anonymous letters containing photographs of his wife and child from an unknown stalker. He became obsessed with protecting his family, but then he found the Millennium Group, who helped him utilize his "gift."

In the show, Black describes his ability this way: "I put myself in [the killer's] head. I become the thing we fear the most. . . . I become capability, I become the horror, what we know we can become only in our heart of darkness. It's my gift; it's my curse." Frank states that his ability is not "psychic," but he can describe events of a crime without examining physical evidence.

The pilot episode established the series' premise. In fear for his family's safety, FBI profiler Frank Black leaves the Bureau and takes his wife, Catherine, and their young daughter, Jordan, back to their hometown of Seattle to live in a nice yellow house. Concerned with the rising bloodshed accompanying the approaching millennium, he joins a mysterious organization known as "The Millennium Group," former law enforcement officers who work to stop the violence, bringing order out of chaos. Catherine, played by Megan Gallagher, is also a Seattle native and a social psychologist who has experience with the criminally insane, although her husband tries to keep her unaware of his involvement in the Millennium Group. She suspects more than her husband wants her to believe. Their five-year-old daughter, Jordan, is played by Brittany Tiplady.

The Millennium Group, from the outside, appears to be a consulting firm, but they work to stop the process leading to an apocalypse at the end of the millennium. It's unclear whether the group subscribes to apocalyptic prophecy. Chris Carter said, "It's not that these guys believe that the world is coming to an end at the year 2000. They believe that, [in] all this random violence we see these days, that there may actually be some order in the chaos. There may be something out there, and these guys think that, if they care enough, that they can stem the tide of this thing."

## "A MAN WITH A NEW IDEA IS A CRANK
### until he succeeds."                    —MARK TWAIN

Carter was inspired in creating the Millennium Group by the Academy Group, a Manassas-based consulting firm. The Academy Group has signed on as a consultant to *Millennium*. The Academy Group is made up of nine behavior and criminal experts, most of whom worked for the FBI behavioral science unit that was depicted in *The Silence of the Lambs*. They have worked with a fascinating array of clients, including a major insurance firm's CEO, when he received anonymous letters from a disgruntled employee, a Texas family that couldn't believe their daughter had committed suicide, and an Arizona resort sued by clients raped in a hotel room. Carter told the *Washington Post*, "The Manassas-based former agents are kind of a mysterious group. They wouldn't return my phone calls for two months."

In reviewing the new show, *Time* said, "*Millennium* suffers from delivering its point too aggressively. The show is constantly contrasting the bleak offices and dark labs in which Black works to hunt the deranged cult leaders and sexual serial killers who are his prey, with the image of his blindingly yellow Seattle home, framed always by a blue sky that is eerie in its brilliance. Yet as over the top as *Millennium* can get, the show does succeed at creating a marvelously unrelenting sense of unease."

If *Time* didn't like *Millennium*, *People*, from the same publisher but different editorial hands, did. The magazine gave the show an A and raved, "With its creepy soundtrack, terrifying visuals, and ingenious plot twists, *Millennium* is far and away the best new show of the year."

Method actor Lance Henriksen was born in either 1940 or 1943 in New York City, the son of a Merchant Marine and a Harvey Girl. Henriksen spent his early years in the South Pacific, military school, on the road, and in jail, working as a fisherman, fruit picker, extra in a Lee Marvin movie, a stunt man, a sailor, an artist, a mime, and (finally) an actor. He first appeared on film, as an FBI agent, in *Dog Day Afternoon*, then in *Aliens*, *The Terminator*, *Close Encounters*, and *Near Dark*.

Henriksen explained how he sees his character on CNN. "It's a guy who did all the suit-and-tie stuff—all the status quo, FBI homicide stuff. Now he doesn't carry a gun and he's not a cop and he doesn't arrest anybody, but what he does do is follow his heart in the things he sees going on."

Megan Gallagher was born in 1960 in Reading, Pennsylvannia. She got her big break in *The Slap Maxwell Story*. She's also appeared on *China Beach* and *The Larry Sanders Show*. Gallagher took the role of Catherine Black because of the reputation Chris Carter had developed for creating strong female characters, which he'd done in *The X-Files*. Gallagher's role is expected to become more prominent as the series progresses.

Carter serves as executive producer, but he also will write several episodes. David Nutter, an *X-Files* alum, is coexecutive producer; Mark Snow is responsible for series music, as he is for *The X-Files*. Stephen Mark is the series editor, Gary Wissner is the production designer, Peter Wunstorf is director of photography, and John Peter Kousakis is supervisory producer.

Clearly, there are similarities between Carter's two series, beyond the fact that virtually all of the crew working on *Millennium* worked on *The X-Files*. Both series cultivate paranoia, featuring heroes struggling against secretive, powerful enemies. Both offer strong statements for the alienated individual in postmodern culture.

Carter told CNN, "I think the similarities between the two shows is really tonal. Both of these shows work in dark worlds. *X-Files* deals with unexplained phenomena. *Millennium* deals with very unexplainable, but sometimes unbelievable phenomena which is the human mind and the human ability to stalk and prey on others."

*Millennium* also has been compared to *The Silence of the Lambs* and *Seven*. Carter has said, "If you liked *The Silence of the Lambs*, you will like *Millennium*, too." The similarities to *Seven* are not coincidental. Series Production Designer Gary Wissner was the art director for *Seven*.

The catch-phrases "Trust no one" and "The truth is out there" appear as the title sequence of *The X-Files*. "Worry" and "Who cares?" play a similar role for *Millennium*. These phrases have significant meaning for Carter. He explains, "It's really, who will care? Who is strong enough to care? Are we going to allow these things to run out of hand or are we going to take action?"

As with *The X-Files*, Carter is pushing the boundaries of network television when it comes to subject matter and visual depictions of violence, but he insists the series doesn't glorify violence, telling CNN, "Really, *Millennium* is about hope. It's about optimism. It's a response, I think, to an overly violent world."

Carter told *TV Guide*, "Lukewarm is not interesting to me. It may be graphic in some cases because it must be. That's what I do. If you just deal with goodness and selflessness, it means nothing—unless it is in jeopardy. That is what people don't understand about the violence. It is irresponsible to just set out to tell sweet stories because I think it is Pollyanna-ish and it does a disservice to the audience."

Bill Smitrovich, who plays homicide Lieutenant Bob Bletcher on *Millennium*, added, "We have to show people the dark side before the light can come out. We have to show the horror before showing that hope exists."

"Yeah, we've gotten some calls from people who find it a little rough," admitted Fox Entertainment president Peter Roth. "But we've gotten an equal number of calls from those who feel it's terrific television. I count myself as one of those."

"This is not a serial killer-of-the-week show," Megan Gallagher told CNN. "It's a show that deals with many themes that have to do with how we deal with the awful things in the world. It seems to be about something otherworldly, but it's not. It's about things that exist—which also makes it scarier."

## THE FUTURE

At the moment, Chris Carter couldn't be more successful. He helms two TV series, *Millennium* and *The X-Files*, and is preparing an *X-Files* movie. Gallagher called him "an absolute perfectionist," while Henriksen told *TV Guide*, "I can only describe him as the Phantom. He arrives if there is a problem. He disappears right after it's solved. The only thing missing is the outfit."

Carter may enjoy the demands of producing two series, and even writing some episodes, but he doesn't like the extracurricular promotional activities generated by their huge popularity. "I don't like being in front of the camera, although I must say I'm getting used to it. Rod Serling used to say that if he dropped his pencil he'd be two weeks behind. That's how I feel," he told *TV Guide*.

Fox is already hinting about a third series with Carter. His commitment to *The X-Files* ends in 1997. Some speculate that Carter might turn the reins over to a new producer, but he insists that there is no chance of this. He does miss having a normal life, though, and told *TV Guide*, "There is no more pressure put on me than the pressure I put on myself. I want to see if I can master something. Someone said, 'Are you having your midlife crisis?' I said, 'I'm having my no-life crisis.' I have a good time most of the time, but there are difficulties, too. I can't wait until I get time to really surf again. I'm anxious to see if I can't, in my forties, ride the big waves in Hawaii. Maybe I've passed that point. But it would be interesting to see if I could do it."

## IMITATION

The world has taken Carter's *The X-Files* to heart. Fans burn up the Internet exchanging messages and paens of praise for its creator. Fanzines and conventions provide lovers of the series with additional outlets to pursue their interest. The series has been nominated for dozens of Emmys and won several coveted Golden Globe Awards.

In *TV Guide*, NBC Entertainment president Warren Littlefield called Carter "a storyteller, but one with a unique, sometimes disturbing vision that has slowly seeped into the collective American consciousness. The articulate visual style of his work, coupled with taut, engaging writing, makes for provocative television."

## "HE WHO NEVER WALKS SAVE WHERE HE sees men's tracks makes no discoveries."

—J. P. HOLLAND

If imitation is deemed the sincerest form of flattery, then the major networks have complimented fledgling Fox indeed, copying Carter's *The X-Files.* It inspired a number of new, supernatural- and conspiratorial-tinged shows in 1995, including *American Gothic, Strange Luck,* and *Nowhere Man.* CBS launched then quickly canceled *EZ Streets,* a crime drama drenched in Celtic gloom, after only one showing. Littlefield's own NBC launched three Saturday night Carter clones, *The Pretender, Profiler,* and *Dark Skies.* They may enjoy greater success.

## The Pretender

*The Pretender* shares a sense of hidden conspiracies and paranoia with *The X-Files.* In *The Pretender,* Michael T. Weiss plays Jarod Russell, a genius pursued by the most dangerous people on earth. Russell, a young genius whose I.Q. is off the chart, was raised in isolation by the Centre, a secret organization that trained him to be a "human chameleon." He can assume any identity and solve any puzzle. Russell had thought he was creating simulated military coups, financial market manipulations, and terrorist strikes, until he learned others were using his results to stage actual misdeeds.

He then fled the Centre on a quest to right these wrongs. He also wants to learn his true identity, and what became of his parents.

Episodes take him to new settings each week as he assumes new identities, including those of a tanker captain who stops toxic dumpers; a surgeon exposing a deadly hospital; and an airline pilot battling unsafe skies. His brilliance and charm help him assume any personality, but genius alone isn't always enough, as Russell has only experienced the world through books, and in some ways, is still a child. The Centre pursues him. While Dr. Sydney Green, played by Patrick Bauchau, once raised him and now wants him back, others want to kill him.

## Profiler

Strong similarities exist between *Profiler* and *Millennium.* Both series share the premise of an FBI profiler leaving the Bureau because their family is stalked, only to be drawn back into the job because of their special talent of entering a criminal's mind.

*Time* has said that *Profiler* and *Millennium* "share the same premise: a central character brings down Hannibal Lecter–type psychopaths by using an uncanny gift to see inside the criminal mind, literally envisioning the evildoers' motivations. In the process both series serve up images unusually brutal for prime-time TV: severed heads, bodies crackling in flames, victims buried alive, near naked women beaten and stabbed to death. Yet beneath the bloody mayhem lies the same knotty issue that the Republican presidential candidate has himself been working hard to articulate: How do we keep home, hearth and the middle-class dream from eroding in a world ravaged by crime, drugs and sexual confusion?"

But *Profiler* has taken a page from the *X-Files* book as well, by featuring a woman as a series heroine. In *Profiler,* created by Cynthia Saunders, Dr. Sam Walters, played by Ally Walker, is a forensic psychologist with the ability to visualize crimes through the eyes of both victims and killers.

A serial killer called Jack of All Trades killed her husband three years before the series begins. He continues to stalk her even though she has been living in seclusion with her daughter, played by Caitlin Wachs, and a close friend, played by Erica Gimpel. Now another longtime friend, Bailey Malone, played by Robert Davis, head of the FBI's Investigative Support Unit, calls Walters back to work. He needs her special talents. The unit, of course, echoes *The X-Files*'s own FBI connection.

Walters investigates a variety of cases that always somehow point back to involvement by Jack of All Trades, and his signature red rose. The series maintains its ongoing theme while offering different stories with each episode. For example, one episode brought on a guest star as a bomb squad dismantler who thawed the usually cool Sam for a case involving a deranged loner bent on destroying Pittsburgh's water supply. The next episode returned to the Jack-of-All-Trades plot line when Walters realizes that all thirteen victims of the serial killer have a connection to herself.

*Time* reported that while "*Profiler* tries hard to create ceaseless tension, it doesn't pull it off. The show is too pat and tidy to make you check under the sofa during the commercial breaks. You are supposed to be scared for mother and daughter—like *Millennium*, *Profiler* switches between images of evil and serenity—but Sam flips her voluminous blond hair back and forth with such perky assurance that you know she will elude the nut by the time the credits roll."

NBC notes that the series has improved the network's dismal record on Saturdays, placing it second in the period and first in the coveted advertising bracket of eighteen-to-forty-nine-year-old viewers.

Executive producers Ian Sande and Kim Moses maintain high production values and the stars work well together. Much as *The Prisoner* once turned an ordinary bicycle into a symbol of dread, *Profiler* has successfully changed innocent red roses into a symbol of death.

## Dark Skies

The most intriguing NBC entry is, without a doubt, *Dark Skies*. If *Profiler* appears similar to *Millennium*, then *Dark Skies* even more closely follows *The X-Files*. It offers a similar scenario, an alternative history of extraterrestrial invasion and government cover-up controlling American events of the past two generations. A young couple—John Loengard, an idealistic congressional aide played by Eric Close, and his girlfriend, Kimberly Sayers, portrayed by Megan Ward—seek to learn the truth.

Just as *The X-Files* involved the recovery of an alien spacecraft in Roswell, New Mexico, in 1947, *Dark Skies* dates the struggle between humans and the alien "Hive" from this event. The conflict continues when the young couple arrive in Washington in 1961. Loengard learns of the off-limits top-secret Majestic-12, a rogue black-operations group headed by Captain Frank Bach, played by J.T. Walsh, while doing routine research for budget hearings.

Physical threats by Majestic-12 agents fail to deter Loengard, so Bach eventually recruits him as a team member, and he is taken to subterranean headquarters. There, he confronts the remains of an alien recovered from the Roswell crash. He then joins Majestic-12 in rooting out human hosts of early-stage alien life-forms.

**"I WOULD SOONER BELIEVE THAT TWO** Yankee professors lied, than that stones fell from the sky." —THOMAS JEFFERSON,

ON HEARING REPORTS OF METEORITES

Loengard decides the public must be told the truth, and he steals a piece of the unworldly craft to show President Kennedy. Majestic-12 forces Loengard and Sayers into hiding until news of Kennedy's assassination sends them on a dangerous journey with the fate of the world at stake. The young couple pursues the truth, learning more and more about the secret alien presence on earth as they live through specific events in American history.

The pilot episode, "The Awakening," which first aired on September 21, 1996, centers around the U2 reconnaissance flight of Lieutenant Francis Gary Powers over the Soviet Union in 1960. Other early episodes include "Moving Targets," which involves them with a turncoat within Majestic-12's ranks; "Mercury Rising," about Cape Canaveral, an abducted astronaut, and a Hive base on the moon; and "Dark Day's Night," in which they meet the Beatles at their historic 1964 New York appearance on *The Ed Sullivan Show* and encounter an alien plot to use the broadcast to send deadly signals to unknowingly abducted humans.

NBC claims that *Dark Skies* blends fact with informed speculation and dramatic license, much as Carter does for *The X-Files*. Cocreator and executive producer Bryce Zabel said, "The series premise is simply this: our future's happening in our past. This is being presented as alternative history." Executive producer James D. Parriott added, "Everyone has their favorite conspiracies, but we will challenge and expand on those by building a framework that adds consistency to the alien-awareness theories."

*Dark Skies* utilizes effects techniques unprecedented for a weekly TV series. Zabel wants the effects to be a tool used to tell the story, not the focus of the show.

The young couple played by Eric Close and Megan Ward act as the focus for the series much as Fox Mulder and Dana Scully do for *The X-Files*, except this pair is romantically involved. As a newlywed and first-time homeowner, Ward senses that a heightened maturity in her personal life has carried over to her acting career. She has graduated from playing teenagers to portraying a "full-bodied" woman. "I am so excited about playing this role," said Ward. "Because I look so young, I've played my share of young, girlish roles. Kimberly is a three-dimensional woman, not just the love interest or object of desire. I've always looked forward to playing those roles where I can put in some of who I am and not just be window dressing. Kimberly is ambitious, honest, and wants to be an equal partner in her relationships, just like me."

Ward has never seen a UFO, but says, "It's an amazingly universal topic. I feel there's no way that we are the only ones around."

Costar and history buff Eric Close regards his role as a way to transport himself back to the era of the Kennedys. "Acting lets you travel around in time periods and locales much like a time machine," said Close. "My generation has always heard about the Kennedys from our parents; there's a definite aura about them. I've done some related research now that I'm going to be 'living' during that time."

All three series clearly arose from NBC's admiration for what Carter has accomplished for the Fox network. But how many of these kinds of shows can survive at once? It remains to be seen whether these shows will be successful and whether Carter can sustain *The X-Files, Millennium,* and a possible third series all at the same time.

# CHAPTER 8

# PRECURSORS TO *THE X-FILES*

Chris Carter, the creator of *The X-Files*, points to his childhood reverence for *Kolchak: The Night Stalker* as the primary influence for his series. Pundits insist *The X-Files* is a direct descendent of *The Twilight Zone*. In my opinion, the show is related to different predecessors entirely. The overwhelming paranoia and sense of futility in attempting to expose a supremely powerful foe motivated by unknown goals more clearly reflects the quest of Richard Kimble, the protagonist of *The Fugitive*, who searched for the mysterious "one-armed man" while eluding the minions of the entire law enforcement establishment. *The X-Files* also bears a strong resemblance to *The Invaders*, in which the protagonist David Vincent valiantly seeks to expose alien invaders to a disbelieving populace, and *The Prisoner*, a series drenched in government paranoia, in which a lone man withholding terrible secrets attempts to escape captivity from "the Village." The daytime terrors of Kafka and not the ghosts, goblins, and little green men of *The Night Stalker* or *The Twilight Zone* lie at the heart of *The X-Files*.

## THE FUGITIVE

Quinn Martin's *The Fugitive* originally aired on ABC from September 17, 1963, until August 29, 1967. The series starred David Janssen as Dr. Richard Kimble, an innocent surgeon accused of murdering his wife. Kimble returns home one night to find his wife being fatally beaten by a one-armed man, who flees after a struggle. However, all of the evidence points to Kimble's guilt, and his story of the intruder is quickly brushed away in court. Kimble is sentenced to death, but he escapes in the hope of finding the one-armed man and clearing his name. During the course of the series, Lieutenant Ger-

ard, played by Barry Morse, persistently pursues Kimble, intent on turning him over to "justice."

That Kimble was an ordinary man who had no idea why the one-armed man had entered his life, or even who he was, added to the sense of overwhelming paranoia. Kimble came to symbolize an Everyman at the mercy of an unknown terror, much as any viewer could stumble upon the terrors of *The X-Files*.

In the series, Kimble travels the country, moving from town to town in fear of discovery and in search of the only man who can purchase his ultimate freedom from pursuit. He becomes involved in the lives and problems of others, including an ailing boxer, a kind rancher, another man wrongly accused of murder, a construction boss with a troubled marriage, a tyrannical hotel owner and his daughter, a nun, an exact double of his dead wife, a seedy mind reader, a computer whiz, a murderous motorcycle gang, a mob boss, and dream researchers. He always sets things right for others, though he is unable to do so for himself. Suspense builds as Kimble consistently eludes pursuit and as he himself closes in on the one-armed man.

Stories that force Kimble to protect Lieutenant Gerard's wife during a hurricane and even to rescue Lieutenant Gerard add a sense of irony. Once, Kimble even has to stop an escaped prisoner from gunning down the one-armed man. As the chase continues, his pursuer, Lieutenant Gerard, becomes convinced of Kimble's innocence, but this conviction remains long unvoiced and ambivalent.

In the final two-part episode, "The Judgement," Kimble nabs the one-armed man and proves that he is innocent of his wife's murder. It became one of the most-watched television episodes in the history of the medium, and it finally brought closure to the series after four years.

Much as the success of *The X-Files* spawned *Dark Skies*, *The Pretender*, and *The Profiler*, the popularity of *The Fugitive* led to the immediate birth of imitators. *Run Buddy Run* added humor to the formula, while *The Invaders* introduced hidden alien invaders from another world. Three decades later, it also led to a movie starring Harrison Ford. Film critic Roger Ebert said the movie was "an allegory about an innocent man in a world prepared to crush him" and that "it only looks realistic while actually functioning on the level of a nightmare." Both these statements could equally apply to *The X-Files*.

## THE INVADERS

Quinn Martin, producer of *The Fugitive*, also launched *The Invaders*, which brought the paranoia a step closer to Chris Carter's *The X-Files*. The words opening each episode of *The Invaders* could easily have come from *The X-Files*:

> *The Invaders . . . alien beings from a dying planet. Their destination . . . the Earth. Their purpose . . . to make it their world. David Vincent has seen them. For him it began one lost night on a lonely country road, looking for a short-cut that he never found. It began with a closed deserted diner, and a man too long without sleep to continue his journey. It began with the landing of a craft from another galaxy. Now, David Vincent knows that the Invaders are here, that they have taken human form. Somehow he must convince a disbelieving world that the nightmare has already begun.*

Fox Mulder could easily sympathize with David Vincent. *The Invaders* chilled television audiences from January 10, 1967 until March 26, 1968. The period piece reflected public concerns of the 1960s, inspired by America's first missions into space and the possibility of contact with life from other planets combined with Cold War fears of hostile foreign infiltration, much as *The X-Files* would reflect public hostility toward government two decades later.

*The Invaders* centered on the efforts of architect David Vincent, played by Roy Thinnes, who, after being awakened in the middle of the night by the landing of an alien ship, dedicates the rest of his days to futilely trying to persuade a skeptical world that the invasion of our planet has begun. Of course, no one believes him, and the invaders devote their efforts to eradicating the hapless hero. These beings have taken human form and are virtually undetectable from human beings. They can only be identified by their lack of a pulse or heartbeat and, in many but not all cases, their mutated fourth finger. The aliens must periodically regenerate themselves. When wounded, they don't bleed, and they find pure oxygen fatal. They self-immolate when they die, leaving virtually no trace, adding to the difficulty of exposing their existence. They also lack emotions.

Paranoia built as the emotionless, powerful aliens relentlessly tracked Vincent, even as all his efforts to expose them prove futile. Each episode lacks closure, since absolute proof of alien existence always disappears or eludes Vincent. Slowly others begin to believe his story, but never enough to bring victory to the architect. Sound familiar? Fox Mulder knows the routine. An unnotable *Invaders* television miniseries produced by Fox appeared in 1995.

Roy Thinnes, star of *The Invaders*, reappeared as Jeremiah Smith in the two-part *X-Files* story "Talitha Cumi" and "Herrenvolk"; these episodes spanned the end of the third and the beginning of the fourth season. It seems clear that David Duchovny and Chris Carter wrote the story in what must have been at least a partial tribute to that show.

## THE PRISONER

Patrick McGoohan created and starred in the British cult hit *The Prisoner*, which first aired in 1967 and 1968 in the U.K. and U.S., and he also wrote several episodes, under his own name as well as under the pen names of Archibald Schwartz and Paddy Fitz Patrick. *The Prisoner* has been repeated many times, including on PBS and the Sci Fi Channel. Unlike *The Fugitive* and *The Invaders*, McGoohan focused on a hidden conspiracy of the rich and the powerful, a danger arising from government itself. It's the government who holds the unnamed prisoner captive, and like the series above, each episode of *The Prisoner* lacks closure, since he can't be allowed to escape until the very end. In many ways, *The Prisoner*, produced by Patrick McGoohan's Everyman Films, comes closest to the spirit of *The X-Files*, if not the detail. When the

Prisoner, known only as Number Six and not by any name despite his protestations, says, "I am not a number. I am a free man," you can almost hear Fox Mulder's desperate pleas for recognition.

Seventeen episodes were made of *The Prisoner*, although it remains unclear if a longer series of twenty-six episodes was originally planned, or whether, as McGoohan claims, he intended to make only seven but was persuaded to make a further ten in order to sell the series to the U.S. It is also unclear whether the first episode is really the beginning and the first appearance of the character.

McGoohan conceived the concept for *The Prisoner* while filming *Danger Man* in Portmeirion, Wales, which became the location of the Village. A companion U.K. series, *Secret Agent*, presented an episode in which a "village" of agents train to become imposters; this also helped form the idea for *The Prisoner*. (The names cause confusion because in the U.K. there were two series, one with each name, while in the U.S. all the episodes from both series ran under the latter name.) Many actors from *Danger Man* and *Secret Agent* appeared in *The Prisoner*. Fans still debate whether *The Prisoner* is a sequel to these two earlier series.

Opening lyrics to the series song, "Secret Agent Man" by Johnny Rivers, written by P. F. Sloan and Steve Barri, lend credence to the sequel theory:

*There's a man who leads a life of danger*
*To everyone he meets, he stays a stranger*
*With every move he makes, another chance he takes*
*Odds are he won't live to see tomorrow.*

*Secret Agent Man, Secret Agent Man*
*They've given you a number and taken away your name.*

The first episode, "Arrival," laid the foundation for the series. McGoohan plays Number Six, a man with priceless secret information, abducted to a beautiful, nameless village where everyone is known by a number and not a name. Following an abortive escape attempt, Number Six meets a colleague who shortly afterward is reported to have committed suicide. At the funeral, Number Six meets a mourner who claims she and his colleague had found a means of escape, and she offers the opportunity to him. He accepts with obvious misgivings. The series builds from here on the themes of paranoia, confusion, philosophical intercourse, manip-

ulations, escape attempts, and confrontation until the final episode, "Fall Out." Up until the end, no episode offered any sense of closure or even of building toward a clearer understanding of what the Village was, why it had been built, why Number Six had been kidnapped, or even, other than breaking him, what his captors wanted.

> "SUCH STARTLING ANNOUNCEMENTS AS these should be deprecated as being unworthy of science and mischievous to its true progress."
> —SIR WILLIAM SIEMENS ON EDISON'S ANNOUNCEMENT OF A SUCCESSFUL LIGHT BULB

In the series finale, "Fall Out," Six is greeted by a scarlet-cloaked, bewigged President as their leader-elect and addressed as "Sir," having earned the right to be an individual. Number Forty-eight and a revived Number Two of the Degree Absolute are tried and found guilty by a jury wearing black and white masks and white hooded cloaks. The President tells Sir he is free either to go or to stay and be their leader, but his speech accepting the former is shouted down by the jury after his first word, "I." Taken to the control room of rocket No. 1, Sir finds a masked and hooded figure. He rips aside the mask only to be confronted by an ape mask. He tears this away to find his own face beneath, and he embarks on a frenzy of destruction and activates the rocket launch control, panicking the Village and allowing Numbers Two, Six, and Forty-eight to escape in the confusion and head for London. Number Six then returns to his home. As the door bearing a large number one opens automatically, a hearse drives by. The Prisoner climbs into his Lotus car and drives to a deserted motorway, repeating his action from the very beginning before he resigned.

If the beginning of *The Prisoner* was unclear, the end was even less clear. Few agree on the proper interpretation of the events of the final episode. But clearly, *The Prisoner* laid the groundwork for *The X-Files* and expanded the possibilities of television. McGoohan explored the themes of government conspiracy and its philosophical implications.

McGoohan talked about the nature of his series in an interview with Warner Troyer in 1978, ten years after completing the series. The talk was sponsored by the Ontario Education Authority to coincide with their University course in *The Prisoner*, entitled The Prisoner Puzzle. McGoohan said, "It was a place trying to destroy the individual by every means possible, trying to break his spirit. This is the one rebel that they can't break. When the last episode came it had one of the largest viewing audiences ever. Everyone wanted to know who Number One was. When they did finally see it, there was a near riot, and I had to go into hiding. They thought they'd been cheated. When that door opens on its own and there's no one behind it, exactly the same as all the doors in the Village open, you know that somebody's waiting in there to start it all over again. There's no final conclusion. People want the word 'The End' put up there. The final two words for that thing should have been 'The Beginning.'" McGoohan is currently writing the script for a movie version of *The Prisoner* for ITC, and he now promises a definite beginning and end!

Like *The X-Files*, *The Prisoner* developed a dedicated fan following, which still meets to discuss the implications of each episode, the philosophy behind the series, and the importance of each character. They publish fanzines and now exchange views on the Internet. For example, the fan club Once Upon a Time has been active since 1978. Their stated philosophy is that they "consider *The Prisoner* to be one of the finest series to appear on TV. We hold all interpretations of *The Prisoner* to be worthy of discussion and we do not advocate any single interpretation of the series in our magazine. We believe interest in *The Prisoner* can be fun. We find the implications of *The Prisoner* storyline to be quite serious. We believe one person can make a difference." Clearly *The Prisoner* fans are as dedicated as X-Philes. They still explore the themes of paranoia and government conspiracy three decades after the series first aired, illustrating the important ways in which the earlier show presaged the current series. And like *The X-Files*, *The Prisoner* has invaded pop culture. For instance, several musicians have included references to *The Prisoner* in lyrics, most significantly, "McGoohan's Blues" by Roy Harper and "The Prisoner" by Iron Maiden.

*The Fugitive*, *The Invaders*, and *The Prisoner* raised many of the issues addressed in *The X-Files*. But the new series combines these elements in a unique way. Only Chris Carter could have created this latest vision.

# PART II

# THE CAST OF *THE X-FILES*

## "THEY HAVE A FILE ON ME"

# CHAPTER 9

# GILLIAN ANDERSON

*"It occurred to me the other day that if I wanted to take a break from this business, I'd be interested in becoming involved with the FBI. When I was a kid, I wanted to be an archaeologist or a marine biologist. I loved investigating."*

—ANDERSON IN TV WEEK

Gillian Leigh Anderson breathes vibrant life into *The X-Files* female lead, Dana Scully. She stands only five feet, two inches tall. She's a pretty woman with a smallish build, auburn hair, hazel eyes, a cute nose, a fair, slightly freckled complexion, and perfect lips.

Anderson was born in Chicago on August 9, 1968, to Ed and Rosemary Anderson, and she was raised in Chicago, Puerto Rico, London, and Grand Rapids, Michigan, where her father now runs a film post-production company. Rosemary, her mother, works as a computer analyst. Anderson is one of three children.

The family left Chicago shortly after she was born. Then, after a brief stay in Puerto Rico, they moved to London when she was two, so that her father could study at the London Film School. Her family still owns a flat there. Anderson enjoyed London, and still has fond memories of the Crouch End neighborhood where they lived until she was eleven. Then the family moved to Grand Rapids, Michigan, where she attended Fountain Elementary School and graduated from City High in 1986.

Moving from London to Grand Rapids was not an easy transition, and these became difficult years for her. "There was a certain feeling of displacement," she told Australia's *TV Week* magazine. "Moving into such a small town after growing up in London gave me a feeling of powerlessness."

A brief trip back to London, shortly after her family moved to Michigan, helped propel Anderson into becoming a rebellious teenager. She told *US*, "One summer when I was twelve or thirteen, I went back [to London] and was suddenly taken by the punks. I would walk sideways around my dad so he wouldn't see it." She pierced her nose, shaved her hair into a mohawk, and joined a band of kindred, combat-booted punks in Michigan. Her favorite bands were the Circle Jerks, Dead Kennedys, and Elvis Costello.

"I was daydreaming, pulling pranks. I got into a heavy punk scene. I had a nose ring, and my hair was purple and black and blue. I dressed in black. I was very confused, and a loner. I was in a relationship with a man ten years older than me when I was fourteen. He was in a punk band, and I used to give him cans of food from our house and buy him Big Gulps and cigarettes," she told *Movieline*.

She told *Entertainment Weekly*, "We'd walk down the street and give the finger to [whoever stared at] us. We'd go hear bands and smash against each other and jump off the stage. It was cool to get hurt. I needed to express my anger, because I had a lot of it—and I still do. I was never very good at expressing other emotions. I did everything I could not to feel pain."

She didn't take school seriously and, as she told *TV Guide*, was "voted class clown, and most likely to be arrested. . . . I was arrested on graduation night for breaking and entering into the high school. I called my boyfriend, who had given up and gone home earlier in the evening. I spent several hours in jail before he came to get me out."

The actress has said that she never felt comfortable in her new home and life, and this created a large pool of anger inside of her, one that hasn't necessarily gone away with time. She told *US*, "My parents were extremely liberal, and I'm very grateful for that, but there were things missing nevertheless. There is a very rebellious nature inside me that will always be there, that kicks in when it needs to." She told Australia's *TV Week*, "It's nothing I've necessarily grown out of."

Anderson auditioned for a community play in Michigan when she was seventeen. She won the part, and the experience changed her life. Theater gave her a sense of belonging. Her grades improved and she was voted most improved student. She quit the punk scene and dropped her interest in marine biology. Instead she continued to act in City High School plays and community theater. She told *Entertainment Weekly*, "[Acting] gave me an outlet to express myself. It was so freeing."

After high school, Anderson went to Ithaca, New York, to study with the National Theater of Great Britain at Cornell University. She graduated from the Goodman Theater School at Chicago's DePaul University with a BFA in 1990. Murphy, one of Anderson's teachers at DePaul University, recalled that once "Gillian had an eight-line part in a French farce, but turned it into a star role just by the attitude she brought to it. She has an incandescence."

Anderson decided to move to New York City after graduation, encouraged by William Morris agents who had witnessed her talent at an actor's showcase at the Goodman Theater School. Anderson later recalled to *B.C. Woman* magazine, "I had it in my mind that I should leave on a certain day, but it took longer to pack than I expected." She left in her Volkswagen Rabbit at eleven o'clock on the appointed night and set out. "The car was packed so high that I couldn't see out the rear-view mirror, and when I stopped to sleep, I had to crouch up in a fetal position."

Once in New York, she worked as a waitress in two different restaurants when she wasn't acting and going on auditions. She made her first film appearance as host in *The Turning*, produced by Robert de Niro's fledgling Tribeca Film Center in 1988. Anderson received a Theatre World Award in 1991 for her off-Broadway performance in Alan Ayckborne's *Absent Friends* at the Manhattan Theater Club; she had taken over the role from Mary-Louise Parker. She also costarred in Christopher Hampton's *The Philanthropist* at the Long Wharf Theater.

Anderson had never intended to leave New York City, but she decided to visit Los Angeles. She told *Movieline*, "I came out to L.A. to visit a man I'd met in a play in New Haven. I was going to stay for two weeks, and I got here and sold my return ticket. William Morris was already my agency, and I went out on three or four film auditions a day for a year and didn't get anything. I didn't have any money, and I was relying on my boyfriend to help me out financially."

Anderson loved theater and performing before a live audience; she never intended to act before an unfeeling camera. "I moved to Los Angeles with the intention of never doing television, because I had no respect for television, the quality of the shows and the work. I actually never watch television, and don't own one," she told the *Philadelphia Inquirer*.

Being out of work for a year changed her mind. Her on-screen career began with *Home Fires Burning*, as April Cavanaugh, for a cable station in 1992, and the audiocassette version of *Exit to Eden*. She had a role in an episode of *Class of '96*, but acting still wasn't paying her bills. She felt that if something didn't happen soon she would have to go back to waitressing.

Then, in 1993, she went to yet another audition, this one for a television pilot. It was the first television series she had ever tried out for, and it happened to be *The X-Files*. She told Australia's *TV Week* that she never thought she would get the job. "I didn't know what it entailed. I didn't even know what a pilot was. I don't think I even cared whether it was going to get picked up or not, but once we did it, and I started to know a little bit more about the whole TV thing, I was hoping we could just get picked up for a year or something like that."

Anderson liked the role of Dana Scully. The rebellious, ex-punker turned actress found herself attracted to the "independent, intelligent," FBI agent, "able to stand up for herself," as she later described the role to *B.C. Woman*. "She's strong-willed, passionate about her work, and a completely capable partner for her brilliant male counterpart."

Apparently, the chemistry between Anderson and Duchovny was instantaneous. She told *Rolling Stone*, "He came over to me in the hallway at the network audition and asked if we could read through the scene together. We did, and it was amazing. Better than anything that we've done since."

Fox executives didn't think she was the right actress, but Carter insisted that she was perfect for the part of Scully. The network finally relented. In 1993, at age twenty-four, Anderson relocated to Vancouver, Canada, to shoot the pilot for *The X-Files*. It was only the third time that Anderson had acted before a camera. She told a *Midday* audience on CBC TV, "I had no idea what was going on. I was just doing what was put right in front of my nose, and I had no idea of how long it would run or really cared. I had a job, and somebody wanted me to act. I was happy with that." When a *Movieline* magazine interviewer asked her if she felt she had paid her dues, she replied, "I feel I've paid a lot of dues, not necessarily in the amount of time I've pounded the pavement, but in my life."

Very quickly, Anderson began to take the job more seriously, delving into her character and the underlying basis of the series. The actress told *SFX* magazine, "Chris [Carter] had a very, very strong idea about who Mulder and Scully were, and he was very particular about how he wanted us to act in terms of their degree of intelligence, seriousness, and what drove them. He was very adamant about that. But in the long run it's the actor who plays the character, and, of course, there are interpretations and flavorings that will come into play. I think we both have a similar idea who the character of Scully is anyway."

Anderson sees Scully as more close-minded than she is about paranormal phenomenon. She told *B.C. Woman* magazine, "I act more on my intuition, and I'm more interested in the paranormal. Actors don't always rely on personal experience. A lot of it is just pretending. When Scully feels angry or afraid, I can draw on experience. But with other things, it's more difficult. The dialogue, for example, is often very technical. It's hard to memorize that kind of material, and even harder to verbalize it in an interesting way."

She told *SFX* magazine, "I'd like to see an alien very much. It wouldn't surprise me if there were a government cover-up. It seems so likely that there's something other than us in this universe. Cover-up is synonymous with government. It just is."

Regarding extraterrestrial life, Anderson told *Los Angeles Daily News*, "I believe that anything is possible. I believe we are living in a vast universe, and it might be rather egotistical of us to think that we are the center of it and the most intelligent people in the universe."

"There is also the theory that we actually have help from spirit beings who are around us constantly," she told the *London Observer*. "I actually believe that. When I was in high school, I was in a very atheist crowd, and it was the consensus that religion was a crutch. But over the past few years I have grown to appreciate that feeling of safety or trust, that there is a light at the end of the tunnel and that there is a reason for us to be here."

## "AERIAL FLIGHT IS ONE OF THAT CLASS OF problems with which man will never be able to cope. —Simon Newcomb, American astronomer, 1903

Anderson's beliefs extend to ESP and psychokinesis, as she told *TV Guide*, "One time, I guess I was fourteen years old, I was dating somebody who lived an hour away. I had seen him the day before, found this black marble, and given it to him. He said on the phone: 'Guess where I put it?' And I said, 'You took the lid off one of your cologne bottles and put it on the neck of the bottle.' He said, 'Oh, my God.' Because that's *exactly* what he had done. We know so little about our brains and our abilities as human and spiritual beings. There could be vast areas of our minds that we're not using on a daily basis, which have the ability to sense—or to know—a whole other level of things."

Even more recently, Anderson experienced another strange occurrence when she moved into a new home. She told *Entertainment Weekly*, "I felt there were spirits there with us. It was really creepy. It felt like there was someone attached to me. We were told by a Native American that we lived near an Indian burial ground. He said there had been a plague years ago that wiped many of them out. There were a lot of souls in unrest. He came to the house and performed this ritual called smudging in which herbs are burned so as to purify the space. It was amazing. Afterward, it was like the house got lighter. Whatever we felt had been there was gone."

Anderson found it hard adjusting to life as a leading actor on a television show, and she battled her self-doubts constantly. Even if she was new to TV, she understood the money and risk involved in casting her, despite Carter's assurance that she was perfect for the role. She told the *London Observer*, "For a long time, there was this feeling that they were going to find out they'd made a really big mistake. Had it been a larger network than Fox, they certainly would not have taken the risk. Even they were interested in getting a typically marketable beauty, although that was not how Scully was written."

Luckily, veteran actor David Duchovny helped support the television novice. She told *Entertainment Weekly*, "David took me under his wing. [His reassurance] meant a lot to me, and still does, because it was a very scary time."

The grind of a weekly series was a difficult adjustment for Anderson. She told the *Washington Times*, "I'm not out much. I work and I go home. I work on the scripts. I wake up and come to work. And in between I try to get my bills paid." In a careless, off-hand moment, she once described her *X-Files* shooting schedule as "a death sentence." She later told *Entertainment Weekly*, "It was a meaningless joke. I felt bad for the people that it affected." Carter admitted to *EW* that the comment upset him at the time. "I called her and said, 'Look, this is a chance of a lifetime. The work is so hard, I'm sure it feels as if you've signed your life away. But if we all felt like that, we might as well go home and pack it up.'"

During the filming of the first season, Anderson also met *The X-Files*'s German-born art director Clyde Klotz, and they began to date. She told *TV Guide*, "I just felt like I had known him for a really long time. Many times before. Other lifetimes. It felt just like that." Anderson elaborated on Regis and Kathie Lee, "He was an art director. . . . He wasn't on the pilot but came on when we started shooting the series. It wasn't love at first sight. I was very attracted to him and assumed he was to me as well. I invited him into my trailer to eat sushi. And when he left, he said he didn't really want the sushi. We went out on a couple dates, and he asked me to marry him. We had a few dates to feel it out—it wasn't bang or anything. . . . I didn't faint."

It wasn't Anderson's first proposal, but this was different. She told *US*, "I had gotten engaged before, with a ring over a fancy dinner, and it was a very uncomfortable thing, but this time it was so fabulously simple." The couple married on New Year's Day in 1994 on the seventeenth hole of a Hawaiian golf course, with a Buddhist priest presiding over the ceremonies. Klotz left the show shortly afterward, and in December 1996 the couple announced they were separating.

One month after they were married, Anderson discovered she was pregnant. This was surprising news, but it shouldn't have been entirely unsuspected. Two months before, at a Fox-sponsored party for the show, Anderson had sat down with a psychic, who had predicted, "You're going to have a little girl." At the time, the young actress wasn't even married!

Regarding her pregnancy, she told *USA Today*, "It was wonderful news, but it scared a lot of people. It scared me. The show was doing relatively well, but it was still very young, and there was the possibility of it going one way or another. It could have crashed, and I would have been somewhat in the middle of that. It was a rough time letting people know I had made this decision and deciding how to work with it."

A worried Anderson feared she would be dropped from the series, but Carter again stuck by her. He became the baby's godfather. Recalling the speed of all the changes in her life, Anderson jokingly told the *Regis and Kathie Lee* audience, "It's actually a prerequisite to a show, you sign a contract and you get a husband and baby as well." She told *Movieline*, "I didn't plan for everything to happen in one year. In the moment, these things didn't seem like they were too much. Eventually it hit me that it was too much. Not that I shouldn't have made the decisions, but that I was going to pay for it."

The actress worked until two days before she gave birth by cesarean section on September 25, 1994. Piper Anderson arrived in the world weighing eight pounds, ten ounces. Anderson remained in the hospital for six days, then returned to work four days later. The veteran stage actress missed just one episode, exemplifying the old adage, "the show must go on."

Anderson said she wants to become pregnant again, but not during this series. She told *B.C. Woman*, "That's hard, too, because the show could run for another five or six years, which means not having another baby for quite a while. But I wouldn't want to do it the same way again. It was one of the hardest things I've ever done."

Morgan summed it up best to an America Online audience, saying, "When she looks back on her life, I'm sure she'll want her children by her side and not an episode of 'Squeeze.'"

Having a daughter has helped the actress put her life into perspective and taught her a new sense of responsibility. Anderson told *Woman's Day*, "Piper keeps me in check. My husband has grounded me as well. At least once a week I lie back in the bathtub and laugh at the ridiculousness of it all."

As Anderson told Australia's *TV Week* magazine, "I got the job when I was twenty-four, so I was still in a period where I was desperately trying to figure out who I was and working very hard at it. The show has really forced me to focus and become much more responsible and make much healthier choices, because there's a responsibility that I have to myself, the show, and most importantly, my daughter. There have been numerous times when I thought that all this was going to break me, but it hasn't, and I feel stronger now than I ever have. I get a lot of fan-mail from women saying how great Scully is as a role model, and even the men think she's cool in a smart way, so that feels really good."

Anderson told a *Midday* audience on CBC TV, "Early on I got a hint that girls of all ages were considering Scully as a role model. Scully is very intelligent; she went ahead with her education; she has a very moral mindframe; she's honest; she's in pursuit of justice . . . all very positive, very strong qualities. I was delighted that women were responding to those attributes."

The ex-punk teenager is now a very intelligent, hardworking, and charming woman with an easygoing and bubbly personality who genuinely enjoys her work. Anderson told the *Philadelphia Inquirer,* "We're on a quality show. I'm trustful of Chris's vision. Everything seems to be heading in the direction it needs to be going."

She has clearly brought to the show everything Carter hoped she would. *Movieline* has called her "a better actress than most of the women you see in movies." In 1997, she won the Golden Globe for best actress in a dramatic series. In 1996, she was nominated for an Emmy, a Golden Globe, and a Quality Award (her second nomination) for best actress in a drama series, and she won the Screen Actors' Guild award. And she is obviously a big reason that the show won the 1995 and 1997 Golden Globe awards for best drama and was nominated for an Emmy and Quality Award for best drama in 1996.

Anderson is pleased with the favorable response she has received from the professional community and from her fans. There are now two Internet online fan clubs, the Gillian Anderson Testosterone Brigade and the Gillian Anderson Fan Club. Anderson is referred to by some fans as IDDG: "Intellectually Drop-Dead Gorgeous." She told the *Washington Times*, "I had a very good feeling that this show would be successful, but I don't think it's really even hit me yet. Once in a

while I'll be driving down the street in Canada and think, 'I'm in Canada. How did I get here?' There is something vulnerable about being in the public eye, to a certain degree. Having that feeling, hearing 'Scully' whispered as you pass people. It reminds you constantly that you're not in your private little world."

She told Australia's *TV Week*, "Los Angeles is such a vast place, and I'm literally shocked when somebody turns around and stares at me, because I forget why they would look at me! In Vancouver, I don't come across it as often. Although now when we shoot on the streets, the entire neighborhood for miles around comes and stands on the sidelines to watch—but that's still only my real contact with fans.

"I have come to L.A. or New York every single weekend since December [1995] for meetings, photo shoots, or media interviews, and not five minutes of that time was spent in a situation where I could step back and take a look at the show through the fan's perspective, or just walk down the street and see what happens."

*Gillian Anderson in character.*

The popularity and recognition can be overwhelming, and a bit unreal. She has said, "I feel like I'm missing something—like something is not quite clocking, and I don't get it. But what surprises me most is that badges I wear can be auctioned for $1,500. It's astounding that people will spend that kind of money on a piece of plastic from *The X-Files*."

In terms of her development in the role, Anderson feels a strong sense of progression. She told the *Washington Post*, "We were spending, I think, the first season figuring out who these [characters] were. And then I got pregnant, and I was trying to figure out who *I* was. And then I think only in the third season have I started to feel really comfortable with her and really feel like she's gotten stronger and more mature. It seems like her relationship with Mulder has gotten stronger, and she's more of a partner than a sidekick."

## "I AM TIRED OF ALL THIS SORT OF THING

called science here . . . We have spent millions in that sort of thing for the last few years, and it is time it should be stopped."

—U.S. SENATOR SIMON CAMERON, ON THE SMITHSONIAN INSTITUTION

Despite all that Scully has seen so far, Anderson assures us that her character's basic skepticism will not change. Anderson said on *RealTime*, "I don't see that changing because there is a dramatic dynamic in that dichotomy between Mulder and Scully that keeps the show moving forward. She has become much more open-minded over the past couple of seasons. She does have a major history and background in the sciences and in medicine. Even though she has witnessed supernatural things, it doesn't necessarily mean that she's going to automatically believe in everything supernatural and paranormal. She's always gonna go back to trying to prove things from a scientific standpoint."

Anderson enjoys playing her role so much, and identifies with her character to such a great degree, that she told *TV Week*, "It occurred to me the other day that if I wanted to take a break from this business, I'd be interested in becoming involved with the FBI. When I was a kid, I wanted to be an archaeologist or a marine biologist. I loved investigating."

However, Anderson is not looking to leave the business. The former stage actress wants to continue expanding her range and avoid becoming typecast, as has happened to some actors on that other cult science fiction series, *Star Trek*. She told *SFX*, "The stuff that's being offered to me at the moment is a far cry from Scully. I haven't had any actual film offers yet, but there have been TV movies. Although I haven't done any; we haven't had the time." Ideally, she's said, she'd prefer her future to be in feature and independent films, rather than TV, but there isn't much to time to worry about that right now.

Anderson doesn't want to work during breaks because, as she told Australia's *TV Week*, she needs the free time to maintain a sense of balance in her life. "When you're working such long hours, it's essential that you rest and have time away from it, but by the time you've had dinner and read your script for the next day, it's time for bed. On weekends, I have a lot of catching up to do with my husband, who's a production designer. Because I work in such a stressful situation, it's very easy to lose touch with who you really are as a person. It's important to have a normal home life. That keeps you sane."

Duchovny told *US* that as a result of the long hours they work together, "We don't spend any time together off the set. It's not because I don't like her. I don't want to see anybody from work."

Anderson also has a social conscience, and she would like to do her part to build a better world than the one she was born into. But, as she told *B.C. Woman*, "Because of the hours involved, a show like this prohibits much volunteer activity beyond sending an autographed picture to a fundraising auction." She favors causes that help battered women, people with AIDS, and sufferers of neurofibromatosis, which is a rare disease that affects nerve endings and causes internal and external deformities, increasing the possibility of other debilitating conditions, like scoliosis, and sometimes leading to early death. Anderson's interest in combating the disease is personal, since her fifteen-year-old brother was diagnosed with it when he was three. Their mother, Rosemary, helped start a clinic for patients in Michigan.

Anderson is also concerned about gender equality, especially in Hollywood. She told *B.C. Woman*, "There are huge differences in the way male and female actors are perceived. Women have to be a certain size in order to get good roles. The only successful, larger-than-average female actor I can think of is Kathy Bates. And once women reach a certain age, they can only expect one or two good roles per year, whereas male actors can continue working regularly well into their forties. Then there are the types of roles available to women. We're constantly depicted as sidekicks, ingenues, and hangers-on, rarely as independent and capable individuals. And the enormous, huge discrepancies in pay. . . . The amounts that some male actors make are astronomically obscene. Women in Hollywood are constantly shown that there's a difference between them and men, and that that's okay. But it's not okay."

Anderson doesn't see herself leaving her adopted country, or the city of Vancouver, any time soon. The actress told *Wrapped in Plastic* magazine, "I really had forgotten how beautiful Vancouver can be in the spring and summertime. It's torturous with all the rain. I don't really have much time to take a look at the city, and I couldn't say I'd be good about finding my way around! . . . I miss L.A. sometimes, not for L.A., but just for the weather. There's a certain sense of freedom when you step outside a plane into a warm and healthy—albeit smoggy—environment. There just seems to be a constant cloud or a constant feeling in this city that gets to you after a while, but otherwise it's great. The people are wonderful."

Anderson told *Movieline* magazine that an extra on one of their shows performed fortune telling by drawing a triangle, a square, and a dot and asking the subject to draw around them. Anderson drew a petal and some leaves around the dot, and the fortune teller told her, "You drew leaves, which are green and represent growth, but you drew only one petal, and this is how you perceive yourself, as not a full flower." Anderson reported that she hadn't previously liked herself and had spent time "overweight, underweight, wearing black, hiding," but that in the past couple of years she had "started to open up in front of millions of people."

# CHAPTER 10

# SPECIAL AGENT DANA KATHERINE SCULLY

NAME: Dana Katherine Scully, M.D.

BADGE NUMBER: JTT03316613

HEIGHT: Five feet, three inches

WEIGHT: Unknown

HAIR: Red

EYES: Blue

DATE OF BIRTH: 23 February 1964

BIRTHPLACE: Unknown

CURRENT ADDRESS: 3170 W. 53rd St., #35, Annapolis, MD

TELEPHONE: (202) 555-6431

E-MAIL: D_Scully@FBI.gov

DISTINGUISHING FEATURES: Tattoo on back

MARITAL STATUS: Unmarried

FATHER'S NAME: William Scully, Captain, US Navy. Served in the Cuban Missile Crisis, 1961. Died December 1993.

MOTHER'S NAME: Margaret Scully

SIBLINGS: Elder brother, William "Bill" Scully, Jr. Elder sister, Melissa Scully (deceased). Younger brother, Charles Scully.

EDUCATION: B.S. Physics, University of Maryland, 1986. Medical degree (unknown), residency in forensic pathology.

PUBLICATIONS: Senior thesis, "Einstein's Twin Paradox: A New Interpretation"

## FBI CAREER HISTORY

1990: Joined the FBI directly from medical school. Taught for two years at Quantico Academy.

1992: Assigned by Section Chief Scott Blevins to the X-Files section.

OCTOBER 1994: Abducted by fugitive Duane Barry (X-File X73317) under unexplained circumstances. Agent Alex Krycek is wanted for questioning in her disappearance.

NOVEMBER 1994: Discovered in deep coma in the Intensive Care Unit of North Georgetown University Hospital; no witnesses or records of her admission are found. Upon her recovery, Agent Scully returned to duty, claiming to have no memory of the events of her disappearance.

APRIL 1995: Agent Scully failed to appear at a hearing called by Walter Skinner into the activities of Agent Mulder. A bungled attempt on her life resulted in the death of her sister, Melissa.

## PROFILE

The FBI recruited Doctor Dana Katherine Scully, M.D., while still in medical school, after she received her undergraduate degree in physics from the University of Maryland. She taught at the FBI Academy in Quantico, Virginia, until assigned to be Agent Fox Mulder's partner by Section Chief Scott Blevins, in order to determine if Mulder had become obsessed with the X-Files.

Scully believes that most supposedly paranormal phenomena actually have logical explanations. She has witnessed several of what she now believes are paranormal activities while assisting Mulder, but these have yet to shake her basic beliefs. Despite a growing openness to paranormal phenomena, she remains determined to search for scientific explanations in all cases. Scully, a Catholic, wears a necklace with a small cross, which she lost when she was abducted. Mulder later returned it to her.

When the X-Files were closed and Scully reassigned to the FBI Academy, she continued to unofficially advise

Mulder on violent crime cases. Mental patient Duane Barry abducted Scully, but she escaped and reappeared in a coma at a Georgetown hospital after a three-month absence. She recovered and was reassigned as Mulder's partner after the X-Files were reopened, although she remains amnesiac regarding the period of her abduction.

Scully and Mulder went into hiding and missed a scheduled meeting with FBI Assistant Director Skinner, placing her career in jeopardy.

Scully, born February 23, 1964, is a middle child. She has one older and one younger brother, and her older sister, Melissa, is deceased. She enjoyed a close relationship with her father, but her family disapproved of her joining the Bureau. Her father died in 1993. She had a year-long relationship with an instructor at the Academy, Jack Willis, but the workaholic agent now has no time to date.

Scully drinks her coffee with cream, but no sugar.

# CHAPTER 11

# DAVID DUCHOVNY

*"I get confused over people's concern with whether or not I'm a nice guy. I work hard to make a good show and I think that's enough."*

—Duchovny in Starlog magazine, June, 1995

The *New York Times* has called David William Duchovny (pronounced "doo-KUV-nee") "the first Internet sex symbol with hair," while the prestigious *New Republic* declared him a "zeitgeist icon." Clearly, David Duchovny has come a long way from his days as a serious, shy intellectual pursuing a teaching career at Yale University.

The actor, whose name means "spiritual" in Russian, was born in Manhattan's Lower East Side, the son of a Russian Jewish father and a Scottish mother, on August 7, 1960. He was raised in New York along with his older brother, Daniel, who has since moved to Los Angeles and become an award-winning director of commercials, and his younger sister, Laurie, who is a New York school teacher.

Duchovny's father, Amram Ducovny—no typo, they spell their last names differently—is a former publicist for the American Jewish Committee and a playwright and novelist. Ducovny wrote the off-Broadway play *The Trial of Lee Harvey Oswald*, which ran in New York City in 1967. David Duchovny later recalled to the U.K.'s *Who* magazine, "It was really long. Oswald just sat there and didn't say anything the whole first act. I remember asking my father how it was possible that he didn't have to go to the bathroom." Ducovny also wrote *The Wisdom of Spiro T. Agnew, David Ben-Gurion in His Own Words*, and *On with the Wind*, a book about Martha Mitchell, the wife of Nixon's attorney general, John Mitchell. He was a Billie Holiday fan who played softball.

If his father is the epitome of a New York Jewish intellectual, his mother, Margaret, is a conservative Presbyterian Scot, who still isn't so sure her son made the right choice to leave academia and become an actor. She worked as a Manhattan grade school teacher.

Recalling the influence of his parents, Duchovny told *Playgirl*, "You get kind of that Protestant work ethic combined with Jewish guilt and introspection. So you get someone to go out and do a lot of stuff and change the world, but he's too busy being depressed and sitting and thinking about it." And, in many ways, despite his success in academia and as an actor, this describes Duchovny in a nutshell.

Duchovny's parents had a difficult marriage, and they eventually divorced in 1972, when he was eleven. As Duchovny told the Copley News Service, his parents couldn't even agree on how to spell their family name. "My father took the 'h' out of our last name because he was tired of having it mispronounced, but when my parents divorced, my mother put the 'h' back in, as a show of solidarity with how a family member spelled the name. I spell it with the 'h'; my brother doesn't use the 'h.' My sister goes back and forth, depending on her mood. Regardless, I think it's a beautiful name. I don't care how people spell the name as long as they get the meaning."

After the divorce, David and his two siblings went to live with their mother in an apartment at Eleventh Street and Second Avenue across from the St. Mark's graveyard. Their father moved to Paris to write novels and sit in cafes.

"The divorce was probably the most important emotional moment in my growing up," Duchovny told *Details*. "I don't think you ever recover from something like that. You are forced into an adult world of emotions that you aren't prepared to deal with. Your parents are trying to explain to you what has gone wrong with adult love. You don't know what that is. They're talking about love that can go away. You're afraid it might go away from you. So it can define the way you deal with love for the rest of your life. Most children feel they caused their parents to split up in some way. I can't whistle. My dad whistled the correct way. I think at eleven I discovered I could make that sound, and I was doing it all the time. I'm sure it was annoying, and at one point my father, dealing with whatever he was dealing with, looked at me and said, 'Will you stop that infernal whistling?' I thought my father left because of my whistling."

Duchovny told *New Weekly*, "It . . . is an experience I've reacted to ever since. It's meant different things to me at different times and will always be very important. As I get older, I deal with it in different ways, as I learn more about relationships between men and women. My aim in life is not to make the same mistakes as my parents."

Growing up, Duchovny learned to hide his feelings, to build a protective wall between himself and the world. He told *US*, "However my family worked itself out, it became a technique of survival not to feel things too deeply. I was always supposed to be the one who didn't have any problems." Duchovny became painfully introverted as a child. "Most people think that New Yorkers are energetic, in-your-face people, but my brother used to tell his friends that I was retarded, because I was so quiet. They would speak very loudly and slowly to me, and that just made me more shy."

Duchovny feels this dynamic has shaped his adult character. He told *Details*, "I'm exoskeletal, like a lobster. It has its bones on the outside and its flesh on the inside. What sticks to the inside is personal. On the outside I express a kind of free-floating irony which appears to have no values at all. Inside I have a free-floating values system, but to say what is meaningful to me would trivialize it. These are not things I express."

As a kid, Duchovny played baseball in the neighborhood church cemetery, using gravestones for bases.

In one of his first acting roles, in the fifth grade he played one of the three Magi in a Christmas play at Grace Church. The young thespian quit acting after that, as he told *Rolling Stone* much later, thinking, "I brought frankincense to the Lord, and now you want me to be a spear carrier?"

Despite his shyness, Duchovny lost his virginity at the early age of fourteen. As he explained to *Woman's Day*, "My buddy was twelve when he lost his virginity—which I'm not condoning. For two long years he taunted me, so I felt like the oldest virgin on the planet. I was anxious to get it over with. My virginity was a burden."

But mostly, Duchovny devoted himself to his studies as a child, and he did so well he earned an academic scholarship to Collegiate, an elite Manhattan prep school, where his fellow students included John F. Kennedy, Jr. Suddenly, Duchovny found himself in a completely different world. "I was a scholarship kid," he told the Associated Press. "I remember going to visit a friend for the first time and seeing the elevator open up into his apartment, which was wild. I'd only seen elevators open into hallways."

In prep school, Duchovny continued to excel at his studies and writing, while also becoming heavily involved in sports. As he told Australia's *TV Hits* magazine, "I was a jock, but I was a reader, a sensitive jock. I wrote poems and considered myself a budding writer. I had a good time in an all-boys high school. I didn't have that frantic, daily search for sex that happens in coed schools. You get a different kind of energy. My teenage years were fun. The hardest years in my life were twenty-five to twenty-nine. The paradigms you create to live your life explode every six to nine years, and that was probably the first time I noticed that. Some people figure life out for themselves, and some people think they have it figured out and lie to themselves and never change."

## "X-RAYS ARE A HOAX." —Lord Kelvin,

### engineer and physicist, c. 1900

Duchovny went to Princeton University for his undergraduate studies. There he played basketball for a year, "until I got fed up with my coach or he got fed up with me," as he later told *US*, and he played baseball for two seasons as a centerfielder. Duchovny then went to Yale University, where he received a masters in English literature and began a graduate fellowship in pursuit of his Ph.D. Famed educator Harold Bloom was one of his teachers at Yale.

"I was a good student and took it really seriously," Duchovny recalled in *Playgirl*. "Looking back on it, I wish I'd had a little more fun. I didn't have those wild and crazy college years that people seem to try to recapture the rest of their lives. I spent no time trying to recapture it. I can just move on. I had a girlfriend I met in my first year. I saw her the first day of school, and decided I must get to know this girl. I joined a politics class just because she was in it. She was my girlfriend for four years and a year after we graduated. If I'd met her a little later we'd probably have stayed together. She was my first long-term relationship."

While pursuing his Ph.D., and working as a teaching assistant, Duchovny began to commute to New York twice a week to take lessons from the Actor's Studio to improve his screenwriting. Duchovny said on *The Late Late Show with Tom Snyder* in 1995, "I was getting a Ph.D. in English literature because I did not yet have the guts to go out and [write] on my own. The plan was to stay in academia and then eventually start to write. I was at Yale. There were all those acting students running around, and they seemed to be having a great time. I wanted to write for the stage or a screenplay, so I thought I should learn something about dialogue, about the stage, so I started taking acting. My heart wasn't involved."

Maggie Wheeler, who dated Duchovny around that time, later told Britain's *Who* magazine, "He made the decision to become an actor in increments. He'd put so much energy into academics and been so successful at it—switching to acting was a big deal."

Jason Beghe, Duchovny's best friend since ninth grade and now a professional actor, persuaded Duchovny to audition for a TV commercial. Beghe recalled, "I thought that because of his credentials, being such a golden boy, he would appeal to the people who were hiring."

Duchovny didn't get the commercial, but he was becoming hooked on acting. He told the Copley News Service, acting gave him "an emotional life really for the first time. It was great. I could scream, yell, and cry on stage without consequences. I could have a full life; nobody would arrest or leave me for [behaving] like that."

"I started acting to stop thinking." Duchovny told *US*, "Well, not really to stop thinking, but I had educated my head about as far as I could."

Two years later, while still teaching at Yale, he finally made his first commercial—for Lowenbrau beer. He earned $9,000 for the spot, earning twice as much money as he made as a teaching assistant. Then, in 1987, he got cast in the feature film *New Year's Day* by Henry Jaglom, and that role finally persuaded him to leave his academic pursuits behind. By 1987, he had only to complete his dissertation to receive his Ph.D., but he was never to finish it. It was provocatively titled, "Magic and Technology in Contemporary Poetry and Prose." Duchovny was twenty-six, and he already felt old to be a beginning actor.

His mother wasn't happy with the decision. Duchovny later told *Who* magazine, "My mom was disappointed. I think she'll always be disappointed, even if she is a little amazed that I was actually able to pull it off. I was never fully convinced that I was meant to be an academic."

As much as Duchovny enjoyed acting, it was his ambivalence about the academic life that precipitated the change. "I would have been a failed academic," he told the *Boston Globe*, "because I was good at it, but I was insecure. I spoke the language, but underneath I was thinking, 'Somebody's going to find out that I don't really care.' In the four months before my orals, I read maybe eight, nine hours a day. The day before, my head felt heavy, like it would roll off my shoulders. . . . I remember thinking, 'I'll never be this smart again.'"

He told the Associated Press, "I enjoyed reading, I enjoyed writing. It was pretty much because I hadn't found anything that moved me, and this was something I could do and I liked in a tepid kind of a way as a career. I wasn't obsessed with actors. I was a sports fanatic, really. Acting gave me a sense of team. [Acting] is where I can be a full human being, a full emotional person, and have none of the dire consequences that you can have in life."

Duchovny is very controlled even as an actor. He told the *Boston Globe*, "I think I'm the kind of actor you have to watch closely. I don't run out to get you. You kind of have to come to me. Luckily, enough people looked closely. The first stuff I went up for, they were saying, 'He doesn't seem to be doing anything.' Now, if somebody says that to me, I say, 'Well, thank you.'"

Duchovny soon began appearing regularly in off-Broadway plays, including *The Copulating Mermaid of Venice, California,* and *Green Cockatoo.* He also appeared in one film, *Working Girl* (1988). At the prompting of his agent, Duchovny moved to Los Angeles in 1989, the year Jaglom's film *New Year's Day* was released, "in case there was any 'heat' when *New Year's Day* opened," the actor told *Who* magazine. "There was a little heat, but the only thing that happened was that I changed agents."

In L.A., Duchovny soon met Perrey Reeves, an actress, at a trendy boutique, Fred Segal's in Santa Monica. He was trying to choose between two suits, and she advised him to buy both. They struck up an "old-fashioned" romance, getting to know each other over the phone, until eventually Duchovny moved in. Duchovny spent the next one and a half years in Hollywood virtually unemployed. Reeves paid the rent, and he helped when he could, with earnings from occasional commercials, writing magazine articles, and working for a catering company.

He told *Starlog,* "I worked so hard as a student for about twelve years to attain some kind of goal and status in that world, and then I started acting and that counted for nothing. For nothing. Other people couldn't care less that I went to Princeton and Yale. Suddenly, all of this work I had done counted for nothing in my professional life, and sometimes I just wanted to cry out, 'But I worked so damn hard! Can't I get a break?'"

Even with his own acting, his academic background was more a hindrance than a help. "Acting is instinctual," Duchovny said on *The Late Late Show with Tom Snyder.* "When I first tried to become an actor, I was almost at a disadvantage because there were so many layers of analytical critical thinking that I had to throw away. It was like all these muscles I had developed were now devalued completely and made me a more boring actor. In terms of breaking down scripts and seeing story arcs, it helped, but not in terms of the heart."

Duchovny won the role of a clubgoer for the 1990 film *Bad Influence,* then he won his first real break, getting cast as the transvestite government investigator Dennis/Denise Bryson in David Lynch's television series *Twin Peaks.* Duchovny told *Starlog,* "I remember showing up on the set and thinking, 'Well, here I am wearing a dress and pantyhose,' and wondering, 'Is this the beginning and end of my career?' That was a pretty scary experience."

Despite his trepidation, "I loved doing that," he told *Seventeen.* "It was a lot of fun. I'm in touch with my feminine side, but the clothes are so uncomfortable! Men can just throw on a pair of jeans and a T-shirt, and that's considered sexy or nice, and women are expected to go with the tight bras and tight pantyhose and the high heels. It's terrible." He said in *Playgirl,* "Bras with wires hurt. I had big tits. I was a large woman, and I had a big rack. They were like a loaf of bread, kind of like Mrs. Doubtfire. I was an unattractive woman, but I had nice legs. My sister was jealous of my legs."

In 1991, Duchovny returned to film in the role of Randy, a biker-philosopher who finds God and becomes an insurance salesman, in *The Rapture,* directed by Michael Tolkin. He starred opposite Mimi Rogers, and one nude scene from that steamy film has come back to haunt him, as stills of the scene have flooded the Internet in recent years.

*David Duchovny between shoots.*

"I was naked in bed with Mimi Rogers, my girlfriend in the movie," he told *New Weekly* magazine. "And she decides to make the bed and turf me out. So the director said, 'Get out of bed and put on your underwear with your back to the camera, because we can't do a frontal shot.' When I got out, I bent over and pulled my shorts up—which is probably one of the least flattering things a man of any age can do. But this is one of the few nude scenes I've done, and it's really haunting me. Earlier in my career, I did a play called *The Copulating Mermaid of Venice, California*, in which I also appeared nude. But I'm pretty sure there aren't any pictures around from that!"

Duchovny also appeared in the film *Julia Has Two Lovers* that year, as a telephone hustler. He told *Playgirl*, "[The movie] was a fun movie because there was no structure. It was mostly improvised, and we had a crew of almost zero. Phone-sex doesn't really interest me. I'm more of a visual person. If they had television phone-sex, I guess that would be exciting."

In 1991, he also played Bruce in *Don't Tell Mom the Babysitter's Dead* and John in *Denial*. His film work continued to grow the following year, 1992; he played Dylan in *Venice/Venice*, Officer Tippit in *Ruby*, Rollie Totherob Roland in Sir Richard Attenborough's *Chaplin* (which starred Robert Downey, Jr.), and Brad, the evil yuppie, in *Beethoven*, costarring opposite Charles Grodin. Duchovny also played David in the television movie *Baby Snatcher*.

In 1993, he costarred with Brad Pitt and Juliette Lewis in *Kalifornia*. Duchovny told *Starlog*, "It was a tough, physical shoot and we were moving around on the road a lot. Working with Michelle [Forbes, of *Star Trek*] was a good experience. Everybody became real close. Working on that film was like a real family thing, and I think it showed in the film."

He won a regular if small role in Showtime's *Red Shoe Diaries* television series, as Jake, the cuckolded architect. Duchovny told *Who* magazine, "I'm the conduit through which America views the soft underbelly of women's erotic desires. Some say it's the part I was born to play." The actor elaborated for *Details*, "I just do a minute in the beginning and in the end, six episodes in a day. I call it my Jack Nicholson day because I figure I'm making Nicholson money for that day."

Then, in 1993, came the most important role in the young actor's life, Agent Fox Mulder in Chris

Carter's *The X-Files* television series for Fox. At the time, however, Duchovny didn't see it in those terms. He told Australia's *TV Hits*, "I think Chris Carter is very instinctual and that he decided immediately that it was going to be me. It probably helped that I wasn't interested in the job. That always helps. I didn't want to do a TV series, and I didn't want to move to Vancouver."

Duchovny quipped to the Copley News Service, "I was chosen for *The X-Files* because of previous experience playing an FBI agent—although it's the first time I'm doing it in a suit. Fortunately, I don't have to use J. Edgar Hoover as a role model this time around."

Not only was Duchovny not interested in TV, he thought *The X-Files* wouldn't last. It was using an anthology format, which hadn't been successful since the 1950s. Even after he signed on, he expected to only do six to twelve episodes, and then move on. He told *Starlog*, "I didn't see this show lasting very long. I didn't see any continuity, and I did see some difficulty in making this series good, in that each show had to stand on its own. I thought there would be a problem in the fact that this show was essentially an anthology, and that the only real constant was these two continuing characters. Needless to say, *The X-Files* is having a longer life than I expected, and I'm really surprised."

The difference, he later told *US*, is that "Chris Carter took it into a different ballpark and made it anything inexplicable. He turned it from the most limited show on TV to the least limited one."

Duchovny likes the fact that Mulder and Scully are not sexually involved. He and Anderson have to do something much more interesting and unusual, create a caring, mature, platonic relationship between a man and woman. Duchovny told *Playgirl*, "Most of the roles I did before *The X-Files* were sexually oriented. One of the things I like about *The X-Files* is that it's different for me in that I'm not really that interested in women or in sex. It's a different muscle to flex."

Duchovny's understated acting style suits Mulder very well. "To make this real," Duchovny told the *Boston Globe*, "you have to believe he is a fairly normal human being who happens to have one area where he goes nuts. You have to like him enough to give him the slack to go there." As he told *Entertainment Weekly*, "An obvious choice would be to make him an oddball, a mad professor. Sometimes I have to fight, because [directors] say, 'Here's this dead body. How come

Mulder's not more emotionally involved?' Everybody's aghast, and I'm detached. Like in the episode with the liver-eating squeeze guy who could elongate himself through chimneys—the director wanted me to be mad about this horrible serial killer. I was like, 'No, this is an amazing discovery! He's not morally culpable, because he's genetically driven.' I judge no one."

Series creator Chris Carter told *Entertainment Weekly*, "It was David who pointed out correctly that if he were a nerd with mechanical-pencil protectors, you wouldn't be interested. But a smart, educated, perfectly sane guy can get you to believe outrageous things."

Duchovny and Carter continue to disagree now and then over how to portray Mulder. Duchovny told *The Prydonian Renegade*, the magazine of the Princeton Dr. Who Fan Club, "Carter's got a very facile mind. Chris is very collaborative. He respects what I have to say. We have different ideas about Mulder from time to time. I'm always trying to make him a little funnier, a little lighter. He's always afraid that that's going to take away from the mystery and suspense, and the scare. He's the boss, but then again, he's not always there. When he's away, I do what I want. Then he comes back and scolds me."

Despite this, Duchovny notes that *The X-Files* does not have room for improvisation because of the quantity of necessary exposition. He says that if an actor pursues an improvisational tangent, it's just going to weaken the show. They're all slaves to the intricate story. He told *Starlog*, "It's like I'm working on a big crochet quilt and doing only one stitch at a time. I don't see the whole blanket. I have to do so much work that I really don't have the luxury to sit back and steer the course. It's going to happen instinctually. And I'll just have to trust that they're going to be the right way."

Duchovny relies on his instincts a lot when playing Mulder. He told *Starlog*, "I couldn't say I have a checklist to go down. I just try to find the physical and psychic center of the character and radiate out from that. I always thought the center of Mulder was a kind of detachment from other people's opinions and views as well as a very deep attachment to what he believes in. He would be kind of difficult to focus on, because he would appear detached and attached at the same time. That's what I try to do. Physically, I felt his center was in the head. He tends to get top-heavy from time to time and to get surprised when his center

moves to other parts of his body. It's moved to the heart and, in one episode, to the groin."

However, when *Details* magazine called Fox Mulder a "geek," Duchovny got a little defensive. He responded, "So I look like a geek? I'm supposed to look a little like one—my character is one. Not only that, I'm a geek among geeks. I'm the outcast." And yet, Duchovny does feel Mulder can be a bit stiff. Duchovny told *TV Guide*, "You want to make him have fun, to feel good. Take Mulder out, buy him cotton candy, and make him smile."

"PEOPLE GIVE EAR TO AN UPSTART astrologer who strove to show that the earth revolves, not the heavens of the firmament, the sun and the moon . . . This fool wishes to reverse the entire scheme of astronomy; but sacred Scripture tells us that Joshua commanded the sun to stand still, not the earth." —MARTIN LUTHER, C. 1540

Hearing Duchovny talk of his struggles with his newfound fame, you sort of wish someone would do that for him, too—take him out, buy him a day off, make him smile. The long hours and pressures have clearly taken their toll on the actor, who never had any dreams of being a TV celebrity and sometimes resents all of the trappings of such success.

He told *Starlog*, "I'm very guarded of my time and of my privacy and of myself. [When I do interviews] bits of myself leak away, are given away. And that's less for me and my loved ones to have. I can't expect anybody to sympathize with that, because they're the fans and they get to do what they want. Celebrities just appear to have power, but they have no power. It's just whoever's watching." Duchovny told *TV Week*, "You become more guarded and have to save your energy for your show, but more people are demanding more parts of you. I think you necessarily become a little more self-conscious as you become the most observed person in the room, and it's not as much fun as being anonymous and observing a room."

Duchovny also feels his work should speak for itself. He told *TV Hits*, "I wouldn't describe Mulder because it's like telling somebody why a painting of mine is great. If I have to describe him, then I haven't done my job. My point of view about the show is the least important."

### "WELL-INFORMED PEOPLE KNOW IT IS

impossible to transmit the voice over wires and that were it possible to do so, the thing would be of no practical value."

—EDITORIAL IN THE BOSTON POST, 1865

Not only do the interviews and the media get to be overwhelming, but the attention of the fans can be suffocating. He told *Playgirl*, "At first, you're like, 'Wow, people know who I am.' Then it's, 'Wow, people know who I am. Let me go home and sit alone.' People are picking you apart and comparing you to their image of you. When you become known on a television show, they identify you with your character rather than if you were a movie actor and had different characters. I'm a little fed up with people saying, 'Oh, look, it's Mulder,' or something like that. I'm not Mulder."

Duchovny said on *Sci-Fi Buzz*, "You should be nice to fans because they're just people, and they like your work and the show. However, I work really hard on the show, and sometimes you just want to relax, and one person coming up and saying, 'Hi, I like your work,' that's one thing, but if you multiply that by 150, then your day is shot."

He told *Starlog*, "People on the outside go, 'What's the big deal? Why can't he just spend an hour in front of a computer screen with people who love him?' I just have an aversion to being coerced into doing anything. Once people start to put pressure on me to either do an interview or go online, I immediately want to do it less than I ever wanted to do it. I would rather give freely than feel strong-armed into doing something. The adoration doesn't register as adoration. Sometimes it registers as pressure. I'm new to the celebrity thing. I'm trying to figure out how I can live a happy life and also not alienate people who have good wishes for me. How could I hate that? What bothers me is people yelling, 'Mulder!' on the street. Or confusing the fact that I'm a human being who may have his own life to lead and doesn't want to be yelled at as a character I

work at fourteen hours a day on the one day I have off. You know what I mean? People don't have to like me, they just have to like the show."

Indeed, many people like the show, and some, Duchovny feels, have clearly become overly obsessed. He told *Cinescape*, "I've seen some of the things that are discussed about the show, and the specificity of the detail kind of distresses me. I have an example. Gillian Anderson got in the car to drive after I had been driving [in an episode]. And the entry [on the Internet] asked why she didn't adjust the car seat—because I'm taller than her. Sometimes I walk away thinking, 'Why am I working so hard? They're looking at things like the car's rear-view mirror.' These are people who are so into the show that they almost go beyond any kind of rational discussion of it. The show itself is kind of taken for granted. It's like a specialist who knows something so well that he is reduced to only talking about the minutiae."

Regarding fame, Duchovny told *US*, "Sometimes it's gratifying, and sometimes I just detour into these rancid, dark moods, and I don't know where they're coming from."

"I'm finally beginning to understand star trips," he told *Who* magazine. "My whole life I've heard about stars doing insane things, and I've been, like, what is their problem? But I obviously have that in me, too. I've felt myself having those Hollywood feelings, these infantile rages, mostly because I can get away with it. So now that I'm finally beginning to understand it—to see it in myself."

Duchovny told an E! OnLine audience, "I get a few days where I just feel I'd like to be completely alone, but then I snap out of it. On the whole, I think I'm winning the battle against turning my life upside down because of being a celebrity. It does get to be a bit much when you hear Actor X or Rocker Y whining about how fame has destroyed their lives. Joe Truck-driver reads about this and says, 'Jesus, like I should have such problems!' On the other hand, fame is a major pain in the ass—and you can't know how much that's true until you're famous."

Clearly, Duchovny feels ill at ease with his new-found celebrity, but unless he decides to quit performing altogether, it's unlikely that the fans will go away. There are already two online Internet groups devoted to him, and he gets piles of adoring fan mail every day.

Duchovny told *Extra* magazine, a newspaper supplement, "I don't know how much fan mail I get. I get a good amount. On days when I feel like a useless human being I'll open my fan mail just to see that people love me. But, selfishly, I don't respond."

What does the actor think of all the paranormal hocus-pocus and government paranoia on *The X-Files?* Predictably, he's put off when people assume that he's just as obsessed as his character, Mulder. And this has given him a reputation as a skeptic. But he told *New Weekly*, "I do believe in ghosts. The living have such a desire for the dead that it's possible we project an energy to recreate them. There is definitely some kind of dialogue between the living and dead. I don't know where that energy comes from but I believe in it."

He told the Copley News Service, "My [Scottish] grandmother said that when she was a little girl, she saw her grandfather—who had drowned a couple of years before—come into the house and go up to the crib where her younger brother was sleeping. The 'ghost' kind of looked in, nodded, and walked out. I believed it happened to my grandmother, and I have definitely felt the presence of loved ones, though I have never seen anyone."

"THE VIEW THAT THE SUN STANDS motionless at the center of the universe is foolish, philosophically false, utterly heretical, because contrary to Holy Scripture. The view that the earth is not the center of the universe and even has a daily rotation is philosophically false, and at least an erroneous belief." —HOLY OFFICE, ROMAN CATHOLIC CHURCH, EDICT OF MARCH 5, 1616

Regarding aliens themselves, Duchovny told *TV Guide*, "There may be something out there. All I ever said was that I don't buy specific stories of UFOs coming down the street. If they did, more of us would have pictures and would know about it. If I were to bet, I would say that it is more likely than not that there are other life forms."

Duchovny has even had a close encounter of his own. He revealed to the Copley News Service, "Actually, I saw something in the sky during the spring of 1982. A student at Princeton at the time, I was running along the beach in Ocean City, N.J., on a bright and sunny morning when I looked up and saw what I thought was a ship or plane, about a hundred yards directly above me. It made no noise; I didn't hear a thing. Thinking it was an odd-looking plane, I took a couple of steps before looking up again. It was gone. Looking back, it seemed triangular in shape, somewhat similar to today's stealth bomber."

"People always ask me if I've been scared by any of the episodes," he told *TV Guide*, tongue-in-cheek, "but the only time I was really scared was when I had to act with my girlfriend [Perrey Reeves]. To show different sides of yourself, to be more honest—that was scary."

Some people have blamed *The X-Files* for spreading a suspicion of the government, but Duchovny doesn't agree. He told *Rolling Stone*, "We didn't create cultural paranoia, we tapped into it, and we've come to symbolize it. I did a course at Yale, and there was a thing about advertising and the fact that the armpit didn't exist as a body part until deodorant companies decided it was a problem. Sometimes I feel that's what we've done. We verbalized a problem people didn't know existed."

Further, Duchovny believes the basic premise of the show speaks to a universal human dilemma. He told *Starlog*, "You have this one man against the assembled forces of the FBI and CIA. But, in real life, there is not just one Fox Mulder out there; there are a lot of groups who believe in many different things. And they're all fighting for the right to get their story told. That's what history is about. Whoever gets to tell the story continues the history. And that's pretty much the idea we're trying to get across with the series. Who is going to tell the story of all these strange happenings? The one man against the world is only a dramatic conceit, but the idea behind it is very real."

Duchovny is a big fan of the original *Star Trek* series, and even considers himself a Trekker, though he has never watched *The Next Generation*. He says he doesn't think that *The X-Files* and *Star Trek* are similar. He views science fiction as paralleling the real world, drawing allegorical morals from the realm of science fiction that apply to this world. In contrast, he sees *The*

*X-Files* as more realistic, existing in a place where the two worlds intersect.

Working so far from his adopted home in L.A. has been difficult for Duchovny, who divides his time between subletting a nondescript shack of weathered, bleached-blond wood with a brick facade on the Pacific Coast Highway in Malibu and subletting a gray, nondescript house in Point Grey, Vancouver. His Vancouver home is filled with shaker furniture, sleazy fifties' Jack Slade movie posters, and, hanging over his bed, an Inuit drawing of a hummingbird. Windows look out on the bay and the mountains beyond.

"It can get cold and lonely in Vancouver," Duchovny told *Starlog*. "We end up in a lot of motels and too many dark woods, and it always seems to be the middle of the night. About half of the episodes have required us to react to things that are added in postproduction. And then there's the fact that my character always gets caught by the bad guys and beaten up. Mulder never gets away with anything. I would like him to get away with something, just once, so I could avoid some bruises. Working with Gillian under these circumstances tends to make the working relationship more like a marriage. We have our good days and our bad days, and we just have to work through it."

## "THERE IS NOT THE SLIGHTEST INDICATION

that [nuclear energy] will ever be obtainable. It would mean that the atom would have to be shattered at will."

—ALBERT EINSTEIN, 1932

The former Princeton and Yale man regrets leaving Los Angeles and misses the live poetry readings of the cafes. He recalled that the readings in Largo Pub, his favorite LA hangout, were different from poetry readings anywhere else. Actors, directors, and writers got up and read poems about how they grew up poor or why they're angry. Duchovny read poems about not belonging, the theme of his life. He once told *Details* magazine, "I think the last place I leave I look on as home, even though while I'm there is doesn't feel that way. It's what Proust said about Milton: 'The only true paradise is paradise lost.'"

The actor has few friends in Canada. He spends most of his time reading and playing with his dog, Blue.

The dog, a border collie/terrier mix, is Duchovny's constant companion. Blue is the daughter of the dog featured in the first-season episode "Ice." The actor told *TV Hits*, "I worked with her father in the show. He's been on a couple of *X-Files*. The trainer told me she was going to have a litter with that great, smart, wonderful dog. She's famous, people are interested in her."

While Duchovny and Perrey Reeves tried to maintain a long-distance relationship for several years, in the end it proved too difficult, and they broke up in 1996. During the relationship, he told the Australian edition of *Woman's Day* magazine, "I do believe in monogamy. Some people have it in their bones—it's their calling. But for others, including me, staying monogamous requires constant vigilance. I'm attracted to the primitive way a woman smells. It's the ultimate aphrodisiac; something each individual woman has that nobody else does." Not only the months apart but the stress in Duchovny's life contributed to the break-up. Duchovny now admits that admiring suggestive letters, photos from female fans, and his roving eye made it difficult for him to stay faithful. He told *Details*, "I didn't have a life in Vancouver, and I fantasized I had a life [in L.A.]. Now I realize I don't have a life anywhere. When I'm faced with myself as a person, I'm unrecognizable to myself. I lost the skill of talking about how I feel, except for stupid actor-needs."

Obviously, Duchovny feels a big reason this has occurred is because of the amount of work required. He told *The Prydonian Renegade* magazine, "TV is so different from movies. We shoot about eight pages of script a day, and in a movie we'd probably shoot two to three pages in a day. It's frustrating that you can't give it the time. You don't agonize over things. You just realize you've got to do it today, and tomorrow it's toilet paper. Move on. Instincts are all you have. You don't have time to prepare. The amount of work has been so intense. I haven't really gotten to see exactly how my life has changed, because I haven't really had a life. I've just been working."

Meanwhile, even as he continues working on *The X-Files* and struggling to live a more balanced life, Duchovny branches out into other projects when he can. In 1995, he appeared on the *Space: Above and Beyond* episode "R&R," as the pool shark on Bacchus's ship. It's possible he played the part as a token of friendship to former *The X-Files* writers Glen Morgan and James Wong, who created the new series.

Duchovny also appeared in *Playing God* (1997), a Disney film. The actor told an E! OnLine audience, "I play a doctor who gets discredited and winds up working for a big-time gangster and fixing up guys who, if they went to a regular doctor or hospital, would wind up in jail. Finally, when the doctor tries to undo the damage he's done to society, it's too late to redeem himself."

And Duchovny has done the rounds of late-night talk shows—appearing on *The Tonight Show* and *The Late Show with David Letterman*—guest hosted the season finale of *Saturday Night Live* on May 13, 1995, and guest starred on an episode of HBO's *The Larry Sanders Show*.

Duchovny misses theater and performing before a live audience. He told *The Prydonian Renegade* magazine, "There's something different about working with an audience. You're making an experience together in the present moment, rather than making something for future use or recorded use. As an actor you're always dealing with nervousness or anxiety and tension. When you're working on film or in television, you're just doing little bits and pieces. You have to deal with your nervousness and tension in each scene or shot. In a play, you come out, say your first few lines, and then you relax. In television you don't get that. I'll have days when all of a sudden, I'll just be a basket case."

Success has not brought Duchovny satisfaction with his career. The actor told *Cinescape* magazine, "When you're trying to envision the career that you want to have—especially before your life has really taken a turn into reality and you're just living in possibility—you have everybody's career. You have Tom Cruise's career. You have Meryl Streep's career. You do all the parts. So there's a certain disappointment when your life becomes just one part. You have to deal with the depression that your life is not limitless, that you won't play every role. On the other hand, this is a great show and it's great to be able to work with such talented people. So maybe I should just shut up."

It's no surprise that the intellectually restless Duchovny is looking for more than a career as an actor. He said on a *Sci-Fi Buzz* show, "I'd like to try different things. I'm not satisfied just acting. I think my life will be a series of attempts at things. I've given up thinking that I'll find one thing that satisfies me, so hopefully I'll be good at something else, too."

One of those things is writing. Duchovny continues to write poetry, but he also hopes to write

screenplays, and Fox has offered Duchovny a few opportunities to expand his talents as a writer and director. Duchovny supplied part of the outline for *The X-Files* two-parter, "Colony" and "End Game," which first aired in February 1995. He told *Starlog* magazine, "I didn't write the story. I had an idea and I told it to Chris. He liked it, and we worked it up together. He was kind enough to give me story credit." Duchovny doesn't think much of these "opportunities" so far, telling *Who* magazine, "Being offered story-lines and directing. It reminds me of playing with my dog. I'll give him a choice between a tennis ball or a Frisbee—whatever it takes to keep him involved."

In any case, Duchovny doesn't feel he'd be able to write and direct well at the same time anyway. "You don't want to spend energy on things when you're writing," he told *The Prydonian Renegade* magazine. "You're conserving everything. You're not even good to the people that you love. When you're acting, it's very similar. You don't know why you're saving it up, but you know you're going to have to put it out at some point. In order to do one of them well, you have to give it everything that you have. I'd like to write. I can't do both at the same time. I don't know how Sam Sheppard does it."

The idea of eventually directing is exciting, but it makes him nervous. He told *Starlog* magazine, "I think directing is like sex. Before you have sex, you can read all the books you want, but doing it is going to teach you a lot more. You can think all you want about it, and then you're thrown into the water. I guess I'll be ready to direct when I get my first job, but I won't feel ready before then."

Between stints in front of the camera, Duchovny jogs, enjoys power workouts, and plays racquetball with Chris Carter. He also maintains his interest in baseball and basketball. Duchovny appeared in MTV's "Rock n' Jock" charity baseball game and in a recent MTV charity basketball game.

He also practices yoga and explores Buddhist philosophy. Duchovny told *Details*, "Yoga silences the buzz in my mind. The idea is to remain mentally calm while you put yourself through this subtle torture. The torture turns off the extraneous buzz and you concentrate on your breathing. I would do it all day long if I could. I think turning off the mind is a good thing. It depends on whether you can turn it back on."

# CHAPTER 12

# SPECIAL AGENT FOX WILLIAM MULDER

NAME: Fox William Mulder

BADGE NUMBER: JTT047101111

HEIGHT: Six feet

WEIGHT: 170 pounds

HAIR: Brown

EYES: Green

DATE OF BIRTH: 13 October 1961

BIRTHPLACE: Chilmark, MA

CURRENT ADDRESS: Unknown. Apartment 42, Alexandria, VA

TELEPHONE: (202) 555-9355

E-MAIL: Unknown

DISTINGUISHING FEATURES: Mole on right cheek.

MARITAL STATUS: Unmarried.

FATHER'S NAME: William "Bill" Mulder. Lived in West Tisbury, Martha's Vineyard, Massachusetts. Assassinated by either Alex Krycek or Hispanic Man.

MOTHER'S NAME: Unknown.

MOTHER'S ADDRESS: 2790 Vine Street, Chilmark, Massachusetts

SIBLINGS: One sister, Samantha Ann Mulder, born 22 January 1964. Disappeared 27 November 1973 (X-File: X-42053)

EDUCATION: Oxford University, A.B. in Psychology, 1982. Quantico Training Academy, 1984

PUBLICATIONS: "On Serial Killers and the Occult," monograph, 1988. Article in *Omni* as M. F. Luder.

## FBI CAREER HISTORY

1983–86: Oxford University

1986: Enters Quantico Academy immediately after graduation from Oxford. Earns nickname "Spooky."

1988: Assigned to the Violent Crimes Unit under the supervision of ASAC Reggie Purdue. On his first case, Agent Mulder distinguishes himself in the pursuit of bank robber John Barnett.

JUNE 16, 1989: Agent Mulder undergoes regression hypnosis with Dr. Heitz Werber, after which Agent Mulder becomes convinced his sister was abducted by extraterrestrial forces.

1991: Agent Mulder persuades his superiors to transfer him to the X-Files section, where he has operated ever since, reporting first to the head of the VCU, Section Chief Blevins, and later to Assistant Director Walter Skinner.

MARCH 6, 1992: Fear that Agent Mulder's work in the X-Files section is getting out of control lead Chief Blevins to assign Agent Dana K. Scully to the X-Files section as Agent Mulder's partner.

1993: Agent Mulder is called in for a hearing with Section Chief Joseph McGrath of the Office of Professional Responsibility after trespassing on a crime scene under military jurisdiction and after accusations of interfering with a military operation and impeding an investigation were lodged against him. All charges later dropped.

APRIL 1994: Assistant Director Walter Skinner investigates charges brought by Eugene Victor Tooms that Agent Mulder was engaging in harassment of Mr. Tooms, who had been released from incarceration. Tooms was later killed in an escalator by Mulder.

MAY 1994: Assistant Director Skinner shuts down the X-Files section and reassigns Agents Mulder and Scully.

OCTOBER 1994: Agent Alex Krycek is partnered with Agent Mulder.

NOVEMBER 1994: Following Agent Scully's abduction by fugitive Duane Barry (X-File X-73317), Assistant

Director Walter Skinner reopens the section. Agent Krycek fails to report to work after Agent Scully's abduction and is wanted for questioning in her disappearance.

MAY 1995: Assistant Director Skinner requests a hearing with Agent Mulder, Agent Scully, and members of the Office of Professional Responsibility after an unprovoked physical assault by Agent Mulder. Agent Mulder does not attend the meeting. The following day, Agent Mulder's father is shot to death in his house while Agent Mulder is present.

## PROFILE

Oxford-trained psychologist Agent Fox William Mulder possesses a photographic memory. Although not held in official favor, Mulder is one of the FBI Violent Crimes Division's best agents. Fellow agents remain suspicious of Mulder's strong interest in the Bureau's X-Files cases, and he has earned the nicknamed "Spooky." Mulder served the Bureau for three years as a crack analyst in the behavioral sciences department before discovering these files, dealing with unexplained phenomena.

A childhood incident, the disappearance of his sister, Samantha, from their home in Chilmark, Massachusetts, when he was twelve and she was eight may have triggered his fascination with the paranormal. Mulder believes she was abducted by aliens. Regressive therapy recalled a memory of hearing his sister cry for help and a paralyzing bright light that told him his sister would be safe. A dream provided a different recollection of the event. Mulder claims that recently both an alien hybrid claiming to be his sister, Samantha, and an alien bounty hunter communicated with him. He has vowed to find his sister.

While attending Oxford, Mulder felt unreciprocated love for a woman now employed by Scotland Yard. His parents separated before his father's death. Mulder's mother confirmed that Samantha had been kidnapped to insure their father's silence about covert activities.

Mulder has high-placed friends in Congress, including SETI proponent Senator Richard Matheson. These contacts shield him from senior Bureau officers, although they assigned Agent Dana Scully as his partner, hoping to discredit Mulder and bring about his dismissal.

Before his murder by an individual known only as "Crew Cut Man," a mysterious individual known only as "Deep Throat" covertly assisted Mulder. Mulder then acquired a new covert ally known only as "X." An additional ally within the Bureau has been identified as Assistant Director Walter Skinner.

During the temporary suspension of the X-Files division, Mulder was reassigned to wiretap surveillance, separated from Agent Scully, and partnered with Special Agent Alex Krycek. Mulder returned to his earlier assignment after Assistant Director Skinner reopened the X-Files department following the disappearance of Agent Scully. Scully later returned and again became Mulder's partner.

Mulder gained possession of a classified Defense Department file purportedly documenting fifty years of covert government operations. His father, Bill, formerly with the State Department, and supposedly once connected to the covert operations, was murdered by either "Hispanic Man" or Krycek before telling Mulder about secrets in his past. Mulder, who had been acting violently due to contamination by a foreign drug, became the prime suspect.

> **"THE MULTITUDE OF BOOKS IS A GREAT**
> evil. There is no limit to this fever for writing; everyone must be an author; some out of vanity, to acquire celebrity and raise up a name, others for the sake of mere gain."
> —MARTIN LUTHER, 1540

Mulder and Scully went into hiding. In New Mexico, Mulder investigated evidence supposedly proving the validity of the secret document. Cigarette-Smoking Man attempted to kill him to prevent his success.

Navajo Indians rescued Mulder and returned him to the East Coast, where he found a suspicious group photo among his dead father's effects. Mulder then joined Scully in Washington, where they received help from the Lone Gunmen and one of the men in the photograph. They uncovered additional secret files, medical records, and tissue samples revealing the covert operation. Skinner later negotiated a truce with

Cigarette-Smoking Man, gaining Mulder and Scully's reinstatement and relative safety.

Mulder recovered a unique weapon while searching for alien clones and confronted an alien who supposedly destroyed clones of his sister living on earth.

Mulder keeps notes for his field reports in a hand-written journal. His favorite alias is George Hale. Mulder wears wild ties to work. The psychologist opposes unnecessary medication and often uses hypnotic regression as a healing tool.

Colorblind Mulder once feared fire, and he habitually eats shelled sunflower seeds, enjoys iced tea, and has a droll sense of humor. He is an ardent supporter of NASA and both the New York Knicks and the Washington Redskins. Mulder enjoys classic rock music and science fiction movies. He keeps physically fit by jogging. It is possible that the agent maintains an interest in pornography.

# CHAPTER 13

# THE OTHER PLAYERS

## MITCH PILEGGI: ASSISTANT DIRECTOR WALTER SERGEI SKINNER

Mitch Pileggi plays FBI Assistant Director Walter Skinner, an ex-Marine. Skinner is Scully and Mulder's boss at the Bureau, and he dislikes Fox Mulder's un-orthodox methods. However, he's also been very supportive of the agents and has stood up for them at critical moments.

Pileggi was born in Portland, Oregon, and raised in Los Angeles, Austin, and Turkey. Pileggi attended Fullerton College and the University of Maryland in Munich, Germany, and he graduated from the University of Texas at Austin. He told *Scarlet Street* magazine, "I lived overseas for a long time. We were over there in Turkey from the time I was ten years old. I graduated high school there, and then I went to school in Germany. Then I ended up working in Saudi Arabia and Iran for the same company as my dad."

"Iran was fun until the revolution—that will always put a damper on things," he told *Entertainment Weekly*. The actor turned to performing regional theater in Austin, Texas, in 1980, appearing in such plays as *Jesus Christ Superstar*, *Lone Star*, and *Bent*. The actor told *Scarlet Street*, " I had done some acting in school and in college. I was in Iran when the revolution began, and it was the third one I had been through. I just got tired of being in jeopardy all the time. So I came back to the States and started doing theater down in Texas."

He began playing small parts on television, then moved to Los Angeles. His film credits include *Basic Instinct*, *Vampire in Brooklyn*, *Guilty as Charged*, and *Shocker*. For television, he appeared in a recurring role on *Dallas* and made guest appearances on such series as *Models Inc.*, *Roc*, *China Beach*, *Hooperman*, and *Get a Life*. He also appeared in such made-for-TV movies as *Absolute Strangers*, *Trapped*, and *Knightrider 2000*. He is less proud of his appearance in *Return of the Living Dead*, which he did before joining *The X-Files*. He was happy to assume the role of FBI Assistant Director Walter Skinner. "After playing so many bad guys," he told *Entertainment Weekly*, "I like playing the guy who has moral values."

Pileggi told *People* Online that his character was created by the producers Jim Wong and Glen Morgan, and that he is very satisfied with the direction they've been taking. Pileggi based his portrayal on his father, Vito, although he didn't realize it immediately. The actor told *Scarlet Street*, "I went in with a kind of an attitude, and fortunately it worked for the character. I base a lot of Skinner on my father and the way he dealt with people in his profession. He worked with the Department of Defense on military contracts overseas, so it was a very similar situation. He had a lot of people he was responsible for and sometimes he had to be very, very tough with them. Yet he had a lot of compassion and was a very fair person. I lost my Dad about a year and a half ago; he was very big in my life. I didn't realize I was doing this with Skinner until I talked to my mom and my brothers and sisters, and they said, 'You know, that's Dad.' I had it down even to the way I sit in the chair and hold my hands. My mom sits there sometimes and cries, because I look a lot like my dad. He was bald, he wore glasses, he wore the suits."

"I had a pretty good grasp when I went in," Pileggi told *Fangoria*. "I was under the impression it was only going to be for one episode from last season, and then it turned out to be more, which I'm pleased about. There was about an eight-episode story arc, when Gillian Anderson had her pregnancy, where they had to take the story line someplace else, and I was part of it."

Pileggi believes that Carter plans to expand the role of his character within the series. He told *Scarlet Street*, "I anticipate that more will be happening. I was talking to David one day and he indicated that Walter Skinner would be getting more of a life. I don't talk to [Carter] much about the character. Until recently, I didn't even know who the cigarette-smoking guy was, what his relationship was to me. I just found out he was my superior!"

"When I first started," Pileggi told People Online, "I thought that he would be a roadblock to their investigations. I thought that was the intention of the character. But as time went by, they saw other possibilities which made the character more valuable to the show."

Pileggi told *Fangoria* he would like to see his character take a more physical part in cases. "I keep on saying, 'Get me out of the office.' They've built me a great set, but get me out. Usually, all of my stuff is hot in that office, and I do my scenes in one or two days. Then I come back to Los Angeles or just hang out in Vancouver for awhile. I don't know how realistic it is to have a director get out in the field, but I'd like to have my own encounters, maybe with some monster besides the 'smoking man.'"

Pileggi enjoys living in Vancouver during shoots. He told *Scarlet Street*, "Vancouver is very comfortable. It's a pretty city, and the people who work on the show are the best I've ever worked with. We have a ball. It's a real treat. Because of the nature of the character, a lot of times I'm in the office and only shoot one or two days, but I usually go up a week before and stay a week during shooting and a week afterward. It's a real struggle to get myself to come back to Los Angeles!" When not in Vancouver, he resides in Valencia, California.

Pileggi enjoys working with both the series stars. He told *Scarlet Street* that Gillian Anderson is "a sweetheart. We goof and do crazy stuff. But she's so right there when you're working with her, and onscreen she's so appealing."

Working with David Duchovny is a more frenetic experience. "David's a good actor, too. We have fun; we get really goofy. David and I really get into it. As a matter of fact, [director] Rob Bowman pulled us both back and said, 'You two, when you get together you start chewing the scenery up.' Our juices really get flowing when we do a scene together."

Pileggi told *People* Online that he feels very fortunate to have been chosen for the role of Skinner, saying, "It's a blessing to be involved in such a quality project as *The X-Files*. And it's something that I will always be proud of."

The actor is also thrilled with the reception his series has received among fans, telling *Scarlet Street*, "The reaction to the show is amazing; I think it's just wonderful. Chris does a tremendous job on it, and I don't know where he keeps coming up with this stuff." He told *People* Online, "I'm very gratified by the response of fans. I'm a fan, too, so I'm on the same page with 'em. People tell me that they like the show, which I appreciate. I enjoy talking to people who watch the show." Pileggi says he worries about lipstick traces left by female fans who kiss the top of his bald head.

In the future, Pileggi says his dream is to play Tevya in *Fiddler on the Roof*. He says he lacks the discipline to write and prefers acting because it is easier, although he has feared typecasting in the past. He says he enjoys the opportunity acting affords to take on other personalities and become another person while making a lot of money.

The divorced and unattached Pileggi plays guitar, works out, in-line skates, and golfs with Nicholas Lea, who plays Krycek. He enjoys reading his favorite authors, Anne Rice, Stephen King, Ernest Hemingway, John Steinbeck, Kurt Vonnegut, and Michael Crichton

He told *Entertainment Weekly* that he believes in extraterrestrial life, saying, "I believe in aliens, but I don't think they're among us."

## NICHOLAS LEA: ALEX KRYCEK

Nicholas Lea plays FBI agent Alex Krycek, whom the Bureau assigned to replace Scully as Mulder's partner after closing the X-Files investigations. Krycek worked to win Mulder's confidence, playing a role as a worshipful junior agent, while actually spying on Mulder and Scully's alien investigations for his real boss, "Cigarette-Smoking Man." The traitor Krycek proved instrumental in the abduction of Scully and the silencing of Duane Barry. He went underground after his treachery was exposed. He then killed Mulder's father, framing Mulder for the murder. He also became an accessory to the murder of Melissa Scully.

After Krycek stole a vital digital tape from Assistant Director Skinner, Cigarette-Smoking Man attempted to have Krycek killed, but he escaped the trap and has vowed revenge on his former mentor. Krycek has since become possessed by an alien, who left him trapped in an abandoned missile silo in South Dakota.

A Vancouver native, Lea is best known for his three seasons as officer Nicky Caruso on *The Commish.* He first appeared on *The X-Files* in the episode "Genderbender," in 1994, playing a barhopper who ends up in a hospital after picking up a sex-switching succubus. Lea returned ten months later as duplicitous FBI agent Alex Krycek in the second-season episode "Sleepless." Originally, Krycek was planned to appear in only three episodes.

Lea, now the father of two daughters, was the lead singer in an alternative rock band called Beau Monde for five years. He also served a hitch in the Canadian Navy and attended art school. He grew up with a love for movies and great stories, and always wanted to be an actor.

When he was twenty-five, he quit his job and started studying acting the day after he met an acting coach. He began playing small parts in Vancouver-based television. He played a low-life alcoholic for *Highlander.* He told *Cinefantastique,* "That was a fun show for me. Usually people in Hollywood tend to cast you because of the way you look. They put you in a little box. But this was great. I got to play an alcoholic. I love doing that kind of stuff, but I don't always get to, because of the way I look, I guess. Playing a real loser, that's always fun."

Then came his role as Caruso in *The Commish.* He told *Cinefantastique,* "I guess what was a big crack for me was three years on *The Commish.* That really gave me a lot of exposure in front of the camera, and I studied all the way through that."

Lea's appearance in the "Genderbender" episode of *The X-Files* followed. His performance stood out for its intensity. Rob Bowman, the director of the episode, was impressed with the scene where Lea's character witnesses Marty, the alien, shifting from female to male. Bowman told *Cinefantastique,* "During that last shot in the car when he sees that the girl has now become a guy, I thought Nick did a beautiful job walking the line in conveying a turning point in his life. He'll never be the same again for the rest of his life, after seeing that. And I thought he found just the right level to play that."

Bowman, who also directed "Sleepless," suggested Lea for Krycek. Lea was the only Vancouver-based actor invited to participate in the prolonged audition process. He read several times. Bowman recalled, "Nick was the best of all. He earned the role. He beat out everybody else." Lea couldn't have been happier, saying, "It was really great. It told me I was doing the right thing after all."

Lea felt his best performance came in "Ascension"— after pistol-whipping a tram operator, he runs his hand back over his head, making sure every hair is still in place. Lea told *Cinefantastique,* "That wasn't the way it was scripted. I was supposed to crack him over the head, and then as his body falls across the frame, they would cut instantly to the tram going up the track. But when I whacked him, they decided to hold on me. I'm glad they kept that, too. I love those kinds of things, the little movements, the little mannerisms that show you more of the person."

### "A WEB OF NAKED FANCIES. WHAT CAN BE more palpably absurd than the prospect held out of locomotives traveling twice as fast as stagecoaches?"

—The Quarterly Review, England, March 1825

Lea enjoys his role as a villain on *The X-Files,* telling *People* Online, "There's less of a distance to fall when you're the bad guy. I love it." Actually he doesn't see his character as bad, just misunderstood. The actor told *Cinefantastique,* "I don't think anybody who does bad things really thinks they're bad. They just think they're doing what they should be doing. And it's either bad guys who are doing wrong and not knowing it, or good guys doing wrong and trying to do good. Those are interesting characters to play."

X-Philes on the Internet have nicknamed him "Ratboy," "Skippy," and "The Weasel." But there is a downside to playing a villain on a series with such dedicated fans. He told the *Toronto Sun,* "I don't need that when, on the Internet, there's people saying, 'Isn't he worried that somebody's going to wait outside the studio with a gun?' I mean, I don't really take that fully seriously but. . . ."

Despite this, Lea told the *Sun,* "It's great to meet the people and to be involved in it. It's great, but you just have to kind of organize it properly. In Reno, they took me in a kind of back way with security guards. Which was cool because you never know. You just never know."

Lea enjoys working with series costar, David Duchovny. He told *Cinefantastique*, "I love all the people that are involved. I worked with David the most. Sometimes I have a tendency to get a little intense in my work, high energy. David's energy, although it's intense, is low-level, and working with him is really great because he makes you just stand there and talk, like people do. I think that's always good for anybody's acting, to just stand there and talk and not do anything outrageous. Less and less is called for. That's really what it's all about for me, doing a good job and learning."

Lea is now working on a pilot for Fox called *Once a Thief*, directed by John Woo. He told *People* Online, "I play an ex-cop who joins together with two ex-thieves that grew up in Hong Kong, to fight crime. John was a wonderful man with quiet charisma. I had to wear knee and elbow pads on the set everyday—because of the stunts, of course."

Lea said it was very important to him to be able to continue to work for *The X-Files*, regardless of whether he has a new series; in fact, it's stipulated in his contract for *Once A Thief*. He may also return to *Sliders*.

His hobbies include drawing, running, and playing guitar. He told *Entertainment Weekly* that he is ambivalent about the paranormal, saying, "I don't know how I feel about werewolves or vampires."

## WILLIAM B. DAVIS: "CIGARETTE-SMOKING MAN"

William B. Davis plays the "Cigarette-Smoking Man," who first convinces Section Chief Scott Blevins to assign Dana Scully as Fox Mulder's partner, in hopes of neutralizing the potentially dangerous agent. Cigarette-Smoking Man plays a key yet mysterious role in hiding government covert operations with alien visitors. He often visits the Pentagon basement to secret evidence in a vast storehouse of classified materials.

Cigarette-Smoking Man has increasingly attempted to manipulate Mulder, and he has repeatedly tried to kill the X-Files agents. Cigarette-Smoking Man and Mulder's father, Bill, were actually both involved during the earliest days of the secret government project, and Cigarette-Smoking Man may be responsible for murdering Bill Mulder.

Davis is a Toronto native and a former Canadian national waterskiing champion. He began acting when he was eleven on a series of radio dramas for the CBC in Toronto in 1948. His early parts included two seasons as the young son on *Life with the Robinsons*, written by Bethune-author Ted Allen. Davis told *Scarlet Street* magazine, "My cousins ran a summer stock company in Ontario. They used to rehearse in our basement, and I spent a fair bit of my youth peering in the window and watching them. At a certain point, though, they needed a young lad in one of their plays and, for no particular reason, I guess, other than that I was reasonably intelligent and I was good at reading, they asked me to do it. And that was my start."

He studied philosophy at the University of Toronto while directing stage productions. Davis revived the legendary summer-theater company, The Straw Hat Players, which eventually featured Donald Sutherland and Gordon Pinsent.

Davis moved to England to study at the London Academy of Music and Dramatic Arts. He also taught with the Royal Shakespeare Company and was hired by Laurence Olivier to be assistant director of the English production of *Miss Julie* with Albert Finney. He turned down an offer to be Finney's assistant on his first film and instead returned to Montreal, where he became artistic director of the National Theatre School and established the Festival Lennoxville in Lennoxville, Quebec.

Davis moved to Vancouver in 1985 to become director of the Vancouver Playhouse's acting school. He opened his own school, the William Davis Centre for Actor's Study, in 1989. Davis told *TV Guide*, "It's important that Canadian actors are getting this kind of recognition. It's been a fight for the Canadian actor in the American film industry to be fully recognized. It's a fight for the Canadian arts community to be recognized at international standards, and not just locally. It's a constant struggle for a small country. But I feel very gratified to have been part of something like *The X-Files*."

Davis returned to acting in the late 1980s, doing some film roles and parts in Vancouver-shot television series, including *MacGyver* and *Airwolf*. He told *Entertainment Weekly*, "I tended to do the nice kindly doctors [as in *Look Who's Talking*] and the gentle grandfathers [as in the cable-TV movie *Circumstances Unknown*]."

The role of "Cigarette-Smoking Man," also known as "Cancer Man," for *The X-Files* followed in 1993. Davis won the part during a general casting call and admitted he saw the character differently than Carter. Davis told the *Edmonton Sun*, "Initially, I wanted to be ironic and use humor, and they wanted it darker than that."

Davis told *Scarlet Street* that he didn't audition for the role. He said that they cast two or three FBI agents for the pilot, including "this guy who just stood around smoking and watching what was going on. So we read the FBI roles, and I was cast in what seemed to be the least of the roles, the nonspeaking part. A friend of mine was cast in the part with lines, as the character who worked with the FBI director and interviewed Scully. They hired me as Cancer Man without telling me anything about it! Not only did I not know that I would be a recurring character, I didn't know that the show would recur!"

As the conspiracy mythology storyline became prominent, so did his character's involvement in the stories. By season three, Cigarette-Smoking Man appeared in one-quarter of the episodes, which was scheduled to increase to one-third of the episodes with season four.

Davis insists that his character is not a villain. He told *TV Guide*, "Everybody gets this show wrong because they think that Mulder's the good guy, but if Mulder succeeds in what he's doing—in revealing 'the truth,' as it were—it will be so terrifying to the population at large that chaos will ensue."

Davis elaborated, telling *TV Guide* Online, "[Cigarette-Smoking Man] would probably think that Mulder was a pretty dangerous man. These people who go off half-cocked, trying to solve the problems of the world without any kind of real perspective of knowledge and experience, are quite dangerous. They're almost like fanatics."

Davis told *Scarlet Street*, "Heroic might be putting it strongly, but I certainly approach it like I'm doing what needs to be done. The world needs me to do what I'm doing, and it does not need Mulder to do what he's doing. If Mulder continues, it will be a very dangerous world. So I don't see it from my actor point of view as villainous. Of course, the audience has to make up its own mind."

Davis doesn't know the history of his character. The actor makes it up as he goes along, telling *TV Guide* Online, "[Carter] gave me no backstory. That's not quite fair; I've had bits and pieces—Bob Goodwin gave me some stuff—but it's kind of changed, and it keeps shifting from how many people have I killed to maybe I haven't killed anybody and I have other people do that sort of work for me. But as the character has evolved, the backstory has enriched, it's deepened. But it has actually in some senses contradicted itself, too. Though as an actor you're constantly absorbing new information and finding new ways to put all the pieces together."

He told *TV Guide*, "I've created background to play certain scenes, and then I get a script later that indicates that background wasn't correct. Who is the Smoking Man? What does he do? Who does he report to? Does he report to anyone? I'm rushing to catch up, just as the viewers are. I still have a tendency to read each new script from the back to the front just to see whether I'm alive at the end."

But Davis also told *TV Guide*, "Somebody asked Chris Carter if he would ever kill 'Cancer Man,' and his reply was, 'You can't kill the Devil.'"

"MEN MIGHT AS WELL PROJECT A VOYAGE to the Moon as attempt to employ steam navigation against the stormy North Atlantic Ocean." —DR. DIONYSUS LARDNER, PROFESSOR OF NATURAL PHILOSOPHY AND ASTRONOMY, UNIVERSITY COLLEGE, LONDON, 1838

The Cigarette-Smoking Man's backstory is growing as Carter and the writers continue to define him. Davis told *Scarlet Street*, "In part of my backstory, I'm the one who fired the shot from the grassy knoll! It was me! I had this line to Mulder: 'You don't scare me. I've watched presidents die.' I puzzled over that for quite awhile. I've been told that I've personally killed a hundred people, and that I've ordered death to many hundreds more. That comment sticks in my mind. There's this connection, too, with Mulder's father and 'Deep Throat' way back when we were all involved in these projects, whatever they were."

Davis is not above a little speculation himself, as he told *Scarlet Street*, "Why is there so much tension between Mulder's father and me? I came up with the notion that perhaps I am Mulder's father! That's Mulder's 'official' father. I had an affair with his wife. He looks more like me than Peter Donat! It could explain why I've let him live all this time! I said, 'If he got knocked off, it would set off a crusade,' but not that many people really know what he's doing!"

It's rare to have a cigarette-smoking character on TV these days, and in fact Davis's character almost had to go on "the patch." After the first episode, in which Cigarette-Smoking Man was shown smoking, Fox network executives asked that he no longer smoke in the future. They sent a memo stating, in part, that "Fox Television is a non-smoking network." Clearly, Cigarette-Smoking Man has a pull with the network, too, since he continues to light up whenever and wherever he pleases.

Davis, though, was once a heavy smoker who quit seventeen years ago. He fears backsliding. He told *Scarlet Street*, "It's a long time since I quit. It would have been really hard to do within a year or two of quitting. When I first started doing it, I was actually smoking real cigarettes, and I found myself thinking, 'Gee, I wonder when I'm gonna get to do another shoot.' At that point, we switched to herbal cigarettes! They don't give me any kick or anything, so they work fine."

Davis said that working for *The X-Files* is unique because everybody works tremendously hard, and there's a conscientiousness and a care and a pulling together that he hasn't encountered before. He told *TV Guide*, "A lot of it stems from Chris, because of who he is and the way he is, which is very open and very positive and very supportive. And so people want to do well by it. And then of course, because it's a success, everybody feels they have a stake in it, whether they're doing makeup or lights or props. Everybody feels connected to it."

Davis's involvement with *The X-Files* has led to convention appearances and guest-starring roles on *The Outer Limits* and the syndicated *Poltergeist*. Davis told a *TV Guide* Online audience, "I'm certainly recognized. Some speak up and some don't, of course. But I've had lots of little benefits. I was at the top of a race course last winter and this guy goes, 'Hey! That's Cancer Man!' And he comes over, and he's a rabid fan, but he's also one of the top ski coaches in Canada. So I got all sorts of extra tips and help and stuff, and he

started taking an interest in my skiing. So these things happen."

Regarding extraterrestrials and government conspiracies, Davis told *Entertainment Weekly*, "I don't fear ghosts and aliens, but I do fear the people who believe that there's a conspiracy."

Explaining his thoughts further, Davis told *Scarlet Street*, "I'm not saying that I think the universe is lifeless or that there isn't something we might contact, but I don't think people are being abducted. They've been running radio telescopes looking for any kind of signal from the universe, and they still haven't got anything they can pin down and say, 'That was created by intelligence.' So it seems we're a long way from something that's really abducting people."

What does Davis like to watch when he isn't busy acting and teaching? He told *TV Guide* Online, "I love Woody Allen's stuff. I'm pretty people-oriented. I like a lot of Mike Nichols' stuff. I'm not a big adventure fan. When the car chase starts, I doze off and wait till that's over. You always know what's going to happen. With Shakespeare I think of myself more as a director than an actor. If you were to ask what is my favorite play, I'd come right back with *The Winter's Tale*, which I think is the greatest play ever written. As a role to play, I keep outgrowing them. You know, I would have loved to have played Romeo, and then I'd have loved to have played Hamlet. I don't know what I can play at my age. There isn't a role I'm bursting to play."

## JERRY HARDIN: "DEEP THROAT"

"I came here to give you some valuable advice."

These are the prophetic first words of "Deep Throat," played by Jerry Hardin, when he introduces himself to Agent Mulder. During the first season, Deep Throat guides Mulder and Scully into involvement with cases they might otherwise overlook, and he directs them away from other lines of investigation. He rarely explains anything about what he wants, who he is, or why he's asking Mulder and Scully to be involved. However, by the end of the first season, he is killed in an attempt to save Mulder's life.

Jerry Hardin has a long resume of television and feature film work that spans two decades. In addition to his most recent work on *The X-Files*, he has appeared in two episodes for *Star Trek: The Next Generation*: as

Radue in "When The Bough Breaks" and as Samuel Clemens in "Time's Arrow." He has also appeared on *Star Trek: Voyager.*

Other television work includes the pilot movie for *L.A. Law* (1986) and guest appearances for *Murphy Brown, Dr. Quinn, Medicine Woman, Remington Steele, Filthy Rich,* and *The Chisholms.* Hardin played a part in the *Celebrity* and *Pandora's Clock* TV miniseries, and he's also appeared the television movies *Baseball in Black and White* (1996), *Bermuda Triangle* (1996), *Where Are My Children?* (1994), *Murder of Innocence* (1993), *Hi Honey—I'm Dead* (1991), *Plymouth* (1991), *Roe vs. Wade* (1989), *Bluegrass* (1988), *Roots: The Gift* (1988), *The Town Bully* (1988), *LBJ: The Early Years* (1987), *Do You Remember Love* (1985), *Attack on Fear* (1984), *Thou Shalt Not Kill* (1982), *Mysterious Two* (1982), *World War III* (1982), *Angel Dusted* (1981), *The Children Nobody Wanted* (1981), and *Gideon's Trumpet* (1980).

Davis's feature film work includes roles in *The Associate* (1996), *The Firm* (1993), *The Hot Spot* (1990), *Pacific Heights* (1990), *Blaze* (1989), *Little Nikita* (1988), *The Milagro Beanfield War* (1988), *Valentino Returns* (1987), *Wanted: Dead or Alive* (1987), *Big Trouble in Little China* (1986), *Let's Get Harry* (1986), *Warning Sign* (1985), *The Falcon and the Snowman* (1984), *Mass Appeal* (1984), *Cujo* (1983), *Honkytonk Man* (1982), *Missing* (1982), *Tempest* (1982), *Heartland* (1981), *Honky Tonk Freeway* (1981), *Reds* (1981), *1941* (1979), *Head Over Heels* (1979), *Wolf Lake* (1978), and *Mitchell* (1975).

## STEVEN WILLIAMS: "X"

Steven Williams plays "X," the mysterious informant who replaced "Deep Throat" during the second season. Although "X" supplies Mulder with information, his motives are less clear, and Mulder does not fully trust him. "X" alternately warns and informs Mulder either in a campaign of disinformation or as an ally in search of the truth. At one point, "X" and Assistant Director Skinner clash after he refuses Scully's request for information on Mulder's whereabouts. Just as "Deep Throat" was murdered for helping Mulder, "X" seems to meet the same fate at the beginning of season four.

Memphis-raised Williams portrayed Captain Fuller on *21 Jump Street* and appeared in the feature films *Cooley High, The Blues Brothers,* and *Twilight Zone: The Movie* before coming to *The X-Files.* The actor told *Entertain-*

*ment Weekly,* "I loved Avery Brooks' character Hawk on *Spenser: For Hire.* X is very similar, only more subdued."

Of his character, Williams told *Entertainment Weekly,* "I'm sort of removed. People have said that I'm cold. Non-caring. By the same token, I'm a very warm, gregarious character. We don't know that 'X' isn't like that in his secret life."

Williams worked as a boxer during a two-year stint in the army. He also modeled briefly in Chicago before turning to acting. As to the possibility of alien life, he believes it would be ridiculous to think we are the only people in the universe.

## THE LONE GUNMEN

*The Lone Gunman* is a publication produced by Byers, Frohike, and Langly. The three believe in the paranormal and in a secret government conspiracy to cover it up; they work to expose it. They assist Mulder and Scully at times.

### Bruce Harwood: Byers

Byers, played by Bruce Harwood, is the most professorial member of the trio, providing military and information systems expertise. He has a sharp, methodical mind and a very ordinary appearance—his beard is neatly clipped and he wears carefully pressed suits. He has an encyclopedic knowledge of conspiracy theories, everything from the Kennedy assassination to the latest in DNA research. He rarely jokes or even smiles, but his calm intelligence adds credibility to the trio.

Born in British Columbia, Harwood made guest appearances on *21 Jump Street* and *Wiseguy,* and he played a recurring role for *MacGyver,* as environmental expert Willis, before joining *The X-Files.* Harwood says he based his character on intellectual, linguist, and political activist Noam Chomsky, telling *Entertainment Weekly,* "I applaud Chomsky's willingness to take a stand. I think of Byers as a university professor. I'm a pretty bookish person, but [Byers is] too weird, intense, paranoid, and I don't wear suits."

The former figure skater now enjoys reading and skiing in his free time. He is married to a high school teacher. Harwood told *Entertainment Weekly,* "I believe there's life on other planets, but I don't believe that UFOs are saucers from another world."

## Tom Braidwood: Frohike

Short, unshaven, and clad in combat boots, Frohike, played by Tom Braidwood, looks like the dirty old man of "The Lone Gunmen." The photographic and surveillance specialist is obviously attracted to Scully, and he once traded Mulder a pair of night-vision goggles for Scully's phone number. He brought Scully her only flowers when she lay dying. Normally quiet, Frohike grows vocal only when Mulder teases him.

Vancouver-native Braidwood has also worked in theater and done some television production work, including for *21 Jump Street*. Besides playing Frohike, he serves as an assistant director on *The X-Files*.

Braidwood told *Entertainment Weekly* that Frohike was an easy character to get a handle on. Frohike's first line upon seeing Scully, "She's hot," he said, "encapsulated the whole character." The actor says that, like his character, "I've got a good sense of humor," but added, "I like pretty and intelligent women, but I have enormous respect for them, whereas Frohike just lusts after them. His mouth is bigger than his mind."

When not working, Braidwood enjoys gardening and spending time with his wife and two daughters. He also writes scripts and watches videos.

But are there aliens? Braidwood told *Entertainment Weekly*, "Something's out there. Whether we've met it or not, I don't know."

## Dean Haglund: Langly

Black-rimmed glasses, long blond hair, and T-shirts from a dozen hard-rock bands conceal the sharp mind of Langly, played by Dean Haglund. Langly is a communications expert who records all incoming phone calls, and, despite his carefree appearance, keeps as current with conspiracy theories as his two companions. Sometimes he feels Mulder's theories go a little too far, such as the idea that UFOs started the Gulf War. When he deems it necessary, Langly will not hesitate to lie.

Haglund, a Winnipeg native, is a stand-up comedian and member of the Vancouver TheaterSports improv group; he's also a veteran of many TV series and movies. The actor played Lorenzo Lamas in HBO's *Mask of Death* and appeared in an episode of *Lonesome Dove: The Series*.

Haglund based his portrayal of Langly on computer-nerd friends and grunge-rocker types. He told *Entertainment Weekly*, "I own a computer, I listen to the Ramones, the long blond hair is for real. I'm not as paranoid and I don't wear glasses."

Although he may be the only Canadian who cannot skate, the married actor practices yoga and can do splits. Haglund told *Entertainment Weekly* that his character's conspiracy theories are "all true—but only to certain people."

# PART
## III

# EPISODE GUIDE

# CHAPTER 14

# SEASON ONE:
# 1993-1994 EPISODES

### 1.1 PILOT: "THE X-FILES"

**Writer:** Chris Carter
**Director:** Robert Mandel
**Original Broadcast:** 9/10/93
**Guest Cast:** Billy Miles (Zachary Ansley), Section Chief Scott Blevins (Charles Cioffi), Cigarette-Smoking Man (William B. Davis), Dr. Jay Nemman (Cliff DeYoung), Theresa Nemman (Sarah Koskoff), and Detective Miles (Leon Russom)

Dr. Scully is assigned to observe Agent Mulder for their FBI superiors. They investigate the murder of Oregon high school students he believes were experimented on by aliens.

### Deconstruction and Notes

Mulder's watch failed to lose the nine minutes while other clocks did. Scully looks at the "I want to believe" poster in Mulder's office, but it changes in the next frame.

### 1.2 "DEEP THROAT"

**Writer:** Chris Carter
**Director:** Daniel Sackheim
**Original Broadcast:** 9/17/93
**Guest Cast:** Section Chief Scott Blevins (Charles Cioffi), Paul Mossinger (Michael Bryan French), Emil (Seth Green), Deep Throat (Jerry Hardin), Col. Robert Budahas (Andrew Johnston), Zoe (Lalainia Lindejerg), Kissell (Vince Metcalfe), Ladonna (Monica Parker), and Anita Budahas (Gabrielle Rose)

A test pilot has disappeared from Ellens Air Force Base in Idaho. Mulder and Scully investigate despite the disapproval of mysterious, powerful people. They find signs of possible experimentation on UFOs by the military.

### Deconstruction and Notes

The rear window reappears after it's shattered.

When one of the MIB's removes the magazine from Scully's gun, there is only one round in the magazine. There should be more than one round in the magazine, unless she had been shooting at street signs as they drove down the road.

### 1.3 "SQUEEZE"

**Writer:** Glen Morgan and James Wong
**Director:** Harry Longstreet
**Original Broadcast:** 9/24/93
**Guest Cast:** Detective Frank Briggs (Henry Beckman), Agent Tom Colton (Donal Logue), and Eugene Victor Tooms (Doug Hutchison)

The scene of an apparently motiveless, gruesome murder shows signs of an X-File killer, but the unsolved file dates back to 1933 and 1963. Mulder and Scully must stop a century-old killer.

### Deconstruction and Notes

Why couldn't Eugene just squeeze himself out of the handcuffs?

When Mulder realizes that Tooms is going after Scully, he tries calling her at home. Tooms has cut off Scully's line, so why didn't Mulder try her cellular?

## 1.4 "CONDUIT"

**Writer:** Alex Gansa and Howard Gordon
**Director:** Daniel Sackheim
**Original Broadcast:** 10/1/93
**Guest Cast:** Sioux City Sheriff (Michael Cavanaugh), Section Chief Scott Blevins (Charles Cioffi), Ruby (Taunya Dee), Pennsylvania Pub Bartender (Don Gibb), Tessa (Shelley Owens), Kevin Morris (Joel Palmer), Darlene Morris (Carrie Snodgress), and Holtzman (Don Thompson)

The signs seem to indicate alien involvement when a woman's daughter disappears while on a camping trip. The mother claims to have seen a UFO as a child, but the key to solving the mystery may be her young son.

### Deconstruction and Notes

There are no mountains on the other side of Spirit Lake.

The address in Samantha Mulder's file, 2790 Vine Street, is the former address of *The X-Files* production offices in Vancouver.

## 1.5 "THE JERSEY DEVIL"

**Writer:** Chris Carter
**Director:** Joe Napolitano
**Original Broadcast:** 10/8/93
**Guest Cast:** Ranger Peter Brullet (Michael MacRae), Dr. Diamond (Gregory Sierra), Creature (Claire Stansfield), and Detective Thompson (Wayne Tippit)

Mulder and Scully go to Atlantic City to investigate a cannibalized human body in New Jersey State Park. Despite obvious police cover-ups, Mulder continues to investigate a possible missing link in human evolution. Scully reflects on her future when she attends her godson's birthday party.

## 1.6 "SHADOWS"

**Writer:** Glen Morgan and James Wong
**Director:** Michael Katleman
**Original Broadcast:** 10/22/93
**Guest Cast:** Robert Dorlund (Barry Primus) and Lauren Kytes (Lisa Waltz)

Mulder and Scully examine very odd corpses in Philadelphia. The investigation leads to a strange force protecting a secretary whose employer recently committed suicide.

### Deconstruction and Notes

Not only did Graves die on the fifth, and Scully's journal in the next episode is dated the fourth, but the security video showing Lauren Kytes being attacked by the Isphahan is dated 09/22/93, even though it is supposed to be about two weeks after Graves had died. Perhaps they mean 10/22/93.

Cars have no license plates, or license plates with the numbers blacked out. This can be seen when Mulder and Scully's car crashes, in the FBI vehicle compound, and in the HTG car park just before Lauren complains about the reassignment of Howard Graves's car parking space.

## 1.7 "GHOST IN THE MACHINE"

**Writer:** Alex Gansa and Howard Gordon
**Director:** Jerrold Freedman
**Original Broadcast:** 10/29/93
**Guest Cast:** Agent Nancy Spiller (Gillian Barber), Agent Jerry Lamana (Wayne Duvall), Deep Throat (Jerry Hardin), Brad Wilczek (Rob LaBelle), and Claude Peterson (Blu Mankuma)

When Mulder's old partner asks for his help investigating the electrocution of a computer company CEO, "Deep Throat," Mulder, and Scully must stop the murderer, the Defense Department, and the apparently sentient building.

### Deconstruction and Notes

How did the Eurisko computer turn on Scully's machine? Devices can turn on computers remotely, but Scully wouldn't have one on her system. Seeing somebody remotely accessing her files, why did she not just unplug the modem from the phone socket?

Scully spools through a DAT tape while sitting at a desk. DAT tape machines do not make that type of spooling noise. The noise used was from an analog tape machine. The sound recorder/dubbing editor would have known the difference.

An elevator's emergency brake is mechanical and cannot be switched off electronically. The person could not have been killed by a falling elevator.

When the Eurisko computer called Scully's computer, the phone rang on Scully's bedside cabinet, she picked it up, and heard the modem squeaking. Scully went to her computer and saw someone, or something, accessing her computer files, then picked up the phone and called for a trace. Wouldn't that telephone be busy also? It's unlikely there is a link between the computer in the workroom and the phone in the bedroom while the phone on the computer table has no link.

When Mulder's ex-partner gets killed as the elevator falls down, he appears to be pushed to the floor by the g-forces when he should be "stuck" to the ceiling.

The town of Crystal City is an allusion to Silicon Valley. Crystal City is, however, an office park just outside of Washington, D.C., in Virginia.

# 1.8 "ICE"

**Writer:** Glen Morgan and James Wong
**Director:** David Nutter
**Original Broadcast:** 11/5/93
**Guest Cast:** Dr. Hodge (Xander Berkeley), Dr. Nancy DaSilva (Felicity Huffman), Dr. Denny Murphy (Steve Hytner), and Bear (Jeff Kober)

A crazed scientist sends "We are not who we are" as the final transmission from the Arctic Ice Core project. Mulder and Scully join the investigative team. Upon arrival at the Alaskan site, they discover a newly unearthed parasite.

## Deconstruction and Notes

When Mulder points the gun at the dog, you hear his cocking the hammer on the gun. The Glock 19 has an internal hammer, so unless it makes that noise when you depress the first stage of the trigger. . . .

When Richter talks into the recorder, he says, "It stops, right here, right now." But when it gets played back to Scully there's a pause that wasn't there before.

At the end of the episode "Ice," Hodge informs Mulder and Scully that the AICP base was torched by a U.S. government agency. Alaska has freezing weather, and Hodge blows into his hands to warm them, while Mulder crosses his arms, shivering, but no one has visible breath.

Alaska is often depicted in films and on TV, but never accurately. Mulder and Scully supposedly take off from Nome airport on a sunny, summer day. There are no trees in Nome. If it is summer in Nome, it is certainly summer one hundred miles north where they went. North of the Arctic Circle, in the summer, it never gets dark, yet when they land at Icy Cape, it is winter, they are caught in a snowstorm, and it is dark. There is no air force base up there.

After the dog is cured, Hodge says he passed both worms in his stool. The worm attached itself to the brain stem, so how did it get to the colon? Both worms were still in one piece, but that is impossible. In order to pass out of the rectum, material first has to pass through the gastrointestinal tract, and there are only two ways to get into that system: through the mouth, which wasn't the case, or through the bile duct, which can only transfer bile, a liquid.

David Duchovny's dog, Blue, is of a litter by the dog in this episode.

---

### Season One Ranking and Awards

Average Nielsen ratings for this season: 6.4

Overall Nielsen ranking: 102nd out of 118 shows.

Best Drama Series given by the Environmental Media Awards for the episode "Darkness Falls"

Nominated for an Edgar Award by the Mystery Writers of America for "The Erlenmeyer Flask"

Endorsed by the Viewers for Quality Television.

Emmy Nominations:

- Outstanding Individual Achievement in Graphics Design and Title Sequence
- Outstanding Individual Achievement for Main Title Theme Music (Mark Snow)

**TAG LINES** "The Erlenmeyer Flask" was the first to change the opening tag line of the credits from "The Truth Is Out There" to "Trust No One." In "Ascension," it was changed to "Deny Everything." In "Anasazi," the tag line displayed the Navajo translation of "The Truth Is Out There" (EI'AANIIGOO 'AHOOT'E). In "731," the opening tag was changed to "Apology Is Policy." In the season four episode premiere, it was again changed to "Everything Dies."

## 1.9 "SPACE"

**Writer:** Chris Carter
**Director:** William Graham
**Original Broadcast:** 11/12/93
**Guest Cast:** Lt. Col. Marcus Aurelius Belt (Ed Lauter) and Michelle Genero (Susanna Thompson)

A NASA worker asks Mulder and Scully to investigate sabotage after a space shuttle launch must be aborted. Something encountered during a spacewalk on a previous mission haunts the former astronaut in charge of the project.

## Deconstruction and Notes

If Dr. Scully is able to tell the paramedics to give Belt 10 milligrams of something-or-other, and warns Mulder of an aneurysm, how come when they first find Belt she just stands there instead of giving first aid? She should have been authoritative before and after the break.

Why did Mulder call for a doctor with Scully present?

Aren't hospital windows made so that people can't jump out of them?

Michelle Genero has a car accident and has quite an amount of blood on her head and a cut on her eyebrow. Later she has no cuts visible.

Lt. Col. Marcus Aurelius Belt is shown on a shuttle mission in 1977, when the space shuttle was first flown in 1981.

## 1.10 "FALLEN ANGEL"

**Writer:** Howard Gordon and Alex Gansa
**Director:** Larry Shaw
**Original Broadcast:** 11/19/93
**Guest Cast:** Col. Calvin Henderson (Marshall Bell), Max Fenig (Scott Bellis), Section Chief Joseph McGrath (Frederick Coffin), and Deep Throat (Jerry Hardin)

"Deep Throat" alerts Mulder to a government cover-up of a crashed UFO. The military obstructs Mulder's investigation while they try to bring in an odd being, and a UFO enthusiast appears on the scene. Mulder's job as an FBI agent is jeopardized.

## Deconstruction and Notes

A "laser fence" is set up around the woodland area to monitor anything entering or leaving. This would need a fantastically stable foundation for the fence posts to be fixed into to ensure alignment of the laser source and target. Assuming that each length between posts was only 50 meters and that each post originated a new beam rather than just reflecting the beam from the last post to the next, then it would only take 0.01 degrees of movement of a source post to cause a deflection error of 1 centimeter at the target post. Simply poking the posts into soft, decomposing woodland undergrowth just wouldn't give the stability required. Of course this doesn't even begin to take into account problems caused by false triggers from birds, rabbits, falling leaves, and so on.

When Max has a seizure and Mulder helps him lie down, Mulder notices a V-shaped scar behind Max's right ear. Later when Mulder is back at the hotel, he tells Scully that Max has a scar behind his *left* ear.

When Mulder gets Max a glass of water, Max tucks his hair behind his right ear and pushes his hair off his shoulder/collar. When Max drinks the water, his hair is once again forward on his shoulder, although still tucked.

At the hospital, the doctor reports that the deputy and the others came in with fifth and sixth degree burns over 90 percent of their body. First-aid classes teach that fourth degree is the worst sort of burn a person can get. In fourth degree the body is burned to the bone. If that's true, then what would be left of a person who had fifth or sixth degree burns over that much of the body? . . . ash?

Scully finds a bottle of pills in Max Fenig's caravan. The drug is Melleril and Scully immediately concludes that Max suffers from schizophrenia, that it is exclusively used for this, but this is not so. It's also used for anxiety, mixed anxiety and depression, tension, psychosomatic disorders, and sleep disturbances. Max could have been taking Melleril for many things other than schizophrenia.

Apparently, the entire episode experiences some "lost time": The caption at the beginning of the episode states, "Townsend, Wisconsin 12:57 a.m. Day 1." At this time the UFO crashes into the forest and causes a fire. A police officer is burned to a crisp. Thirty-five minutes later, the fire crew arrives, and they too are burned. Fox Mulder is briefed by "Deep Throat" as to the situation, and leaves for Wisconsin. Then, the first scene of Mulder in Townsend, outside of his hotel. The caption reads: "Budget Rest Motel Townsend, Wisconsin. 12:57 a.m. Day 1." Same day, same time.

UFO chaser Max Fenig's cap can be seen hanging on various coat racks in various following episodes.

# 1.11 "EVE"

**Writer:** Kenneth Biller and Chris Brancato
**Director:** Fred Gerber
**Original Broadcast:** 12/10/93
**Guest Cast:** Deep Throat (Jerry Hardin), Dr. Sally Kendrick/Eve 6,7,8 (Harriet Harris), Cindy Reardon (Erika Krievens), and Teena Simmons (Sabrina Krievens)

Mulder and Scully investigate the murder of a Connecticut man and uncover another man in California killed simultaneously in the same manner. The men's daughters could be identical twins. They watch the remaining child after the first child disappears.

## Deconstruction and Notes

Where did they put the blood they drained out of the bodies? Mulder mentioned that the first murder occurred right before it rained and the blood was washed away. But if that was the case, why wasn't the body soaking wet?

If Teena Simmons had the Eve-strength to get her father into the swing without leaving signs of a struggle,

how did Mulder restrain her with one arm and Cindy with the other?

Sally Kendrick, the adult Eve, said she had extra chromosomes (aneuplody) of normal chromosome sets, which is absolutely fatal in higher animals, except for X, 13,18 and/or 21, all of which lead to severe retardation. Multiple extra chromosomes would result in spontaneous abortion of the fetus long before birth.

When Eve 8 enters the Litchfield prison, she is handed no flashlight, whereas the importance of the flashlight had been stressed with Mulder and Scully.

It took "Deep Throat" to get two FBI agents into that place; so how did Eve 8 enter that far?

Didn't anyone notice that Sally Kendrick looked an awful lot like the prisoner she was going to see?

When the girls and Eve are in the motel room, their drinks are in takeaway paper cups. However when Mulder later picks up a cup, it has miraculously turned to glass. Granted it may have been easier to see the green residue in a glass, but they should have corrected the earlier scene.

The two little "Eve" girls were named Cindy and Teena, after the wives of writers/producers Glen Morgan and James Wong.

# 1.12 "FIRE"

**Writer:** Chris Carter
**Director:** Larry Shaw
**Original Broadcast:** 12/17/93
**Guest Cast:** Sir Malcolm Marsden (Dan Lett), Lady Marsden (Laurie Paton), Inspector Phoebe Green (Amanda Pays), and Bob/Cecil L'Ively (Mark Sheppard)

Mulder's ex-lover solicits his protection for a visiting member of Parliament and ignites jealousy in Scully. Mulder must overcome his fear of fire to defeat a pyrokinetic serial killer.

## Deconstruction and Notes

When Scully is typing on the computer, this is the exact same shot they used when she was typing in "Squeeze." Even the photos on the desk are the same.

While on the phone requesting a fax of the suspect's composite drawing, Scully looks at her watch. It's the type of watch with both analog and digital display. Initially the digital display reads "4:22:11," but the analog display reads "5:05." Then, five seconds later, the analog display is seen to read "4:50."

## 1.13 "BEYOND THE SEA"

**Writer:** Glen Morgan and James Wong
**Director:** David Nutter
**Original Broadcast:** 1/7/94
**Guest Cast:** Captain William Scully (Don S. Davis), Luther Lee Boggs (Brad Dourif), Lucas Jackson Henry (Lawrence King), and Margaret Scully (Sheila Larken)

When a death row psychic offers to help Scully capture a kidnapper after her father dies, her skepticism is tested. She must determine whether to believe the man's visions without Mulder's aid.

## Deconstruction and Notes

When Scully is in her car waiting at the intersection and looks around, she notices the "water falling" and the angel. Shots of the things she sees are interposed with shots of her as she notices them. In one of those shots of her, she is reversed, her hair suddenly parted on the wrong side. She looks up at her rear-view mirror, which is now to her left, and the car lights behind her can also be seen over her left shoulder. It now looks as though she is driving a car with the steering wheel on the right side and not the left.

Captain Scully is wearing an admiral's rank badge.

"Beyond the Sea" is the Bobby Darin record played at Scully's father's funeral.

## 1.14 "GENDERBENDER"

**Writer:** Larry Barber and Paul Barber
**Director:** Rob Bowman
**Original Broadcast:** 1/21/94
**Guest Cast:** Sister Abigail (Michele Goodger), Brother Andrew (Brent Hinkley), Marty [Male] (Peter Stebbings), and Marty [Female] (Kate Twa)

The two agents cannot determine the gender of a perpetrator of sexually related serial killings. Clues point to a small Massachusetts community called the "Kindred."

## Deconstruction and Notes

Why are the Kindred hanging out their laundry and chopping wood when it's raining outside?

After the head Kindred woman tells Mulder and Scully, "I asked you not to interfere," Mulder leads Scully away. From one camera angle, he is leading her away by the hand. In the same scene, but from a different camera angle, he has his arm around her. When we go back to the first camera angle, he is once again leading her away by the hand.

Steveston, Massachusetts, was named after a small community south of Vancouver beloved by *The X-Files*'s location manager for its diversity of settings.

## 1.15 "LAZARUS"

**Writer:** Alex Gansa and Howard Gordon
**Director:** David Nutter
**Original Broadcast:** 2/4/94
**Guest Cast:** Agent Jack Willis (Christopher Allport), Agent Ruskin (Jackson Davies), Warren James Dupree (Jason Schombing), and Lula Phillips (Cec Verrell)

Scully's friend, and fellow agent, is shot by a criminal when they set a trap set for a bank robber, whom Scully shoots in turn. The agent apparently returns from death, but actually he has absorbed the persona of the dead criminal. Scully sticks by him, but Mulder doubts his real identity.

## Deconstruction and Notes

The kidnappers use Scully's cellular phone, and Mulder says they can't trace it, yet "Cigarette-Smoking Man" finds Mulder in "Anasazi."

When Scully is trying to convince Jack to be Jack and not Dupree, she reminds him of his birthday—February 23, 1957. Then, when she is looking at the "Happy 35th" watch, she says that she gave it to him three years ago, which would be 1991. If Jack Willis was born in 1957, he would have only been 34 in 1991, not 35.

If Jack was a diabetic, why did it take so long for him to go into a coma without insulin?

How did he pass his medical and psychological tests without blood and urine tests? If this was an "FBI approved" doctor who had the agent's history, wouldn't she or he have asked Jack how his diabetes was getting along, which would have been a clue to the dude inhabiting Jack's body that his new body had a problem he had to deal with?

"Dupree" cut the fingers off his old body in order to get his wedding ring. Why did it perfectly fit his "new" body?

When Willis is practicing at the target range, we see eight bullet holes in a close-up of the cardboard target, including one almost on the white dot in the center of the target. Immediately after this we see Willis fire five more shots, but there are still only eight holes in the target when he retrieves it. When Willis signs the birthday card on top of the target, the pattern of bullet holes has changed, most noticeably, his near-bullseye is missing.

## 1.16 "YOUNG AT HEART"

**Writer:** Scott Kaufer and Chris Carter
**Director:** Michael Lange
**Original Broadcast:** 2/11/94
**Guest Cast:** Young John Barnett (Alan Boyce), Agent Henderson (Christine Estabrook), Deep Throat (Jerry Hardin), Doctor at N.I.H. (Graham Jarvis), Dr. Joe Ridley (Robin Mossley), Older John Barnett (David Petersen), Joe Crandall (Gordon Tipple), and Agent Reggie Purdue (Dick Anthony Williams)

A criminal Mulder captured shortly after graduating from the academy returns to take vengeance against the agent. An older, wiser Mulder must elude his seemingly unaged opponent.

## Deconstruction and Notes

When Mulder and Scully are in the opera building near the end, in the near full-body camera shot, Mulder is wearing his black ear piece, but when the camera goes to the close-up shot of his head and his gun, he is not wearing it.

## 1.17 "E.B.E."

**Writer:** Glen Morgan and James Wong
**Director:** William Graham
**Original Broadcast:** 2/18/94
**Guest Cast:** Frohike (Tom Braidwood), Langly (Dean Haglund), Byers (Bruce Harwood), Deep Throat (Jerry Hardin), and Ranheim/Frank Druce (Peter LaCroix)

An unmarked truck carrying the occupant of a UFO that crashed near Iraqi airspace is assailed in Tennessee. After a rash of UFO sightings, "Deep Throat" helps and hampers Mulder and Scully's investigation of the truck.

## Deconstruction and Notes

When Mulder and Scully breach the power plant with the help of the lone gunmen, they come across an MP guarding a door. The MP is wearing the rank of Sergeant Major on his uniform. An SGM would never guard a door himself. They occupy staff level positions.

When Mulder pushes past the MP, a whole squad of MP's mysteriously appears to chase him. The SGM never alerted them. If back-up responded based on the original call, only a few soldiers would have responded, not a squad.

All MP's are in class "A" uniform. Places where MP's still work in class As are few and far between. It would have been more believable to dress them in BDUs, with the ugly green pistol belts, not the nice leather gear.

When Mulder and Scully are about to go into the truck with the "rescued" alien in it, in one camera shot Scully has her flashlight, and in the next she doesn't have it and has moved one step forward.

Scully and Mulder follow a truck that might contain alien devices. They are stopped by a white flash. As soon as the flash disappears, they can see the truck in front of them. One detail is quite strange: the truck is facing them. We can see the front of the truck facing the front of their car as if it was driving the opposite way. The flash shuts down all electrical devices but doesn't turn around trucks.

When Mulder and Scully pull out to follow the truck, something appears briefly in the back window. It appears to be the camera and a light or mirror.

## 1.18 "MIRACLE MAN"

**Writer:** Howard Gordon and Chris Carter
**Director:** Michael Lange
**Original Broadcast:** 3/18/94
**Guest Cast:** Samuel Hartley (Scott Bairstow), Sheriff Maurice Daniels (R. D. Call), Reverend Calvin Hartley (George Gerdes), and Leonard Vance (Dennis Lipscomb)

Multiple mysterious deaths propel Mulder and Scully onto the trail of a Bible Belt faith healer. The miracle worker retains faith in his gift, and Mulder experiences the boy's power.

## 1.19 "SHAPES"

**Writer:** Marilyn Osborn
**Director:** David Nutter
**Original Broadcast:** 4/1/94
**Guest Cast:** Ish (Jimmy Herman), Sheriff Charles Tskany (Michael Horse), Lyle Parker (Ty Miller), Gwen Goodensnake (Renae Morriseau), and Jim Parker (Donnelly Rhodes)

The assailant of a Native American believed he had shot an animal. Mulder investigates an Indian myth and possible lycanthropy, the subject of the first X-File.

## Deconstruction and Notes

During the investigation of Joe Goodensnake's death, Mulder finds tracks in the mud—human steps, and then animal steps, all on the same track. From the description that Ish gave Mulder, and what we saw Lyle go through in the bathroom, transforming from man to beast was very painful and took a couple of minutes. It doesn't seem possible that when Joe Goodensnake was possessed he could go through the transformation and still continue walking a normal path.

When Lyle is in the bathroom transforming into the beast, he tears the shower curtain with his nails. Minutes later, his hand is split open, the nails are short and dull. How did he rip the curtain?

When Scully is outside the bathroom, why can he hear her say, "I want to take you to the hospital," and yet she can't hear him when he's howling incredibly loudly? The keyhole should have let her hear him.

When Mulder and the sheriff are talking to the old Indian man, the sheriff turns into the light and his makeup line is clearly visible.

Why couldn't Mulder call Scully on the cellular? If he can call her from inside a boxcar buried in a canyon, she would be able to pick up his call from within a car.

When the old Indian describes his childhood experience with the creature, he describes what happens later to Parker. Then he ends his description with, "But his eyes, they were still human. And they begged me to kill him." However, when Parker changes into the Manitou, his eyes are the first thing to change!

## 1.20 "DARKNESS FALLS"

**Writer:** Chris Carter
**Director:** Joe Napolitano
**Original Broadcast:** 4/15/94
**Guest Cast:** Larry Moore (Jason Beghe), Perkins (Barry Greene), Steve Humphreys (Tom O'Rourke), Dyer (Ken Tremblett), and Doug Spinney (Titus Welliver)

Thirty missing loggers illegally cutting trees in Washington State suffer a horrible punishment. While investigating, Mulder and Scully face the same danger.

## Deconstruction and Notes

Why did Spinney get killed by the bugs when he was standing in the headlights of the car? If the bugs swarmed on Spinney's unlit side when he was in the headlights, then the bugs should have swarmed on everyone's unlit side. They only had one light bulb left so they must have had shadows on their backs. Unless they are in soft light, there would be a shadow and a dark place for them to swarm.

Why didn't they build a fire?

When they are riding in the jeep down the hill, it looks like there's another vehicle following them. This reflection off the camera lens looks pretty weird.

When they find the ancient felled tree, the stump that Mulder clambers up onto to investigate the growth rings has a distinctive crack at the center and the growth rings are irregular in shape. However the stump close up has no crack and regular circular rings.

Jason Beghe, playing Ranger Larry Moore, got David Duchovny interested in acting in the first place. The two tended bar and took acting classes together.

## 1.21 "TOOMS"

**Writer:** Glen Morgan and James Wong
**Director:** David Nutter
**Original Broadcast:** 4/22/94
**Guest Cast:** Detective Frank Briggs (Henry Beckman), Smoking Man (William B. Davis), Eugene Victor Tooms (Doug Hutchison), and Dr. Aaron Monte (Paul Ben Victor)

Mulder and Scully capture Eugene Tooms, a mutant killer. He is released due to lack of evidence and a psychiatric reevaluation. Tooms then seeks a fifth, and final, human liver to eat. Mulder tries to stop him while Scully searches for new evidence, and both agents struggle to overcome their superiors' insistence that they follow the rules.

## Deconstruction and Notes

Tooms lived at 66 Exeter for sixty years, coming out every twenty years to eat five livers and then hibernate. How did he pay the rent while he was hibernating? The building was sold and turned into a mall, and he wouldn't have sold his hibernating place.

Tooms built a nest under the base of an escalator, which led to his eventual demise when the escalator was turned on, dragging him under to his death. The escalator was traveling down to pull him back under the escalator base, but, before the episode ended, the camera shows a trail of blood traveling up the escalator on the top side.

Just how long was Tooms locked up? In "Squeeze," 66 Exeter Street was shown as a derelict condemned building. In "Tooms," it's this shiny new shopping mall. Wouldn't it take longer than the seemingly few months Eugene was locked up to build something like this?

## 1.22 "BORN AGAIN"

**Writer:** Howard Gordon and Alex Gansa
**Director:** Jerrold Freedman
**Original Broadcast:** 4/29/94
**Guest Cast:** Dr. Sheila Braun (P. Lynn Johnson), Anita Fiore (Mimi Lieber), Michelle Bishop (Andrea Libman), Tony Fiore (Brian Markinson), Detective Sharon Lazard (Maggie Wheeler), and Judy Bishop (Dey Young)

A little girl may have murdered two Buffalo policemen. Mulder and Scully investigate the eight year old, discovering clues to an unsolved, nine-year-old murder, possibly that of the girl in a previous life.

## Deconstruction and Notes

Why did Mulder, a trained psychologist, and another psychologist confuse multiple personality syndrome with schizophrenia?

When Michelle is working with Mulder and the computer guy, Harry, on the computerized mugshot, Mulder asks her if the guy's hair is dark like his or lighter like hers. Michelle says it's like hers, which was blond. Harry then gives the picture dark hair and no one corrects him.

How do Mulder and Scully get to Buffalo so soon after the guy went out the window? They're still taking pictures and examining the scene when Mulder and Scully get to Buffalo. The female cop had to call the FBI, and someone had to assign them the case. That's not even including travel time.

## 1.23 "ROLAND"

**Writer:** Chris Ruppenthal
**Director:** David Nutter
**Original Broadcast:** 5/6/94
**Guest Cast:** Dr. Keats (Garry Davey), Roland Fuller/Dr. Arthur Grable (Zeljko Ivanek), Mrs. Stodie (Micole Mercurio), Tracy (Kerry Sandomirsky), Dr. Frank Nollette (James Sloyan), and Dr. Ronald Surnow (Matthew Walker)

All signs lead to a mentally handicapped janitor as the murderer of two propulsion researchers, yet evidence of advanced theoretical work seems to close the possibility. Then Mulder and Scully discover the janitor's relationship to a cryogenically preserved scientist.

## Deconstruction and Notes

Why did a fluid mechanic run to stand in front of the fan as it started up? He would have known to stand in the corner to one side of the fan, out of the direct line of the wind, in an area of "stagnant flow." The wind will be at its maximum where he stands, but the flow will be at a minimum, and quite possibly calm, to one side.

## 1.24 "THE ERLENMEYER FLASK"

**Writer:** Chris Carter
**Director:** R.W. Goodwin
**Original Broadcast:** 5/13/94
**Guest Cast:** Cigarette-Smoking Man (William B. Davis), Dr. Anne Carpenter (Anne DeSalvo), Crew Cut Man (Lindsey Ginter), Deep Throat (Jerry Hardin), Dr. Terrance Allen Berube (Ken Kramer), Captain Roy Laceri (Jim Leard), and Dr. William Secare (Simon Webb)

"Deep Throat" alerts Mulder to a news story about a drowned fugitive, but Mulder and Scully fail to understand why. They then discover evidence of secret government experimentation with extraterrestrial DNA—and soon not only the evidence but everyone who has seen it begin to vanish.

## Deconstruction and Notes

The sign glimpsed briefly during the opening car chase reads: "Vancouver Drydock Company Ltd."

Before Scully hands over the alien fetus, why doesn't she take a tissue sample for further research?

Why would Scully try to pet an animal research subject? No one in the medical or scientific community would do such a thing where they lacked details of the research and the condition of the animal.

# CHAPTER 15

# SEASON TWO:
# 1994–1995 EPISODES

## 2.1 "LITTLE GREEN MEN"

**Writer:** Glen Morgan and James Wong
**Director:** David Nutter
**Original Broadcast:** 9/16/94
**Guest Cast:** Senator Richard Matheson (Raymond J. Barry), Cigarette-Smoking Man (William B. Davis), Jorge Concepcion (Mike Gomez), Samantha Mulder [Age 8] (Vanessa Morley), and Fox Mulder [Age 12] (Marcus Turner)

After the X-Files division closes, an old friend gives Mulder new reason to believe when Mulder follows him to an abandoned SETI program site in Puerto Rico.

## Deconstruction and Notes

In the pilot Mulder told Scully that he and his sister were in bed when Sam was abducted. In this episode, they were arguing in the living room.

Scully wears her trench coat in sunny Miami—she needed it to hide the actress' pregnancy.

The Radio Telescope at Arecibo is not closed as depicted in the episode. They even have a home page on the World Wide Web.

If Mulder had to climb the locked fence to get in, how did Scully get her truck in so it would be conveniently waiting for their getaway?

A wide bandwidth does not mean a radio transmission source is close by, but that the transmission covers many frequencies, just as narrow bandwidth radio transmissions cover a small range of frequencies. Distance has nothing to do with this!

When Scully is trying to find out what happened to Mulder, she types in his computer password as "trustno1." This has eight digits, but she types nine keys and hits return.

In the beginning, Mulder cuts open the chain that keeps the door locked to the interior of the lab. The Hispanic guy is already in the windowless bathroom. How did he get there?

Scenery slip up: Too many pines and evergreens for Puerto Rico.

Someone reads a newspaper in the "Miami" airport. The front page has the name of a Miami newspaper, but the back page is unmistakably the *Toronto Globe and Mail*.

Senator Richard Matheson is named after the sci-fi/horror author.

X-Philes whose names appeared on the airline passenger list: Paulette Alves, Donald Anglin, Sylvia Bartle, Kinh Berreman, Sarah Brice, Kelly Brown, Tere Carstensen, Gail Celio, Cliff Chen (Keeper of the *X-Files* Episode Guide), Hayden Dawson, Lori Dawson, Harle Erickson, Garn Ferguson, Jodi Giannini, Jan Gompf, Pat Gonzales (Keeper of the *X-Files* FAQ), Jeff Gostin, Charles Grant (*X-Files* author), Betty Grant, George E. Hale (One of Mulder's pseudonyms), George Ellery Hale, Andrew Harrison, Melissa Harris, Linda Lee Hill, Scott Hill, and Eliza Hofmann

## 2.2 "THE HOST"

**Writer:** Chris Carter
**Director:** Daniel Sackheim
**Original Broadcast:** 9/23/94
**Guest Cast:** Detective Norman (Freddy Andeiuci), Agent Brisentine (Marc Bauer), and Flukeman (Darin Morgan)

Scully's autopsy turns up a parasite living inside a decomposed human body found in the sewers of Newark, New Jersey. Then something bites a sewer worker.

## Deconstruction and Notes

Scully is quoting to Mulder from a book all about flukes (trematodes). However, the stuff she is quoting is wrong. She states that flukes or flatworms have a scolex with hooks and suckers. That is the distinguishing characteristic of cestodes (tapeworms), not flukes.

A and A Anderson Tank doesn't exist in Newark, but it does exist with the same phone number in Vancouver.

The impellers in sewage-sucker-trucks chop their load into tiny pieces, which should have chopped up Mr. Flukeman.

They depict Newark police uniforms and cars incorrectly, and Newark does not have that many trees.

The man who played the Flukeman is Darin Morgan, brother of writer Glen Morgan. Darin Morgan is famous among X-Philes for humorous script writing of some of the episodes.

The autopsy Scully performs is case number DP112148 (Dori Pearson's, Chris Carter's wife, initials and birthdate) of John Doe number 101356 (Chris Carter's birthdate).

## 2.3 "BLOOD"

**Writer:** Glen Morgan and James Wong
**Original Story:** Darin Morgan
**Director:** David Nutter
**Original Broadcast:** 9/30/94
**Guest Cast:** Frohike (Tom Braidwood), Sheriff Spencer (John Cygan), Harry McNally (Andre Daniels), Mrs. McRoberts (Kimberly Ashlyn Gere), Langly (Dean Haglund), Taber (John Harris), Byers (Bruce Harwood), Edward Funsch (William Sanderson), and County Supervisor Larry Winter (George Touliatos)

Mulder goes to Franklin, Pennsylvania, to investigate killings. All the victims died in berserker rages, although they had no prior history of violent actions. Also electronics and an unknown organic substance are destroyed.

---

### Season Two Ranking and Awards

Average Nielsen rating for this season: 11.5

Overall Nielsen ranking: 64th out of 141 shows.

Best TV Drama Series by the Environmental Media Awards for the episode "Fearful Symmetry"

Cinematographer John Bartley nominated for an Outstanding Achievement Award by American Society of Cinematographers for his work on "Duane Barry."

Nominated for the Writer's Guild Award for Best TV Drama Writing on "Duane Barry" (Chris Carter).

Endorsed by the Viewers for Quality Television Quality Awards nominations:

- Best Drama
- Best Actor in a Drama (David Duchovny)
- Best Actress in a Drama (Gillian Anderson)

Nominated by Television Critic's Association for Best Drama.

Golden Globe Award for Best Television Series—Drama.

Emmy nominations:

- Outstanding Individual Achievement in Editing for a Series—Single Camera Production (James Coblentz, "Duane Barry")
- Outstanding Individual Achievement in Editing for a Series—Single Camera Production (Stephen Mark, "Sleepless")
- Outstanding Sound Editing for a Series (Supervising Sound Editor: Thierry Couturier; Dialogue Editors: Machiek Malish, Chris Reeves, Marty Stein, and Jay Levine;

Sound Effects Editors: Stuart Calderon, Michael Kimball, David Van Slyke, Susan Welsh, Chris Fradkin, and Matt West; Music Editor: Jeff Charbonneau; ADR Editor: Debby Ruby Winsberg, "Duane Barry")

- Outstanding Individual Achievement in Cinematography for a Series (John Bartley, "One Breath")
- Outstanding Guest Actress in a Drama Series (C.C.H. Pounder, "Duane Barry")
- Outstanding Individual Achievement in Writing in a Dramatic Series (Chris Carter, "Duane Barry")
- Outstanding Drama Series

## Deconstruction and Notes

After the woman kills the mechanic, Mulder goes over the crime scene. Mulder takes the clipboard off the wall to examine it. Like a good agent, he's wearing white rubber gloves. But when he runs his finger down the page, his right hand is bare. And the very next line is a Mulderism—he goes to shake hands and says, "Pardon my rubber."

The Franklin Community College tower really stands at the University of British Columbia.

Writers Glen Morgan and James Wong began with a single note, "Postal Workers," that they subsequently combined with the controversy in Southern California over malithion spraying. Carter wanted to incorporate digital readouts in a scary way.

The final transmission—"ALL DONE, BYE BYE"—later served as the final shot in the blooper reel.

Ken Hawryliw operated the appliances off-camera. Mrs. McRoberts's microwave was a mockup.

Glen Morgan's brother, Darin Morgan, contributed the idea of the subliminal messages.

The nurse rings morse code for "kill" on the mailman's door. Coexecutive produer Glen Morgan confirmed this on AOL.

## 2.4 "SLEEPLESS"

**Writer:** Howard Gordon
**Director:** Rob Bowman
**Original Broadcast:** 10/ 7/94
**Guest Cast:** Cigarette-Smoking Man (William B. Davis), Salvatore Matola (Jonathan Gries), Agent Alex Krycek (Nicholas Lea), Augustus Cole (Tony Todd), and X (Steven Williams)

Mulder and his new partner, Alex Krycek, investigate after a scientist burns to death, despite no signs of flames or burns.

## Deconstruction and Notes

Scully teaches a class around a corpse. Her students take notes. One of the student's notebooks is totally blank.

## 2.5 "DUANE BARRY"

**Writer:** Chris Carter
**Director:** Chris Carter
**Original Broadcast:** 10/14/94
**Guest Cast:** Agent Alex Krycek (Nicholas Lea), Agent Kazdin (C.C.H. Pounder), Duane Barry (Steve Railsback), and Dr. Hakkie (Frank C. Turner)

After escaping from a mental hospital, an ex-FBI agent holds hostages in a travel agency. Mulder and Krycek investigate when the man claims to have been a UFO abductee. This is the first of two parts.

## Deconstruction and Notes

Duane forgot "Resolution" when listing FBI strategy.

When Duane walks away from Mulder to talk to the doctor, we hear him say, "'I'm tired of all the B.S.!" but his lips form "bullshit!"

A scanner at the supermarket wouldn't read out an alien code. It would get to the end of the digits used in UPC codes then hit an error, even if it proved to be compatible systems. It's like trying to read a diskette with a CD player.

Duane lived in Pulaski, Virginia. After his alleged abduction, he was sent to a mental health hospital in Marion, Virginia. There he kidnaps a doctor and drives into downtown Richmond, then holds several workers in a travel agency hostage. It's more than a five-hour drive from Marion to Richmond. Wouldn't the Virginia State police have set up roadblocks?

How come Duane Barry was talking with the police on a Sanyo cordless phone when there was no electricity?

## 2.6 "ASCENSION"

**Writer:** Paul Brown
**Director:** Michael Lange
**Original Broadcast:** 10/21/94
**Guest Cast:** Cigarette-Smoking Man (William B. Davis), Margaret Scully (Sheila Larken), Agent Alex Krycek (Nicholas Lea), Duane Barry (Steve Railsback), and X (Steven Williams)

Mulder unsuccessfully goes after Duane Barry after hearing Scully's phone message. A police video from a traffic violation provides a clue. Second of two parts.

## Deconstruction and Notes

A "stomach pump" starts out just metal on flesh, but after a cut-away, medical tape/gauze appears on Scully's midsection where the pump is connected.

Route 229 does not lead to the Blue Ridge Parkway. It leads to Route 211, which does go to the Blue Ridge Parkway. Route 229 doesn't appear anywhere near the town where the cop was shot.

The time is given as 11:45 A.M. in the hallway scene with X. Why is it so dark?

In the very next scene, in Skinner's office, the time is given as 8:11 A.M. No date change is given, and everyone is dressed the same. Has everyone just experienced twenty-one hours of "lost time"?

Gillian Anderson was pregnant while filming, so when Scully goes to the store in the episode, they have her buying pickles and ice cream.

**THE GUNS OF THE X-FILES** In the pilot, Mulder carried a Taurus 92 automatic, firing 9mm rounds. Scully carried a Bernadelli 7.65. Mulder later switched to a Glock 19 and Scully changed to a Walther PPK 7.65. In the first few episodes of the second season, they were both carrying Sig Sauer weapons; Mulder carried a Sig Sauer 226 and Scully a 228. They are now carrying the FBI standard weapons, Smith and Wesson 1076 with 10mm round.

## 2.7 "3"

**Writer:** Glen Morgan and James Wong
**Original Script:** Chris Ruppenthal
**Director:** David Nutter

**Original Broadcast:** 11/4/94
**Guest Cast:** Detective Nettles (Frank Ferrucci), Detective Munson (Tom McBeath), The Son aka John (Frank Military), The Father (Gustavo Moreno), Kristen (Perrey Reeves), and The Unholy Spirit (Justina Vail)

When he works on a recently reopened X-File, Mulder recognizes a Los Angeles killing as the work of the Trinity murderers, a trio of killers with a fetish for drinking blood.

## Deconstruction and Notes

If the sun is creeping toward John, then the sun's setting, not rising.

## 2.8 "ONE BREATH"

**Writer:** Glen Morgan and James Wong
**Director:** R.W. Goodwin
**Original Broadcast:** 11/11/94
**Guest Cast:** Frohike (Tom Braidwood), Dr. Daly (Jay Brazeau), Nurse G. Owens (Nicola Cavendish), Captain William Scully (Don S. Davis), Cigarette-Smoking Man (William B. Davis), Langly (Dean Haglund), Byers (Bruce Harwood), Margaret Scully (Sheila Larken), Melissa Scully (Melinda McGraw), and X (Steven Williams)

Machines keep Scully alive after she reappears in a Washington, D.C., hospital. Mulder hunts for the people responsible.

## Deconstruction and Notes

Mulder signs the sheet for Scully while she is in a coma and the signature is different to the one on his F.B.I. card in the credits.

How come the doctors didn't notice the large hole in her belly or the branched DNA?

Mulder's laser printer has the "Hewlett Packard" portion of the name taped over. Only LaserJet 4 can be seen.

The Thinker is modeled after fan and America Online member Yung Jun Kim (also known as "Duh-Thinker").

The Lone Gunmen invite Mulder to come over and jump on the Internet to "nitpick the scientific inaccuracies of Earth 2." This is a nod to the Internet X-Philes community and quite possibly to the Net-picker's Guide to *The X-Files*, maintained by Kymber-lee Ricke.

## 2.9 "FIREWALKER"

**Writer:** Howard Gordon
**Director:** David Nutter
**Original Broadcast:** 11/18/94
**Guest Cast:** Peter Tanaka (Hiro Kanagawa), Eric Parker (David Kaye), Vosberg (David Lewis), Dr. Adam Pierce (Tuck Milligan), Jason Ludwig (Leland Orser), Technician (Torben Rolfsen), Jesse O'Neil (Shawnee Smith), and Dr. Daniel Trepkos (Bradley Whitford)

A lifeform living in a cave causes the death of a research team member. A malfunctioning robot provides a clue. Mulder and Scully investigate.

## Deconstruction and Notes

The scientists are exposed to a silicon-based, fungus-like parasite that is completely undetectable until it bursts out of their neck to spread spores. There are several problems with the science in this. The fungi are silicon based, but since there is nearly no silicon in the human body, the scientists would have had to be munching on beer bottles.

The extremely efficient fungi must have evolved as parasites, but the scientists were the first humans to visit the volcano. There must have been earlier natural hosts, but no sign remains.

The parasites burst out from the neck, but the crowded human neck already contains the spine, wind-pipe, esophagus, and major arteries and veins. Where did the parasites live without causing distressing pressure on these organs?

When O'Neil dies, a puff of spores flew out of the crack in the door. At least one should have gotten Scully.

## 2.10 "RED MUSEUM"

**Writer:** Chris Carter
**Director:** Win Phelps
**Original Broadcast:** 12/ 9/94

**Guest Cast:** Beth Kane (Gillian Barber), Sheriff Mazeroski (Steve Eastin), Crew Cut Man (Lindsey Ginter), Richard Odin (Mark Rolston), and Gird Thomas (Paul Sand)

Mulder and Scully travel to investigate underwear-clad Wisconsin teens with "He is one" scrawled on their backs.

## Deconstruction and Notes

A camcorder films through a peephole.

When Mulder and Scully are eating dinner, Mulder goes outside to see what the kids are yelling at. He removes his napkin once, then again as he's walking along.

## 2.11 "EXCELSIUS DEI"

**Writer:** Paul Brown
**Director:** Stephen Surjik
**Original Broadcast:** 12/16/94
**Guest Cast:** Dorothy (Frances Bay), Stan Phillips (Eric Christmas), Hal Arden (David Fresco), Michelle Charters (Teryl Rothery), and Gung Bittouen (Sab Shimono)

Mulder and Scully investigate the rape of a nurse in a Massachusetts convalescent home. She claims her attacker was invisible.

## Deconstruction and Notes

When the episode aired, it was titled "Excelsius Dei," but on the show the name on the metal gate at the entrance says "Exclesis Dei."

The doctor tells Scully and Mulder that he has been experimenting on the Alzheimer's patients with a drug called Deprenyl. There is such a drug, and it has been studied as a possible treatment for Alzheimer's due to its memory, intelligence, and mood-elevating effects. The doctor also tells Scully and Mulder that the drug increases acetylcholine levels. Acetylcholine is a chemical that acts as a neurotransmitter (it carries messages between nerve cells). There is another chemical in the brain called dopamine that also acts as a neurotransmitter. Deprenyl primarily effects dopamine levels in the nervous system, not acetylcholine. Scully later announces that the doctor is right, and that elevated acetylcholine levels can cause psychosis. That may be true at very high levels, but Deprenyl doesn't influence acetylcholine metabolism.

Why don't they break the window when the bathroom was filling with water? When Mulder and Scully leave the bathroom after viewing Hal Arden's "plumbing," the light from a large window can be seen on the wall.

A bathroom of that size would hold tons of water. Wouldn't the floor have collapsed under the weight?

Gung refers to his "prefecture," which is the administrative term for a district in China, but he is eventually repatriated to Malaysia, where there are no prefectures.

## 2.12 "AUBREY"

**Writer:** Sara Charno
**Director:** Rob Bowman
**Original Broadcast:** 1/6/95
**Guest Cast:** Mrs. Thibedeaux (Joy Coghill), Lieutenant Brian Tillman (Terry O'Quinn), Detective B.J. Morrow (Deborah Strang), and Harry Cokely (Morgan Woodward)

A dreaming policewoman experiences the memory of a fifty-year-old serial killing and unearths the body of the FBI investigator. Mulder and Scully work with the detective to determine the killer's identity after the murderer strikes again.

## Deconstruction and Notes

Mulder drives while Scully rides shotgun. They pull over to the right side of the road. As soon as Mulder stops, Scully heads for the house, but Mulder gets there first, after putting the car in park, killing the engine, unbuckling his seatbelt, getting out of the car, and going around the car.

When B. J. is digging for the body down in the cellar, Mulder and Scully come down the stairs. Scully trips and Mulder grabs her.

In the beginning, when Mulder and Scully are in the office talking, Scully is reading a file. Several times, she flips the page over, but when we see her from Mulder's point of view, the page is not overturned.

If the body was that close to the surface, why hadn't it been discovered sooner?

Why didn't Scully and Mulder call Mrs. Thibedeaux and warn her not to be home when they "discovered" that B. J. had become Cokely? It would have been a lot faster than driving.

## 2.13 "IRRESISTIBLE"

**Writer:** Chris Carter
**Director:** David Nutter
**Original Broadcast:** 1/13/95
**Guest Cast:** Donald Eddie Pfaster (Nick Chinlund), Toews (Robert Thurston), Agent Bocks (Bruce Weitz), Agent Karen E. Kosseff (Christine Willes), and Marilyn (Denalda Williams)

A Minnesota agent brings an unearthed, mutilated female corpse to Mulder's attention, claiming it is the work of aliens. A similarly mutilated prostitute is found.

## Deconstruction and Notes

Cars and a bus run down the street Donny cruises. The sign on the bus says UBC, which is the University of British Columbia in Vancouver!

How did Mulder and Bocks know that it was Donny Pfaster who ran Scully off the road?

Ray Soams's grave from the pilot appears in the graveyard at the beginning.

At the beginning, Mulder, Scully, and Bocks look over an unearthed grave in the rain. Wouldn't they have needed to cover the grave to keep evidence from washing away?

Pfaster committed murder with a knife. He didn't seem to have a gun. Why didn't Scully shoot Pfaster when he ran her off the road?

Scully pushed Pfaster backward into the bath tub. He is soaked from the waist down, his left arm soaked to the elbow. In the next shot he is dry!

## 2.14 "DIE HAND DIE VERLETZT"

**Writer:** Glen Morgan and James Wong
**Director:** Kim Manners
**Original Broadcast:** 1/27/95

**Guest Cast:** Phyllis H. Paddock (Susan Blommaert), Jim Ausbury (Dan Butler), Pete Calcagni (Shaun Johnson), and Shannon Ausbury (Heather McComb)

A teenager is murdered when a group feigns an occult ritual. The town's real occultists hide their tracks from Mulder and Scully.

## Deconstruction and Notes

"Die Hand Die Verletzt" means "the hand that wounds."

The Coriolis Effect is subject to many myths, including that it supposedly causes water to flow down a drain clockwise. Actually it causes certain systems, for example, low-pressure systems, to rotate counterclockwise. It does not, however, have much effect on systems smaller than a hurricane. This is why 80 percent of tornadoes rotate counterclockwise, just like hurricanes, but 20 percent of tornadoes rotate clockwise.

When Shannon dies from slitting her wrists after Mrs. Paddock's demonic suggestion, Paddock says that she ran in when she heard the girl fall off the stool. Dying from slitting one's wrists would have taken a long time even after she passed out and fell off the stool. Unless she nearly cut her hands off, the wounds would have started to clot before she died.

How did the python get Ausbury's hand out of the handcuffs when it swallowed him? Pythons dissolve their prey and cannot chew. The handcuffs still looked okay afterward and remained locked. There was no blood on the floor or on the handcuffs.

Toads are from the family *Bufonidae*, and frogs from the family *Ranidae*. Most documented cases of falls are toads.

Pythons only grow to twelve feet, with a head the size of a hand, fingers extended. How could such an animal eat a full grown man in one piece? Snakes can dislocate their jaws, but a snake that size would have to have so much extra skin around its mouth that it would look like a basset hound. Also snakes eat their prey head first.

When Mulder and Scully are in the basement of the teacher's house, Mulder was holding the flashlight pointed at Scully, yet he jerked his head to call her over. If his flashlight was in her eyes, she couldn't see him move his head in the pitch black.

Mulder and Scully broke the law when they looked to see who checked out the witchcraft book from the library. Patron records are confidential and require a warrant to look at them.

After finding Shannon's stepfather, why weren't the agents concerned about the location of a missing, ferocious, man-eating python?

Why would Mrs. Paddock feed an embalmed pig embryo to the snake? Snakes only eat live prey.

This is the last episode written by Glen Morgan and James Wong, who left the series for Fox's *Space: Above and Beyond*. The writers used Paddock's line on the chalkboard, "It's been nice working with you," to say goodbye to the cast and crew.

The producers, San Diego Chargers fans, indulged an in-joke listing themselves in the opening credits as James "Chargers" Wong and Glen "Bolts, Baby" Morgan in this episode that first aired on the eve of Super Bowl XXIX.

"Crowley" High School was named after Aleister Crowley, whose theories on "magick" shocked his contemporaries and heavily influenced the development of modern Wicca.

The characters "Paula Vitaris" and "Deborah Brown" are named after online X-Philes. The Ausbury family were named after Jill Ausbury, which has had a prominent place in the show. Murdered Jerry is named after Jerry Jones, host of the AOL X-Files forum, school pscychologist Pete Calcagni after the husband of another AOL fan.

## 2.15 "FRESH BONES"

**Writer:** Howard Gordon
**Director:** Rob Bowman
**Original Broadcast:** 2/3/95
**Guest Cast:** Colonel Wharton (Daniel Benzali), Private Jack McAlpin (Kevin Conway), Private Kittel (Roger Cross), Robin McAlpin (Katya Gardner), Private Harry Dunham (Matt Hill), Lieutenant Foyle (Peter Kelamis), Groundskeeper (Callum Keith Rennie), Chester Bonaparte (Jamil Walker Smith), X (Steven Williams), and Pierre Bauvais (Bruce Young)

A soldier in a Haitian resettlement camp drives into a tree. His widow calls Mulder and Scully, fearing a voodoo curse reinforced by the local residents, including other soldiers.

## Deconstruction and Notes

The design painted on the tree into which McAlpin crashes his car is a "vever," a sign belonging to the *loa* or spirits honored in the voudoun. Bauvais explains the vever as a *loco-miroir*, or mirror of the soul.

# 2.16 "COLONY"

**Writer:** Chris Carter
Story: Chris Carter and David Duchovny
**Director:** Nick Marck
**Original Broadcast:** 2/10/95
**Guest Cast:** CIA Agent Ambrose Chapel (Tom Butler), Mulder's Father (Peter Donat), Dr. Landon Prince/Gregor's (Dana Gladstone), FBI Agent (David L. Gordon), Field Doctor (Bonnie Hay), Federal Marshall (Tim Henry), Agent Barry Weiss (Andrew Johnston), Samantha Mulder (Megan Leitch), Military Policeman (Michael McDonald), First Jailer (Capper McIntyre), Mrs. Mulder (Rebecca Toolan), and Pilot/Bounty Hunter (Brian Thompson)

A newspaper ad asking the whereabouts of a doctor triggers murders of lookalikes. Scully and Mulder race the killer to locate another. Mulder receives unexpected assistance. The first of two parts.

## Deconstruction and Notes

Scully couldn't call Mulder's cellular because it was destroyed when he was hit by the car. Why didn't Mulder call Scully on her cellular when he reached her machine? Chris Carter couldn't give an answer at the Pasadena *X-Files* convention.

Scully gets on the bus for Germantown alone, but when she sits down and calls Mulder, the Alien is already on her bus. How did he know what bus she'd be on?

Sorry, Wrong Number: Scully dials 1225, not 1236, to check the V-mail. Also, they take off after the first message, not bothering with the rest.

Mulder brings in the report for Skinner, but walks right out still holding the thing!

Wrong Messages: While Mulder's away, there are two different messages on his machine: "Hi, this is Fox Mulder. Please leave me a message and I'll get back to you as soon as I can," and "Hello, this is Fox Mulder, leave a message please."

In the beginning, Mulder is wearing an oxygen mask when he's in the tub. Scully comes in and talks to the doctor and, in the background, Mulder wears no oxygen mask. The mask is back in the next shot.

"Samantha" and "Gregor" enter the apartment and take off their coats. Gregor hears a door slam and looks out the window to see Mulder and Scully getting out of the car and coming to their building. Exactly five seconds pass as Gregor looks up at Samantha and she hides—and the doorbell rings! How did they and "Agent Chapel" get up to the second floor so fast?

# 2.17 "END GAME"

**Writer:** Frank Spotnitz
**Director:** Rob Bowman
**Original Broadcast:** 2/17/95
**Guest Cast:** Lieutenant Terry Wilmer (Colin Cunningham), Mulder's Father (Peter Donat), Samantha Mulder (Megan Leitch), Pilot/Bounty Hunter (Brian Thompson), X (Steven Williams), and Paramedic (Beatrice Zeilinger)

The Bounty Hunter takes Scully captive. Mulder exchanges a loved one, then tracks the hunter. Second of two parts.

## Deconstruction and Notes

In the episode "End Game," the day after Samantha fell in the river, the people drag the body out of the lake. Soon Scully is called over to look at the body because it's deteriorating. The fumes don't bother her. In "Colony," the policeman was killed by the fumes after shooting the clone, and it effected Mulder at the end. Wouldn't it also effect Scully?

Scully uses the X sign in Mulder's window to signal "X" because she wants to know where Mulder is. He appears but won't speak to her, so, since he already knows where Mulder is, why did he turn up?

## 2.18 "FEARFUL SYMMETRY"

**Writer:** Steven De Jarnatt
**Director:** James Whitmore, Jr.
**Original Broadcast:** 2/24/95
**Guest Cast:** Ray Floyd (Charles Andre), Willa Ambrose (Jayne Atkinson), Frohike (Tom Braidwood), Kyle Lang (Lance Guest), Byers (Bruce Harwood), and Ed Meecham (Jack Rader)

An escaped elephant seems responsible for killing a federal construction worker and destroying property. Witnesses saw no animals. Mulder and Scully investigate a zoo.

## Deconstruction and Notes

Willa said Sophie signed, "Baby/ go flying/ light," but it looked more like "Baby/ finish/ light," with no sign for "flying." Mulder shows Willa what Sophie said before disappearing as "he/ god/ help/ he/ god," but the sign in the middle was "save" not "help."

The aliens would have to take animals twice, to artificially inseminate them and then "harvest" the embryo. There would be little evidence of a pregnancy only a few hours after the insemination. Why didn't the aliens have problems returning them the first time?

Why were all the kidnapped animals returned outside the zoo except for the tiger returned inside while

---

## Episode Locations

1. Bellefleur, OR (Pilot)
2. Ellens Air Force Base, ID (Deep Throat)
3. Baltimore, MD (Squeeze)
4. Sioux City, IA (Conduit)
5. Atlantic City, NJ (Jersey Devil)
6. Philadelphia, PA (Shadows)
7. Crystal City, VA (Ghost in the Machine)
8. Icy Cape, AK (Ice)
9. Houston, TX (Space)
10. Townsend, WI (Fallen Angel)
11. Marin County, CA (Eve)
12. Cape Cod, MA (Fire)
13. Raleigh, NC (Beyond the Sea)
14. Steveston, MA (Genderbender)
15. Baltimore, MD (Lazarus)
16. Tashmoo Prison, PA (Young at Heart)
17. Mattawa, WA (E.B.E.)
18. Kenwood, TN (Miracle Man)
19. Browning, MT (Shapes)
20. Olympic National Forest, WA (Darkness Falls)
21. Baltimore, MD (Tooms)
22. Buffalo, NY (Born Again)
23. Colson, WA (Roland)
24. Georgetown, MD (Erlenmeyer Flask)
25. Arecibo, Puerto Rico (Little Green Men)
26. Newark, NJ (The Host)
27. Franklin, PA (Blood)
28. New York, NY (Sleepless)

29. Marion, VA (Duane Barry)
30. Skyland Mountain, VA (Ascension)
31. Los Angeles, CA (3)
32. Georgetown, MD (One Breath)
33. Mt. Avalon, WA (Firewalker)
34. Delta Glen, WI (Red Museum)
35. Worcester, MA (Excelsis Dei)
36. Aubrey, MO (Aubrey)
37. Minneapolis, MN (Irresistible)
38. Milford Haven, NH (Die Hand Die Verletzt)
39. Folkstone, NC (Fresh Bones)
40. Germantown, MD (Colony)
41. Deadhorse, AK (End Game)
42. Fairfield, ID (Fearful Symmetry)
43. Tildeskan, Norway (Dod Kalm)
44. Gibsonton, FL (Humbug)
45. Arlington, VA (The Calusari)
46. Cumberland Prison, VA (F. Emasculata)
47. Richmond, VA (Soft Light)
48. Dudley, AR (Our Town)
49. Farmington, NM (Anasazi)
50. New Mexico and Washington, DC (The Blessing Way)
51. Washington, DC and West Virginia (Paperclip)
52. Connerville, OK (D.P.O.)
53. St. Paul, MN (Clyde Bruckman's Final Repose)

54. Leon County, FL (The List)
55. Cleveland, OH (2Shy)
56. Ft. Evanston, MA (The Walk)
57. Seattle, WA (Oubliette)
58. Knoxville, TN/Allentown, PA (Nisei)
59. Perkey, WV (731)
60. Coveland, OH (Revelations)
61. Miller's Grove, MA (War of the Coprophages)
62. Town of Comity, Caryl County, NH (SYZYGY)
63. George Washington University, Washington, D.C., and Virginia (Grotesque)
64. Pacific Ocean, Latitude 42 degrees N, Longitude 141 degrees E., San Diego and San Francisco, CA (Piper Maru)
65. (Flashback) Navy Hospital, Pearl Harbor, Hawaii.(Current Time) Mostly Washington, D.C. (Apocrypha)
66. Multiple locations in Virginia (Pusher)
67. Ecuadorian Highlands, South America/Boston, MA (Teso Dos Bichos)
68. Chinatown, San Francisco, CA (Hell Money)
69. Klass County, WA (Jose Chung's 'From Outer Space')
70. Washington, D.C. (Avatar)
71. Striker's Cove, GA (Quagmire)
72. Braddock Heights, MA (Wet Wired)
73. Arlington, VA (and Providence) (Talitha Cumi)
74. Bond Mill Road, MA (Herrenvolk)

that WAO guy was prowling around. How did it get outside of the zoo gates?

If Willa hits the tiger with the dart gun, the cat won't arrive for another few minutes, so walking in by herself was stupid, especially for a zookeeper.

Mulder explains why the animals reappear some distance from the zoo, and says something about the aliens not having the astrological coordinates right. If Mulder doesn't know the difference between astrology and astronomy, how can anyone take his alien theories seriously?

The title of the episode is from the William Blake poem "The Tyger." The building where the tiger is eventually captured is owned by Blake Towers.

## 2.19 "DOD KALM"

**Writer:** Howard Gordon and Alex Gansa
Story: Howard Gordon
**Director:** Rob Bowman
**Original Broadcast:** 3/10/95
**Guest Cast:** Halverson (Mar Anderson), Lieutenant Richard Harper (Dmitry Chepovetsky), Captain Barclay (David Cubitt), Ionesco (Stephen Dimopoulos), Olafsson (Vladimir Kulich), Sailer (John McConnach), Nurse (Bob Metcalfe), Burke (Claire Riley), and Henry Trondheim (John Savage)

A boat is found with survivors of the *U.S.S. Argent*, a ship lost in the Norwegian counterpart to the Bermuda Triangle. Mulder notices that the sailors aged decades in days.

## Deconstruction and Notes

Eliminating free-radicals would stop aging, but how did they reverse it at the end of the show?

If Mulder's dehydration, due to his seasickness, contributes to his aging to the point where even untainted water won't help him, why would drinking alcohol, something that can seriously dehydrate you, extend the life of the captain? It can't be that he didn't drink the water, since he was obviously exposed to the agent.

The ship they were on was not American, but Canadian.

Why cast a Russian as a Norwegian? When Henry Trondheim interrogates Halvorsen, supposedly in

Norwegian, it took Norwegian subtitles to understand what he said. The guy playing Trondheim was easier to understand.

The ship is decrepit, the engine is unrecognizable, everything is covered with residue, and people turn into salt, but the flashlights don't corrode, decay, or run out of power.

Mulder is looking at a map and talking about the disappearances of several boats, when he says that one of the boats left Leeds and points at Great Britain. Leeds lies inland and lacks a port.

## 2.20 "HUMBUG"

**Writer:** Darin Morgan
**Director:** Kim Manners
**Original Broadcast:** 3/31/95
**Guest Cast:** Mr. Nutt (Michael Anderson), Curator (Alex Diakun), Sheriff Hamilton (Wayne Grace), Jerald Glazebrook (John Payne), Dr. Blockhead aka Jeffrey Swaim (Jim Rose), Lanny (Vincent Schiavelli), Waiter (Debis Simpson), Glazebrook [older] (Blair Slater), Hepcat Helm (George Tipple), and Glazebrook [younger] (Devin Walker)

Mulder and Scully investigate ritualistic killings, including the most recent death of the "alligator man," a sideshow act.

## Deconstruction and Notes

Scully pretends to eat a bug. She takes the bug with her right hand, but when she shows Mulder the bug, it is in her left hand.

## 2.21 "THE CALUSARI"

**Writer:** Sara Charno
**Director:** Michael Vejar
**Original Broadcast:** 4/14/95
**Guest Cast:** Charlie/Michael Holvey (Joel Palmer), Golda (Lilyan Chauvin), Maggie Holvey (Helena Clarkson), Dr. Charles Burk (Bill Dow), Head Calusari (Kay E. Kuter), Steve Holvey (Ric Reid), Teddy Holvey (Oliver and Jeremy Isaac Wildsmith), and Agent Karen E. Kosseff (Christine Willes)

A photograph of a recently murdered two-year-old boy points to supernatural intervention. After the dead boy's grandmother dies, the remaining grandchild requests the aid of Romanian ritualists to cleanse the home of evil.

## Deconstruction and Notes

In the scene at the amusement park, Charlie's dad has two ice cream cones in his left hand. One has two scoops on it, the other has one. He begins to hand the one with two scoops to Charlie. The camera then cuts to an angle from Charlie's perspective, and Charlie takes the one-scoop cone from his Dad's hand.

When Charlie is questioned by Karen Kosseff, the FBI social worker, they sit in a playschool. A big yellow toy fish "faces" the door. Mulder appears behind the two-way mirror, then the big yellow fish tail faces the door. Behind the mirror, through the glass, the yellow fish head faces the door. Later when Charlie suffers an attack, Mulder and Scully rush into the room and the yellow fish tail faces the door.

# 2.22 "F. EMASCULATA"

**Writer:** Chris Carter and Howard Gordon
**Director:** Michael Bowman
**Original Broadcast:** 4/28/95
**Guest Cast:** Cigarette-Smoking Man (William B. Davis), Paul (John Pyper-Ferguson), U.S. Marshal Tapia (Dean Norris), Dr. Simon Auerbach (Morris Panych), Dr. Osbourne (Charles Martin Smith), Steve (John Tench), and Angelo Garza (Angelo Vacco)

Mulder and Scully watch the retrieval of two escaped convicts in a penitentiary. They find that a highly contagious, lethal disease has infected inmates, and possibly the two escapees.

## Deconstruction and Notes

Wrong Aseptic Technique Part I: Scully puts on a mask and gloves. She should wear a surgical suit.

Wrong Aseptic Technique Part II: Scully reaches out with her tweezers to pick up the bug out of the pustule on the dead prisoner, without her mask on. When she looks at the bug, she has her mask on.

The guy in the jungle at the beginning finds an animal with pustules. The animal has a gray elephant-like hide and tusks, yet there are no elephants in the rain forests of Costa Rica, nor warthogs or wild boar. A feral pig would have hair.

Huge beetlelike critters crawl on the corpses of the animal and the scientist. These insects are called "Madagascar hissing cockroaches," but the island of Madagascar lies off the coast of Africa, not Central America.

# 2.23 "SOFT LIGHT"

**Writer:** Vince Gilligan
**Director:** James Contner
**Original Broadcast:** 5/5/94
**Guest Cast:** Government Scientist (Forbes Angus), Second Officer (Steve Bacic), Detective Barron (Nathaniel Deveaux), Barney (Guyle Frazier), Dr. Christopher Davey (Kevin McNulty), Doctor (Robert Rozen), Dr. Chester Ray Banton (Tony Shalhoub), Detective Kelly Ryan (Kate Twa), X (Steven Williams), and Night Nurse (Donna Yamamoto)

Mulder and Scully are asked by one of Scully's ex-students to help with her first investigation concerning disappearances. They investigate spontaneous human combustion.

## Deconstruction and Notes

When a person stepped into Chester's shadow, the person and their clothes were swallowed by the "dark matter." Why didn't the moving black hole swallow other matter it contacted, including the floor?

When Mulder and Scully are chasing Chester, train markings indicate it's for VIA rail. VIA only runs in Canada!

Dr. Banton unscrews two burning light bulbs with his bare hands.

When the two cops confront Banton in the alley, his strong shadow shines only one way. A cop steps on it and vaporizes. Then the other cop on the other side dies the same way, but the lighting didn't change.

When Banton's former partner at Polarity Magnetics tells Scully about their experiments with quarks and gluons and mesons, and such, she says that nobody knows for sure whether they exist. Every physics student knows they do.

After the meeting with Dr. Chris Davey, Mulder sits in the train station trying to figure out what Dr. Benton was doing in the video. An overhead shot of the station shows a column in the far distance. The shot never loses sight of the column, and random passersby walk toward the column, but no Scully appears. As the camera moves downward to focus on Mulder in the foreground, Scully suddenly appears from behind the column, as if she had been walking toward it all this while.

The rookie detective became a small pile of ash, but there was a coffin at the funeral.

When Mulder and Scully are interrogating Banton, he says his shadow "changes matter into energy." Assuming the average person weighs at least 140 pounds, this would produce about 6 million million million joules of energy, a bit more than a faint blue glow on the ground. It would blast a large chunk out of the planet.

## 2.24 "OUR TOWN"

**Writer:** Frank Spotnitz
**Director:** Rob Bowman
**Original Broadcast:** 5/12/94
**Guest Cast:** Sheriff Tom Arens (Gary Grubbs), Doris Kearns (Caroline Kava), George Kearns (John MacLaren), Creighton Jones (Hrothgar Matthews), Walter Chaco (John Milford), Paula Gray (Gabrielle Miller), Dr. Vance Randolph (Robin Mossley), and Jess Harold (Timothy Webber)

Mulder and Scully go to Dudley, Arkansas, to find a missing poultry inspector. An insane poultry worker is shot after giving a lead.

## Deconstruction and Notes

When Scully is doing the autopsy, the scene shows her looking at a slide of Paula's brain through a microscope. How did she obtain brain matter without cutting her head open?

Scully said that the disease wasn't communicable or degenerative, so how did the people in the town get

it if they didn't eat the heads that were cut off and locked up in Mr. Chaco's cupboard?

The people contracted Creutzfeldt-Jakob disease (CJD), and it showed up in the brain tissue within a matter of weeks, but it takes several years to show up.

## 2.A "THE SECRETS OF THE X-FILES"

**Writer:** Ron Scalera and Bart Montgomery
**Original Broadcast:** 5/19/95
**Narrator:** Richard Courtney

A one-hour retrospective on the show.

## 2.25 "ANASAZI"

**Writer:** Chris Carter
Story: David Duchovny and Chris Carter
**Director:** R.W. Goodwin
**Original Broadcast:** 5/19/95
**Guest Cast:** Frohike (Tom Braidwood), Thinker aka Kenneth Soona (Bernie Coulson), Cigarette-Smoking Man (William B. Davis), Antonio (Aurelio Dinunzio), Bill Mulder (Peter Donat), Langly (Dean Haglund), Byers (Bruce Harwood), Agent Alex Krycek (Nicholas Lea), Agent Kautz (Paul McLean), Father (Byron Chief Moon), Josephine Doane (Renae Morriseau), Senior Agent (Michael David Simms), and Albert Hosteen (Floyd "Red Crow" Westerman)

Mulder acts strangely, risking Scully's trust. The Lone Gunmen direct him to a hacker who broke into secret files. Scully investigates Mulder's actions, while the Cigarette-Smoking Man becomes involved. The first of three parts.

## Deconstruction and Notes

When the Lone Gunmen visit Mulder, they hear a gunshot from outside, and Mulder immediately rushes out to investigate. He runs to the old woman's apartment and finds that she has shot her husband. The police arrive about ten to fifteen seconds after Mulder. How could they get there so quickly?

Scully goes to see the woman at the Navajo nation offices to have the file translated. As Scully stands up to leave, the reflection of a boom mike moves in one of the picture frames on the wall directly in front of her.

When Mulder and Scully are looking at the coded files in their office, after Mulder goes to see Skinner, he does not have his suit coat, but when he sees Skinner, he has it on.

Mulder decks Skinner, gets hauled in front of the FBI's version of a court martial, and is threatened with suspension without a chance for reinstatement. Wouldn't the FBI conduct a mental and physical exam before invoking such extreme punishment? Wouldn't a physical include blood and urine tests, indicating the foreign substance?

What happens after Scully shoots Mulder? How does a petite woman handle an unconscious six-foot-tall man?

When Mulder wakes up after being shot by Scully, she states that he's been out for thirty-six hours. He was pretty well shaven for a guy who's been out of commission for that long.

Mulder calls Scully from his father's house after he was killed. He has blood over his hands, but when he gets to Scully's place, his hands are clean. When did he wash?

When the boy opens the door to the boxcar, there is dirt everywhere, but when the army stands on the top of the car, all the dirt has been swept away.

Scully's name still isn't on the door to the basement office, even after two years of being teamed with Mulder.

# CHAPTER 16

# SEASON THREE:
# 1995–1996 EPISODES

## 3.1 "THE BLESSING WAY"

**Writer:** Chris Carter
**Director:** R. W. Goodwin
**Original Broadcast:** 9/22/95
**Guest Cast:** M.D. (Forbes Angus), Frohike (Tom Braidwood), Luis Cardinal aka Hispanic Man (Lenno Britos), Camouflage Man (Mitchell Davies), Cigarette-Smoking Man (William B. Davis), William Mulder (Peter Donat), Security Guard (Ernie Foort), Tour Guide (Benita Ha), Deep Throat (Jerry Hardin), Eric Hosteen (Dakota House), Dr. Mark Pomerantz (Alf Humphreys), Margaret Scully (Sheila Larken), Agent Alex Krycek (Nicholas Lea), Melissa Scully (Melinda McGraw), Well-Manicured Man (John Neville), Senior FBI Agent (Michael David Simms), Mrs. Mulder (Rebecca Toolan), Minister (Ian Victor), Albert Hosteen (Floyd "Red Crow" Westerman), and Elder (Don S. Williams)

A supposed dead man stops Cigarette-Smoking Man from recovering stolen computer files. Mulder fights for survival while Scully turns to her family for help. The second of three parts.

## Deconstruction and Notes

In the "Anasazi," a bullet intended for Mulder grazed Scully across the forehead, shedding blood. In "Blessing Way," no scar or mark of any kind appears.

Soldiers get out of a helicopter to search Scully's car, but it's a civilian helicopter. They're all wearing desert camouflage BDU's, but permission to wear them is rare. The male soldier searches Scully, while the female checks the trunk. The female should've performed the search of a woman.

In both "The Blessing Way" and "Paper Clip," everyone searches for the computer backup tape referred to as a DAT (digital audio tape), but the tape is a DC2120 tape, commonly used in QIC-80-style drives, such as the Colorado and Conner, not a DAT.

There is an easy way to copy any tape using commercial programs or shareware programs for the job. Simply tap the stream of characters going to the screen. Even if the reading program uses direct hardware access, there is still an IRQ activated to acknowledge the character, so you either tap the character stream before running the program or the ACK IRQ and dump it to a file. Most computer magazines have advertisements for Renju, Last Resort, Dumper, and so on that are used when something doesn't save or crashes.

Mulder displayed the secret files on screen. Doesn't his computer have a "Print Screen" key?

If the Thinker's purpose was to distribute the information, why did he encode his copy?

Navajo scholars alerted the producers to cultural inaccuracies in "Anasazi," and they invited Carter to attend a Navajo night chant and the Native American Church Peyote Ritual in preparing "Blessing Way," which is named for an actual chant.

Krycek, played by Nicholas Lea, helped shoot Melissa Scully, played by his real-life girlfriend, Melinda McGraw.

A tag at the end reads: "In Memoriam. Larry Wells. 1946–1995." Wells was a costume designer for *The X-Files*.

## 3.2 "PAPER CLIP"

**Writer:** Chris Carter
**Director:** Rob Bowman
**Original Broadcast:** 9/29/95
**Guest Cast:** Frohike (Tom Braidwood), Cigarette-Smoking Man (William B. Davis), Victor Klemper (Walter Gotell), Langly (Dean Haglund), Byers (Bruce Harwood), Margaret Scully (Sheila Larken), Agent Alex Krycek (Nicholas Lea), Well-Manicured Man (John Neville), Mrs. Mulder (Rebecca Toolan), and Albert Hosteen (Floyd "Red Crow" Westerman)

Mulder and Scully encounter a pardoned ex-Nazi scientist with valuable information. The last of three parts.

### Deconstruction and Notes

The big secret had an unlocked back door. If they needed the code to get in the front, the back entrance would be similarly guarded; instead it just had a clap-trap wooden door.

Skinner claimed he couldn't copy or print out the encrypted data downloaded by the hacker, but Scully and Mulder gave the Navaho code talker a copy of the file to decode. Did Scully and Mulder hand copy the entire file in code off the screen while Mulder was still recovering? How then did Scully get a hard copy for both the woman in the office in Washington, D.C., and the code talker to look at?

Werner von Braun was not a part of Paperclip, but defected before the end of the war.

If Albert knows what the file says, why doesn't he tell Mulder and Scully?

The "Well-Manicured Man" directs Mulder and Scully to the mining company in West Virginia, and he even hints at the access code. He asks, "Do you know what Napier's constant is?" Scully replies, "Yes." When the agents get to the mining company, they start entering the code "27828" as the PIN access code, explaining that Napier's constant is the base for all natural logarithms. This is true. However, Napier's constant is 2.71828; the five-digit code should have been 27182, not 27828.

Mulder was shot in the shoulder and then stranded in the desert for over a day. Then he kicks in his door and aims a gun at Skinner as if nothing had happened. When Mulder runs outside to see the spacecraft, he leaves the door open, but when he goes back to the door, it is closed. There was no wind.

At the mine, Mulder drives a blue car similar to Scully's, but later, when they escape, it is not shown how they got to the diner. Later yet, at the diner, Skinner takes them home in his car. What became of their car?

In "Conduit," the X-File on Samantha Mulder's disappearance gives her name as Samantha T. Mulder. The medical file in the mountain in "Paper Clip" has her listed as Samantha Ann Mulder. In "Conduit," her birthdate was shown as 1/22/64. Here it is 11/21/65.

This episode ends with a dedication: "In Memoriam. Mario Mark Kennedy. 1966-1995." Kennedy was a major fan of the series who had organized America Online discussion sessions. He died about a month after getting hit by a car.

## 3.3 "D.P.O."

**Writer:** Howard Gordon
**Director:** Kim Manners
**Original Broadcast:** 10/6/95
**Guest Cast:** Stan Buxton (Peter Anderson), Jack Hammond (Mar Andersons), Zero (Jack Black), Traffic Cop (Brent Chapman), First Paramedic (Jason Anthony Griffith), Night Nurse (Bonnie Hay), Sheriff Teller (Ernie Lively), Frank Kiveat (Steve Makaj), Darren Peter Oswald (Giovanni Ribisi), Mrs. Oswald (Kate Robbins), and Sharon Kiveat (Karen Witter)

Mulder and Scully investigate a person killed by lightning in a small Oklahoma town, the fifth in a series. Their investigation leads to the only person to have survived a lightning strike.

### Deconstruction and Notes

DPO shows control over electrical appliances, including changing the traffic lights and restarting someone's heart. This would require knowledge of circuitry and voltage. Darren, a remedial student, is unlikely to know this information.

## 3.4 "CLYDE BRUCKMAN'S FINAL REPOSE"

**Writer:** Darin Morgan
**Director:** David Nutter
**Original Broadcast:** 10/13/95
**Guest Cast:** Photographer (Greg Anderson), Clyde Bruckman (Peter Boyle), The Stupendous Yappi (Jaap Broeker), Detective Cline (Frank Cassini), Puppet (Stu Charno), Tarot Dealer (Alex Diakun), Madame Zelma (Karin Konoval), Detective Havez (Dwight McFee), Mr. Gordon (David McKay), and Clerk (Ken Roberts)

A psychic predicts the murder of prognosticators.

## Deconstruction and Notes

In his dream, Clyde Bruckman says he is "lying naked in a field of red tulips," but he's wearing a T-shirt and underwear in the dream.

Bruckman asks Mulder if a blue piece of cloth he holds is from his New York Knicks T-shirt, a reference to "Beyond the Sea."

Clyde Bruckman plays poker with Scully and holds a "dead man's hand," aces and eights.

Clyde Bruckman worked with silent film star Buster Keaton. The episode included many references to Keaton, who, along with Bruckman, Jean Havez, Eddie Kline (Havez and Kline were used as names for detectives in the episode), and Joseph Mitchell, formed a team of silent film writers and gagmen. Keaton usually directed, but Bruckman sometimes codirected. Keaton's film *The General* was based on a book he received from Bruckman. The real Bruckman also committed suicide.

## 3.5 "THE LIST"

**Writer:** Chris Carter
**Director:** Chris Carter
**Original Broadcast:** 10/20/95
**Guest Cast:** Key Guard (Denny Arnold), Guard (Craig Brunanski), Napoleon "Neech" Manley (Badja Djola), Chaplain (Joseph Patrick Finn), Vincent Parmelly (Ken Foree), Danielle Manley (April Grace), Fornier (Mitch Kosterman), Perry Simon (Bruce Pinard), Ullrich (Paul Raskin), Danny Charez (Greg Rogers), John Speranza (John Toles-Bey), Warden Leo Brodeur (J.T. Walsh), and Sammon Roque (Bokeem Woodbine)

A man threatens to return from the dead to avenge his execution. After a prison guard dies, everyone fears they are on his list of five targets.

## Deconstruction and Notes

An electrocution causes eyes to protrude and bleed from the corners. Neech's eyes remain shut. A mouthguard prevents biting the protruding tongue. Neech gritted his teeth. They don't fasten an electrode on each side of the head, but put one on the head and the other on the lower leg, so electricity will flow through and stop the heart.

## 3.6 "2 SHY"

**Writer:** Jeffrey Vlaming
**Director:** David Nutter
**Original Broadcast:** 11/3/95
**Guest Cast:** Virgil Incanto (Timothy Carhart), Monica (Glynis Davies), Detective Alan Cross (James Handy), Jennifer (Suzy Joachim), Lauren MacKalvey (Randi Lynne), Agent Kazanjian (William MacDonald), Jesse (Aloka McLean), Ellen Kaminsky (Catherine Paolone), and Joanne Steffen (Kerry Sandomirsky)

A serial killer seduces shy women met through an online service. A strange substance that digests fatty acids in flesh coats the victims.

## Deconstruction and Notes

The First District Police Headquarters building in Washington, D.C., fills in as the establishing shots for the Cleveland police headquarters.

The substance stuck in people's mouths gave one woman chemical burns. Scully pulls the goo out of the woman's mouth but doesn't get burned. Later Mulder and Scully touch hydrochloric acid, which should immediately eat through their skin.

Scully says the autopsy date is August 29, but DPO and Clyde Bruckman's Final Repose are set in September.

The first victim's roommate tells Mulder about the online service. He immediately calls Scully and tells her that he has already called the online service! When did he have time to do that?

Why did Ellen lock Encanto in her apartment when she was nervous about having him coming late at night?

## 3.7 "THE WALK"

**Writer:** John Shiban
**Director:** Rob Bowman
**Original Broadcast:** 11/10/95
**Guest Cast:** Frances Callahan (Andrea Barclay), Quinton "Roach" Freely (Willie Garson), Army Doctor (Deryl Hayes), General Thomas Callahan (Thomas Kopache), Trevor Callahan (Brennan Kotowich), Amputee (Rob Lee), Ward Nurse (Paula Shaw), Captain Janet Draper (Nancy Sorel), Lt. Colonel Victor Stans (Don Thompson), Leonard "Rappo" Trimble (Ian Tracey), and Burly Nurse (Beatrice Zeilinger)

A "phantom soldier" prevents an attempted suicide in a military hospital. The General opposes an FBI investigation until the invisible killer stalks him. The primary suspect is a quadraplegic.

## Deconstruction and Notes

The two-star general wears unit crests on shoulder loops on green class "A"s. According to AR (Army Regulation) 670-1, general officers wear only rank on the shoulder loops, but GO's do have freedom to modify their uniforms.

---

### Season Three Awards

Cinematographer John Bartley nominated for an Outstanding Achievement Award by American Society of Cinematographers for his work on "731"

Cinema Audio Society Award nomination for Outstanding Series for "Humbug"

Nominated for an Edgar Award by the Mystery Writers of America for "Humbug" (Darin Morgan)

British Academy of Film and Television Arts award for Best TV Show

Producer's Guild Award nomination for Best Episodic Show

Director's Guild award nomination for Best Television Drama for the episode "The List" (Chris Carter)

Screen Actor's Guild Award nomination for Outstanding Performance by a Male Actor in a Dramatic Series (David Duchovny)

Screen Actor's Guild Award for Outstanding Performance by a Female Actor in a Dramatic Series (Gillian Anderson)

Telegatto Award (Italy) for best television show

Quality Awards nominations:

- Best Drama
- Best Actor in a Drama (David Duchovny)
- Best Actress in a Drama (Gillian Anderson)

Golden Globe Awards:

- Best Actor in a Dramatic Series (David Duchovny)
- Best Actress in a Dramatic Series (Gillian Anderson)
- Best Dramatic Series

Emmy nominations:

- Outstanding Individual Achievement in Art Direction for a Series (Art Director: Graeme Murray; Set Decorator: Shirley Inget—"Jose Chung's 'From Outer Space'")
- Outstanding Drama Series

- Outstanding Lead Actress in a Drama Series (Gillian Anderson)

Emmy awards (5 total wins, the most for a drama series in 1996):

- Outstanding Sound Editing for a Series ("Nisei")
- Outstanding Sound Mixing for a Drama Series (Production Mixer: Michael Williamson; Re-Recording Mixers: David J. West, Nello Torri, and Doug Turner—"Nisei")
- Outstanding Writing in a Drama Series (Darin Morgan—"Clyde Bruckman's Final Repose")
- Outstanding Guest Actor in a Drama Series (Peter Boyle—"Clyde Bruckman's Final Repose")
- Outstanding Individual Achievement in Cinematography for a Series (John S. Bartley—"Grotesque")

The female adjutant appears to be wearing infantry branch insignia on her green class As. Women cannot enlist or be commissioned into the infantry.

Everyone calls the lieutenant colonel, "Lieutenant Colonel," but AR 670-1 states that the proper way to address a lieutenant colonel is "Colonel."

Uniformed MP's and plainclothes security agents would guard the threatened general's quarters.

Trees surround the exterior of the police station labeled "substation B." The Allentown, Pennsylvania, police station has no trees and is not sectioned off alphabetically.

## 3.8 "OUBLIETTE"

**Writer:** Charles Grant Craig
**Director:** Kim Manners
**Original Broadcast:** 11/17/95
**Guest Cast:** Myra Jacobs (Sidonie Boll), Carl Wade (Michael Chieffo), Lucy Householder (Tracey Ellis), Mr. Larken (David Fredericks), Henry (Jacques LaLonde), Special Agent Walt Eubanks (Ken Ryan), Fast Food Supervisor (Dolly Scarr), Amy Jacobs (Jewel Staite), and Tow Truck Driver (Dean Wray)

A former kidnap victim experiences everything another young girl who's been kidnapped miles away feels. Mulder believes she may be the key to finding the missing girl.

### Deconstruction and Notes

Mulder and Scully talk about the blood on Lucy's blouse. Amy is B+. Mulder claims that one in five people have this blood type (20 percent). This is not true. According to the American Association of Blood Banks Technical Manual (11th Edition), only 6.6 percent of the population would be B+.

They stop CPR on the drowned girl after just a few seconds. Drowning victims, particularly cold-water drowning, have been revived up to forty-five minutes after commencing CPR. Dr. Scully should have known this.

## 3.9 "NISEI"

**Writers:** Chris Carter, Howard Gordon, and Frank Spotnitz
**Director:** David Nutter
**Original Broadcast:** 11/24/95
**Guest Cast:** Penny (Gillian Barber), Senator Richard Matheson (Raymond J. Barry), Agent Pendrell (Brendan Beiser), Frohike (Tom Braidwood), Langly (Dean Haglund), Byers (Bruce Harwood), Dr. Takeo Ishimaru (Robert Ito), Lottie Holloway (Corrine Koslo), Red-Haired Man (Stephen McHattie), Coast Guard Officer (Paul McLean), Kazuo Sakurai (Yasuo Sakurai), Diane (Lori Triolo), and X (Steven Williams)

A high-ranking Japanese diplomat apparently murders the distributor of a mail-order videotape showing an alien autopsy. Mulder tries to learn more about the video while complete strangers recognize Scully. The first of two parts.

### Deconstruction and Notes

The murderer appears to go into the women's bathroom at the bus depot. The stick figure on the door of the bathroom wears a dress.

When Senator Richard Matheson tells Mulder that four Japanese Nationals have been murdered, Matheson says that the murders had occurred several weeks before, but Mulder later tells Scully that someone must have identified the four doctors who performed the autopsy because they were murdered the day before.

Mulder now has a strap-on gun because so many people on the Internet newsgroup had mentioned the fact that Mulder is constantly losing his gun.

## 3.10 "731"

**Writer:** Frank Spotnitz
**Director:** Rob Bowman
**Original Broadcast:** 12/1/95
**Guest Cast:** Agent Pendrell (Brenden Beiser), Escalante (Colin Cunningham), Cigarette-Smoking Man (William B. Davis), Dr. Shiro Zama aka Dr. Takeo Ishimaru (Robert Ito), Red-Haired

Man (Stephen McHattie), Conductor (Michael Puttonen), Elder (Don S. Williams), and X (Steven Williams)

Mulder is trapped on a train with a Japanese scientist and the man sent to kill him, while Scully investigates the implant removed from her neck. The second of two parts.

## Deconstruction and Notes

Mulder runs the card through the door lock backwards, but if the magnetized strip isn't in contact with the scanner, there's nothing to scan.

The producers only wrote one page of text, then they copied it over and over again to make up the rest of the Japanese scientist's diary. The one page, however, is authentic Japanese written for the production; the word *uchuu-jin*, meaning "alien" (lit., "outer space-person"), appears in the text.

## 3.11 "REVELATIONS"

**Writer:** Kim Newton
**Director:** David Nutter
**Original Broadcast:** 12/15/95
**Guest Cast:** Owen Lee Jarvis (Michael Berryman), Michael Kryder (Sam Bottoms), Priest (Fulvio Cecerk), Reverend Finley (R. Lee Ermy), Carina Maywald (Lesley Ewen), Mrs. Tynes (Nicole Robert), Susan Kryder (Hayley Tyson), Simon Gates (Kenneth Welsh), and Kevin Kryder (Kevin Zegers)

Mulder and Scully protect a young stigmatic boy in Ohio from a fanatic who murdered eleven alleged stigmatics.

## Deconstruction and Notes

Why was Kevin removed from his mother's custody so quickly after he started bleeding in school? The teacher and all the kids saw him start to bleed in front of the classroom, when he hadn't been bleeding before that. The mother was not around, so how could they think she caused it? It takes more than one question-able incident before social services will remove a child.

People were not crucified by having nails hammered through the palms of their hands to a cross. Victims were nailed just below the wrist, since this is the place that can support a human body. The marks on the boy are in the wrong place.

The stigmata appeared on both sides of the little boy's hands, just like the wounds of Jesus. However, when the rich guy falls into the grinder, and Scully rescues the boy, the bandages are on the back of his hand.

The boy's father is in an institution, presumably in the U.S. His medication list includes haloperidol, loxapine, and chlorpromazine, which make sense, but the fourth medication, Largactil, is in error. It is a brand-name of chlorpromazine, thus a duplication, and not available in the United States.

When Scully is in the school nurse's office with the little boy whose hands are bleeding, she asks the school nurse if the boy's temperature has been taken. The nurse pulls out a red-tipped thermometer and sticks it in the boy's mouth. That's a rectal thermometer. Blue thermometers are oral.

## 3.12 "WAR OF THE COPROPHAGES"

**Writer:** Darin Morgan
**Director:** Kim Manners
**Original Broadcast:** 1/5/96
**Guest Cast:** Customer #2 (Sean Allan), Sheriff Frass (Dion Anderson), Dr. Jeff Eckerle (Raye Birk), Dr. Bugger (Alex Bruhanski), Dude (Alan Buckley), Dr. Newton (Bill Dow), Customer #1 (Maria Herrera), Resident #1 (Tom Heaton), Dr. Inanov (Ken Kramer), Stoner (Tyler Labine), Chick (Nicole Parker), Dr. Bambi Berenbaum (Bobbie Phillips), Orderly (Wren Robertz), Customer #5 (Fiona Roeske), Resident #2 (Bobby L. Stewart), Customer #4 (Dawn Stofer), and Reporter (Norma Wick)

Cockroaches kill residents of a Massachusetts town.

## Deconstruction and Notes

The credits list Dr. Bambi as "Chick."

Mulder tells Scully about the roach exterminator being killed by roaches, and mentions two other deaths. Later he says she was right about all the deaths, only listing the ones shown and making no mention of the first two.

It's hard to distinguish error from joke in this episode. Dr. Ekerle's office window at the Alternative Fuel Research Plant reads: "Dr. Jeff Ekerle—chief science officer." Shouldn't it be: "Chief Research Scientist"? Don't know what he would be an officer of.

This episode paid homage to the film *War of the Worlds*. The town, Miller's Grove, mirrors Grover's Mill in the movie. The mass hysteria is the same in both instances. The sailor grabbing chocolate and pantyhose recalls World War II imagery.

*Breakfast at Tiffany's*, the book Scully reads, is an in-joke. David Duchovny missed this *Final Jeopardy* answer. It cost him the game.

The television news reporter, Skye Leikin, is that of an AOL X-Phile, whose screen name is Leikin Skye. She won an AOL trivia contest to get her screen name on an episode.

Robotics researcher, A. Ivanov, is named in tribute to science fiction writer Isaac Asimov, creator of the "laws of robotics."

Dr. Bambi Berenbaum is named for Dr. May R. Berenbaum, head of the Entomology Department at the University of Illinois and author of many books on insects.

## 3.13 "SYZYGY"

**Writer:** Chris Carter
**Director:** Rob Bowman
**Original Broadcast:** 1/26/96
**Guest Cast:** Margi Kleinjan (Wendy Benson), Minister (Ryk Brown), Bob Spitz (Garry Davey), Dr. Richard W. Godfrey (Tim Dixon), Terri Roberts (Lisa Robin Kelly), Brenda Summerfield (Gabrielle Miller), Scott Simmons (Russell Porter), Eric Bauer (Jeremy Radick), Jay "Boom" DeBoom (Ryan Reynolds), Detective Angela White (Dana Wheeler-Nicholson), and Zirinka (Denalda Williams)

A Satanic cult may have murdered small town high school students. An astrologer insists conflict between the investigating Mulder and Scully and the townsfolk is written in the stars.

## Deconstruction and Notes

Scully says she has been working with Mulder for two years. The pilot aired in March of 1992; they've been working together for four years.

Stellar objects do not follow human time schedules. Mulder looks at the clock on the wall as the two girls are dueling it out. At the exact sound of midnight, everything stops.

Syzygy means planetary alignment or other cosmic alignments that have significance in many different professions. This is usually an astronomy term.

## 3.14 "GROTESQUE"

**Writer:** Howard Gordon
**Director:** Kim Manners
**Original Broadcast:** 2/2/96
**Guest Cast:** Agent Sheherlis (Susan Bain), Young Agent (Kasper Michaels), John Mostow (Levani Outchaneichvili), Agent Bill Patterson (Kurtwood Smith), Agent Greg Nemhauser (Greg Thirloway), and Peter (Zoran Vukelic)

The arrest of an artist claiming possession by an evil force completes the investigation of the murder of an FBI behavioral scientist. Then the chain of murders continues, forcing Mulder to confront the killer.

## Deconstruction and Notes

When Scully and Mulder enter John Mostow's cell, Scully asks why he is on the floor. Mulder says, "He's been busy." The ground has a drawing of a gargoyle. The man says he drew it. He is in a straitjacket, so how could he draw on the floor, especially without drawing supplies?

Mulder describes a gargoyle as a mythical beast that swam in the Seine. There never was any such legend. Gargoyle is from the French for "water spout," and it gained common usage from the water spouts at Notre Dame. The proper name for what we know as a gargoyle is "grotesque"—the name of the episode.

## 3.15 "PIPER MARU"

**Writers:** Frank Spotnitz and Chris Carter
**Director:** Rob Bowman
**Original Broadcast:** 2/9/96
**Guest Cast:** Jeraldine Kallenchuk (Jo Bates), Dr. Seizer (Paul Batten), Hispanic Man aka Luis Cardinal (Lenno Britos), Commander Johansen (Robert Clothier), Medic (Russell Ferrier), Waitress (Rochelle Greenwood), Alex Krycek (Nicholas Lea), World War II Pilot (Robert F. Maier), Wayne Morgan (Stephen E. Miller), Young Dana (Tegan Moss), Navy Base Guard (David Neale), Gray-Haired Man (Morris Panych), Young Johansen (Tom Scholte), First Engineer (Joel Silverstone), Bernard Gauthier (Ari Solomon), and Joan Gauthier (Kimberly Unger)

Mulder and Scully are interested in the *Talypus* and the *Piper Maru*, ships that suffered mysterious fates after visiting the same location. The crew of the latter ship returned with severe radiation burns. Scully pursues information about the undersea location at the naval base where she grew up. The first of two parts.

## Deconstruction and Notes

The episode was named after Gillian Anderson's daughter.

## 3.16 "APOCRYPHA"

**Writers:** Frank Spotnitz and Chris Carter
**Director:** Kim Manners
**Original Broadcast:** 2/16/96
**Guest Cast:** Agent Pendrell (Brenden Beiser), Frohike (Tom Braidwood), Hispanic Man aka Luis Cardinal (Lenno Britos), First Government Man (Dmitry Chepovetsky), Armed Man (Jeff Chivers), Cigarette-Smoking Man (William B. Davis), Major Domo (Martin Evans), Nurse (Frances Flanagan), Langly (Dean Haglund), Byers (Bruce Harwood), Alex Krycek (Nicholas Lea), Navy Doctor (Barry Levy), Agent Caleca (Sue Mathew), Agent Fuller (Kevin McNulty), Well-Manicured Man (John Neville), Sick Crewman (Peter Scoular), and Elder (Don S. Williams)

Krycek escapes Mulder while Scully investigates Skinner's attacker to solve her sister's murder case. The second of two parts.

**L**anguages Other than English Spoken in The X-Files Creole (Fresh Bones), French (Fresh Bones, Piper Maru), Russian (The Host), Italian, Japanese, and Navajo (Anasazi), Rumanian (The Calusari), Transylvanian (3), Latin and German (Die Hand Die Verletzt), Spanish (Little Green Men, Piper Maru), Norwegian (Dod Kalm), Japanese alone (Nisei, 731), and Chinese (Hell Money).

## Deconstruction and Notes

The miniature submarine in the black-and-white flashback looks like a toy. As it moved away from the camera, it slowly lost focus, something a large ship wouldn't do.

Skinner gets a blood transfusion, but the blood is not on an intravenous delivery pump as it should be. He has cardiac telemetry leads attached to his chest, but no cardiac monitor. The naso-gastric tube (N-G tube) from his nose is placed and taped very poorly, is not attached to a drainage canister, and shows no drainage coming from the tube. If there's nothing there to drain, why place an N-G tube?

Scully says, "Looking for a male . . . with blood type B+ . . . know that from the waitress's description." The waitress can tell the guy's blood type just by looking at him?

Mulder wears a telemetry (cardiac) monitor after being hospitalized for observation after a head injury. This is a young, healthy man with a head injury. Unless he has a cardiac dysrhythmia, he would not have these leads on.

Scully finds Skinner has just been transferred, yet the room is already clean and totally made-up. Skinner is alone in the back of the ambulance with an IV infusing. A nurse accompanies patients with IVs.

The only other person in this "Advanced Life Support Unit" is the driver. There should have been two paramedics/EMTs on the crew, one to drive and one to initiate or administer life support if necessary.

Mulder had passed out when the car crashed into the ditch. He woke up in time to see the bright flash, but wasn't conscious when the agents took Krychek out of the car. Later, in the hospital, Mulder recalls seeing this.

## 3.17 "PUSHER"

**Writer:** Vince Gilligan
**Director:** Rob Bowman
**Original Broadcast:** 2/23/96
**Guest Cast:** Holly (Julia Arkos), Agent Collins (Steve Bacic), Defense Attorney (Meredith Bain Woodward), SWAT Lieutenant (Roger R. Cross), Lobby Guard (Ernie Foort), Lead SWAT Cop (Darren Lucas), Judge (Don MacKay), Deputy Scott Kerber (D. Neil Mark), Agent Frank Burst (Vic Polizos), Prosecutor (Brent Sheppard), and Robert Patrick Modell aka Pusher (Robert Wisden)

An apprehended man escapes after claiming he killed fourteen people for pay, whose deaths had previously been ruled as suicides. The man can control others. He challenges Mulder and Scully by leaving clues.

## Deconstruction and Notes

When Scully, Mulder, and the local police department search the suspect's apartment, the Pusher calls the local detective on the phone and proceeds to "talk the guy to death." Mulder and Scully try to intervene, but are physically restrained by other local police. Odd that low-ranking local officers would interfere with the FBI.

Mulder, Scully, and the SWAT team go to Fairfax Mercy Hospital, actually Fairfax Hospital. The electronic map indicated it on/near Chain Bridge Road in Fairfax County, Virginia, but it is on Gallows Road.

Mulder radioed that he had heard two gunshots and ran toward the sound. He found a hospital technician and the hospital security guard dead of gunshot wounds to the head and guessed that Pusher had willed the guard to shoot the technician and himself. When Mulder viewed the bodies, he saw the guard's revolver and more than two spent casings on the ground near the bodies. Two shots were heard, but there are more than two spent casings, and revolvers don't eject casings. Someone had to open the revolver and empty the spent casings out.

At the end, if the room was full of oxygen for that patient on life support, wouldn't they risk blowing up the room when Mulder shot Pusher?

Scully shows X rays of DNA to Skinner in the hospital. She says they're PCRs. PCR is a DNA replication technique. It creates more DNA. The X rays looked more like RFLPs (Restriction Fragment Length Polymorphisms), a series of bands that constitute a molecular "fingerprint."

The front page of the tabloid newspaper in the grocery store shows a picture of Flukeman from "The Host."

Nirvana drummer and Foo Fighter member Dave Grohl and his wife, Jennifer Youngblood-Grohl, make a cameo appearance.

## 3.18 "TESO DOS BICHOS"

**Writer:** John Shiban
**Director:** Kim Manners
**Original Broadcast:** 3/8/96
**Guest Cast:** Dr. Winters (Garrison Chrisjohn), Dr. Lewton (Tom McBeath), Mona Wustner (Janne Mortil), Dr. Carl Roosevelt (Alan Robertson), Tim Decker (Ron Sauve), Shaman (Gordon Tootoosis), and Dr. Alonzo Bilac (Vic Trevino)

Mulder and Scully investigate a curse caused by unearthing the remains of an amaru, a female shaman, after two people disappear. They suspect a dig team member who uses a native hallucinogen to pray to the spirit.

## Deconstruction and Notes

The only museum of natural history in Boston is called the Peabody Museum or the Harvard Museum.

The Peabody Museum isn't surrounded by houses, but large brick buildings containing labs, a coffee shop, and other Harvard facilities.

## 3.19 "HELL MONEY"

**Writer:** Jeff Vlaming
**Director:** Tucker Gates
**Original Broadcast:** 3/29/96
**Guest Cast:** Detective Neary (Doug Abrahams), Large Man (Stephen M.D. Chang), Vase Man (Donald Fong), Dr. Wu (Diana Ha), Organ Procurement Org. Staffer (Ellie Harvik), Hard-Faced Man (James Hong), Johnny Lo (Derek Loke), Kim Hsin (Lucy Alexis Liu), Detective Glen Chao (B.D. Wong), Li Oi-Huan (Paul Wong), and Hsin Shuyang (Michael Yama)

Mulder and Scully investigate the deaths of Chinese immigrants in the San Francisco Bay Area. A Cantonese-speaking detective helps them find clues to a potentially lethal game.

## 3.20 "JOSE CHUNG'S 'FROM OUTER SPACE'"

**Writer:** Darin Morgan
**Director:** Rob Bowman
**Original Broadcast:** 4/12/96
**Guest Cast:** The Stupendous Yappi (Jaap Broeker), Dr. Fingers (Alex Diakun), Sergeant Hyrek (Michael Dobson), Harold (Jason Gaffney), Roky Crikenson (William Lucking), Dr. Hand (Mina E. Mina), Detective Manners (Larry Musser), Lieutenant Jack Schaeffer (Daniel Quinn), Jose Chung (Charles Nelson Reilly), Chrissy Giorgio (Sarah Sawatsky), Alex Trebek (Alex Trebek), CIA Man (Andrew Turner), Man in Black (Jesse Ventura), and Blaine Faulker (Darin Morgan)

Scully meets Jose Chung, a famous writer, when he wants to interview her and Mulder for his latest book on alien abduction, especially concerning their reaction to the apparent abduction of two teenagers and two gray aliens by the Lord Kinbote.

## Deconstruction and Notes

In this self-mocking episode, a plethora of in-jokes and references abound. Lord Kinbote is named after David Kinbote, a character in Vladimir Nabokov's *Pale Fire*, the commentator on a long and obscure poem that he completely distorts.

Klass County, setting for the episode, was named in tribute to Philip J. Klass, a UFO debunker and author of *UFOs Explained*.

Military abductees Robert Vallee and Jack Schaffer, and Sergeant Hynek, all carry names of authors. Trading the first names of Robert Vallee and Jack Schaffer gives Robert Schaffer, an author on the paranormal, and Jaques Vallee, who, along with Allen Hynek, wrote *The Edge of Reality: A Progress Report on UFO's*.

The autopsy movie Chung shows Scully, *Dead Alien: Truth or Humbug*, recalls *Alien Autopsy: Fact or Fiction*, a real show. The music during the video is a lighter version of *The X-Files* theme by Mark Snow.

Roky Crikenson, the witness to the kids' abduction, was named after Roky Erickson, the psychedelic lead singer for the 13th Floor Elevators, who formed the band, Roky Erickson and the Aliens.

The actor who plays "The Stupendous Yappi," Jaap Broeker, is David Duchovny's stand-in for scene blocking and lighting.

Mr. Chung mentions an earlier book, *The Caligari Candidate*, a reference to *The Manchurian Candidate*, about a brainwashed soldier manipulated into believing in alternate versions of reality by political enemies, and *The Cabinet of Dr. Caligari*, a German silent film also dealing with mind control.

### The Top Three

*Chris Carter's Top Three Picks:*
1. "Ice"
2. "Beyond the Sea"
3. "The Erlenmeyer Flask"

*Gillian Anderson's Top Three Picks:*
1. "Beyond the Sea"
2. "Irresistible"
3. "Piper Maru"

*David Duchovny's Top Three Picks:*
1. "Ice"
2. "Duane Barry"
3. "Anasazi"

Darin Morgan, who plays Blaine, wears a *Space: Above and Beyond* T-shirt, a show created by two *X-Files* writers, including Glen Morgan, Darin Morgan's brother. That night, Duchovny appeared on *Space*, and the *Space* episode referenced the *X-File* episode "Clyde Bruckman's Final Repose," written by Darin Morgan.

Jose Chung calls Mulder "Reynard Muldrake." The French word for "fox" is *renard*.

Detective Manners is named for producer Kim Manners.

*Close Encounters of the Third Kind* also used a mountain of mashed potatoes. The pie referenced *Twin Peaks*, Duchovny's earlier series.

Alex Trebek played one of the Men in Black.

Roky has relocated to El Cajon, California, where Darin and Glen Morgan were born and raised.

## 3.21 "AVATAR"

**Writer:** Howard Gordon
Story by: David Duchovny and Howard Gordon
**Director:** James Charleston
**Original Broadcast:** 4/26/96
**Guest Cast:** Agent Pendrell (Brendan Beiser), Judy Fairly (Stacy Grant), Sharon Skinner (Jennifer Hetrick), Detective Waltos (Tom Mason), Grey-Haired Man (Morris Panych), Old Woman (Bethoe Shirkoff), Senior FBI Agent (Michael David Simms), Jane Cassal (Tasha Simms), Special Agent Bonnecaze (Malcolm Stewart), Carina Sayles (Amanda Tapping), and Lorraine Kelleher (Jamie Woods-Morris)

Assistant Director Skinner signs divorce papers and spends the night with a prostitute only to wake the next morning and find her dead. He believes he may have killed her.

## 3.22 "QUAGMIRE"

**Writer:** Kim Newton
**Director:** Kim Manners
**Original Broadcast:** 5/3/96
**Guest Cast:** Ted Bertram (Mark Acheson), Ansel Bray (R. Nelson Brown), Sheriff Lance Hindt (Chris Ellis), Dr. Bailey (Peter Hanlon), Stoner (Tyler Labine), Snorkel Dude (Terrance Leigh), Fisherman (Murray Lowry), Chick (Nicole Parker), and Dr. Farraday (Timothy Webber)

Mulder and Scully go to Georgia in search of "Big Blue," an aquatic dinosaur reputed to inhabit the local lake, after a federal wildlife official disappears.

## Deconstruction and Notes

Heuvelman's Lake was named after Van Heuvels, a Dutch cryptozoologist who wrote *In the Wake of the Sea Serpents.*

Dr. Faraday is named for chemist and physicist Dr. Michael Faraday, who discovered the principle of electromatic induction, the basis for generating electric power.

The photographer is named after photographer Ansel Adams.

Kim Newton wrote this episode and "Revelations." "Revelations" uses a character called Simon Gates, perhaps named after Bill Gates, while the "Quagmire" lake monster is "Big Blue," a common nickname for IBM.

*Moby Dick*'s Queequeg was a cannibal.

## 3.A "MORE SECRETS OF THE X-FILES"

**Original Broadcast:** 5/10/96
**Narrator:** Mitch Pileggi

This second retrospective recaps highlights, focusing on the ongoing government conspiracy.

## 3.23 "WETWIRED"

**Writer:** Mat Beck
**Director:** Rob Bowman
**Original Broadcast:** 5/10/96
**Guest Cast:** Joseph Patnik (Linden Banks), Frohike (Tom Braidwood), Dr. Henry Stroman (Colin Cunningham), County Coroner (Andre Danyliu), Jimmy (Joe DeSorro), Langly (Dean Haglund), Byers (Bruce Harwood), Plain-Clothed Man (Tim Henry), Margaret Scully (Sheila Larken), Motel Manager (Joe Maffei), Duty Nurse (Heather

McCarthy), Officer #1 (John McConnach), Dr. Lorenz (Crystal Verge), and X (Steven Williams)

Mulder and Scully investigate murders in Maryland caused by television.

## 3.24 "TALITHA CUMI"

**Writer:** Chris Carter
**Story by:** David Duchovny and Chris Carter
**Director:** R.W. Goodwin
**Original Broadcast:** 5/17/96
**Guest Cast:** Paramedic (Cam Cronin), Cigarette-Smoking Man (William B. Davis), Detective (Stephen Dimopoulos), William Mulder (Peter Donat), Deep Throat (Jerry Hardin), Night Nurse (Bonnie Hay), Doctor (John Maclaren), Galen Muntz (Hrothgar Mathews), Jeremiah Smith (Roy Thinnes), Pilot/Bounty Hunter (Brian Thompson), Mrs. Mulder (Rebecca Toolan), Doorman (Angelo Vacco), and X (Steven Williams)

Mulder and Scully investigate a man who heals four people after they are shot, then disappears. Mulder learns that his mother was admitted to the hospital after meeting the Cigarette-Smoking Man. The first of two parts.

## Deconstruction and Notes

In the Bible, *talitha cumi* means "Little girl—arise," or "Arise, maiden." Mark 5:41 records these words spoken by Jesus in an Aramaic dialect to the apparently dead daughter of a Jewish leader.

The scene between Jeremiah and Cigarette-Smoking Man pays homage to *The Brothers Karamazov* by Dostoyevsky. In the book, in "The Legend of the Grand Inquisitor," Jesus returns and is arrested by church leaders. The Grand Inquisitor tells Jesus that he shouldn't have returned because he burdened man with too much freedom, which the church has taken away because man prefers to be led.

The Cigarette-Smoking Man mentions water-skiing, something at which actor William B. Davis excels.

# CHAPTER 17

# SEASON FOUR:
# 1996–1997 EPISODES

## 4.1 "HERRENVOLK"

**Writer:** Chris Carter
**Director:** R.W. Goodwin
**Original Broadcast:** 10/4/96
**Guest Cast:** Agent Pendrell (Brendan Beiser), Second Senior Agent (Ken Camroux), Repairman (Garvin Cross), Marita Covarrubius (Laurie Holden), Gray-Haired Man (Morris Panych), Senior FBI Agent (Michael David Simms), Jeremiah Smith (Roy Thinnes), Pilot/Bounty Hunter (Brian Thompson), Mrs. Mulder (Rebecca Toolan), Elder (Don S. Williams), and X (Steven Williams)

Mulder tracks Jeremiah Smith while eluding the alien assassin to Alberta, Canada, an apparent nursery for drones—both bees and mute adolescent clones of Mulder's sister, Samantha. He also must save his mother's life and learn the fate of his sister, while Scully analyzes data from Jeremiah's files to learn of his work at the Social Security Administration. The second of two parts.

## 4.2 "HOME"

**Writer:** Glen Morgan and James Wong
**Director:** Kim Manners
**Original Broadcast:** 10/11/96
**Guest Cast:** Catcher (Neil Denis), Batter (Cory Fry), Sherman Nathaniel Peacock (Adrian Hughes), Radio Singer (Kenny James), Mrs. Peacock (Karin Konoval), Barbara Taylor (Judith Maxie), Right Fielder (Lachlan Murdoch), George Raymond Peacock (Chris Nelson Norris), Sheriff Andy Taylor (Tucker Smallwood), Pitcher (Douglas Smith),

Deputy Barney Paster (Sebastian Spence), and Edmund Creighton Peacock (John Trottier)

Mulder and Scully go to small-town Pennsylvania to investigate a deformed baby found in a shallow grave only to find a home of genetically induced depravity. Mulder and Scully consider parenthood.

**QUARANTINES** Mulder and Scully have been quarantined three times after potential contact with an infectious organism—at the end of the episodes "Ice," "Darkness Falls," and "Firewalker."

## 4.3 "TELIKO"

**Writer:** Howard Gordon
**Director:** Jim Charleston
**Original Broadcast:** 10/18/96
**Guest Cast:** Samuel Aboah (Willie Amakye), Agent Pendrell (Brendan Beiser), Flight Attendant (Maxine Guess), Marita Covarrubius (Laurie Holden), Marcus Duff (Carl Lumbly), Bus Driver (Bill MacKenzie), Minister Diabira (Zakes Mokae), Dr. Simon Bruin (Bob Morrisey), Lieutenant Madson (Michael O'Shea), and First Officer (Danny Wattley)

African-American men are turning up dead, and without pigmentation, prompting Scully to help the Center for Disease Control. Mulder believes that their suspected disease carrier may be a murderer, a metamorphic ghost creature from West African folklore.

## 4.4 "UNRUHE"

**Writer:** Vince Gilligan
**Director:** Rob Bowman
**Original Broadcast:** 10/27/96
**Guest Cast:** Mary Louise LeFante (Sharon Alexander), Inspector Puett (Ron Chartier), Officer Corning (Michael Cram), Alice Brandt (Angela Donahue), Billy (Scott Heindl), ER Doctor (Michele Melland), Officer Trott (William MacDonald), Druggist (Walter Marsh), Photo Technician (Christopher Royal), and Gerry Thomas Schnauz (Pruitt Vince)

Scully believes a photograph has been misdeveloped; Mulder does not. He believes it is the only clue to the mind of Gerry Schnauz, a paranoid schizophrenic-turned-kidnapper, who lobotomizes young women he deems troubled.

## 4.5 "THE FIELD WHERE I DIED"

**Writer:** Glen Morgan and James Wong
**Director:** Rob Bowman
**Original Broadcast:** 11/3/96
**Guest Cast:** Harbaugh (Doug Abrahams), Melissa Riedal Ephesian (Kristen Cloke), BATF Agent (Michael Dobson), FBI Agent Riggins (Anthony Harrison), Vernon Warren aka Vernon Ephesian (Michael Massee), and Therapist (Donna White)

Mulder discovers religious cultists hidden in a civil war bunker and must find evidence by interrogating one of the sect leader's six wives' past lives. Mulder becomes convinced he's shared a life with her.

## 4.6 "SANGUINARIUM"

**Writer:** Valerie Mayhew and Vivian Mayhew
**Director:** Kim Manners
**Original Broadcast:** 11/10/96
**Guest Cast:** Attorney (Andrew Airlie), ER Doctor (Norman Armour), Dr. Jack Franklyn (Richard Beymer), Dr. Hartman (Martin Evans), Rebecca Waite, R.N. (O-Lan Jones), Dr. Harrison Lloyd (John Juliani), Dr. Shannon (Arlene Mazerolle), Dr. Eric Ilaqua (Paul Raskin), and Doctor (Gregory Thirloway)

A doctor in a hospital plastic surgery unit murders patients. Mulder and Scully investigate his claim that he was possessed and find a nurse practicing magic.

## 4.7 "MUSINGS OF A CIGARETTE SMOKING MAN"

**Writer:** Glen Morgan
**Director:** James Wong
**Projected Broadcast:** 11/17/96
**Guest Cast:** Corporal (Anthony Ashbee), Soldier (Dean Aylesworth), Matlock (Marc Baur), Frohike (Tom Braidwood), Cuban Man (Gonzalo Canton), Cigarette-Smoking Man (William B. Davis), Director (David Fredericks), Aide (Peter Hanlon), Deep Throat (Jerry Hardin), Byers (Bruce Harwood), James Earl Ray (Paul Jarret), Troop Leader (Colin Lawrence), Mob Man (Peter Mele), Lydon (Laurie Murdoch), Supervisor (Steve Oatway), Young Cigarette-Smoking Man (Chris Owens), General Francis (Donnelly Rhodes), Major General (Michael St. John), Jones (Jude Zachary), and Agent Man (Dan Zukovic)

Cigarette-Smoking Man reviews his life. He joined the side of darkness while an army officer and played a role in most major recent historical events, including President John Fitzgerald Kennedy's assassination in 1963. Fellow army officer Bill Mulder reveals his son Fox's first word was "JFK." Cigarette-Smoking Man's real dream was to become a writer of Tom Clancy-esque spy novels under the penname Raul Bloodworth.

## 4.8 "TUNGUSKA"

**Writers:** Chris Carter and Frank Spotnitz
**Director:** Kim Manners
**Broadcast:** 11/24/96

A space rock crashed to earth in Russia in 1908. Mulder encounters a right-wing militia group in Queens, New York, and cellmates in a Russian gulag, among others, during his quest for the rock, which contains four-billion-year-old liquid lifeforms that transmit a deadly "black cancer." America and Russia want the rock. U.N. operative Marita Covarrubias draws closer to becoming X's heir as mysterious benefactor, while

Mulder shares an intimate moment with Scully. The first of two parts.

## 4.9 "TERMA"

**Writers:** Chris Carter and Frank Spotnitz
**Director:** Rob Bowman
**Original Broadcast:** 12/1/96

Mulder escapes from the Siberian Gulag and makes his way back to the United States. A former KGB operative, Vassily Peskow, comes out of retirement to kill everyone who knows about, or had contact with, the rock. A second rock surfaces in Terma, North Dakota, but Mulder and Scully get there too late to prevent Peskow from destroying the evidence. Krycek is revealed to be a high-ranking KGB mole.

## 4.10 "PAPER HEARTS"

**Writer:** Vince Gilligan
**Director:** Rob Bowman
**Original Broadcast:** 12/15/96

Mulder has a vivid dream that leads him to unearth the skeleton of a murdered child. Mulder recognizes the technique of mass-murderer, John Lee Roche. Scully and Mulder question Roche in jail, and Roche notices that Mulder is taking the case personally—Mulder believes Roche might have abducted and murdered Samantha. Roche escapes captivity, and Mulder must hunt Roche down. Mulder is forced to shoot Roche to save a little girl's life.

## 4.11 "EL MUNDO GIRA"

**Writer:** John Shiban
**Director:** Tucker Gates
**Original Broadcast:** 1/12/97

The mutilated corpses of a migrant farm worker and her goats surface following a thunderous deluge of hot, yellow rain. The laborers of the migrant camp are convinced she was killed by Eladio Buente, whom they believe to be El Chupacabra (the Goatsucker, a Mexican folk tale of a small gray creature with a large head, a tiny mouth, and prominent black eyes). Scully's autopsy of the woman's body exposes the truth: Maria passed away on account of a monstrous fungal infection. However, Eladio is a carrier for the fungus, which alters his appearance so radically it transforms him into the very image of El Chupacabra.

## 4.12 "LEONARD BETTS"

**Writers:** Vince Gilligan, John Shiban, and Frank Spotnitz
**Director:** Kim Manners
**Projected Broadcast:** 1/26/97

## 4.13 "NEVER AGAIN"

**Writers:** Glen Morgan and James Wong
**Director:** Rob Bowman
**Projected Broadcast:** 2/2/97

## 4.14 "MEMENTO MORI"

**Writers:** Vince Gilligan, John Shiban, and Frank Spotnitz
**Director:** Rob Bowman
**Projected Broadcast:** 2/9/97

## 4.15 "KADDISH"

**Writer:** Howard Gordon
**Director:** Kim Manners
**Projected Broadcast:** 2/16/97

## 4.16 "UNREQUITED"

**Writers:** Howard Gordon and Chris Carter
**Director:** Michael Lange
**Projected Broadcast:** 2/23/97

## 4.17 "TEMPUS FUGIT"

**Writers:** Chris Carter and Frank Spotnitz
**Director:** Rob Bowman
**Projected Broadcast:** 3/9/97

# CHAPTER 18

# CONSPIRACY

I am still doing a cult show; it's just that more people are watching it," Chris Carter told *Entertainment Weekly*. Carter wants to introduce a mainstream audience to his paranoid fantasies without diluting the cult favorite to please their sensibilities. *The X-Files* remains as bizarre as ever despite its high ratings and winning several Golden Globe Awards.

## THE MYTHOLOGY

The show requires the viewer to concentrate on the intricacies of plot and to recall threads of storylines months, even years, after they first appear. It defies casual viewing. The audience must not only suspend disbelief, accepting the paranormal, the extraterrestrial, and all manner of government deceptions and cover-ups, but pay rapt attention.

"In a way, Mulder and Scully are tour guides to the postwar chaos that we're having to navigate," executive producer and writer Howard Gordon told *Entertainment Weekly*. "The show is really about the power of the individual and the necessity of the individual in that context. It's a testament."

The so-called "mythology" episodes form the core of the series around which all else takes a rightful place. When stand-alone episodes air, they are merely entertaining interludes in the larger story. Humor has a place, but only as relief from the dark paranoid atmosphere so prevalent in the series as a pair of Don Quixotes, including one distaff, tackle an alien and government conspiracy while avoiding all types of perils.

"Chris has described the conspiracy as the scaffolding on which the series hangs," continued Gordon. "It's actually a conceit that the audience has permitted . . . for this huge conspiracy to be going on and yet we're allowed to deal with an albino vampire or three mutant brothers in Pennsylvania."

Unlike most traditional television, the primary storylines never quite resolve. The government continues its deception, perhaps colluding with extraterrestrials, good guys die, evidence disappears, and the viewer is otherwise denied the satisfaction of seeing good triumph. It brings viewers back week after week.

LOST TIME   Mulder has lost time in the pilot (nine minutes), "Deep Throat" (undetermined), "E.B.E." (undetermined), and "Little Green Men" (undetermined). Scully has lost time in the pilot (nine minutes), "E.B.E." (undetermined), and "Ascension/One Breath" (approximately three months).

*The X-Files* frustrates, baffles, and angers viewers, but like a good lover, keeps them crawling back for more. The producers have created a paranoid universe without clear answers in their conspiracy-packed "mythology" shows. They fill it with alien corpses, mutant DNA, green toxic blood, and devious vaccines. Carter told *Entertainment Weekly*, "I would like to think that because we can never truly know all the answers in life, that the show might follow that same route. I liken it to Lewis and Clark. I know the direction I'm headed, but I don't know quite what I'll find on the way."

## THE BLACK HATS

The Project, a secret joint venture between the Syndicate and villainous extraterrestrials, lies at the heart of the "mythology" stories. Echoing Nazi scientists, together they hope to create a super race, or herrenvolk (master race). Under the guise of providing smallpox vaccinations, they have injected everyone born since 1954 with a DNA identification tag. They then gave each subject a number and stored the codes in the Social Security system. Although both the vaccination and the Social Security number are public knowledge, their real purpose is not. Hide in plain sight much as Poe's purloined letter.

**TEN THIRTEEN'S PRODUCTION CREW CAMEOS** First Assistant Director Tom Braidwood appears as Lone Gunman photographer Frohike in a recurring role, and his name was used as the person taking over Howard Graves's parking spot in "Shadows" and as Mulder's alias to get into the secured government compound in Washington State in "E.B.E." Ken Kirzinger, stunt coordinator, appeared as Richter in "Ice." Hair Stylist Malcolm Marsden's name was used for the British PM in "Fire." Vladimir Stefoff, first assistant director, had his name (as Val Stefoff) used as Scully's alias to get into the compound in "E.B.E." Chris Carter appeared in "Anasazi" in the same episode as an FBI agent (the third one) grilling Scully. Angelo Vacco, who plays "Angelo Garza" in "F. Emasculata," is a production assistant in the offices of Ten Thirteen Productions in Los Angeles.

They followed this by secretly abducting thousands of human guinea pigs for invasive experiments and planted electronic tracking devices/memory collectors in their gums, nasal passages, and necks. Using techniques perfected by Nazi scientists during World War II, they combine human and extraterrestrial DNA, and also create clones. Finally, they cover up their operation by destroying all evidence and dumping the hybrid bodies (code name: "the merchandise") into mass graves or buried boxcars.

Jeremiah Smith, an alien clone, led Fox Mulder to a Canadian compound filled with killer bees and clones, duplicates of his missing sister, Samantha. Fox's father, Bill Mulder, had worked with "Cigarette-Smoking Man" and "Well-Manicured Man" in the secret project to create alien-human hybrids. "Cigarette-Smoking Man" once even referred to it as "Bill Mulder's project."

Unlike his companions, Bill's conscience led him to threaten to expose the experiments. The others then abducted his daughter. His wife left him, and much later, he was murdered when he tried to reveal his secrets to his son, Fox.

Mulder has dedicated his life to finding his abducted sister, Samantha. He joined the FBI and became obsessed with so-called "X-Files" cases, which involved seemingly inexplicable paranormal phenomena. His passion to find the truth began when aliens abducted his eight-year-old sister when he was twelve.

The clones in the Canadian compound weren't the first such to enter his life. A woman who claimed to be his grown sister once warned him that aliens live among us and are colonizing our world, because humans "have failed in their stewardship of the planet."

Aliens come in all shapes and sizes, including gender-bending sexaholics, light-warping predators, body-jumpers, parasitic worms, and even benign friends.

No one knows for sure why they come. Most labor for the secret joint project they began with the Syndicate, a group of elderly white men who control the world from their smoky, badly lit HQ on West 46th Street in New York City. They include "Fat Man," "Well-Manicured Man," and "Cigarette-Smoking Man." They secretly control much of the government, especially the CIA and the military, with powerful connections in most countries. They've carried out bizarre plans since World War II.

Their connection with the aliens began when a UFO crashed into the Pacific Ocean in 1953. The Syndicate joined forces with the shape-shifters, and recovered DNA from the alien.

## THE GRAY HATS

"Cigarette-Smoking Man" currently plays the most visible role. The "black-lunged son of a bitch," as Mulder once called him, was personally involved in everything from shooting JFK to rigging Buffalo Bills games and writing bad spy novels. His trademark is the cigarette butts he leaves behind after chain-smoking. He answers to the Syndicate, spends his time at FBI HQ, and frequently visits the Pentagon. Yet, on occasion, he seems to help Mulder and doesn't try to kill him, even after Mulder learned most of the Syndicate's darkest secrets.

"Cigarette-Smoking Man" has said, "You risk turning one man's religion into a crusade," if you kill him. But that hardly seems sufficient reason considering the FBI agent's lack of power and visibility and his existing reputation as being more than a little off-the-wall. If they could kill a president of the United States, they could certainly slaughter an FBI agent. The connection between "Cigarette-Smoking Man" and Mulder appears far more personal. The actor playing the chain-smoking villain has speculated that his character is secretly Fox's father, and had an affair with Bill Mulder's wife. Cigarette-Smoking Man worked with Mulder's father (since the early fifties, at least), and there was a possible romantic encounter between Cancer Man and Mulder's mother.

"Deep Throat," a graying, trench-coated character named after the Watergate informant, was a high-ranking official involved in the alien cover-up with Cancer Man who regularly fed Mulder valuable tips, along with the occasional lie. "There are some secrets that should remain secrets," he said once, after throwing Mulder off the track with a fake UFO photo. "Truths that people are just not ready to know."

"X" assumed the job of assisting Mulder after the Syndicate killed "Deep Throat." "X" worked for Cigarette-Smoking Man. Eventually, the Syndicate also killed him, but not before he scrawled the name of a United Nations division (SRSG) in his own blood. There, Mulder found Marita Covarrubias, probably X's heir apparent.

## THE WHITE HATS

While the world is plagued with evil aliens and humans engaged in a vast conspiracy, and an occasional additional monster-of-the-week, as well as more dubious characters such as "Deep Throat" and "X," Mulder also has allies who wear white hats. Besides his partner, the exemplary Dr. Dana Scully, Assistant Director Skinner is Mulder's staunchest supporter. Skinner has risked his life to protect Mulder and Scully. The Lone Gunmen, Byers, Langly, Frohike, publishers of an underground newsletter, occasionally provide guidance. They are obsessed conspiracy theorists whose allegations are sometimes suspect, though. "We like you because your theories are even crazier than ours," Frohike once told Mulder.

Alex Krycek, the former "Cigarette-Smoking Man" henchman who killed Mulder's father, has become a freelance "player" selling secrets to foreign governments. He will continue to play both sides, plaguing both the Syndicate and Mulder.

### Eleven X-File Facts

1. Adult Video News: Porno publication Mulder is said to read in his free time

2. Spooky: Derisive nickname given to Mulder by fellow FBI agents

3. Stratego: Board game played by Mulder as a kid on Martha's Vineyard

4. X-Files: Unexplained FBI cases; the first one was opened in 1946 by J. Edgar Hoover

5. "SRSG": Written in X's dying hand and in his own blood, a clue for Mulder to find another ally. SRSG stands for Special Representative to the Secretary General.

6. Starbuck: Pet name given to Scully by her Navy captain father

7. Sneaky Fox: Native American name given to Mulder; a.k.a. Running Fox ("Shadows")

8. TRUSTNO1: Mulder's computer password

9. Club Tepes: Hollywood Boulevard hangout frequented by vampires ("3")

10. Drawstring pants: Recurring fashion trend Mulder cited as the reason he doesn't want to live forever

11. "I made this": Said by Nathan Couturier, son of supervising sound editor Thierry Couturier

# PART
# IV

# THE WORLD OF THE X-FILES
## "I WANT TO BELIEVE"

# CHAPTER 19

# THE X-PHILES

The fans made *The X-Files*, and the series' creators know it. Many of these fans, known as X-Philes, communicate on the Internet, where the number of dedicated websites and the amount of chat about the series is only surpassed by *Star Trek*. In fact, many X-Philes are also Trekkers, and these highly dedicated, and in some cases even obsessive, fans have created phenomenons out of both shows.

*The X-Files* failed to catch fire when it first aired. It finished its first season ranked 102 out of 118 series on the air, very near the bottom of the list. But the bizarre show caught the attention of the online community, and by the end of the second season, the show's cult following had pushed its year-end rating up to 64 out of 141. The third season saw the cult favorite transformed into a genuine mainstream hit, and its periodic Nielsen ratings sometimes put it in the top 10.

Seventy-five-hundred fans belong to the official *X-Files* fan club alone, run by Glendale-based Creative Entertainment. Thousands attended more than twenty conventions hosted in 1995.

Paula Mackey, president of the major fan club devoted to Mitch Pileggi, told the *Los Angeles Times* that she has attended so many conventions—four and counting—that "I'm going to start asking Creative (Entertainment) if they have a season pass."

Every day Mackey visits the Internet to check her e-mail and the bulletin boards devoted to her favorite series. She's got plenty of company. The official World Wide Web page (www.TheX-Files.com) has had eight million hits; 150,000 new hits normally arrive on the night *The X-Files* airs. There are over nine hundred unofficial sites dedicated to *The X-Files* on the Web. This lively and busy X-Philes community is also where the series creators go when they want some feedback from their fans. A production assistant also regularly culls relevant bits off the Internet and passes them on to production people.

## ONLINE AND TUNED-IN

But just who are these X-Philes? They have frequently been compared to Trekkers, who have developed a bad popular image. Two British sociologists from the University of Northumbria have even recently reported that 10 percent of *Star Trek* fans interviewed at conventions were maladjusted and suffered from obsessive addiction to the program. X-Philes guard their own image, perhaps a little defensive about being seen in the same light.

Mackey told the *Los Angeles Times*, "We don't want to get stuck with that stereotype. I'm a normal person. Honest." Only about half of the fans believe in the paranormal—not inconsistent with Gallup polls during the last twenty years, which have consistently found that half of Americans believe UFOs are real. Carter told the *Times*, "People are always sure that I'm having to deal with the weirdos who have crawled out of the woodwork. That just is not the case."

Guy Jackson, thirty-nine, an aerospace software engineer and an X-Phile who's been to four conventions, provides a healthy example. He told the *Times*, "It's one of the few shows out there that doesn't cater to the lowest common denominator. They try to stay on a higher level, [and say] 'Let's make you think a little about this.'"

Another recent survey seems to confirm that X-Philes are, in the main, educated and well adjusted. Charles McGrew, of Rutgers University (mcgrew@cs.rutgers.edu), and Shana Walton, of the University of Southern Mississippi (swalton@whale.st.usm.edu), conducted a demographic survey of X-Philes on three Usenet newsgroups (rec.arts.tv.sf, rec.arts.tv., and rec.arts.tv.x-files) and the America Online *X-Files* discussion group. They found the typical X-Phile respondent to be either male (60 percent) or female (40 percent), most likely between the ages of eighteen and thirty-five, and either in college or having at least a bachelor's degree. The X-Phile is most likely to live in the Northeast (here defined as north of Virginia) and enjoy *Star Trek* second only to *The X-Files*. As the researchers noted, clearly the new series "has successfully tapped into the *Star Trek* audience."

One notable difference among X-Philes—as opposed to fans of other shows loosely termed sci-fi—is the relative high percentage of women. Males between sixteen and thirty-five are the expected audience for this type of show, but *The X-Files* has drawn a large number of female viewers, and this has clearly made a big difference in terms of marketing and advertisers. Many women say they are drawn to Scully, who, unlike most female characters on network TV, is strong, competent, smart, and equal to her male partner.

Oddly, despite the finding that the heaviest concentration of X-Philes may be found in the Northeast, the series enjoys higher ratings in rural areas, while falling behind more of the sitcoms in urban areas.

While there is a significant overlap with *Star Trek* fandom, some insist there is a difference. Some think *Star Trek* is pure science fiction, and *The X-Files* is only partly science fiction, with many plots and stories based firmly in our present world. Many X-Philes claim this creates a different outlook altogether. Examining the reality of an episode, as well as deconstructing on-going plotlines, and even checking small details—also activities of *Trek* fans—are favorite pastimes of X-Philes.

Online fan Mike Quigley told CBC's *Afternoon Show*, a Canadian radio talk show, "That's part of the fascination with the show, the nitpicking, or as they call it on the Internet, the 'netpicking.'"

Trekkers are known for their fan fiction, having published literally thousands of fan magazines placing their favorite characters into every situation imaginable. Perhaps the most infamous group of these stories are the so-called Kirk-Spock pairings, which romantically and sexually involve the starship captain and everyone's favorite Vulcan.

X-Philes have duplicated this as well. There is a "fanfic" mailing list for X-Philes who supplement the weekly saga by contributing plots of their own. Some scripts take more liberties than the series itself, with a subgenre devoted to gay and lesbian plot developments and gleefully X-rated contributions from the "Gillian Anderson Testosterone Brigade." As Quigley told the *Afternoon Show*, "There's actually two Internet newsgroups. One is called alt.tv.x-files, the other is alt.tv.x-files.creative, which is where people can upload their own stories, which they've based on *X-Files*-type themes. It gets pretty bizarre, and some of it has been quite tasteless."

Illustrating the devotion X-Philes have to their favorite series, fellow online fan Alexa Deans added, "Several of us plan our schedules so Friday nights, that's where we are, watching it, and if, for some unforeseeable reason, we can't be home, someone tapes it for us."

## CONVENTIONS

As if watching every single *X-Files* episode and spending some amount of time every day communicating online were not enough, many X-Philes attend conventions. The first Official X-Files Convention was held by Creation Entertainment in participation with FOX Television on Sunday, June 11th, 1995 in San Diego, California. Three thousand people attended.

Fans entered a lobby packed with memorabilia and venders selling newly released posters, T-shirts, hats, coffee mugs, books, and comics; a gaggle of psychics, vampirologists, and UFO enthusiasts were on hand to answer questions. Guests included *X-Files* creator Chris Carter, writer Frank Spotnitz, Doug Hutchison (the notorious "Tooms"), Brad Dourif ("Beyond the Sea"'s Luther Boggs), vampirologist Hal Bodner, *UFO* magazine publisher Don Ecker, and renowned psychic Sylvia Browne. They opened with a musical montage of *X-File*-inspired songs and clips. The X-Files prop and costume display included such items as Mulder and Scully's snow suits from "End Game," skeletal remains from "Aubrey," Tooms's dog-catching suit, Boggs's penetentiary suit from "Beyond the Sea," and "evidence"—bizarre items and alien specimens from assorted episodes.

Hutchison recalled to the *Sacramento Bee*, "I didn't anticipate how big it was. I signed my hand off. The line snaked all around the convention center. When they told me it was time to go to make my flight, I said, 'No way, these poor folks have been standing in line for hours.' I took a midnight flight home to L.A."

The second convention attracted eighteen hundred people to Seattle the following week. Sacramento, which has a history of being a strong science-fiction market, has been *The X-Files* highest-rated TV market several times. Sacramento, San Diego, Seattle, and more than a dozen other cities were selected as convention sites because of high TV ratings for *The X-Files* and the amount of mail each city generated in response to a convention ad that ran during a Fox special on *The X-Files*. That fifteen-second ad prompted more than ten thousand cards and letters, which gave organizers the zip codes they needed to target specific cities.

Burbank provided series' star Anderson's first convention experience. Perhaps illustrating the spirit of these conventions, at one point, Hutchison, posing as a fan, asked Anderson what it was like lying under the handsome Tooms character. Surprised, she replied that he was a "Great Guy" and that it was her birthday when they filmed the scene. Hutchison, still in his fan persona, added, "I'd love to take you out for some liver."

## THE WEB

The core of *The X-Files* fandom exists on the Internet, and *The X-Files* is the first show to experience this type of response from the beginning. *Star Trek* fandom lacked such a tool when it first began in the late sixties and early seventies, although it is now certainly the largest fandom on the Web for any television series. The emergence of the Internet and its ability to support online communities has the potential to change society. Many "experts" and pundits argue over the hows, the whens, and the whats of this (or even if it will all blow over and amount to very little), but when it comes to entertainment, the Internet is a force to be reckoned with. *Feed On-line* magazine devoted much space to analyzing the nature of community on the Web and questioned whether it will replace more traditional communities. "Up until recently, communities were rooted in neighborhoods and fostered in certain kinds of places . . . or they evolved from an issue that brought believers together. . . . These kinds of communities, though founded on a particular issue or common faith, traditionally occupied distinct spaces: political rallies and marches on Washington, churches, mosques and synagogues. Right now, virtual communities are largely built around text; is this just a primitive, stop-gap solution to inadequate bandwidth, or is there something about carving out worlds with words that enhances or permits the development of community? Are we witnessing the birth of a new kind of interaction that loosely resembles community but, in fact, merits a new, more descriptive name?"

Carter would assert that the Web does offer the possibility for the formation of communities. He told a Clnet online audience, "[The Web] solidified that hard-core science fiction audience. [*The X-Files* is] a show that has found devotees, and they've found a way to communicate with each other. So it's strengthened the core audience of the show, which is the most important audience. Those are the people who take it the most seriously, and you must listen to their voices and see what they like and don't like, whether you agree with them or not. I only use it as a kind of mood barometer. Any thoughtful criticism I take to heart. I listen to it. If there are enough voices out there, you'd be ridiculously stupid not to heed them or at least take them seriously."

Carter added that he believed fans of *The X-Files*, and of other similar series such as *Star Trek*, are fundamentally different than fans of other television series, such as *Seinfeld* or *Murphy Brown*. Carter said on Clnet, "There are people for whom sci-fi is a way of life, and these shows are telling stories that have some kind of personal resonance with them. And they take them very seriously. With *Seinfeld*, it's less so—it's more traditional entertainment. It becomes a kind of mythology in a way, and that's what people respond to. I've never done a real analysis of it, nor do I think I will for a long time to come. I just try to do good work and hope that people keep responding to it the way they do."

Carter offered his online fans a special reward unique in the history of television. Although a season of *The X-Files* runs twenty-four episodes on TV, a twenty-fifth episode was created on the Web. The episode featured specially shot footage and offered full interactivity, with the viewer taking the role of an FBI agent to help Mulder and Scully investigate spooky goings-on. *The X-Files* website (http://www.thexfiles.com) and Fox hoped this experiment would lead to a whole new market.

However, popularity on the Web is not sufficient to guarantee success for a television series. *Briscoe County*, *Eerie, Indiana*, and dozens of other shows have had strong Internet followings, but they failed to reach a wider audience and were canceled.

The Internet has also become a focal point over issues of copyright infringement, and this debate has recently affected X-Philes. According to Hotwired, the Fox network has ordered all Web pages devoted to *Millennium* (Carter's follow-up series after *The X-Files*) to shut down their unofficial websites. The edict followed the show's impressive debut to thirty-two million viewers.

Online X-Phile Gil Trevizo told Hotwired that he picked up his e-mail after a Fox-sponsored IRC chat, part of the much-hyped "cyberpremiere" of *Millennium* the Wednesday before the Friday airing of the first episode, only to learn that his Internet service provider, the University of Texas at El Paso, had blocked his online access. According to Trevizo, Fox's David Oakes had called the dean of students and threatened to sue the university if it didn't shut down Trevizo's unofficial *Millennium* site before that weekend.

Fox claimed this action was taken because of the use of pirated copyrighted images on commercial sites, but none of the sites on Fox's list were using the images for commercial gain. "We have an official *Millennium* site, with network-approved content, and these people don't work for the network," said Oakes. He added, "we've had significant problems with *The X-Files* about this." Fox received so much outraged mail from fans that their mail server crashed. Trevizo told Hotwired, "The online community has been a boon to *The X-Files*. *X-Files* merchandising wouldn't have taken off without the Internet, which has replaced [conventions] as the main gathering place for fans."

"Basically, Fox is shooting themselves in the butt," added Virginia Eveland, the sixteen-year-old founder of the Smart Young X-Philes Web Circle. "Somebody must have told Fox that they could make money with their official website, which was their first mistake," said Eveland. "You make fans with a website, not money."

# CHAPTER 20

# NOVELS, COMICS, AND MORE

The popularity of *The X-Files* and its huge cult following made an onslaught of merchandising inevitable. Everything from cups to T-shirts to books, comics, and videos have appeared.

HarperCollins, a division of the same Rupert Murdoch company that owns Fox, the producer of *The X-Files*, obtained the rights to publish the television series in book form. The books include brand-new adventures aimed at an adult audience and adaptations of aired episodes targeted to a juvenile audience. There are also several authorized and unauthorized nonfiction books about the television series.

## ADULT NOVELS

The original full-length novels are published under HarperPrism.

Charles Grant is known for both his original science fiction stories and his talented adaptation of movie and television heroes to the printed page. He wrote the first two books in the series, *Goblins* and *Whirlwind*. The owners of *The X-Files* property and the publisher felt they had placed the franchise in competent hands. They were not disappointed.

The story in *Goblins*, the series' first entry, begins with Mulder and Scully investigating two inexplicable murders near Fort Dix, New Jersey, where they encounter an old woman raving about goblins. Grant's second novel, *Whirlwind*, begins with the discovery of corpses and carcasses near a Konochine Indian community. People and cattle have been slaughtered and skinned in seconds. Both the Indians and local authorities erect a wall of silence when Mulder and Scully arrive to investigate.

The third novel in the series, *Ground Zero*, marked the beginning of writer Kevin Anderson's affiliation with the book series. Anderson told *SFX* magazine how he approaches creating a new *X-Files* novel. He said, "I submit a batch of ideas and proposals, work with the editors at HarperCollins as well as the licensing folks at Twentieth Century Fox and the *X-Files* production offices, until we've finally hammered down the best potential book we can develop."

In *Ground Zero*, Mulder and Scully investigate nuclear weapons testing when people are found burned and dead from what seems to have been a small atomic blast. HarperPrism also published the novel as an audiotape, with actress Gillian Anderson (Dana Scully in the series) reading the text.

As he had in his first entry, Anderson added some new background information for the lead characters in his second novel, *Ruins*. This required close coordination with all involved. Anderson told *SFX* magazine, "In my first *X-Files* novel, *Ground Zero*, I had planted details of Scully's background and her early years in college. In *Ruins* I wanted to do the same for Mulder, describing some events of the first days after his sister Samantha had disappeared, his desperate efforts to find her. Defining any such landmark events in the characters' lives required careful consultation with Chris Carter and his extremely sharp associates Mary Astadourian and Frank Spotnitz, seeing just what fine line we could walk. Sometimes it involved only a word change, sometimes it required a new way of looking at things, but we managed to strike the perfect balance."

One drawback involved with using characters owned by other creators is that they can require unexpected changes, even at the last moment. Anderson said, "I learned that the *X-Files* people had some ideas on how to change a couple of the last scenes in the book, and could I rewrite it over the phone? Readers don't realize what a harrowing experience it is to write one of these books! I believe the end result is worth all the hardships, though."

*Ruins* involves Scully and Mulder with Mayan ruins. As with his earlier novel, this book was also made into an audiotape, this time performed by Mitch Pileggi, who portrays FBI Assistant Director Walter Skinner in the series.

## NOVELIZATIONS OF EPISODES

Les Martin adapted several episodes, including the pilot, into book format for the juvenile audience. The adaptation of the pilot was titled *X Marks the Spot;* "Fearful Symmetry" became *Tiger Tiger.* He has also adapted "Darkness Falls"; "Humbug"; "Blood," under the title *Fear;* and "War of the Coprophages," under the title *E.B.E.*

Other writers have contributed to the series of children's books. Ellen Steiber adapted the episodes "Squeeze" and "Shapes"; Easton Royce contributed "D.P.O.," under the title *Voltage.*

## NONFICTION BOOKS

HarperPrism has released several nonfiction books about the television series, beginning with *The Truth Is Out There: The Official Guide to The X-Files* by Brian Lowry, an official guidebook including synopses of episodes up to "Paper Clip" (3.2) and background information about the cast and crew. The same author also released *Trust No One: The Official Third Season Guide to The X-Files.*

Other official books from HarperPrism include *The X-Files Book of the Unexplained: Volume I* by Jane Goldman, a hardcover first released in the U.K. that offers background on the paranormal topics around which first-season episodes are based. Presumably subsequent volumes will cover the following seasons.

*The Unofficial X-Files Companion* by Ngaire E. Genge is an unauthorized paperback offering a brief look at the show and episode synopses. Like the U.K. book, this volume is dedicated to delivering a detailed look at the paranormal events and circumstances upon which the episodes are based. A second volume, to be entitled *The Unofficial X-Files Companion II,* was

planned by the same author to cover additional episodes that did not appear in the first volume.

Other unauthorized books have been announced, such as *X-Files Confidential* by Ted Edwards and *The X-Files Declassified* by Robert Lovece.

## COMIC BOOKS

*The X-Files* has leapt from the television screen into several different forms, including four-color comic books. This jump was made amidst an atmosphere of controversy, however. David Campiti, co-owner of the comic book packaging and production company Glass House Graphics, told *The Comics Journal* magazine that he and Topps Comics Editor-in-Chief Jim Salicrup made an oral agreement in early 1994 concerning the acquisition of the rights to and the production of *The X-Files* comic book. The arrangement between the two men allegedly stipulated that Campiti, having proposed *The X-Files* property to Topps, would be compensated for negotiating the TV show's licensing, and that Glass House would receive the writing, art, lettering, and coloring assignments.

However, Topps Comics released the first issue of *The X-Files* comic book in November 1994 without using or consulting Glass House. Campiti alleged he was owed $1,500 for negotiating the license as well as approximately $15,000 for a kill fee as a result of Topps not using Glass House Graphics creators. Topps refused comment on the dispute.

Regardless of the merits of the allegations, the comic book series became a sales success, by some measures the twenty-third most popular comic book published in the United States.

The comic book series offers all-new original stories based on the characters from the television series and set in the universe Chris Carter and crew created for their show. The conspiracy/alien intervention "mythology" plays a central role in the comic book.

The first issue presented a story titled, "Not to Be Opened until Xmas," written by Stefan Petrucha and drawn by Charles Adlard with a cover by Miran Kim. Mulder and Scully investigate when the final Fatima Prophecy is stolen from the Vatican and linked to a murder in New York City. A black and white version of the first half of this book appeared in *Star Wars Galaxy #2.*

The creative team on the comic book remained consistent until the seventeenth issue, dated May 1996, a year and a half later. To date, Topps has published the following comic books:

## #2 "A Dismembrance of Things Past"

Month: February 1995
Writer: Stefan Petrucha
Artist: Charles Adlard
Cover: Miran Kim

Witnesses to a forty-seven-year-old UFO crash are being murdered. Mulder and Scully investigate to protect retired General Palmer. First of two parts.

## #3 "A Little Dream of Me"

Month: March 1995
Writer: Stefan Petrucha
Artist: Charles Adlard
Cover: Miran Kim

The general commits suicide. Mulder investigates a mysterious individual who offers to deliver Mulder's sister, Samantha, if he will steal Pentagon computer access codes. Second of two parts.

## N/A "A Trick of the Light"

Month: April 1995
Writer: Stefan Petrucha
Artist: Charles Adlard
Cover: Jim Salicrup

This special insert appeared as an advertising promotion in *Hero Illustrated* #22. An artist's models disappear.

## #4 "Firebird Part One: Khobka's Lament"

Month: April 1995
Writer: Stefan Petrucha
Artist: Charles Adlard
Cover: Miran Kim

Mulder and Scully investigate when a scientist involved in research into the Tunguska meteorite is found dead in an overturned truck in New Mexico. His bones have aged thousands of years. First of three parts.

## #5 "Firebird Part Two: Crescit Eundo"

Month: May 1995
Writer: Stefan Petrucha
Artist: Charles Adlard
Cover: Miran Kim

This is the second of three parts.

## Special Edition #1

Month: June 1995
Writer: Stefan Petrucha
Artist: Charles Adlard
Cover: Miran Kim

This special edition combined the first three comics in the series.

## #6 "Firebird Part Three: A Brief Authority"

Month: June 1995
Writer: Stefan Petrucha
Artist: Charles Adlard
Cover: Miran Kim

Mulder speaks with Khobka on behalf of the cabal, in an effort to stop the Firebird. The last of three parts.

## N/A "Circle Game"

Month: July 1995
Writer: Stefan Petrucha
Artist: Charles Adlard

Mulder investigates crop circles in this five-page insert in the July 15–21, 1995, issue of *TV Guide*.

## #7 "Trepanning Opera"

Month: July 1995
Writer: Stefan Petrucha
Artist: Charles Adlard
Cover: Miran Kim

Victims of trepanning have a hole drilled into their heads, creating a "third eye." Mulder investigates, but the killer appears to see into the future.

## Annual #1 "Hallow Eve"

Month: August 1995
Writer: Stefan Petrucha
Artist: Charles Adlard
Cover: Miran Kim

Everyone who handles the bones of the female progenitor of the human race dies. Scully tries to stop the angry spirit of all humankind.

## #8 "Silent Cities of the Mind: Part One"

Month: August 1995
Writer: Stefan Petrucha
Artist: Charles Adlard
Cover: Miran Kim

A doctor believes a lost city can be found in the mountains of Alaska; Mulder investigates, and then he disappears. The first of two parts.

## #9 "Silent Cities of the Mind: Part Two"

Month: September 1995
Writer: Stefan Petrucha
Artist: Charles Adlard
Cover: Miran Kim

Agent Scully's radio call for help brings unfriendly guests. The cannibalistic doctor decides to be more cooperative, though. The second of two parts.

## N/A Collected Edition

Month: September 1995
Writer: Stefan Petrucha
Artist: Charles Adlard
Cover: Miran Kim

This special collected edition reprints the first six issues in paperback.

## #10 "Feelings of Unreality: Part One—Wheels within Wheels"

Month: October 1995
Writer: Stefan Petrucha
Artist: Charles Adlard
Cover: Miran Kim

Mulder investigates a conspiracy with the help of a strange informant while Scully tries to help. The first of three parts.

## #11 "Feelings of Unreality: Part Two— The Ancient of Days"

Month: December 1995
Writer: Stefan Petrucha
Artist: Charles Adlard
Cover: Miran Kim

Mulder guards the Ilbal. Scully investigates how it affects the human mind. The second of three parts.

## Special Edition #2

Month: December 1995
Writer: Stefan Petrucha
Artist: Charles Adlard
Cover: Miran Kim

This special edition reprints the fourth through sixth issues.

## #12 "Feelings of Unreality: Part Three— Nightmare of History"

Month: January 1996
Writer: Stefan Petrucha
Artist: Charles Adlard
Cover: Miran Kim

While suffering faulty memories, Mulder and Scully find the person who masterminded nearly all of the cases they've recently investigated. The third of three parts.

## #½ "Tiptoe through the Tulpa"

Month: January 1996
Writer: Stefan Petrucha
Artist: Charles Adlard
Cover: Miran Kim

Murders lead to a comatose man. Published only as an insert in *Wizard* #53.

### #13 "One Player Only"

Month: February 1996
Writer: Stefan Petrucha
Artist: Charles Adlard & Miran Kim
Cover: Miran Kim

Mulder and Scully investigate a newly insane computer programmer who killed three coworkers.

### #14 "Falling"

Month: April 1996
Writer: Stefan Petrucha
Artist: Charles Adlard
Cover: Miran Kim

Mulder and Scully investigate a UFO crash in a small town, until children trap Mulder, believing him to be the alien from the ship.

### #15 "Home of the Brave: Part One— The New World"

Month: May 1996
Writer: Stefan Petrucha
Artist: Charles Adlard
Cover: Miran Kim

Mulder and Scully investigate a crashed UFO, but survivalists attack them. The first of two parts.

### #16 "Home of the Brave: Part Two— A Question of Ownership"

Month: May 1996
Writer: Stefan Petrucha
Artist: Charles Adlard
Cover: Miran Kim

Scully and Mulder escape. The second of two parts.

At this point, the creative team responsible for the comic book series changed. John Rozum began to write most of the issues, replacing Petrucha, while Adlard returned to the art chores after missing an issue. Gordon Purcell and Josef Rubinstein filled in.

### #17 "Thin Air"

Month: May 1996
Writer: John Rozum
Pencils: Gordon Purcell
Inks: Josef Rubinstein
Cover: Miran Kim

Mulder and Scully investigate when a pilot reappears in Greece after disappearing in the Bermuda Triangle in 1945. He hasn't aged.

### #18 "Night Lights: Part One"

Month: June 1996
Writer: John Rozum
Artist: Charles Adlard
Cover: Miran Kim

Scientists disappear while studying ball lightning. Two students reproduce the phenomenon, but only one survives. The first of two parts.

### #19 "Night Lights: Part Two"

Month: June 1996
Writer: John Rozum
Artist: Charles Adlard
Cover: Miran Kim

Local police don't believe Mulder's theory that an atmospheric organism killed the scientists. The second of two parts.

Purcell and Rubinstein again replace Adlard on the art while Kevin Anderson takes over the writing. Anderson, a science-fiction writer, has contributed to *The X-Files* book series as well.

### #20 "Family Portrait: Part One—Gallery"

Month: July 1996
Writer: Kevin Anderson
Pencils: Gordon Purcell
Inks: Josef Rubinstein
Cover: Miran Kim

Mulder and Scully investigate a serial killer after a photographer dies, noting his odd camera. The first of two parts.

**#21 "Family Portrait: Part Two—
The Camera Eye"**

Month: August 1996
Writer: Kevin Anderson
Pencils: Gordon Purcell
Inks: Josef Rubinstein
Cover: Miran Kim

Mulder photographs Scully with the strange camera. She then rests while Mulder reads the photographer's journals until the original owner of the camera returns. Second of two parts.

## *The X-Files* Digest

In December of 1995, while the comic book series was still in the hands of the original creative team, Topps expanded the comics line with a smaller digest format publication. Petrucha, Adlard, and Kim also provided the creative team for this new publication, which offered original stories combined with adaptations of Ray Bradbury short stories.

**#1 "Big Foot, Warm Heart"**

Month: December 1995
Writer: Stefan Petrucha
Artist: Charles Adlard
Cover: Miran Kim

This contained a new *X-Files* story and three Ray Bradbury stories adapted into comic form. Skinner sends Mulder and Scully to investigate a missing FBI agent kidnapped by Bigfoot.

**#2 "Dead to the World"**

Month: April 1996
Writer: Stefan Petrucha
Artist: Charles Adlard
Cover: Miran Kim

Mulder investigates an alchemist who claims to have lived for centuries.

## *The X-Files* Magazine

In the winter of 1996, Topps launched a short-lived official magazine for *The X-Files*. The publication included original comic stories by the usual creative team.

**#1 "The Pit"**

Season: Winter 1996
Writer: Stefan Petrucha
Artist: Charles Adlard

Mulder and Scully investigate a haunted digging site and a hostage situation in Canada.

**#2 "The Silent Blade"**

Season: Fall 1996
Writer: Stefan Petrucha
Artist: Charles Adlard

A man purchases a haunted blade.

## *The X-Files* Season One

Pleased with the sales of their X-Files comic series, Topps added a series based on actual episodes.

**#0 "The X-Files"**

Month: August 1996
Adapted by: Roy Thomas
Artist: John Van Fleet
Cover: John Van Fleet

This comic adapted the pilot episode.

# THE CD-ROM

In addition to print versions of *The X-Files* adventures, Seattle-based multimedia producer HyperBole Studios is working to create entirely new, interactive episodes of *The X-Files* for Fox Interactive, featuring the show's regular cast, to be released on CD-Rom. HyperBole's CEO and creative director, Greg Roach, produced two earlier CD-Rom science-fiction movies, *Quantum Gate* and *Quantum Gate II: The Vortex*, as well as a multimedia novel, *The Madness of Roland*, since founding HyperBole five years ago.

Roach will employ the latest version of a software engine specifically devised for creating interactive, dramatic works: VirtualCinema. VirtualCinema, which Roach designed and first employed on *Quantum Gate*, is designed to make watching a story on a PC as much like going to the movies as possible. There's no frame surrounding the video image, no icons or toolbars. Icons are brought up by placing the mouse pointer on a certain part of the screen. VirtualCinema responds to the viewer's actions indirectly.

*The X-Files* CD-Rom represents a chance to develop the VirtualCinema technology free from financial worries. The CD-Rom industry has never achieved a significant market. Many multimedia companies, such as Redmond-based Medio, have collapsed, or been absorbed by their investors, such as Splash Inc. HyperBole shelved any major projects while preparing smaller pieces on contract for websites such as the London-based *New Scientist* magazine. Fox Interactive frees HyperBole to develop the art of digital storytelling without money worries.

## THE ALBUMS

Besides the stories and characters, the music of *The X-Files* is also collected by fans of the series. Warner Bros. released the first *X-Files* album, *Songs in the Key of X.*

Songs on the album contained only one composition by series composer Mark Snow and primarily included contemporary works that had never been heard on the show.

*The Truth and the Light*, Warners' second spin-off album, consists entirely of original music created by Snow. The album contains two dozen individual pieces taken from Snow's work over the first three seasons of *The X-Files*, interspersed with dialogue excerpts from series stars David Duchovny and Gillian Anderson. The album also includes an introduction by the show's creator, Chris Carter.

## TRIPLE-X FILES

*SFX* magazine found the oddest *X-Files*-related product of all: a pornographic movie based on the popular television series but completely unaffiliated with Twentieth Century Fox. *The Breast Files* is a hardcore video about a government plot to insert silicon chips into women's breasts that will cause men to lose control. The more obvious titles, *The Sex Files* and *The XXX Files*, appear only to have been used in comedy spoofs.

# CHAPTER 21

# THE X-FILES JOKEBOOK

Any cult phenomenon inevitably generates self-parodying humor. Trekkers have logged many, many pages of jokes on themselves, and X-Philes have done likewise. And any show that, on the surface, takes itself as seriously as *The X-Files* just seems to be asking for a poke in the ribs now and then. In addition, X-Philes have created poems, limericks, and folk songs that celebrate their beloved series, and collecting Mulderisms and Scullyisms has become something of a sport.

Below, in no particular order, are some of the better jokes that have been gathered. Many are built up over a period of time, as people pass around these lists online.

## YOU KNOW YOU'RE AN X-PHILE WHEN...

1. You steal your neighbor's newspaper every morning for an entire week—just to cut out the "Fox Trot" comic, and replace it on their doorstep as if nothing had happened.
2. You deny that you had anything to do with the big hole on the comics page of your neighbor's newspaper, and suggest it must have been a government conspiracy.
3. You wake up in the middle of the night with a nose-bleed, and insist to be taken to the hospital for an X-ray.
4. You decorate your room and workplace with assorted pictures of Mulder and Scully.
5. You create a new folder in your filing cabinet, labeling it, "X-Files."
6. You compulsively read and respond to articles posted in Alt.tv.x-files, and go through withdrawal symptoms when you can't get to the computer.

7. You change the message on your answering machine to "Hi, this is Dana Scully. Leave a message and I'll get back to you as soon as I can"—using Gillian Anderson's voice from the episode "Colony."
8. You spend all ten of your allocated online hours downloading anything with reference to *The X-Files* or seeking new *X-Files* links for your Home Page.
9. You go to the public library with the intent of checking out all of *The X-Files* magazine articles you have missed, and are planning to scan the pictures.
10. You purchase three copies of *The X-Files* featured *TV Guide* on the first day it comes out . . . even though you know your subscription copy will be there in two days.
11. Your friends abandon you, your roommates think you've been brainwashed, and your family institutionalizes you for rambling endlessly about last Friday's episode.
12. Your watch stops and you get all happy about it!

## MULDER'S LAWS

**Mulder's Laws No. 1:**
"Never put anything up your nose not from this planet."

**Mulder's Laws No. 2:**
"Never hibernate under an escalator."

**Mulder's Laws No. 3:**
"To Mulder, it's a ritually beheaded corpse with fifth-degree burns, to the rest of us it's a Thanksgiving turkey."

**Mulder's Laws No. 4:**

"Score: Loggers–0, MonkeyWrenchers–0, Bugs–34."

**Mulder's Laws No. 5:**

"Have an alibi handy. The police won't believe that your dead ex-boss is responsible when everyone you dislike keeps being murdered."

**Mulder's Laws No. 6:**

"If time is not a universal invariant in your zip code, then your mail delivery may be somewhat erratic."

**Mulder's Laws No. 7:**

"A man with a thing about unsecured lines is either paranoid or calls 1-900-BONDAGE numbers."

## EVERYTHING I NEEDED TO KNOW I LEARNED FROM *THE X-FILES....*

1. The truth is out there.
2. I want to believe.
3. Trust no one.
4. Deny everything.
5. Apology is policy.
6. Don't hang around people who smoke.
7. Don't sleep with your coworkers.
8. Don't eat at restaurants where the motto is: "Good People, Good Food."
9. If it's iced tea, it could be love.
10. If it's root beer, it's fate.
11. If you find an audiocassette in your car, ten-to-one you can't dance to it.
12. To conquer fear, face it.
13. Always make back-ups of your important data.
14. If there's a white van in your driveway, don't drink the water.
15. Don't look for romance online.
16. Don't accept dinner invitations from bald, tattooed, half-naked guys.
17. "Bambi? Her name is Bambi?"
18. Smart is sexy.
19. Brush or you will get calcium deposits.
20. Beware of anyone who uses the royal/pontifical "we" in conversation.
21. Never scan unidentified metal.
22. Make certain you remember the birthdays of people who are important to you.
23. Sometimes you just gotta say, "Sure. Fine. Whatever."
24. Sometimes you just gotta say, "Go with it."
25. Beware you don't become the monster you are hunting.
26. "The cat ate the rat." "The dog ate the cat."
27. The "ordinary" murderer next door can be as horrifying as a hideous mutant or alien.
28. It's never just a "nice trip to the forest."
29. "Pardon my gender type."
30. Sometimes those mysterious bumps are just mosquito bites.
31. Keep your friends close, but keep your enemies even closer.
32. Always have a second gun, especially if you're tired of losing the first one.
33. It is difficult to maintain a cool exterior, especially when you have bile on your fingers.
34. If you're stranded on a rapidly rusting ship, don't drink the water.
35. The truth is out there, but so are lies.
36. Once you've seen the truth, you'll want the answers.
37. "Sometimes the need to mess with their heads outweighs the millstone of humiliation."
38. On long trips, take turns driving.
39. Miracles happen.
40. Everyone has an uncle who is an amateur magician.
41. Even friends will point guns at you.
42. Never, ever go into the bathroom.
43. Sometimes we are not who we are.
44. Truth has no court.
45. Just because something is pure and good does not make it trite and silly.
46. Anger is a luxury we cannot always afford.

## TOP TEN LINES NEVER HEARD ON *THE X-FILES*

10. "The alien is speaking, Agent Mulder. . . . I think it wants to phone home."
9. "Sure, we could have these people killed to protect what they know . . . but isn't that a little harsh?"

8. "I've seen this one before, Scully. His name is Casper, and he's what we call a 'friendly' ghost."

7. "Look under the mask. This is no swamp monster. It's Mr. Handy, the owner of the old country store!"

6. "My Lord! This conspiracy involves all three of the Gabor sisters!"

5. "Well, Agent Mulder., you caught us. We'll cooperate fully, of course. What would you like to know?"

4. "You'll be happy to hear, Assistant Director Skinner, that I've switched over to the nicotine patch."

3. "The president wants to see you two immediately. His cheeseburger is possessed."

2. "And it would have worked, too, if it hadn't been for you meddling FBI agents!"

1. "Gosh, I guess we were wrong . . . the government did have our best interests at heart, after all!"

# PART

# V

# APPENDIXES
"DENY EVERYTHING"

# THE FEDERAL BUREAU OF INVESTIGATION

This "Overview of the Federal Bureau of Investigation" was prepared by the Office of Public and Congressional Affairs, Federal Bureau of Investigation.

## FBI MISSION STATEMENT

The Mission of the FBI is to uphold the law through the investigation of violations of federal criminal law; to protect the United States from foreign intelligence and terrorist activities; to provide leadership and law enforcement assistance to federal, state, local, and international agencies; and to perform these responsibilities in a manner that is responsive to the needs of the public and is faithful to the Constitution of the United States.

The Federal Bureau of Investigation is the principal investigative arm of the United States Department of Justice. Title 28, United States Code (U.S. Code), Section 533, which authorizes the Attorney General to "appoint officials to detect . . . crimes against the United States," and other federal statutes give the FBI the authority and responsibility to investigate specific crimes. At present, the FBI has investigative jurisdiction over violations of more than two hundred categories of federal crimes.

The Bureau also is authorized to investigate matters where no prosecution is contemplated. For example, under the authority of several Executive Orders, the FBI conducts background security checks concerning nominees to sensitive government positions. In addition, the FBI has been directed or authorized by Presidential statements or directives to obtain information about activities jeopardizing the security of the Nation.

Information obtained through an FBI investigation is presented to the appropriate U.S. Attorney or Department of Justice official, who decides if prosecution, or other action, is warranted. Top priority has been assigned to the five areas that affect society the most: counterterrorism, drugs/organized crime, foreign counterintelligence, violent crimes, and financial crimes.

The FBI also is authorized to provide other law enforcement agencies with cooperative services, such as fingerprint identification, laboratory examinations, police training, Uniform Crime Reports, and the National Crime Information Center.

## A BRIEF HISTORY OF THE FBI

The agency now known as the Federal Bureau of Investigation was founded in 1908 when Attorney General Charles J. Bonaparte appointed an unnamed force of Special Agents to be the investigative force of Department of Justice. Prior to that time, Department of Justice borrowed Agents from the U.S. Secret Service to investigate violations of federal criminal laws within its jurisdiction.

By order of Attorney General George W. Wickersham, the Special Agent force was named the Bureau of Investigation in 1909. Following a series of changes in name, the Federal Bureau of Investigation officially received its present title in 1935.

During the early period of the FBI's history, its Agents investigated violations of some of the comparatively few existing federal criminal violations, such as bankruptcy frauds, antitrust crime, and neutrality violations. During World War I, the Bureau was given responsibility for espionage, sabotage, sedition, and draft violations. Passage of the National Motor Vehicle Theft Act in 1919 further broadened the Bureau's jurisdiction.

The Gangster Era began after passage of Prohibition in 1920. Criminals engaged in kidnapping and bank robbery, which were not federal crimes at that time. This changed in 1932 with the passage of a federal kidnapping statute. In 1934, numerous other federal criminal statutes were passed, and Congress gave Special Agents the authority to make arrests and to carry firearms.

The FBI's size and jurisdiction during World War II increased greatly and included intelligence matters in South America. With the end of that war and the advent of the Atomic Age, the FBI began conducting background security investigations for the White House and other government agencies, as well as probes into internal security matters for the Executive Branch.

Civil rights and organized crime became major concerns of the FBI in the 1960s, as did counter-terrorism, financial crime, drugs, and violent crimes, during the 1970s and 1980s.

In addition to its five priority programs, the FBI also concentrates significant investigative resources into applicant and civil rights matters.

## ORGANIZATIONAL STRUCTURE

The FBI is a field-oriented organization in which nine divisions and four offices at FBI Headquarters (FBIHQ) in Washington, D.C., provide program direction and support services to fifty-six field offices, approximately four hundred satellite offices known as resident agencies, four specialized field installations, and twenty-three foreign liaison posts. The foreign liaison offices, each of which is headed by a Legal Attache or Legal Liaison Officer, work abroad with American and local authorities on criminal matters within FBI jurisdiction.

The FBI has approximately 10,100 Special Agents and 13,700 other employees who perform professional, administrative, technical, clerical, craft, trade, or maintenance operations. About 7,300 employees are assigned to FBIHQ; approximately 16,000 are assigned to field installations.

## DIVISIONS AND OFFICES AT FBI HEADQUARTERS

The FBI is headed by a Director, who is supported by a Deputy Director. An Assistant Director heads each of the nine Headquarters divisions. The four offices are headed by executives with varying titles. An Inspector in Charge manages the Office of Public and Congressional Affairs, and the Office of the General Counsel is headed by the FBI's General Counsel. The Office of Equal Employment Opportunity Affairs is administered by the Equal Employment Opportunity Officer.

Assistant Directors of each division are supported by Deputy Assistant Directors (DADs). FBIHQ divisions and offices usually are arranged along broad functional lines into sections, and then into smaller, more specialized work groups known as units.

FBI field offices are located in fifty-six major cities. Of those, fifty-five are in the United States, and one is in Puerto Rico. The locations were selected according to crime trends, the need for regional geographic centralization, and the need to efficiently manage resources.

Each FBI field office is overseen by a Special Agent in Charge (SAC), except for those located in New York City and Washington, D.C. Due to their large size, those offices each are managed by an Assistant Director in Charge (ADIC). The ADICs are assisted by DADs and by SACs responsible for various programs.

The SACs in all field offices, including those in New York City and Washington, D.C., are aided by one or more managers called Assistant Special Agents in Charge. The SACs also are assisted by Squad Supervisors in charge of investigative work and Administrative Officers, who manage support operations.

FBI field offices conduct their official business both directly from their headquarters facilities and through approximately four hundred satellite offices, known as resident agencies. The number of resident agencies under each field office varies, as does the number of employees assigned to a resident agency. They range from one to a dozen or more employees. Each of the larger resident agencies is managed by a Supervisory Senior Resident Agent, who reports to the field office which covers the area. Resident agencies, like field offices, are located where crime trends and available resources require.

The FBI also operates specialized field installations: two Regional Computer Support Centers—one in Pocatello, Idaho, and one at Fort Monmouth, New Jersey—and two Information Technology Centers (ITCs)—one at Butte, Montana, and one at Savannah, Georgia. The ITCs provide information services to support field investigative and administrative operations. In addition, the FBI provides support for the National Drug Intelligence Center (NDIC) in Johnstown, Pennsylvania. The NDIC collects and consolidates drug-trafficking intelligence developed by law enforcement and other official users. The facility is overseen by Department of Justice.

The FBI also works with the Drug Enforcement Administration (DEA) to combat drug trafficking through the DEA's El Paso Intelligence Center in El Paso, Texas.

The FBI's role in international investigations has expanded due to the authority granted by the congressional application of extraterritorial jurisdiction and the growth in international criminal activity. FBI investigations abroad require the approval of the host country and coordination with the U.S. Department of State and any other involved agency through the FBI's Legal Attache Program.

Legal Attaches are overseen by the International Relations Branch of the Criminal Investigative Division at FBIHQ. That Branch also is responsible for contacts with other Executive Branch agencies; Interpol; foreign police and security officers based in Washington, D.C.; and national law enforcement associations.

Given the expanded extraterritorial responsibilities of the FBI and increasing international demands in drugs/organized crime, foreign counterintelligence, terrorism, and financial crime, the FBI establishes and maintains liaison with principal law enforcement and intelligence/security services in many foreign countries. Liaison is maintained in accordance with Executive Orders, statutes, Attorney General guidelines, and FBI policy.

There are twenty-three Legal Attache offices in countries around the world. They are located in the U.S. embassies in the countries to which they are accredited. The Special Agent representatives abroad carry the title of Legal Attache, Deputy Legal Attache, or Assistant Legal Attache. The Special Agents assigned to the Honolulu; Miami; and San Juan, Puerto Rico, Liaison Offices are called Liaison Officers.

## FBI PERSONNEL AND EMPLOYMENT

The FBI is a unique institution in the federal government in that it is responsible for sensitive foreign counterintelligence matters, important civil investigations, background inquiries on persons nominated for high public office, and criminal investigations which may involve prominent figures in both the public and private sectors. In recognition of these diverse responsibilities, the FBI has traditionally been provided broader discretion in personnel matters than is afforded most other federal agencies.

All persons and positions in the FBI are in the excepted service (Title 28, USC, Section 536). This places all FBI employees outside the general civil service population and allows the Director to take various personnel actions relating to hiring, promotion, qualifications, discipline, and other matters with a greater degree of discretion than would be the case if FBI personnel were included in the competitive service.

Positions in the FBI work force are governed by regulations issued by the Office of Personnel Management (OPM), an independent agency in the Executive Branch of the federal government. Most of the FBI's positions are white-collar occupations and can be classified into five broad white-collar job categories established by OPM: Professional, Administrative, Technical, Clerical, and "Other."

For ease of reference the FBI, like many other law enforcement entities, classifies its employees into the categories of Special Agent or Professional Support personnel, in accordance with actual job classifications.

## CURRENT HIRING ACTIVITY

The FBI will be hiring men and women as Special Agents in the foreseeable future. In addition, a limited number of support personnel will be hired to fill positions at Headquarters, in Washington, D.C., or in FBI Field Offices throughout the United States.

Most FBI white-collar personnel are paid according to the General Schedule contained in Title 5, USC, Section 5332(A). Some General Schedule personnel in specialized or competitive job categories are paid at a higher level under a Special Pay Rate System. The highest-ranking FBI personnel are paid under the SES Schedule or the Executive Schedule.

In addition, special geographic locality rates apply; therefore, the pay scales used in different parts of the country vary. The highest-ranking FBI personnel are paid under the SES Schedule or the Executive Schedule.

Recruitment: The FBI is authorized to hire its own personnel directly; it does not hire through the Office of Personnel Management as do many federal agencies. The Bureau recruits candidates through its fifty-six field offices and tenders all appointments by means of a centralized hiring system at FBI Headquarters. The FBI is an equal opportunity employer. Women, minorities, and the handicapped are encouraged to apply.

Prior to employment, all candidates must complete a rigorous application process. Successful completion of written tests and an interview are followed by a thorough background investigation that includes: checking credit and arrest records; interviewing associates; contacting personal and business references; interviewing past employers and neighbors; verifying educational achievements; drug testing; a polygraph examination; and a physical examination may be required.

The completed background investigation is then assessed for a final decision on hiring. Use of marijuana in the last three years, or of any illegal drug or combination of illegal drugs during the last ten years, or the sale of any of these drugs disqualify an applicant from employment.

## EQUAL EMPLOYMENT OPPORTUNITY AFFAIRS

The FBI is an equal opportunity employee. Women, minorities, and the handicapped are encouraged to apply.

The FBI believes that all of its employees should have equal opportunities and the entitlement to work in a professional environment. The FBI strongly endorses the initiatives pertaining to affirmative recruitment and increasing the number of women and minorities among its Special Agent and support personnel ranks, particularly in supervision and management.

## FBI INVESTIGATIVE RESPONSIBILITIES

The FBI's investigative authority is the broadest of all federal law enforcement agencies. The FBI therefore has adopted a strategic approach which stresses long-term, complex investigations. The FBI investigative philosophy also emphasizes close relations and information sharing with other federal, state, local, and foreign law enforcement and intelligence agencies. A significant number of FBI investigations are conducted in concert with other law enforcement agencies or as part of joint task forces.

## CATEGORIES OF INVESTIGATIVE PROGRAMS

As part of this process, the FBI has divided its investigations into seven programs: Applicant Matters, Civil Rights, Counterterrorism, Financial Crime, Foreign Counterintelligence, Organized Crime/Drugs, and Violent Crimes and Major Offenders.

These programs represent the FBI's responsibilities as assigned by law. Individual cases in a particular program may receive extensive investigative attention because of their size, potential impact, or sensitivity.

Investigations are conducted within the Attorney General's Guidelines which pertain to racketeering enterprises, general criminal investigations, undercover operations, criminal informant matters, extraterritorial investigations, and domestic security/terrorism matters. The Guidelines afford centralized direction, which allow for greater uniformity and control of a national and international law enforcement effort.

Some sensitive investigative methods, such as undercover activities and electronic surveillance, are subject to specific review and approval procedures.

## EXAMPLES OF INVESTIGATIVE MATTERS

The following pages present examples of some investigative matters in each of the above programs. Note that the same violation may appear in more than one program.

**Applicant Program:**
Department of Energy and Nuclear Regulatory Commission Applicants
Department of Justice candidates
FBI Special Agents and Support Applicants
U.S. Court candidates
White House Staff candidates

**Civil Rights Program:**
Civil Rights Act of 1964
Discrimination in Housing
Equal Credit Opportunity Act

**Counterterrorism Program:**
Domestic Terrorism
Hostage Taking
Overseas Homicide/Attempted Homicide (U.S.
    Persons)
Protection of Foreign Officials and Guests
Sabotage
Domestic Security
Attempted or Actual Bombings
Nuclear Extortion
Sedition

**Financial Crime Program:**
Bank Fraud and Embezzlement
Environmental Crimes

Fraud Against the Government
Corruption of Public Officials
Health Care Fraud
Election Law Violations

**Foreign Counterintelligence Program:**
Espionage
Foreign Counterintelligence Matters

**Organized Crime/Drug Program:**
Drug Matters
Racketeer Influenced and Corrupt Organizations
    Criminal Enterprise Investigations
Labor Racketeering
Money Laundering
Organized Crime/Drug Enforcement Task Force Matters

**Violent Crimes and Major Offenders Program:**
Fugitives Wanted as a Result of FBI Investigations
Escaped Federal Prisoners (some instances)

## FBI Fact Sheet

**DIRECTOR:**
Louis J. Freeh

**HEADQUARTERS ADDRESS:**
Federal Bureau of Investigation
J. Edgar Hoover Building
935 Pennsylvania Avenue, N.W.
Washington, D.C. 20535-0001
*Telephone:* (202) 324-3000

**ESTABLISHED:**
An investigative agency under the Department of
Justice was formed in 1908; after various changes in
name, it became known as the FBI in 1935.

**ORGANIZATION:**
The FBI is headed by a Director and Deputy Director.
Headquarters is comprised of nine divisions and
four offices. The FBI maintains fifty-six field offices,
approximately four hundred resident agencies, four
specialized field installations, and twenty-three
foreign liaison posts.

**EMPLOYEES:**
Special Agents: 10,529
Support Personnel: 15,398

**INVESTIGATIVE PROGRAMS:**
Applicant Matters
Civil Rights
Counterterrorism
Financial Crimes
Foreign Counterintelligence
Organized Crime/Drugs
Violent Crimes and Major Offenders

**BUDGET:**
The FBI's total annual funding for all operations,
salaries, and expenses is approximately
$2.5 billion.

**MISSION:**
To uphold the law through the investigation of
violations of federal criminal law; to protect the
United States from foreign intelligence and terrorist
activities; to provide leadership and law enforcement
assistance to federal, state, local, and international
agencies; and to perform these responsibilities in a
manner that is responsive to the needs of the public
and is faithful to the Constitution of the United
States.

**TRAINING FACILITY:**
The FBI Academy is located in Quantico, Virginia. It
occupies 385 acres and is approximately forty miles
south of Washington, D.C.

**TERM OF FBI DIRECTOR:**
Public Law 94-503, section 203, enacted on October
15, 1976, provides for the appointment of the FBI
Director by the President with the advice and
consent of the Senate. In addition, the term of an
FBI Director was limited to ten years.

**FBI MOTTO:**
Fidelity, Bravery, Integrity

Probation/Parole Violations (some instances)
Unlawful Flight to Avoid Prosecution (including
parental kidnapping fugitives)
Crime on Indian Reservations
Theft of Government Property
Interstate Transportation of Stolen Motor Vehicles
Interstate Transportation of Stolen Property
Theft from Interstate Shipments
Assaulting, Kidnapping, or Killing the President,
Vice President, or Member of Congress
Bank Robbery, Burglary, or Larceny
Crime Aboard Aircraft
Kidnapping—Extortion
Sexual Exploitation of Children
Tampering with Consumer Products

## MAJOR RECENT INVESTIGATIVE ACCOMPLISHMENTS

A February 26, 1993, explosion in the World Trade Center's parking garage resulted in six deaths and 1,042 injuries. The blast, caused by a bomb made of about twelve thousand pounds of explosives, resulted in a five-story crater with damage of over $500 million. On March 4, 1994, Muhammad Amin Salameh, Nidal Ayyad, Mahmud Abouhalima, and Ahmed Ajaj were convicted for their roles in the bombing. On April 25, 1994, each received a 240-year prison term and a $500,000 fine. Also, money they may receive from interviews or books must be turned over to the families of the six people killed in the bombing.

Salameh's roommate, Ramzi Ahmed Yousef, also was found to be involved in the conspiracy. However, he left this country for Pakistan the day after the bombing on board a Pakistan International Airlines flight. On February 7, 1995, Yousef, a "Top Ten" fugitive, was arrested in Pakistan and was then turned over to the FBI.

### Ames Espionage Investigation

Aldrich Hazen Ames and Maria Del Rosario Casas Ames were arrested on February 21, 1994, and charged with conspiracy to commit espionage. Ames had been an employee of the Central Intelligence Agency (CIA) for over thirty-one years and served as Chief, Soviet Operational Review Branch in the Operational Review and Production Group of the Soviet/East European (SE) Division of the Directorate of Operations (DO) of the CIA from 1983 through 1985. In the fall of 1985, until his departure for Rome in July 1986, Ames attended Italian language classes and worked with the Europe Branch, External Operations Group, SE Division, in preparation for his tour. At the time of his arrest, he was assigned to the Directorate of Intelligence Counternarcotics Center. His wife was a university student and had been a paid source for the CIA in Mexico City. Ames was sentenced on April 28, 1994, to life in prison without parole for conspiracy to commit espionage. On October 21, 1994, Mrs. Ames was sentenced to sixty-three months for conspiracy to commit espionage and ten concurrent months for income tax evasion.

### Operation Disconnect

Operation Disconnect, involving eighteen FBI field offices, focused on identifying and prosecuting illegal telemarketers. It is considered to be the most significant federal investigation ever directed at illegal telemarketing. As of November 1994, over 300 people had been charged and over 220 were convicted. Also, $6.5 million in property was seized for potential forfeiture.

### Polar Cap

Polar Cap was a joint investigation into one of the most significant international money-laundering organizations operating in the United States. This group was responsible for laundering an estimated $150 million each year for the Cali and Medellin drug cartels of Colombia, moving millions of dollars through bank accounts in the United States, Austria, Belgium, Colombia, the United Kingdom, Panama, and Switzerland. As of November, 1994, forty-five persons had been arrested, and asset seizures totaled over $50 million. Polar Cap was conducted by the FBI, Drug Enforcement Administration (DEA), Internal Revenue Service, and U.S. Customs Service.

### Violence Against Clinics Providing Reproductive Health Services

Following the FBI's investigation, Paul Hill was found to be responsible for the anti-abortion-related shooting deaths of Dr. John Britton and James Barrett and for gunshot injuries to Mrs. June Barrett, which occurred on July 29, 1994. Hill was convicted on three counts of violating Title 18, U.S. Code, Section 248, the Freedom of Access to Clinics Entrances Act of 1994. Also, on November 2, 1994, a Florida state jury found him guilty of murder, attempted murder, and firing a gun into an occupied vehicle. Hill was sentenced to die in Florida's electric chair.

## Investigation into Beating of Rodney King

On April 17, 1993, after extensive FBI investigation and federal prosecution, a jury convicted Los Angeles police officers Laurence Powell and Stacey Koon of one count, each, of violating Title 18, U.S. Code, Section 242 (Color of Law), in connection with the beating of Rodney King while he was being arrested. Both

## Frequently Asked Questions About the FBI

**1. Is the FBI a type of national police force?**

No. The FBI is a fact-finding organization which investigates violations of federal law, and its authority is strictly limited to matters within its jurisdiction.

**2. Does the FBI investigate all violations of federal and constitutional law?**

No. The FBI can investigate a matter only when it has authority to do so under a law passed by Congress or on instructions of the President or the Attorney General.

**3. What does the FBI do with facts and evidence gathered during an investigation?**

If a possible violation of federal law under the jurisdiction of the FBI has occurred, the FBI conducts an investigation. The facts of the case are then presented to the appropriate U.S. Attorney or Department of Justice official, who determines whether or not prosecution or further action is warranted. The FBI does not give an opinion or decide whether an individual is to be prosecuted.

**4. If a crime is a violation of both local and federal laws, does the FBI "take over" the investigation?**

No. State and local agencies are not subordinate to the FBI, and the FBI has no authority over them. The investigative resources of the FBI and the local agency are pooled in a common effort to solve the case.

**5. Can the FBI be "called in" to investigate a serious crime, such as murder, when local police cannot solve the case?**

No. The FBI has no authority to investigate local crimes that are not within FBI jurisdiction. The FBI will, however, render all possible assistance to local police through the FBI Laboratory, Criminal Justice Information Services Division, and the National Center for the Analysis of Violent Crime.

**6. What authority do FBI Agents have to make arrests?**

Agents may make arrests without a warrant for any federal offense committed in their presence, or when they have reasonable grounds to believe that the person to be arrested has committed or is attempting to commit a felony violation of U.S. laws. Agents also may make arrests by warrant.

**7. If someone claims to be an FBI Agent, how can one positively identify him or her as such?**

Each Special Agent carries a commission card, which identifies him or her as a Special Agent of the FBI and which bears the Agent's name, signature, and photograph. Each Agent is also issued a gold FBI Badge in the shape of a shield surmounted by an eagle.

**8. What is the function of the FBI in civil rights?**

It is to objectively investigate alleged violations of the civil rights statutes within FBI jurisdiction and to furnish the results of these investigations to the Department of Justice for a determination as to whether further action or prosecution is desired.

**9. If a child is missing under circumstances indicating a kidnapping has occurred, but no interstate transportation is known, will the FBI begin an investigation?**

Yes. The law provides that unless the victim is located or released within 24 hours, it is presumed that he or she has been transported interstate.

**10. How can I get an FBI security clearance?**

The FBI does not issue security clearances except for its own employees. It does conduct applicant investigations in certain cases at the request of other government agencies for people requiring security clearances. The results of these investigations are furnished to the requesting agency, which then decides whether or not to grant the person a security clearance.

**11. How does the FBI select its "Ten Most Wanted Fugitives"?**

This selection is based on several items, including the fugitive's past criminal record, the threat posed to the community, the seriousness of the crime for which he/she is sought, and whether nationwide publicity is likely to assist in the apprehension.

**12. How may I take the FBI tour in Washington, D.C.?**

The FBI tour is open Monday through Friday, except holidays, from 8:45 A.M. to 4:15 P.M. A reservation is not required, although one may be made for groups of fifteen or more by calling (202) 324-3447.

officers were sentenced to serve thirty months in federal prison.

## Gang Violence

As a result of an FBI investigation, the entire leadership of a violent street gang, the "LA Boys" or "Cali Boys," headed by Donald "Sly" Green and Darryl "Reese" Johnson, was convicted of racketeering, as well as racketeering and narcotics conspiracy, on March 30, 1994. Green also was found guilty of conducting a Continuing Criminal Enterprise. Prior to the trial, twenty-six of thirty-two defendants pleaded guilty to Racketeer Influenced and Corrupt Organization charges. Therefore, the most powerful and violent drug-distribution group in western New York was dismantled. Johnson faces a capital death penalty charge, as authorized by the Attorney General.

## Operation Horsecollar

A task force comprised of the FBI and New York City police targeted heroin distribution networks in Harlem, which has the highest concentration of heroin addicts in this Nation. Investigation resulted in about 222 arrests, 167 people convicted, over $8 million seized, 15 organizations dismantled, and 30 groups identified, as of November 1994. The operation also has been responsible for a marked decrease in murders in New York and the solution of forty murders, including the assassination of a New York police officer by a group under investigation.

## MAJOR RECENT ORGANIZATIONAL INITIATIVES

The FBI's Safe Streets Program targets violent crime and drug trafficking identified by state or local authorities as a significant local concern. As of October, 1995, 133 Safe Streets Task Forces had been established in 54 field offices. These task forces include 916 state and local officers, 719 FBI Agents, and 150 persons from other federal agencies. Between fall 1992 and September 1994 over 57,000 arrests had been made, and 23,900 complaints or warrants had been filed, which resulted in over 24,400 indictments and 21,088 convictions.

## Project Forge

Project Forge, initiated in February 1992, was a comprehensive internal evaluation designed to review the FBI's organizational structure and design; the role, responsibilities, and authority of FBIHQ managers; communications networks; and management ties between FBIHQ and field offices. As a partial result of Project Forge, completed in early 1994, the Director approved organizational changes, which have significantly improved the FBI's ability to accomplish its mission. The changes include: reconfiguring several FBIHQ divisions along functional lines to improve operation, reducing the number of management "layers" at FBIHQ; consolidating or removing redundant FBIHQ administrative/operational functions; and delegating additional operating authority to field offices.

## Recruitment

As a result of recent appropriations, the FBI is starting one of the most significant recruiting/hiring efforts in its history to attract qualified applicants. In that regard, the FBI is implementing a national advertising strategy for minority and female Special Agent and support applicants, as well as implementing new and validated selection procedures for both Special Agent and support applicants. The FBI expects to hire hundreds of Agents and support employees in each of the next few fiscal years.

## Rapid Start Team

This team is a pool of FBI Special Agents and support personnel from which deployable groups are formed to provide on-site automation for major cases and crises. The team travels to the jurisdiction investigating such crimes as murders, kidnappings, bombings, or other task force cases. The investigation is automated by entering all pertinent facts into one database. The information may be sorted, filtered, and analyzed, allowing for effective lead management, as well as directing investigators toward more effective approaches. The Rapid Response Team has been responsible for automating facts in many investigations, including the bombing of the World Trade Center.

## DNA Technology

The FBI began DNA analysis of evidence in 1988. In April 1992 and August 1994, the FBI Laboratory began using new DNA casework tests based on a technique for amplifying small quantities of DNA often found in crime scene evidence. The Combined DNA Index System (CODIS) is a database containing DNA profiles of convicted sex offenders and other violent offenders, as well as missing persons. CODIS allows state and local crime laboratories to match DNA profiles from serial rape cases having unknown suspects to each other to help in refocusing investigative efforts. Full CODIS development was scheduled for early 1995; however, DNA-matching software from the system had previously been used to solve cases. The full CODIS system will take advantage of the existing twenty thousand convicted offender DNA records when it is deployed in the Nation's forty-five DNA crime laboratories.

## FBI Disaster Squad

The nucleus of the Disaster Squad consists of the FBI Laboratory's Latent Fingerprint Specialists. Since its 1940 inception, the Squad had assisted in identifying almost four thousand deceased persons in over 180 incidents by securing fingerprints, palm prints, and footprints from an estimated sixty-nine hundred victims, as of November 1994. Recent incidents requiring Disaster Squad assistance included two separate airplane crashes, the accidental downing of two military aircraft, an overseas military conflict, and the unearthing of grave sites at two cemeteries due to flooding.

## National Crime Information Center (NCIC) 2000

Established in 1967, NCIC is a nationwide computerized information system to provide law enforcement with ready data regarding wanted persons, stolen property, and other information. The enhanced NCIC 2000 will incorporate advanced technologies such as capture, transmission, retrieval, and printout of fugitives' photographs and fingerprint images, as well as other improvements.

## Integrated Automated Fingerprint Identification System (IAFIS)

The IAFIS, intended to improve identification services such as fingerprint identifications and criminal history information, will be a rapid-response paperless system to receive and process electronic fingerprint images, criminal histories, and related data. New services will include remote searches of crime scene fingerprints and remote access to fingerprint images. IAFIS is scheduled to become operational in early 1999.

## Uniform Crime Reports (UCR)

UCR provides criminal statistics, based upon data reported to the FBI by law enforcement agencies across the Nation. The program is being improved through the implementation of the National Incident-Based Reporting System (NIBRS), which will collect data in twenty-two crime categories made up of forty-six specific crimes. Data will be collected on each single crime and its components. NIBRS will provide the ability to quantify drug seizures in relation to drug arrests; address issues such as hate crimes; and report the age, sex, race, etc., of victims and witnesses of all crimes. NIBRS is expected to be implemented by the end of the decade.

## Regional Drug Intelligence Squads (RDIS)

These multi-agency information-gathering groups are located in eight geographic regions—all key U.S. transshipment centers for illegal drugs. The intelligence information uncovered by RDISs is often used to predicate major drug investigations. Squad members, using the Racketeering Enterprise Investigation concept, focus on getting information about the most serious drug-trafficking organizations operating in their areas—including their composition, scope, magnitude, internal/external dynamics, and drug-trafficking patterns. Once collected, the information is analyzed and provided to the law enforcement agency—federal, state, or local—best suited to handle the case.

## DRUGX

This joint FBI-DEA drug index database became operational in 1995 after the Office of Investigative Agency

Policies—headed by FBI Director Louis J. Freeh—issued a resolution mandating its creation in order to enhance interagency coordination. Over 4.4 million FBI drug records—more precisely, case index information—have been merged with more than 4.1 million DEA records. Now, when the FBI contemplates opening an investigation on a subject, it can first check to see if DEA has an investigation on the same subject (or vice versa). DRUGX, by reducing duplicate efforts, will save valuable resources and man-hours for both the FBI and DEA.

## National Drug Intelligence Center (NDIC)

The FBI is one of many federal law enforcement, intelligence, and military agencies participating in the NDIC, which was established in 1993 to provide a strategic picture of drug distribution organizations. NDIC's Intelligence Priorities Board—created last year after a mandate by the Office of Investigative Agency Policies—sets the organization's collection and analysis requirements. NDIC analysts—after gathering information from the field and from the various agencies' headquarters—review the information and prepare reports, studies, and other products on requested drug trafficking–related topics. NDIC is also in the process of developing an electronic library which would enable participating agencies to search specific topics. These library services should eventually be available to state and local law enforcement as well.

## El Paso Intelligence Center (EPIC)

This is a multi-agency, round-the-clock electronic monitoring post on the U.S.-Mexican border that keeps tabs on drug-trafficking organizations and serves a national network of law enforcement agencies. Its primary focus is on drug-trafficking activities along the Southwest border, but EPIC investigators and analysts from the fifteen or so participating agencies also collect and analyze tactical drug intelligence from other areas—including foreign countries—whose drug activities impact on the United States. EPIC personnel also prepare periodic threat assessments of drug-trafficking organizations worldwide. During the normal course of their everyday work, EPIC agencies share their automated drug data bases with one another—a move which results in better coordinated investigative efforts.

## INTERNATIONAL ACTIVITIES

The Bureau's Legal Attaches receive information from national and local police agencies that is sometimes relevant to FBI OC/Drug cases in the United States, and the Legats pass on certain FBI information that might help the investigations of national and local police agencies. The FBI participates in international working groups with countries such as Italy, Australia, Canada, and Mexico. The Bureau participates in the exchange of mid-level supervisory personnel with police agencies in such countries as Germany, Italy, Australia, and Japan, and in INTERPOL, which facilitates the rapid exchange of criminal investigative information on drug smuggling and other international crimes.

## COOPERATIVE LAW ENFORCEMENT SERVICES

The FBI's Laboratory Division is one of the largest and most comprehensive crime laboratories in the world. It provides leadership and service in the scientific solution and prosecution of crimes throughout the United States and is the only full-service federal forensic laboratory.

FBI Laboratory scientific examinations support criminal, counterterrorism, and espionage field investigations for the FBI and other federal agencies. Forensic disciplines include chemistry, DNA, trace evidence, photography, document examinations, firearms, and latent fingerprints among others. Other services include the FBI's Disaster Squad, which identifies deceased persons at major disaster scenes, and the expert preparation of demonstrative evidence to enhance court testimony for law enforcement.

Examinations of evidence submitted in connection with criminal investigations and prosecutions with necessary expert court testimony are performed, free of charge, for all duly constituted law enforcement agencies in the United States that do not have access to the sophisticated instrumentation and/or expertise to perform the necessary examination(s). In addition, state and local crime laboratory and law enforcement personnel receive FBI Laboratory training from FBI personnel in courses carefully selected and developed after consultations throughout the law enforcement and crime laboratory communities. Much of this training is not available anywhere else in the United States, and, without it, jurisdictional laboratories would find it difficult to improve and expand their capabilities.

## CRIMINAL JUSTICE INFORMATION SERVICES

The Criminal Justice Information Services (CJIS) Division serves as the focal point and central repository for criminal justice information services in the FBI. Because the FBI recognized a need to better meet law enforcement's increasing fingerprint and information demands, the CJIS Revitalization and Relocation Project was initiated. This revitalization is being pursued through initiatives, including the development and implementation of the Integrated Automated Fingerprint Identification System, augmentation of the current National Crime Information Center (NCIC) to NCIC 2000, and the conversion of the summary-based Uniform Crime Reporting Program to the National Incident-Based Reporting System.

As a result of several factors, including insufficient space requirements to house these new technological systems and the desire to create improved working conditions for a large number of employees, the FBI explored relocation options. Following a thorough and in-depth relocation study, a site in Clarksburg, West Virginia, was selected for the new facility. In January 1991, the FBI purchased a 986-acre site. The main office building is of modular construction, consists of approximately 500,000 square feet, and provides office space for 2,500 employees. The complex now is complete, and 1,300 employees work there. FBI employees began to occupy the space in 1995.

## TRAINING PROGRAMS

Much of the training given to FBI employees takes place at the FBI Academy, located in Quantico, Virginia. New Agent training is a core initiative. Other law enforcement personnel also attend training programs at this facility.

This complex, managed by the Training Division, of twenty-one major buildings incorporates dormitory, classroom, research, and other ancillary training facilities to provide a unique law enforcement academy. One of the most recent additions is Hogan's Alley, a mock town where practical training exercises are conducted.

### Executive Training for State and Local Police

The FBI offers mid-level law enforcement officers the opportunity to attend the FBI National Academy, a comprehensive balanced, eleven-week program of advanced professional instruction. The curriculum consists of such courses as Management Science, Behavioral Science, Law, Law Enforcement Communication, Forensic Science, and Health/Fitness. Throughout this training, particular emphasis is placed on leadership

## Three Key Questions for X-Philes

Answers from former FBI supervisory special agent Gregg O. McCrary as published in *Entertainment Weekly* (#355, November 29, 1996).

**1. Does the FBI maintain a real "X-Files" division?**

As close as we come is the unit I was in, the "Profiling Unit." It deals with the behavioral sciences, and bizarre and unusual crimes—sex crimes, serial killers, etc. There isn't any real need for an "X-Files" because there aren't any aliens running around—but there's enough bizarre human behavior to keep us busy.

**2. Do powerful, independent rogue groups exist within the United States government or military?**

Not that I'm aware of. The only thing I've been sworn to secrecy about is foreign intelligence. Within the FBI, there's certainly subterfuge and sensitive, undercover work in foreign counterintelligence.

**3. What is the official FBI position on UFOs?**

We certainly acknowledge the reports, and there are a lot. But whether they are indeed flying saucers is the critical issue. For the FBI to get involved with UFOs, there would have to be "statutory jurisdiction," and I don't know why [they] would have it, unless the UFOs were committing a federal crime.

development. The impressive number of graduates who have achieved top executive positions in their respective agencies is a continuing source of pride to the National Academy staff.

The National Executive Institute (NEI) is a fifteen-day training program designed for chief executive officers of the largest law enforcement agencies in the United States. The majority of NEI participants are current executives that belong to the Major City Chiefs Association. Each year up to five federal law enforcement officials are invited along with an equal number of internationally known law enforcement officials. The two primary goals of the NEI are to act as a vehicle to enhance cooperation and coordination of policing throughout the law enforcement community and to promote individual learning.

The Law Enforcement Executive Development Seminar is designed for law enforcement executives of medium-sized departments. The two-week program is offered twice each year and provides instruction on a wide variety of timely subjects of interest and concern to the chief executive.

## FBI/Local Police

The Violent Crime/Fugitive Task Force Survival Awareness In-Service is part of the Safe Streets Program that promotes a coordinated effort between FBI field offices and their respective local counterparts to locate and apprehend violent fugitives and to attack street gangs and drug-related violence. The In-Service is designed to enhance street survival of the FBI Agents and local law enforcement officers involved in the associated task forces. The training consists of firearms, survival, and tactical movements.

## International Training

In a recent fiscal year, the FBI provided training to approximately 1,200 international students who took part in thirty-two separate international training initiatives. Of this number, approximately 870 students received training from FBI instructors who traveled outside the United States. In April 1995, the International Law Enforcement Academy at Budapest began operating within the Hungarian National Police Academy facility. Representatives of twenty-seven

countries from Central and Eastern Europe, Russia, and the newly independent states of the former Soviet Union had expressed interest in sending students to the facility, which has a curriculum modeled after the FBI National Academy and focuses on areas including organized crime, economic crime, and nuclear nonproliferation. The International Law Enforcement Academy hosts fifty students during each eight-week session, and at least five sessions are to be held each year. At the same time, topical seminars and courses are conducted for an additional fifty students. Academy instructors come from the ranks of the FBI and other federal law enforcement agencies. However, law enforcement agencies from such countries as Canada, the United Kingdom, Germany, Italy, Denmark, Norway, and Sweden have expressed interest in joining the United States in this unprecedented training effort.

## OPERATIONAL ASSISTANCE

In addition to course offerings, FBI Academy faculty members conduct research and provide assistance to federal, state, and local law enforcement on many topics and investigative techniques, including psycholinguistics, forensic hypnosis, psychological profiling, hostage negotiations, crisis management, and major case strategy consultations.

## Critical Incident Response Group (CIRG)

This group was formed to address hostage-taking, barricade situations, terrorist activities, and other critical incidents requiring an emergency response by diverse law enforcement resources. The CIRG provides training and operational support in such areas as crisis management, negotiations, criminal profiling, and special weapons and tactics (SWAT). The FBI Hostage Rescue Team and the Field SWAT Programs are part of the CIRG, and nine enhanced SWAT Teams are strategically located around the country.

## National Center for the Analysis of Violent Crime

The National Center for the Analysis of Violent Crime (NCAVC), formed at the FBI Academy in 1985, is a law enforcement–oriented resource center that consolidates research, training, investigative, and operational support functions to provide assistance to law enforcement agencies confronted with unusual, high-risk, vicious, or repetitive crimes. NCAVC's research activities include the study of serial and violent crimes, such as homicide, rape, child abduction, arson, threats, and computer crimes, as well as hijacking, crisis management, and areas of interest relating to hostage negotiation and special weapons and tactics team operations. Investigative support is also offered through the Violent Criminal Apprehension Program to alert law enforcement agencies which may be seeking the same offender for crimes in their jurisdictions.

# REAL-LIFE X-FILES AND THE ORGANIZATIONS THAT INVESTIGATE THEM

## PART I: ALIEN VISITORS

The search for extraterrestrial life has centered on attempting to detect radio transmissions. NASA funded a coordinated effort to scan over a wide range of frequencies. The SETI (Search for Extraterrestrial Intelligence) project was cut from the 1994 NASA budget; however, donations from private will allow it to continue.

Currently, UFO contactee and abductee reports are the only evidence of alien visitors. The Drake Equation, an attempt to estimate the number of civilizations in the universe, would support the existence of intelligent extraterrestrial life. Recent discoveries on our own planet provide proof of the existence of life on Mars. While planets have been detected in other star systems, there is a lack of verifiable information on the structure or conditions on these planets, and it is not known if any of these worlds could support life.

The evidence from abductee and contactee reports remains inconclusive. Many theories exist as to what they actually observe. One theory of electromagnetic effects maintains that all reports of paranormal incidents, including UFOs, ghosts, ESP, sasquatch, and religious fervor, can be explained as being caused by seismic activity generating electromagnetic radiation which in turn makes people think they are witnesses to an anomalous event. Alternatively, the EMM radiation can luminesce so that it appears as a UFO. The chief proponent of this theory is Michael Persinger. Paul Devereux has offered a variant theory known as the "Earth Lights" hypothesis.

Researchers involved with contactee, abduction and other cases associated with flying saucers or other UFOs have produced reports describing twelve types of alien.

They claim that Arcturus natives are members of the Confederation of Humans, supposedly an organization of alien groups born out of positive energy, that help the human race. In addition, the Confederation is said to include natives from Vega, Sirius, and Pleiades.

Aryans, or Blondes, are reportedly blond Nordic Humanoids who are said to switch their loyalties between the Reptoids and the Confederation.

The Blues, or Star Warriors, are said to have translucent skin, large almond shaped eyes, and small stature. Robert Morningsky, a Hopi/Apache dancer, provided most of the information about the Blues. He claimed the Greys contacted the U.S. Government about 1947–1948 to form a treaty, but the Blues advised the government not to deal with the Greys, insisting it would only lead to disaster.

The Blues supposedly offered to teach peace and harmony if men would disarm, then left when the military rejected their offer. A few reportedly remained in Northern Mexico and Arizona and entered a treaty with the Hopi Indians. Hopi supposedly know these aliens as Star Warriors. When the Greys began monitoring the Blues, the Blues fled the reservation, along with a few Elders.

Greys are the most frequently reported alien race. Scientific UFOlogists maintain that they are the most common abductors of human victims. Their motives are not known, but they are said to be abducting, studying, testing, and using humans. The New Age Movement offers a different interpretation, defining them as an evil race with bad energy often associated with the Reptoids and of unknown motives.

Various conspiracy theories involve the Greys, mixing Scientific and New Age views. The standard theory says the Greys crashed and were found by the

U.S. government then entered a secret treaty allowing them to abduct humans in exchange for technology. Some conspiracy theories state that the Greys later violated the treaty.

Descriptions of several types of Greys exist. They are said to be humanoid in appearance, with a head, a torso, two arms, hands, legs, and feet. The most commonly reported Grey is two to four feet tall, very slender, with delicate features, penetrating black slanted eyes, and no pupils, an almost vestigial mouth and nose, and a very large head with a pointed chin. Reportedly, their skin color varies, and they have no hair on their bodies.

Another commonly seen Grey is described similarly as above, except they're usually six inches taller. A variation includes eyes like big, rounded, black buttons.

Another reported type of Grey are stocky, small robotic beings with a smooth, rounded hat on top, dark, deep set eyes, and a very round mouth, and possessing a square breastplate with concentric circles. They have a sulfuric smell and mushroom grey skin. Still other variations are described as reptilian. There have also been reports of cross breeds with humans.

The Orion Empire groups are said to be born out of negative energy similar to the Reptoids and Greys.

Pleiadians are a collective of extraterrestrials from the star system Pleiades and the future, ranging from 500 years from now to millions of years from now. The ancient Pleiadian culture was "seeded" from a universe of love long before Earth was created. Supposedly Pleiadians started a project to contact and inspire Earth humans to create a better reality for themselves and are here as ambassadors from another universe to help Earth through her transition from the third dimension to the fourth dimension.

Pleiadians reportedly speak as a collective with no identifiable individuals and do not appear in physical form. Billie Meier claimed to have been contacted over 130 times between 1976 and 1982 by a female named Samjese. He published their conversations in four books.

Reptoids are reportedly a reptilian race from Draco bent on conquest, and possibly controlling the Greys by means of an implant similar to that the Greys implant in humans. Their master plan supposedly involves using half-breed humans with implants to defeat the Confederations of Humans. Reptoids eat humans.

# PART 2: GLOSSARY

**Adamski, George:** A UFO hoaxer most famous for the Adamski photographs later revealed to be fake. He also claimed to have met Venusians in 1952 and advocated Cosmic Philosophy.

**AFOSI:** US Air Force Office of Special Investigations.

**Anomaly (AN Rating):** See VALLE CLASSIFICATION SYSTEM.

**APRO:** US-based Aerial Phenomenon Research Organization.

**Area 51:** Groom Dry Lake area of Nellis Air Force Range and Nuclear Test Site in the Nevada desert, about 80 miles NNW of Las Vegas. US government may be test-flying BLACK PROJECT aircraft, including UFOs, for a number of years.

**Arnold, Kenneth:** Pilot who reported observing nine boomerang-shaped craft flying over the Cascade Mountains in Washington on June 24, 1947.

**Bennewitz, Paul:** Albuquerque businessman who monitored electromagnetic pulses from craft flying above Manzano Nuclear Weapons Storage Facility near Kirtland Air Force Base in the late 1970s. Concluded that the pulses possibly controlled implanted abductees. Attempted to decode the pulses and contacted APRO, then AFOSI in October 1980. Communicated with RICHARD DOTY. Bennewitz filled out forms and supplied videotape of possible UFOs flying over the Nuclear Storage Facility. Doty presumably fed Bennewitz DISINFORMATION about US government involvement with extraterrestrial intelligences, including pacts, alien bases, and hybrid experimentation, which Bennewitz accepted at face value. Doty instigated WILLIAM MOORE to supply further disinformation. Bennewitz grew paranoid and then insane. JOHN LEAR included Bennewitz' story in his DARK SIDE HYPOTHESIS.

**Black Projects:** Government projects declared secret due to advanced technology.

**BUFORA (British UFO Research Organization):** Major UFO group in United Kingdom organized in 1964. Conducts research and issues a bimonthly publication, *UFO TIMES*.

**Cash/Landrum Case:** Betty Cash, Vickie Landrum, and her grandson, Colby Landrum, were driving along a road in Huffman, Texas in December

1980, and reported encountering a bright light in the sky and a diamond shaped UFO. Exhaust from the vessel forced them to stop their car near the craft. Vickie and Colby remained with their car, while Betty moved closer to the vessel. Her skin burned because of heat from the flames. She returned to the car when the object rose and unmarked black helicopters followed the UFO. They suffered sunburn, diarrhea, and vomiting after returning home. Some claim this was a US government manufactured UFO due to the presence of flames and helicopters (See PROJECT SNOWBIRD).

**Cattle Mutilations:** Cattle carcasses missing various parts with blood drained through incisions apparently made by laser. No trace of blood is found near the body. UFO sightings have been linked with these mutilations.

**Close Encounters (CE Rating):** See HYNEK CLASSIFICATION SYSTEM and VALLEE CLASSIFICATION SYSTEM.

**Collins, Robert:** See "CONDOR."

**Condon Report:** Dr. Edward Condon conducted investigation into PROJECT BLUE BOOK in 1969. Began as a debunker insisting that Blue Book wasted government resources. His report concluded that all UFO sightings were explainable and did not pose a defense threat.

**"Condor":** Also known as Robert Collins who reportedly took part in a DISINFORMATION program with WILLIAM MOORE and RICHARD DOTY against PAUL BENNEWITZ.

**Cooper, Milton William:** Also known as Bill Cooper, he is disliked by the UFO community. Formerly US Air Force, later reportedly joined Naval Intelligence. First appeared within the UFO community on PARANET reporting a UFO sighting observed while on the *USS Tiru*, a US Naval submarine. Later added details about alleged US government secret projects. Replied abusively to requests for evidence. Eventually barred from Paranet, he sent reports to various computer bulletin boards anonymously, accusing UFO researchers of working for the government to spread DISINFORMATION. Now a highly paid lecturer who claims JFK was assassinated because he wanted to make UFOs public and that we had bases on the Moon and Mars since the 1950s. Further claims that aliens in US TV series *Alien Nation* are real aliens employed as part of an indoctrination program. Mixes claims by PAUL BENNEWITZ, BILL MOORE, JOHN LEAR, and BOB LAZAR with personal theories. During *Billy Goodman's Happening* phone-in radio show, on November 21, 1989, Cooper called in to declare that Lazar's claims were genuine. Cooper later declared Lazar a fraud.

**CUFOS (The Centre for UFO Studies):** Founded in 1973 by Dr. J. Allen Hynek four years after concluding work at PROJECT BLUE BOOK. Publishes bimonthly *International UFO Reporter* and annual *JOURNAL OF UFO STUDIES.*

**Dark Side Hypothesis:** JOHN LEAR hypothesis that many flying saucer crashes have been recovered by the US government leading to Project Redlight in 1962, a program implemented to discover how to fly these craft and was carried out in S-4 at AREA 51. Lear claims that aliens later took over this area, leading to a US government pact with the aliens, trading them control of part of S-4 and abductees for advanced technology and prior approval authority over abduction subjects. The US government accused the aliens of unauthorized abductions in 1973. The aliens captured, then killed, 44 top scientists and Delta Force troops in 1978, ending the pact. The aliens continued abducting as many as 10% of Americans to use in experiments, replacing mutilated abductees with androids. The US government and the aliens later entered a new pact granting the US access to additional alien technology. Lear claims the US government now supervises abductions and that abductees are implanted with control devices. MJ-12 supposedly heads the secret government project. Lear's sources include PAUL BENNEWITZ, BOB LAZAR, and BILL COOPER. Bob Lazar publicly stated on US TV in 1989 that he did not believe Lear's claims.

**Daylight Disk:** See HYNEK CLASSIFICATION SYSTEM.

**Disinformation:** A strategy of supplying false information to mislead.

**Doty, Richard:** AFOSI Special Agent who supplied PAUL BENNEWITZ with DISINFORMATION and employed WILLIAM MOORE to observe prominent UFOlogists. Moore may have given him the code name "FALCON" when they appeared on *UFO Cover-Up . . . Live* with "CONDOR" in the US, embarrassing the UFO community when they claimed EBE's live in secret hideaways and like strawberry ice cream and Tibetan music.

**Dreamland:** Common name for AREA 51.

**EBE (Extra-terrestrial Biological Entities):** Common name for aliens first used in the MJ-12 briefing document.

**ET (Extra-terrestrial):** Common term for aliens.

**ET Exposure Law:** (Title 14, Section 1211 of the Code of Federal Regulations) A regulation prohibiting contact with aliens enacted in 1969. Since revoked.

**"Falcon":** Possibly former AFOSI Special Agent RICHARD DOTY.

*Fire in the Sky:* Film based on the TRAVIS WALTON ABDUCTION CASE fictionalized for entertainment purposes.

**Fly-By (FB Rating):** See VALLEE CLASSIFICATION SYSTEM.

**Flying Saucer:** Term created by a newspaper covering Kenneth Arnold's possible witnessing of nine boomerang-shaped UFOs in 1947 because Arnold described their movements as similar to a saucer skipping across the surface of a lake.

*Flying Saucer Review:* Oldest currently published UFO journal, begun in the 1950s. No longer considered authoritative due to changes of editors.

**FOIA (Freedom of Information Act):** Law guaranteeing public access to classified documents by having all or a portion declassified by order of a federal judge. The judge may refuse declassification if such action would be detrimental to national security.

**Foo Fighters:** Shiny metallic-looking sphere reported floating in the skies during World War II. After the war, both sides denied ownership. Americans called them "foo fighters," a term derived from a comic-strip phrase, "Where there's foo, there's fire."

**Ghost Rockets:** Over two thousand UFOs were reported flying above Scandinavia in 1946. Reports claimed some had landed and exploded. Neither East nor West admitted ownership. Western scientists said fragments were composed of an organic substance that resembled carbide. Allegedly, the Greek Army closed an investigation after it publicly announced that these were not missiles in 1967.

**Good, Timothy:** Author of *Above Top Secret, Alien Liaison, Alien Update,* and *The UFO Report. Above*

*Top Secret* claimed to document worldwide government cover-up of UFOs, and published a fake MJ-12 briefing document. *Alien Liaison* added coverage of DISINFORMATION, CATTLE MUTILATIONS, and the ROBERT LAZAR . It was heavily influenced by the MJ-12 documents, and the claims of BILL MOORE and BOB OESCHLER.

**Greys:** Humanoids ranging from two to five feet in height, usually exhibiting black bug-like eyes, with little or no nose, and a small slit mouth, frequently reported in CLOSE ENCOUNTER incidents.

**Gulf Breeze Sightings:** UFO sightings in Gulf Breeze, Florida since 1987, concentrated between November 1987 and May 1988. Ed Walters claimed aliens attempted to abduct him and his wife, Frances, with a blue ray, but failed. He later claimed to know when a UFO arrival was imminent because he would feel a humming noise in his head. The Walters took forty photos with various cameras over that period.

**Hill Abduction Case:** Abduction case relying on information gained through HYPNOTIC REGRESSION on Betty and Barney Hill. The Hills were returning from a holiday on a New Hampshire road in September 1961 when they saw a bright moving light. A coin-shaped craft with blue lighted windows approached their car, so they stopped. Two wings emerging from the craft convinced the pair to resume their journey home. When they returned, they learned that two hours were missing from their lives. Betty later had a series of disturbing dreams relating to a possible UFO abduction. The couple then underwent hypnotic regression. They recalled stopping the car because it was stalled by the UFO, then being taken off of the road onto a ramp into the UFO. They were put into different rooms and underwent an examination. Betty witnessed a three-dimensional holographic star map she drew at a regression session. An amateur astronomer calculated that the aliens identified the ZETA RETICULI system.

**Hynek Classification System:** Dr. J. Allen Hynek developed this system to categorize types of UFO sightings. The categories follow:

• Nocturnal Light: Any anomalous light(s) seen in the night sky whose description rules out the possibilities of aircraft lights, stars, meteors and the like.

- Daylight Disk: UFOs seen in the distant daytime sky. Various shapes.
- Radar-Visuals: UFOs tracked on radar and visually at the same time.

*Close Encounters . . .*

- Of the First Kind (CEI): A UFO in close proximity (within approx. 500 feet) to the witness.
- Of the Second Kind (CEII): A UFO that leaves markings on the ground, causes burns or paralysis to humans, frightens animals, interferes with car engines or TV and radio reception.
- Of the Third Kind (CEIII): A CEI or CEII with visible occupants.

*Additional unofficial classes*

- Of the Fourth Kind (CEIV): Abduction cases.
- Of the Fifth Kind (CEV): Communication between a person and an alien.
- Hypnotic Regression: Attempted access to subconscious memory by use of hypnotism, but proven unreliable because it is possible to lie during regression or confuse memories. Interpretation is also difficult.

**Journal of UFO Studies (JUFOS):** CUFOS' annual journal containing scholarly papers on UFOlogy.

**Just Cause:** A journal published quarterly by CAUS (Citizens Against UFO Secrecy) since 1984.

**Lazar, Robert Scott:** Robert Lazar holds two masters degrees, in physics and electronics. He wrote his thesis on magnetohydrodynamics (MHD), and has worked in Los Alamos as a technician and then as a physicist in the Polarized Proton Section dealing with particle accelerators. Lazar appeared on KLAS-TV in March 1989 in shadow with his voice altered, under the pseudonym "Dennis," claiming to have worked in an above Top Secret installation known as S-4, ten miles south of Area 51 in the Nevada desert to examine a captured flying saucer. He claimed witnessing nine different saucers at S-4 that used a gravity waves propulsion system powered by irradiating Element 115, an element not found on Earth, and which cannot be synthesized. He further claimed to have entered a craft and witnessed a test flight. He took three friends, including John Lear, to the edge of S-4 to observe UFO test flights through a telescope on March 29, 1989. They filmed a craft hovering in the air, briefly disappearing, and reappearing a few feet higher, and then going down in the same way. A security guard caught them when they returned on June 4, 1989, and a record was entered on a computer in Area 51. They were ordered to leave the area. Lazar was ordered to go to Area 51 the following day for a meeting with security guards and an FBI agent. He resigned and left, then went on television under his own name after being fired at on an interstate highway. He told his full story in November of 1989; he hoped that publicity would protect him from reprisal.

**Lear, John:** The estranged son of Bill Lear, inventor of the Lear Jet, and the only pilot holding every airman certificate awarded by the Federal Aviation Administration. He has flown over 160 types of aircraft and, reportedly, many missions for the CIA. He is a friend of Paul Bennewitz who told Lear everything that he had heard from Richard Doty and William Moore. Lear was also a friend of Robert Lazar. Moore showed him the documents from Doty, and he began to create the Lear Hypothesis, also known as the Dark Side Hypothesis. He then subscribed to Paranet and befriended Bill Cooper. Cooper helped create the hypothesis and sent it to the Paranet Bulletin Board. Later, Lear and Cooper were barred from Paranet and their friendship ended, Cooper accused Lear of being a government agent. Lear now lectures about his Hypothesis.

**Majestic:** Reportedly, the highest security level, thirty-eight levels higher than Top Secret due to the compartmentalization of information. Documents about S-4/Area 51 are classified as "Majestic."

**Maneuver (MA Rating):** See Vallee Classification System.

**Men in Black (MIBs):** Allegedly, people who dress in black suits and travel in black cars and helicopters threatening UFO witnesses.

**Missing Time:** An unaccounted for period of time ranging from minutes to days missing from memory after returning from a UFO sighting.

**MJ-12 (also known as Majic-12, Majority-12, Majesty-12):** Mystery begun with the 1987 publication of an alleged briefing document from ex-US President Harry Truman to President-Elect Dwight Eisenhower dated November of 1953 revealing government knowledge of UFOs, aliens, and above secret projects. The document listed Dr. Lloyd Berkner, Dr. Detlev Bronk, Dr. Vannevar Bush, James Forrestal, Gordon Gray, Vice Admiral Roscoe Hillenkoetter, Dr. Jerome Hunsaker, Dr. Donald Menzel, General Robert Montague, Rear Admiral Sidney Souers, General Nathan Twining, and General Hoyt Vandenberg as the twelve. James Forrestal had a mental breakdown and committed suicide in 1949 and allegedly was replaced by General Walter Smith. The twelve supposedly headed a research and development/intelligence operation answerable only to the US President. All members had died before the briefing document was publicized, so none could verify the report. The briefing document was proved to be a fake when it was found that the signature was identical in ratio to a 1947 memo from President Truman to Vannevar Bush. However the MJ-12 controversy continued with partisans claiming the document was deliberate DISINFORMATION, therefore proving it was true. The document included information relating to the ROSWELL CASE, as well as PROJECTS SIGN, GRUDGE, and BLUE BOOK, and KENNETH ARNOLD's sighting. UFOlogists divided as to belief in the existence of a Majestic 12. Some say it only evaluated PROJECT BLUE BOOK reports, while others claim it runs the CIA, FBI, and world drugs market, and plans world domination in partnership with the GREYS.

**Moore, William:** This ex-teacher became a writer in 1979 and investigated the 1947 ROSWELL CASE. He worked with APRO before joining the APRO board. He learned of PAUL BENNEWITZ's claims from fellow board member Jim Lorenzen, but didn't become interested. He received phone calls from a nearby Air Force Base sergeant while promoting his book, *The Roswell Incident*. He then met RICHARD DOTY. Doty told him that he, and nine other military people, would supply him with information about the US government's activities with UFOs if he spied on APRO and passed DISINFORMATION on to Paul Bennewitz. All ten used the code names derived from birds. Moore gave Bennewitz doctored documents from Doty and, in exchange, was given documents about PROJECTS SIGMA, Redlight, AQUARIUS, GALILEO, POUNCE, and SNOWBIRD by Doty and the others. These documents purportedly claimed that the US government worked with aliens in advancing US space technology, and that three EBEs had been kept in various Air Force Bases. Moore went on the TV show, *UFO Cover-Up . . . Live*, with "FALCON" and "CONDOR" in October 1988, a show considered to be the worst embarrassment suffered by the UFO community. Moore was devastated and confessed at the 1989 MUFON annual conference that he had passed on disinformation from Doty to Bennewitz and had spied on UFOlogists.

**MUFON (The Mutual UFO Network):** Established in 1969 and now the world's largest international UFO organization. It publishes the monthly *MUFON UFO Journal*.

**Nocturnal Light:** See HYNEK CLASSIFICATION SYSTEM.

**Oeschler, Robert:** Bob Oeschler joined the US Air Force and the American Forces Radio and Television service in 1968 filming classified prototype weapons systems during the Vietnam War. He spent eighteen months at Wright-Patterson AFB before working for NASA after he returned to the US. He specialized in missions technical analysis as a prototype designer of control and mobile surveillance systems at NASA. He is allegedly connected with the US Intelligence Community. He claimed to have worked on a government project called "Cosmic Journey," an exhibition of US space missions, including a section on aliens which was going to exhibit a cryogenically preserved alien body. This project was then shelved due to the 1988 US presidential election. Then, in October 1993, on BBC Radio One, he adopted ROBERT LAZAR's story, claiming that everything Lazar heard and saw, he heard and saw too.

**Paranet:** A moderated forum founded by Jim Spieser in 1986 originally dedicated to the paranormal as well as UFOs. Originally distributed as a newsletter via E-mail, it now consists of a set of newsgroups on Usenet. It was the first organization to offer the ROBERT LAZAR story and the forum in which MILTON WILLIAM COOPER made his debut.

**Project Aquarius:** Allegedly started in 1953 to accumulate and distribute data about alien life forms. First reported by WILLIAM MOORE when he released three pages of a "Project Aquarius Executive Briefing Document" to the public. This document is now thought to be a fake. Moore refused to release more proof that Project Aquarius existed.

**Project Blue Book:** The last publicly acknowledged USAF investigation into UFOs, which started in March 1952. Its aims were to assess UFO sightings as to national security, and determine if UFOs used advanced technology. Reports were collected, analyzed, and filed until an investigator sent in his own sighting. It was filed, but later allegedly disappeared. Blue Book ended in 1969 as a result of the CONDON REPORT. Dr. J. Allen Hynek, an investigator, went on to form the first scientific-based UFO group, the Center for UFO Studies, in 1973.

**Project Galileo:** A purported S-4 project dealing with flying recovered discs.

**Project Grudge:** Alleged successor to PROJECT SIGN launched to denounce UFOlogists, and encourage articles saying UFOs didn't exist. The final report said that all sightings could be dismissed on psychological ground and further investigation should be downgraded. Project Grudge supposedly was shut down in 1950.

**Project Pounce:** A project allegedly launched in 1953 to evaluate UFOs to gain space technology.

**Project Sigma:** Supposedly, an ongoing 1954 project that looked into how to communicate with aliens, revealed in the PROJECT AQUARIUS Briefing Document and said to have succeeded in 1964 when a USAF intelligence officer met two aliens in the New Mexico desert. A "Project Sigma" is listed in the 1986 Defense Marketing Services Code Name Directory as a "Top Secret Air Force program involving Rockwell International" and has been officially identified as a laser weapons project.

**Project Sign:** The first official USAF UFO investigation, started in January 1948 to determine what UFOs were. It lasted until February 1949.

**Project Snowbird:** An alleged ongoing 1972 project that researched, developed, and implemented alien spacecraft technology and test flew recovered UFOs. It is possible that the UFO involved in the CASH/LANDRUM CASE was built as part of this project; however, another "Project Snowbird" has been found described as a "Joint Army/Air Force peacetime military exercise in the sub-arctic region in 1955" in the 1963 Gale Research's Code Names Dictionary. Project Snowbird is another project supposedly revealed in the PROJECT AQUARIUS Briefing Document.

**Project Twinkle:** A highly secret study into green fireballs in New Mexico. Fireballs persistently disappeared before an investigator arrived, so they couldn't be examined, and Project Twinkle was shut down.

**Radar-Visuals:** See HYNEK CLASSIFICATION SYSTEM.

**Roswell Case:** An alleged flying saucer crashed near Corona, New Mexico during a violent thunderstorm in July of 1947. Mac Brazel found unidentifiable wreckage on his ranch the next morning. He showed it to the local sheriff, George Wilcox, who contacted Major Jesse Marcel at Roswell Air Army Field. Marcel reported to his commanding officer, William Blanchard. Counterintelligence gathered wreckage from the ranch to fly to Washington, via Fort Worth. Marcel and Cavitt returned to the ranch the next day to collect more wreckage to take back to Roswell Air Force Base. Marcel showed his family a small piece of tin-foil-like material which readily folded but returned to its original shape leaving no crease, and a light plastic-like material that wouldn't scratch, cut, burn or melt. Meanwhile, Lydia Sleppy at Roswell Radio station KSWS transmitted a story about the crashed saucer over the teletype until transmission was interrupted by someone claiming to represent the FBI. The Army initially released a story to the press saying they had captured a flying saucer, but then quickly insisted it was a weather balloon. Mac Brazel was placed under house arrest for a week while his ranch was combed for debris. Supposedly, authorities then found the main saucer body, and four aliens, including two dead, one seriously injured, and another attending to it. Mac Brazel was told never to tell anyone what he had found.

**S-4:** Three S-4s exist in the Nevada Test Site home of AREA 51, a nuclear reactor, an area south of the Tonopah test range, and one called Papoose Dry Lake Bed, ten miles south of Area 51. ROBERT LAZAR claims to have worked in the latter area.

**Sagan, Carl:** The late science popularizer and UFO skeptic who believes that no UFO would cross light years of distance due to the large amount of fuel and time needed. ROBERT LAZAR claimed that alternative methods of travel using gravity waves propel UFOs without significant cost in time or resources.

**SETI (The Search for Extra-Terrestrial Intelligence):** US government-funded project that monitors electromagnetic wave emissions from space. If they detect abnormal emissions, they will determine where they originate from. UFO researchers are skeptical. According to an article by Dr. Pierre Guerin in FLYING SAUCER REVIEW, the government already knows aliens don't use electromagnetic waves. The failed SETI project was given the order to close down by US Congress in October 1993 due to budget cuts. It wasn't a success.

**SVP Rating:** See VALLEE CLASSIFICATION SYSTEM.

**UFO:** Abbreviation for "Unidentified Flying Object." The USAF defines a UFO as: Anything that relates to any airborne object which by performance, aerodynamic characteristics, or unusual features does not conform to any presently known aircraft or missile type, or which cannot be identified as a familiar object. (USAF Regulation 200-2)

**UFO Times:** BUFORA journal containing British and European reports.

**UFOlogy:** The study of the UFO phenomena.

**Vallee, Jacques:** French astrophysicist and UFOlogist who believes that UFOs come from both a physical and psychic origin and that some characters in folklore, like elves, could have originated from aliens. He expanded the HYNEK CLASSIFICATION SYSTEM.

**Vallee Classification System:** A system used to categorize types of UFO and paranormal experiences invented by Dr. Jacques Vallee which replaced the HYNEK CLASSIFICATION SYSTEM. The categories follow:

*AN Rating:* Anomalous behavior.
- AN1: Anomalies without lasting physical effects.
- AN2: Anomalies with lasting physical effects.
- AN3: Anomalies with associated entities.
- AN4: Witness interaction with the AN3 entities.
- AN5: Anomalous reports of injuries and deaths.

*MA Rating:* Describes behavior of a UFO. Analogous to the Nocturnal Light, Daylight Disk, and Radar Visual Hynek classifications.
- MA1: UFO observed traveling in a discontinuous trajectory.
- MA2: MA1 plus physical effects.
- MA3: MA1 plus entities observed on board.

- MA4: Maneuvers accompanied by a sense of reality transformation for the observer.
- MA5: A maneuver that results in a permanent injury or death.

*FB Rating:* Fly-by rating.
- FB1: UFO traveling in a straight line across the sky.
- FB2: FB1 accompanied by physical evidence.
- FB3: A fly-by where entities are observed on board.
- FB4: A fly-by where the witness experiences a transformation of reality.
- FB5: A fly-by in which the witness suffers permanent injuries or even death..

*CE Rating:* Close Encounter rating. Similar to the Hynek Close Encounter ratings.
- CE1: UFO comes within 500 feet of the witness, but no after effects are suffered by the witness or the surrounding area.
- CE2: A CE1 that leaves landing traces or injuries to the witness.
- CE3: Entities observed on the UFO.
- CE4: The witness abducted.
- CE5: A CE4 which results in permanent psychological injuries or death.

*SVP Rating:* Credibility rating based on source reliability (first digit), site visit (second digit), and possible explanations (third digit). A rating of 222 or higher indicates the case was reported by a reliable source, the site has been visited, and a natural explanation would require a major alteration of at least one parameter.

*Source Reliability Rating*
- + 0: Unknown or unreliable source.
- + 1: Report attributed to a known source of unknown or uncalibrated reliability.
- + 2: Reliable source, secondhand.
- + 3: Reliable source, firsthand.
- + 4: Firsthand personal interview with the witness by a source of proven reliability.

*Site Visit Rating*
- + 0: No site visit, or answer unknown.
- + 1: Site visit by a casual person not familiar with the phenomena.
- + 2: Site visited by persons familiar with the phenomena.
- + 3: Site visit by a reliable investigator with some experience.
- + 4: Site visit by a skilled analyst.

*Possible Explanations Rating*

- + 0: Data consistent with one or more natural causes.
- + 1: Natural explanation requires only slight modification of the data.
- + 2: Natural explanation requires major alteration of one parameter.
- + 3: Natural explanation requires major alteration of several parameters.
- + 4: No natural explanation possible, given the evidence.

**Vimanas:** Flying devices in Hinduism. Ancient Sanskrit texts found by Westerners in a South Indian temple showed Vimanas as open-topped flying devices restricted to the Earth's atmosphere. Dr. Roberto Pinotti, an Italian scientist, referred to several Hindu texts and Indian gods and heroes fighting in the skies using piloted vehicles armed with weapons, when he spoke at the World Space Conference in Bangalore, India. The "Pinjula Mirror" offered a form of "visual shield" protecting the pilots from "evil rays," while the "Marika" shot enemy craft. Dr. Pinotti said the "principles of propulsion as far as the descriptions were concerned, might be defined as electrical and chemical, but solar energy was involved as well." Other scientists said that the craft were driven by a mercury ion propulsion system. Dr. Pinotti concluded that the Vimanas, written about hundreds, even thousands, of years ago, resembled modern UFOs, suggesting India had a ". . . superior but forgotten civilization. In the light of this, we think it will be better to examine the Hindu texts and subject the descriptive models of Vimanas to more scientific scrutiny." UFOlogists claim this indicates extraterrestrial visitors rather than indigenous advanced civilization.

**Walton, Travis, Abduction Case:** In November 1975, six tree-trimmers were in a truck in the Sitgreave-Apache National Forest in Arizona, USA. The driver stopped when he noticed a flying saucer hovering above nearby trees. Travis Walton approached on foot, and was knocked to the ground by a blue and white light. The terrified men in the truck sped off leaving him for dead. They later returned and couldn't find Travis or the flying saucer. Five days later, Travis returned wondering what had happened to him. He underwent hypnotic regression and recalled lying on his back on a table watched by aliens that looked like five-foot tall fetuses with mushroom-white skin, wearing tight-fitting, tan robes. A more human-looking alien wearing a helmet took him for a guided tour of the ship, ignoring questions. They walked into a hangar containing three saucers and met three other human-like aliens. Travis was then put onto a table with a mask over his face. He next remembered waking on a pavement in a village a few miles away from his home.

**Zeta Reticuli:** A binary star system 37 light years from Earth. Betty and Barney Hill (see HILL ABDUCTION CASE) allegedly were abducted by aliens from a planet in this system, and ROBERT LAZAR claimed that the nine UFOs he saw in S-4 came from one of the planets in this system.

# PART 3: AIR FORCE CADET MANUAL

Physics 370
United States Air Force Academy
Introductory Space Science

## Chapter XXXIII: Unidentified Flying Objects

What is an Unidentified Flying Object (UFO)? Well, according to United States Air Force Regulation 80-17 (dated 19 September 1966), a UFO is "Any aerial Phenomenon or object which is unknown or appears to be out of the ordinary to the observer." This is a very broad definition which applies equally well to one individual seeing his first noctilucent cloud at twilight as it does to another individual seeing his first helicopter. However, at present most people consider the term UFO to mean an object which behaves in a strange or erratic manner while moving through Earth's atmosphere. That strange phenomenon has evoked strong emotions and great curiosity among a large segment of our world's population. The average person is interested because he loves a mystery, the professional military man is involved because of the possible threat to national security, and some scientists are interested because of the basic curiosity that led them into becoming researchers.

The literature on UFO's is so vast, and the stories so many and varied, that we can only present a sketchy outline of the subject in this chapter. That outline includes description classifications, operational domains (temporal and spatial), some theories as to the nature of the UFO phenomenon, human reactions, attempts to attack the problem scientifically, and some tentative conclusions. If you wish to read further in this area, the references provide an excellent starting point.

## 33.1 Descriptors

One of the greatest problems you encounter when attempting to catalog UFO sightings, is selection of a system for cataloging. No effective system has yet been devised, although a number of different systems have been proposed. The net result is that almost all UFO data are either treated in the form of individual cases, or in the forms of inadequate classification systems. However, these systems do tend to have some common factors, and a collection of these factors is as follows:

a. Size
b. Shape (disc, ellipse, football, etc.)
c. Luminosity
d. Color
e. Number of UFO's

### Behavior
a. Location (altitude, direction, etc.)
b. Patterns of paths (straight line, climbing, zig-zagging, etc.)
c. Flight characteristics (wobbling, fluttering, etc.)
d. Periodicity of sightings
e. Time duration
f. Curiosity or inquisitiveness
g. Avoidance
h. Hostility

### Associated Effects
a. Electro-magnetic (compass, radio, ignition systems, etc.)
b. Radiation (burns, induced radioactivity, etc.)
c. Ground disturbance (dust stirred-up, leaves moved, standing wave peaks on surface of water, etc.)
d. Sound (none, hissing, humming, roaring, thunder-claps, etc.)
e. Vibration (weak, strong, slow, fast)
f. Smell (ozone or other odor)
g. Flame (how much, where, when, color)
h. Smoke or cloud (amount, color, persistence)
I. Debris (type, amount, color, persistence)
j. Inhibition of voluntary motion by observers
k. Sighting of "creatures" or "beings"

### After Effects
a. Burned areas or animals
b. Depressed or flattened areas
c. Dead or missing animals
d. Mentally disturbed people
e. Missing items

We make no attempt here to present available data in terms of the foregoing descriptors.

## 33.2 Operational Domains— Temporal and Spatial

What we will do here is to present evidence that UFO's are a global phenomenon which may have persisted for many thousands of years. During this discussion, please remember that the more ancient the reports the less sophisticated the observer. Not only were the ancient observers lacking the terminology necessary to describe complex devices (such as present day helicopters) but they were also lacking the concepts necessary to understand the true nature of such things as television, spaceships, rockets, nuclear weapons and radiation effects. To some, the most advanced technological concept was a war chariot with knife blades attached to the wheels. By the same token, the very lack of accurate terminology and descriptions leaves the more ancient reports open to considerable misinterpretation, and it may well be that present evaluations of individual reports are completely wrong. Nevertheless, let us start with an intriguing story in one of the oldest chronicles of India . . . the Book of Dzyan.

This book is a group of "story-teller" legends which were finally gathered in manuscript form when man learned to write. One of the stories is of a small group of beings who supposedly came to Earth many thousands of years ago in a metal craft which orbited Earth several times before landing. As told in the Book "These beings lived to themselves and were revered by the humans among whom they had settled. But eventually differences arose among them and they divided their numbers, several of the men and women and some children settling in another city, where they were promptly installed as rulers by the awe-stricken populace.

"Separation did not bring peace to these people and finally their anger reached a point where the ruler of the original city took with him a small number of his warriors and they rose into the air in a huge shining metal vessel. While they were many leagues from the city of their enemies, they launched a great shining lance that rode on a beam of light. It burst apart in the city of their enemies with a great ball of flame that shot up to the heavens, almost to the stars. All those who were in the city were horribly burned and even those who were not in the city—but nearby—were burned also. Those who looked upon the lance and the ball of fire were blinded forever afterward. Those who entered the city on foot became ill and died. Even the dust of the city was poisoned, as were the rivers that flowed through it. Men dared not go near it, and it gradually crumbled into dust and was forgotten by men.

"When the leader saw what he had done to his own people he retired to his palace and refused to see anyone. Then he gathered about him those of his warriors who remained, and their wives and children, and they entered into their vessels and rose one by one into the sky and sailed away. Nor did they return."

Could this foregoing legend really be an account of an extraterrestrial colonization, complete with guided missile, nuclear warhead and radiation effects? It is difficult to assess the validity of that explanation . . . just as it is difficult to explain why Greek, Roman and Nordic Mythology all discuss wars and conflicts among their "Gods." (Even the Bible records conflict between the legions of God and Satan.) Could it be that each group recorded their parochial view of what was actually a global conflict among alien colonists or visitors? Or is it that man has led such a violent existence that he tends to expect conflict and violence among even his gods?

Evidence of perhaps an even earlier possible contact was uncovered by Tschi Pen Lao of the University of Peking. He discovered astonishing carvings in granite on a mountain in Hunan Province and on an island in Lake Tungting. These carvings have been evaluated as 47,000 years old, and they show people with large trunks (breathing apparatus? . . . or "elephant" heads shown on human bodies? Remember, the

Egyptians often represented their gods as animal heads on human bodies.).

Only 8,000 years ago, rocks were sculpted in the Tassili plateau of Sahara, depicting what appeared to be human beings but with strange round heads (helmets? or ii sun" heads on human bodies?). And even more recently, in the Bible, Genesis (6:4) tells of angels from the sky mating with women of Earth, who bore them children. Genesis 19:3 tells of Lot meeting two angels in the desert and his later feeding them at his house. The Bible also tells a rather unusual story of Ezekiel who witnessed what has been interpreted by some to have been a spacecraft or aircraft landing near the Chebar River in Chaldea (593 B.C.).

Even the Irish have recorded strange visitations. In the Speculum Repali in Konungs Skuggsa (and other accounts of the era about 956 A.D.) are numerous stories of "demonships" in the skies. In one case a rope from one such ship became entangled with part of a church. A man from the ship climbed down the rope to free it, but was seized by the townspeople. The bishop made the people release the man, who climbed back to the ship, where the crew cut the rope and the ship rose and sailed out of sight. In all of his actions, the climbing man appeared as if he were swimming in water. Stories such as this makes one wonder if the legends of the "little people" of Ireland were based upon imagination alone.

About the same time, in Lyons (France) three men and a woman supposedly descended from an airship or spaceship and were captured by a mob. These four foreigners admitted to being wizards, and were killed. (No mention is made of the methods employed to extract the admissions.) Many documented UFO sightings occurred throughout the Middle Ages, including an especially startling one of a UFO over London on 16 December 1742. However, we do not have room to include any more of the Middle Ages sightings. Instead, two "more-recent" sightings are contained in this section to bring us up to modern times.

In a sworn statement dated 21 April 1897, a prosperous and prominent farmer named Alexander Hamilton (Le Roy, Kansas, U.S.A.) told of an attack upon his cattle at about 10:30 p.m. the previous Monday. He, his son, and his tenant grabbed axes and ran some 700 feet from the house to the cow lot where a great cigar-shaped ship about 300 feet long floated some 30 feet above the cattle. It had a carriage underneath which was brightly lighted within (dirigible and gondola?) and which had numerous windows. Inside were six strange looking beings jabbering in a foreign language. These beings suddenly became aware of Hamilton and the others. They immediately turned a searchlight on the farmer, and also turned on some power which sped up a turbine wheel (about 30 ft diameter) located under the craft. The ship rose, taking with it a two-year old heifer which was roped about the neck by a cable of one-half inch thick, red material. The next day a neighbor, Link Thomas, found the animal's hide, legs and head in his field. He was mystified at how the remains got to where they were because of the lack of tracks in the soft soil. Alexander Hamilton's sworn statement was accompanied by an affidavit as to his veracity. The affidavit was signed by ten of the local leading citizens.

On the evening of 4 November 1957 at Fort Itaipu, Brazil, two sentries noted a "new star" in the sky. The "star" grew in size and within seconds stopped over the fort. It drifted slowly downward, was as large as a big aircraft, and was surrounded by a strong orange glow. A distinct humming sound was heard, and then the heat struck. One sentry collapsed almost immediately, the other managed to slide to shelter under the heavy cannons where his loud cries awoke the garrison. While the troops were scrambling towards their battle stations, complete electrical failure occurred. There was panic until the lights came back on but a number of men still managed to see an orange glow leaving the area at high speed. Both sentries were found badly burned . . . one unconscious and the other incoherent, suffering from deep shock.

Thus, UFO sightings not only appear to extend back 47,000 years through time but also are global in nature. One has the feeling that this phenomenon deserves some sort of valid scientific investigation, even if it is a low level effort.

# 33.3 Some Theories as to the Nature of the UFO Phenomenon

There are very few cohesive theories as to the nature of UFOs. Those theories that have been advanced can be collected in five groups: a. Mysticism b. Hoaxes, and rantings due to unstable personalities c. Secret weapons d. Natural Phenomena e. Alien visitors

**Mysticism**

It is believed by some cults that the mission of UFO's and their crews is a spiritual one, and that all materialistic efforts to determine the UFO's nature are doomed to failure.

**Hoaxes and Rantings due to Unstable Personalities**

Some have suggested that all UFO reports were the results of pranks and hoaxes, or were made by people with unstable personalities. This attitude was particularly prevalent during the time period when the Air Force investigation was being operated under the code name of Project Grudge. A few airlines even went as far as to ground every pilot who reported seeing a "flying saucer." The only way for the pilot to regain flight status was to undergo a psychiatric examination. There was a noticeable decline in pilot reports during this time interval, and a few people interpreted this decline to prove that UFO's were either hoaxes or the result of unstable personalities. It is of interest that NICAP (The National Investigations Committee on Aerial Phenomena) even today still receives reports from commercial pilots who neglect to notify either the Air Force or their own airline.

There are a number of cases which indicate that not all reports fall in the hoax category. We will examine one such case now. It is the Socorro, New Mexico sighting made by police Sergeant Lonnie Zamora. Sergeant Zamora was patrolling the streets of Socorro on 24 April 1964 when he saw a shiny object drift down into an area of gullies on the edge of town. He also heard a loud roaring noise which sounded as if an old dynamite shed located out that way had exploded. He immediately radioed police headquarters, and drove out toward the shed. Zamora was forced to stop about 150 yards away from a deep gully in which there appeared to be an overturned car. He radioed that he was investigating a possible wreck, and then worked his car up onto the mesa and over toward the edge of the gully. He parked short, and when he walked the final few feet to the edge, he was amazed to see that it was not a car but instead was a weird egg-shaped object about fifteen feet long, white in color and resting on short, metal legs. Beside it, unaware of his presence were two humanoids dressed in silvery coveralls. They seemed to be working on a portion of the underside of the object. Zamora was still standing there, surprised, when they suddenly noticed him and dove out of sight around the object. Zamora also headed the other way, back toward his car. He glanced back at the object just as a bright blue flame shot down from the underside. Within seconds the egg-shaped thing rose out of the gully with "an earsplitting roar." The object was out of sight over the nearby mountains almost immediately, and Sergeant Zamora was moving the opposite direction almost as fast when he met Sergeant Sam Chavez who was responding to Zamora's earlier radio calls. Together they investigated the gully and found the bushes charred and still smoking where the blue flame had jetted down on them. About the charred area were four deep marks where the metal legs had been. Each mark was three and one-half inches deep, and was circular in shape. The sand in the gully was very hard-packed so no sign of the humanoids' footprints could be found. An official investigation was launched that same day, and all data obtained supported the stories of Zamora and Chavez. It is rather difficult to label this episode a hoax, and it is also doubtful that both Zamora and Chavez shared portions of the same hallucination.

## Secret Weapons

A few individuals have proposed that UFO's are actually advanced weapon systems, and that their natures must not be revealed. Very few people accept this as a credible suggestion.

## Natural Phenomena

It has also been suggested that at least some, and possibly all, of the UFO cases were just misinterpreted manifestations of natural phenomena. Undoubtedly this suggestion has some merit. People have reported, as UFO's, objects which were conclusively proven to be balloons (weather and skyhook), the planet Venus, manmade artificial satellites, normal aircraft, unusual cloud formations and lights from ceilometers (equipment projecting light beams on cloud bases to determine the height of the aircraft visual ceiling). It is also suspected that people have reported mirages, optical illusions, swamp gas and ball lightning (a poorly-understood discharge of electrical energy in a spheroidal or ellipsoidal shape . . . some discharges have lasted for up to fifteen minutes but the ball is usually no bigger than a large orange). But it is difficult to tell a swamp dweller that the strange, fast-moving light he saw in the sky was swamp gas; and it is just as difficult

to tell a farmer that a bright UFO in the sky is the same ball lightning that he has seen rolling along his fence wires in dry weather. Thus accidental misidentification of what might well be natural phenomena breeds mistrust and disbelief; it leads to the hasty conclusion that the truth is deliberately not being told. One last suggestion of interest has been made, that the UFO's were plasmoids from space . . . concentrated blobs of solar wind that succeeded in reaching the surface of Earth. Somehow this last suggestion does not seem to be very plausible; perhaps because it ignores such things as penetration of Earth's magnetic field.

## Alien Visitors

The most stimulating theory for us is that the UFO's are material objects which are either "Manned" or remote-controlled by beings who are alien to this planet. There is some evidence supporting this viewpoint. In addition to police Sergeant Lonnie Zamora's experience, let us consider the case of Barney and Betty Hill. On a trip through New England they lost two hours on the night of 19 September 1961 without even realizing it. However, after that night both Barney and Betty began developing psychological problems which eventually grew sufficiently severe that they submitted themselves to psychiatric examination and treatment. During the course of treatment hypnotherapy was used, and it yielded remarkably detailed and similar stories from both Barney and Betty. Essentially they had been hypnotically kidnapped, taken aboard a UFO, submitted to two-hour physicals, and released with posthypnotic suggestions to forget the entire incident. The evidence is rather strong that this is what the Hills, even in their subconscious, believe happened to them. And it is of particular importance that after the "posthypnotic block" was removed, both of the Hills ceased having their psychological problems.

The Hills' description of the aliens was similar to descriptions provided in other cases, but this particular type of alien appears to be in the minority. The most commonly described alien is about three and one-half feet tall, has a round head (helmet?), arms reaching to or below his knees, and is wearing a silvery space suit or coveralls. Other aliens appear to be essentially the same as Earthmen, while still others have particularly wide (wrap-around) eyes and mouths with very thin lips. And there is a rare group reported as about four feet tall, weight of around 35 pounds, and covered with thick hair or fur (clothing?). Members of this last group are described as being extremely strong. If such beings are visiting Earth, two questions arise: 1) why haven't there been accidents which have revealed their presence, and 2) why haven't they attempted to contact us officially? The answer to the first question may exist partially in Sergeant Lonnie Zamora's experience, and may exist partially in the Tunguska meteor discussed in Chapter XXIX. In that chapter it was suggested that the Tunguska meteor was actually a comet which exploded in the atmosphere, the ices melted and the dust spread out. Hence, no debris! However, it has also been suggested that the Tunguska meteor was actually an alien spacecraft that entered the atmosphere too rapidly, suffered mechanical failure, and lost its power supply and/or weapons in a nuclear explosion. While that hypothesis may seem far fetched, samples of tree rings from around the world reveal that, immediately after the Tunguska meteor explosion, the level of radioactivity in the world rose sharply for a short period of time. It is difficult to find a natural explanation for that increase in radioactivity, although the suggestion has been advanced that enough of the meteor's great kinetic energy was converted into heat (by atmospheric friction) that a fusion reaction occurred. This still leaves us with no answer to the second question: why no contact? That question is very easy to answer in any of several ways: 1) we may be the object of intensive sociological and psychological study. In such studies you usually avoid disturbing the test subjects' environment; 2) you do not "contact" a colony of ants, and humans may seem that way to any aliens (variation: a zoo is fun to visit, but you don't "contact" the lizards); 3) such contact may have already taken place secretly; and 4) such contact may have already taken place on a different plane of awareness and we are not yet sensitive to communications on such a plane. These are just a few of the reasons. You may add to the list as you desire.

## 33.4 Human Fear and Hostility

Besides the foregoing reasons, contacting humans is downright dangerous. Think about that for a moment! On the microscopic level our bodies reject and fight (through production antibodies) any alien material; this process helps us fight off disease but it also sometimes results in allergenic reactions to innocuous materials.

On the macroscopic (psychological and sociological) level we are antagonistic to beings that are "different." For proof of that, just watch how an odd child is treated by other children, or how a minority group is socially deprived, or how the Arabs feel about the Israelis (Chinese vs Japanese, Turks vs Greeks, etc.). In case you are hesitant to extend that concept to the treatment of aliens let me point out that in very ancient times, possible extraterrestrials may have been treated as Gods but in the last two thousand years, the evidence is that any possible aliens have been ripped apart by mobs, shot and shot at, physically assaulted (in South America there is a well-documented case), and in general treated with fear and aggression. In Ireland about 1,000 A.D., supposed airships were treated as "demon-ships." In Lyons, France, "admitted" space travelers were killed. More recently, on 24 July 1957 Russian anti-aircraft batteries on the Kouril Islands opened fire on UFO's. Although all Soviet anti-aircraft batteries on the Islands were in action. no hits were made. The UFO's were luminous and moved very fast. We too have fired on UFO's. About ten o'clock one morning, a radar site near a fighter base picked up a UFO doing 700 mph. The UFO then slowed to 100 mph, and two F-86's were scrambled to intercept. Eventually one F-86 closed on the UFO at about 3,000 feet altitude. The UFO began to accelerate away but the pilot still managed to get to within 500 yards of the target for a short period of time. It was definitely saucer shaped. As the pilot pushed the F-86 at top speed, the UFO began to pull away. When the range reached 1,000 yards, the pilot armed his guns and fired in an attempt to down the saucer. He failed, and the UFO pulled away rapidly, vanishing in the distance. This same basic situation may have happened on a more personal level. On Sunday evening 21 August 1955, eight adults and three children were on the Sutton Farm (one-half mile from Kelly, Kentucky) when, according to them, one of the children saw a brightly glowing UFO settle behind the barn, out of sight from where he stood. Other witnesses on nearby farms also saw the object. However, the Suttons dismissed it as a "shooting star," and did not investigate. Approximately thirty minutes later (at 8 p.m.), the family dogs began barking so two of the men went to the back door and looked out. Approximately 50 feet away and coming toward them was a creature wearing a glowing silvery suit. It was about three and one-half feet tall with a large round head and very long arms. It had large webbed hands which were equipped with claws. The two Suttons grabbed a twelve gauge shotgun and a .22 caliber pistol, and fired at close range. They could hear the pellets and bullet ricochet as if off of metal. The creature was knocked down, but jumped up and scrambled away. The Suttons retreated into the house, turned off all inside lights, and turned on the porch-light. At that moment, one of the women who was peeking out of the dining room window discovered that a creature with some sort of helmet and wide slit eyes was peeking back at her. She screamed, the men rushed in and started shooting. The creature was knocked backwards but again scrambled away without apparent harm. More shooting occurred (a total of about 50 rounds) over the next 20 minutes and the creatures finally left (perhaps feeling unwelcome?). After a two hour wait (for safety), the Suttons left too. By the time the police got there, the aliens were gone but the Suttons would not move back to the farm. They sold it and departed. This reported incident does bear out the contention though that humans are dangerous. At no time in the story did the supposed aliens shoot back, although one is left with the impression that the described creatures were having fun scaring humans.

## 33.5 Attempts at Scientific Approaches

In any scientific endeavor, the first step is to acquire data, the second step to classify the data, and the third step to form hypotheses. The hypotheses are tested by repeating the entire process, with each cycle resulting in an increase in understanding (we hope). The UFO phenomenon does not yield readily to this approach because the data taken so far exhibits both excessive variety and vagueness. The vagueness is caused in part by the lack of preparation of the observer . . . very few people leave their house knowing that they are going to see a UFO that evening. Photographs are over-exposed or underexposed, and rarely in color. Hardly anyone carries around a radiation counter or a magnetometer. And, in addition to this, there is a very high level of "noise" in the data. The noise consists of mistaken reports of known natural phenomena, hoaxes, reports by unstable individuals and mistaken removal of data regarding possible unnatural or unknown natural phenomena (by overzealous individuals who are trying to eliminate all data due to known natural phenomena). In addition, those data, which do appear to be valid, exhibit an excessive amount of variety relative to the statistical samples available. This has led to very clumsy classification systems, which in turn provide quite unfertile ground for formulation of hypotheses.

One hypothesis which looked promising for a time was that of ORTHOTENY (i.e., UFO sightings fall on "great circle" routes). At first, plots of sightings seemed to verify the concept of orthoteny but recent use of computers has revealed that even random numbers yield "great circle" plots as neatly as do UFO sightings.

There is one solid advance that has been made though. Jacques and Janine Vallee have taken a particular type of UFO—namely those that are lower than tree-top level when sighted—and plotted the UFO's estimated diameter versus the estimated distance from the observer. The result yields an average diameter of 5 meters with a very characteristic drop for short viewing distances, and rise for long viewing distances. This behavior at the extremes of the curve is well-known to astronomers and psychologists as the "moon illusion." The illusion only occurs when the object being viewed is a real, physical object. Because this implies that the observers have viewed a real object, it permits us to accept also their statement that these particular UFO's had a rotational axis of symmetry.

Another, less solid, advance made by the Vallees was their plotting of the total number of sightings per week versus the date. They did this for the time span from 1947 to 1962, and then attempted to match the peaks of the curve (every 2 years 2 months) to the times of Earth-Mars conjunction (every 2 years 1.4 months). The match was very good between 1950 and 1956 but was poor outside of those limits. Also, the peaks were not only at the times of Earth-Mars conjunction but also roughly at the first harmonic (very loosely, every 13 months). This raises the question: why should UFO's only visit Earth when Mars is in conjunction and when it is on the opposite side of the sun? Obviously, the conjunction periodicity of Mars is not the final answer. As it happens, there is an interesting possibility to consider. Suppose Jupiter's conjunctions were used; they are every 13.1 months. That would satisfy the observed periods nicely, except for every even data peak being of different magnitude from every odd data peak. Perhaps a combination of Martian, Jovian, and Saturnian (and even other planetary) conjunctions will be necessary to match the frequency plot . . . if it can be matched.

Further data correlation is quite difficult. There are a large number of different saucer shapes but this may mean little. For example, look at the number of different types of aircraft which are in use in the U.S. Air Force alone.

It is obvious that intensive scientific study is needed in this area; no such study has yet been undertaken at the necessary levels of intensity and support. One thing that must be guarded against in any such study is the trap of implicitly assuming that our knowledge of physics (or any other branch of science) is complete. An example of one such trap is selecting a group of physical laws which we now accept as valid, and assume that they will never be superseded. Five such laws might be:

1 Every action must have an opposite and equal reaction.
2 Every particle in the universe attracts every other particle with a force proportional to the product of the masses and inversely as the square of the distance.
3 Energy, mass and momentum are conserved.
4 No material body can have a speed as great as c, the speed of light in free space.
5 The maximum energy, E, which can be obtained from a body at rest is $E=mc^2$, where m is the rest mass of the body.

Laws numbered 1 and 3 seem fairly safe, but let us hesitate and take another look. Actually, law number 3 is only valid (now) from a relativistic viewpoint; and for that matter so are laws 4 and 5. But relativity completely revised these physical concepts after 1915, before then Newtonian mechanics was supreme! We should also note that general relativity has not yet been fully verified. Thus we have the peculiar situation of five laws which appear to deny the possibility of intelligent alien control of UFO's, yet three of the laws are recent in concept and may not even be valid Also, law number 2 has not been tested under conditions of large

relative speeds or accelerations. We should not deny the possibility of alien control of UFO's on the basis of preconceived notions not established as related or relevant to the UFO's.

## 33.6 CONCLUSION

From available information, the UFO phenomenon appears to have been global in nature for almost 50,000 years. The majority of known witnesses have been reliable people who have seen easily-explained natural phenomena, and there appears to be no overall positive correlation with population density. The entire phenomenon could be psychological in nature but that is quite doubtful, However, psychological factors probably do enter the picture as "noise." The phenomenon could also be entirely due to known and unknown natural phenomena (with some psychological "noise" added in) but that too is questionable in view of some of the available data.

This leaves us with the unpleasant possibility of alien visitors to our planet, or at least of alien controlled UFO's. However, the data are not well correlated, and what questionable data there are suggest the existence of at least three and maybe four different groups of aliens (possibly at different stages of development). This too is difficult to accept. It implies the existence of intelligent life on a majority of the planets in our solar system, or a surprisingly strong interest in Earth by members of other solar systems.

A solution to the UFO problem may be obtained by the long and diligent effort of a large group of well-financed and competent scientists; unfortunately there is no evidence suggesting that such an effort is going to be made. However, even if such an effort were made, there is no guarantee of success because of the isolated and sporadic nature of the sightings. Also, there may be nothing to find, and that would mean a long search with no proof at the end. The best thing to do is to keep an open and skeptical mind, and not take an extreme position on any side of the question.

## References

33-1. Davidson, L. *Flying Saucers: An Analysis of the Air Force Project Blue Book Special Report No. 24.* (Third

Edition) Ramsey, New Jersey: Ramsey-Wallace Corp., July 1966.

33-2. Edwards, F. *Flying Saucers—Serious Business.* New York: Bantam Press, 1966.

33-3. Fuller, J. "Flying Saucer Fiasco," Look. 14 May 1968, 58.

33-4. *The Interupted Journey.* New York. Dial Press, 1966.

33-5. Hall, R. (editor). *The UFO Evidence.* Washington, D.C.: National Investigations Committee on Aerial Phenomena, May 1964.

33-6. Jung, C. *Flying Saucers: A Modern Myth of Things Seen in the Skies.* Translated by R.F. Hull. New York: Harcourt, Brace and Company, 1959.

33-7. Keyhoe, D. *The Flying Saucer Conspiracy.* New York: Henry Holt, 1955.

33-8. *Flying Saucers: Top Secret.* New York: G.P. Pumam's Sons, 1960.

33-9. Lorenzen, C. *The Great Flying Saucer Hoax.* New York: William-Frederick Press, 1962.

33-10. Markowitz, W. "The Physics and Metaphysics of Unidentified Flying Objects," Science. 15 September 1967, 1274.

33-11. Menzel, D. and L. Boyd. *The World of Flying Saucers: A Scientific Examination of a Major Myth of the Space Age.* Garden City, New York: Doubleday, 1963.

33-12. Michel, A. *Flying Saucers and the Straight-Line Mystery.* New York: Criterion Books, 1958.

33-13. Ruppelt, E. *The Report on Unidentified Fly-by Objects.* Garden City, New York: Doubleday, 1956.

33-14. Tacker, L. *Flying Saucers and the U.S. Air Force.* Princeton, New Jersey: D. Van Nostrand, 1960.

33-15. Terry, D. "No Swamp Gas for Him, Thank You," St. Louis Post-Dispatch. 2 June 1966, 4F.

33-16. VaRee, J. *Anatomy of a Phenomenon: Unidentified Objects in Space—A Scientific Appraisal.* Chicago: Henry Regnery, 1965.

33-17. Vallee, J. and J. VaUee. *Flying Saucers a Challenge to Science.* New York: Henry Regnery, 1966.

33-18. Whitney, D. *Flying Saucers.* New York: Cowles Communications, 1967.

# PART 4: FEDERAL REGULATIONS REGARDING EXTRATERRESTRIALS

## 1211.100 Title 14—Aeronautics and Space

Part 1211—Extra-terrestrial Exposure

## 1211.100—Scope

This part establishes:

(a) NASA policy, responsibility and authority to guard the Earth against any harmful contamination or adverse changes in its environment resulting from personnel, spacecraft and other property returning to the Earth after landing on or coming within the atmospheric envelope of a celestial body; and

(b) security requirements, restrictions and safeguards that are necessary in the interest of national security.

## 1211.101—Applicability

The provisions of this part to all NASA manned and unmanned space missions which land or come within the atmospheric envelope of a celestial body and return to the Earth.

## 1211.102—Definitions

(a) "NASA" and the "Administrator" mean, respectively the National Aeronautics and Space Administration and the administrator of the National Aeronautics and Space Administration or his authorized representative.

(b) "Extra-terrestrially exposed" means the state of condition of any person, property, animal or other form of life or matter whatever, who or which has:

(1) Touched directly or come within the atmospheric envelope or any other celestial body; or

(2) Touched directly or been in close proximity to (or been exposed indirectly to) any person, property, animal or other form of life or matter who or which has been extra-terrestrially exposed by virtue of paragraph (b)(1) of this section. For example, if person or thing "A" touches the surface of the Moon, and on "A's" return to Earth, "B"

touches "A" and, subsequently, "C" touches "B," all of these—"A" through "C" inclusive—would be extra-terrestrially exposed ("A" and "B" directly; "C" indirectly).

(c) "Quarantine" means the detention, examination and decontamination of any persons, property, animal or other form of life or matter whatever that is extra-terrestrially exposed, and includes the apprehension or seizure of such person, property, animal or other form of life or matter whatever.

(d) "Quarantine period" means a period of consecutive calendar days as may be established in accordance with 1211.104 (a).

## 1211.107 Court or other process

(a) NASA officers and employees are prohibited from discharging from the limits of a quarantine station any quarantined person, property, animal or other form of life or matter whatever during order or other request, order or demand an announced quarantine period in compliance with a subpoena, show cause or any court or other authority without the prior approval of the General Counsel and the Administrator.

(b) Where approval to discharge a quarantined person, property, animal or other form of life or matter whatever in compliance with such a request, order or demand of any court or other authority is not given, the person to whom it is directed shall, if possible, appear in court or before the other authority and respectfully state his inability to comply, relying for his action on this.

## 1211.108 Violations

Whoever willfully violates, attempts to violate, or conspires to violate any provision of this part or any regulation or order issued under this part or who enters or departs from the limits of a quarantine station in disregard of the quarantine rules or regulations or without permission of the NASA quarantine officer shall be fined not more than $5,000 or imprisoned not more than 1 year, or both.

*From the Federal Register, Volume 56, Number 81, Friday, April 26, 1991, "Rules and Regulations."*

National Aeronautics and Space Administration
14 CFR Part 1211
Extraterrestrial Exposure
Agency: National Aeronautics and Space Administration (NASA).
Action: Final rule.

Summary: NASA is removing 14 CFR part 1211 since it has served its purpose and is no longer in keeping with current policy.
Effective Date: April 26, 1991.
List of Subjects in 14 CFR Part 1211: Extraterrestrial exposure, environmental protection, security measures, space transportation, and exploration.
PART 1211 [REMOVED]
14 CFR part 1211 (consisting of paragraphs 1211.100 through 1211.108) is hereby removed and reserved.
Richard H. Truly. Administrator
[FR Doc. 91-9904 Filed 4-25-91: 8:45 am]

## PART 5: GENERAL ACCOUNTING OFFICE REPORT ON THE ROSWELL INCIDENT

*The following is the complete text of the GAO Report to Congressman Steve Schiff having to do with the Roswell incident. It also includes related documents.*

*The actual hard copy of this report can be ordered by calling the GAO publications ordering desk at (202) 512-6000.*

United States
General Accounting Office
Washington, D.C. 20545

National Security and International Affairs Division

B-262046
July 28,1995

The Honorable Steven H. Schiff House of Representatives

Dear Mr. Schiff:

On July 8, 1947, the Roswell Army Air Held (RAAF) public information office in Roswell, New Mexico, reported the crash and recovery of a "flying disc." Army Air

Forces personnel from the RAAF's 509th Bomb Group were credited with the recovery. The following day, the press reported that the Commanding General of the U.S. Eighth Air Force, Fort Worth, Texas, announced that RAAF personnel had recovered a crashed radar-tracing (weather) balloon, not a flying disc.

After nearly 50 years, speculation continues on what crashed at Roswell. Some observers believe that the object was of extraterrestrial origin. In the July 1994 "Report of Air Force Research Regarding the Roswell" Incident, the Air Force did not dispute that something happened near Roswell, but reported that the most likely source of the wreckage was from a balloon-launched classified government project designed to determine the state of Soviet nuclear weapons research. The debate on what crashed at Roswell continues.

Concerned that the Department of Defense (DoD) may not have provided you with all available information on the crash, you asked us to determine the requirements for reporting air accidents similar to the crash near Roswell and identify any government records concerning the Roswell crash.

We conducted an extensive search for government records related to the crash near Roswell. We examined a wide range of classified and unclassified documents dating from July 1947 through the 1950s. These records came from numerous organizations in New Mexico and elsewhere throughout DoD as well as The Federal Bureau of Investigation (FBI), the Central Intelligence Agency (CIA), and the National Security Council. The full scope and methodology of our work are detailed at the end of this report.

## Results in Brief

In 1947, regulations required that air accident reports be maintained on air accidents reported by the Army Air Forces in New Mexico during July 1947. All of the accidents involved military aircraft and occurred after July 8, 1947—the date the RAAF public information office first reported the crash and recovery of a "flying disc" near Roswell. The Navy reported no air accidents in New Mexico during July 1947. Air Force officials told us that according to record-keeping requirements in effect during July 1947, there was no requirement to prepare a report on the crash of a weather balloon.

In our search for records concerning the Roswell crash, we learned that some government records covering RAAF activities had been destroyed and others had not. For example, RAAF administrative records (from Mar. 1945 through Dec. 1949) and RAAF outgoing messages (from Oct. 1946 through Dec. 1949) were destroyed. The document disposition form does not indicate what organization or person destroyed the records and when or under what authority the records were destroyed.

Our search for government records concerning the Roswell crash yielded two records originating in 1947—a July 1947 history report by the combined 509th Bomb Group and RAAF and an FBI teletype message dated July 8, 1947. The 5O9th-RAAF report noted the recovery of a "flying disc" that was later determined by military officials to be a radar-tracking balloon. The FBI message stated that the military had reported that an object resembling a high-altitude weather balloon with a radar reflector had been recovered near Roswell.

The other government records we reviewed, including those previously withheld from the public because of security classification, and the Air Force's analysis of unidentified flying object (1) sightings from 1946 to 1953 (Project Blue Book Special Report No. 14), did not mention the crash or the recovery of an airborne object near Roswell in July 1947. Similarly, executive branch agencies' responses to our letters of inquiry produced no other government records on the Roswell crash.

**Footnote**

(1) According to Air Force regulations, an unidentified object is an airborne object that by performance, aereodynamic characteristics, or unusual features, does not conform to known aircraft or missiles, or does not correspond to Air Force definitions of familiar or known objects or unidentified aircraft.

## Reporting Air Accidents

According to press accounts from July 1947, Army Air Forces personnel from RAAF were involved in the recovery of an airborne object near Roswell. Therefore, if an air accident report was prepared, it should have been prepared in accordance with Army regulations. According to an Army records management official, in 1947 Army regulations required that air accident reports be maintained permanently. An Air Force official said there was no similar requirement to report a weather balloon crash.

According to an Air Force official who has worked in the records management field since the mid-1940s, air accident reports prepared in July 1947 under Army regulations should have been transferred to Air Force custody in September 1947, when the Air Force was established as a separate service.

The Air Force Safety Agency is responsible for maintaining reports of air accidents. We examined its microfilm records to determine whether any air accidents had been reported in New Mexico during July 1947. We identified four air accidents during this time period.(2) All of the accidents involved military fighter or cargo aircraft and occurred after July 8, 1947—the date the RAAF public information office first reported the crash and recovery of a "flying disc" near Roswell. According to the Army Air Forces' Report of Major Accident, these four accidents occurred at or near the towns of Hobbs, Albuquerque, Carrizozo, and Alamogordo, New Mexico. Only one of the four accidents resulted in a fatality. The pilot died when the aircraft crashed during an attempted take-off.

**Footnote**

(2) These records do not include information regarding mishaps of air vehicles belonging to civilian or other government agencies. These records also do not include mishaps involving unmanned air vehicles such as remotely piloted aircraft, low-speed cruise missiles, and most balloons.

## Search for Records

In searching for government records on the Roswell crash, we were particularly interested in identifying and reviewing records of military units assigned to RAAF in 1947—to include the 509th Bomb Group, the 1st Air Transport Unit, the 427th Army Air Force Base Unit, and the 1395th Military Police Company (Aviation).

Document disposition forms obtained from the National Personnel Records Center in St. Louis, Missouri, indicate that in 1953, the Walker Air Force Base (formerly RAAF) records officer transferred to the Army's Kansas City records depository the histories of units stationed at Walker Air Force Base. These histories included the 509th Bomb Group and RAAF for February 1947 through October 1947; the 1st Air Transport Unit for July 1946 through June 1947;

and the 427th Army Air Force Base Unit for January 1946 to February 1947. We could not locate any documentation indicating that records of the 1395th Military Police Company (Aviation) were ever retired to The National Personnel Records Center or its predecessor depositories.

The July 1947 history for the 509th Bomb Group and RAAF stated that the RAAF public information office "was kept quite busy . . . answering inquiries on the 'flying disc,' which was reported to be in [the] possession of the 509th Bomb Group. The object turned out to be a radar tracking balloon." By his signature, The RAAF's commanding officer certified that the report represented a complete and accurate account of RAAF activities in July 1947. (Excerpts from the report are contained in app. I.)

In addition to unit history reports, we also searched for other government records on the Roswell crash. In this regard, The Chief Archivist for the National Personnel Records Center provided us with documentation indicating that (1) RAAF records such as finance and accounting, supplies, buildings and grounds, and other general administrative matters from March 1945 through December 1949 and (2) RAAF outgoing messages from October 1946 through December 1949 were destroyed. According to this official, the document disposition form did not properly indicate the authority under which the disposal action was taken. The Center's Chief Archivist stated that from his personal experience, many of the Air Force organizational records covering this time period were destroyed without entering a citation for the governing disposition authority. Our review of records control forms showing the destruction of other records—including outgoing RAAF messages for 1950—supports the Chief Archivist's viewpoint.

During our review of records at FBI headquarters, we found a July 8, 1947, teletype message from the FBI office in Dallas, Texas, to FBI headquarters and the FBI office in Cincinnati, Ohio. An FBI spokesperson confirmed the authenticity of the message. According to the message, an Eighth Air Force headquarters official had telephonically informed the FBI's Dallas office of the recovery near Roswell of a hexagonal-shaped disc suspended from a large balloon by cable. The message further stated that the disc and balloon were being sent to Wright Field (now Wright-Patterson Air Force Base, Ohio) for examination. According to The

Eighth Air Force official, the recovered object resembled a high-altitude weather balloon with a radar reflector. The message stated that no further investigation by the FBI was being conducted. (A copy of the teletype message appears in app. II.)

To follow up on the July 8th message, we reviewed microfilm abstracts of the FBI Dallas and Cincinnati office activities for July 1947. An abstract prepared by the FBI Dallas office on July 12, 1947, summarized the particulars of the July 8th message. There was no mention in the Cincinnati office abstracts of the crash or recovery of an airborne object near Roswell.

Because the FBI message reported that debris from the Roswell crash was being transported to Wright Held for examination, we attempted to determine whether military regulations existed for handling such debris. We were unable to locate any applicable regulation. As a final step, we reviewed Air Materiel Command (Wright Held) records from 1947 to 1950 for evidence of command personnel involvement in this matter. We found no records mentioning the Roswell crash or the examination by Air Materiel Command personnel of any debris recovered from the crash.

## Queries to Federal Agencies Regarding Records on the Crash

We sent letters to several federal agencies asking for any government records they might have concerning the Roswell crash. In this regard, we contacted DoD, the National Security Council, the White House Office of Science and Technology Policy, the CIA, the FBI, and the Department of Energy.

The National Security Council, the White House Office of Science and Technology Policy, and the Department of Energy responded that they had no government records relating to the Roswell crash. (Copies of their responses appear in app. III, IV, and V.) The FBI, DoD, and the CIA provided the following information.

### Federal Bureau of Investigation

The FBI informed us that all FBI data regarding the crash near Roswell had been processed under Freedom of Information Act (FOIA) requests previously received by the Bureau. We reviewed the FBI's FOIA material and identified the July 8, 1947, FBI teletype message

discussing the recovery near Roswell of a high-altitude weather balloon with a radar reflector. (A copy of the FBI's response appears in app. VI.)

### Department of Defense

DoD informed us that the U.S. Air Force report of July 1994, entitled "Report of Air Force Research Regarding the Roswell Incident," represents the extent of DoD records or information concerning the Roswell crash. The Air Force report concluded that there was no dispute that something happened near Roswell in July 1947 and that all available official materials indicated the most likely source of the wreckage recovered was one of the project MOGUL balloon trains. At the time of the Roswell crash, project MOGUL was a highly classified U.S. effort to determine the state of Soviet nuclear weapons research using balloons that carried radar reflectors and acoustic sensors. (A copy of DoD's response appears in app. VII.)

### Central Intelligence Agency

In March 1995, the CIA's Executive Director responded to our letter of inquiry by stating that earlier searches by the CIA for records on unidentified flying objects produced no information pertaining to the Roswell crash. The Executive Director added, however, that it was unclear whether the CIA had ever conducted a search for records specifically relating to Roswell. In the absence of such assurance, the Executive Director instructed CIA personnel to conduct a comprehensive records search for information relating to Roswell. On May 30, 1995, the CIA's Executive Director informed us that a search against the term "Roswell, New Mexico," in all CIA databases produced no CIA documents related to the crash. (A copy of CIA's response appears in app. VIII.)

### Agency Comments

A draft of this report was provided to DoD for comment. DoD offered no comments or suggested changes to the report. The Chief Archivist, National Personnel Records Center offered several comments clarifying matters dealing with records management. These comments have been incorporated into the final report where appropriate.

The CIA, the Department of Energy, the FBI, the National Security Council, and the White House

Office of Science and Technology Policy also received excerpts from the report discussing the activities of their respective agencies. They had no substantive comments and made no suggested changes to the report.

## Scope and Methodology

To determine the requirements for reporting all accidents in 1947, we interviewed military service records management officials, reviewed military record-keeping regulations in effect during this time period, and examined Army Air Forces and Navy air accident reports.

We also sought to identify any government records related to the Roswell crash. In this regard, we visited and reviewed records at the locations listed in table 1.

Our search of government records was complicated by the fact that some records we wanted to review were missing and there was not always an explanation. Further, the records management regulations for the retention and disposition of records were unclear or changing during the period we reviewed.

We also queried the National Security Council, the White House Office of Science and Technology Policy, the Department of Energy, the FBI, DoD, and the CIA to determine what government records they have on the Roswell crash. We did not independently verify the information provided to us in their written responses.

In addition to physically examining government records, we contacted the following federal activities to determine whether they had any information about the Roswell crash: Air Force Historical Research Agency, Maxwell Air Force Base, Alabama; Air Force Aeronautical Systems Center, Wright-Patterson Air Force Base, Ohio; Army Center for Military History, Washington, D.C.; and 509th Bomb Wing, Office of the Historian, Whiteman Air Force Base, Missouri.

We conducted our review from March 1994 to June 1995 in accordance with generally accepted government auditing standards.

Unless you publicly announce its contents earlier, we plan no further distribution of this report until 30 days after its issue date. At that time, we will make copies available to other interested parties upon request.

If you or your staff have any questions about this report, please call me. A major contributor to this report is Gary K. Weeter, Assistant Director.

Sincerely yours,

/s/ Richard Davis

Director, National Security
Analysis

## Combined History for July 1947

Combined History 509th Bomb Group and Roswell Army Air Field
1 July 1947 through 31 July 1947

**Restricted**
The other three briefings were those which were given to the VIP and a simulated briefing to a large group of Air Scouts representing all of the troops in New Mexico which was given on 15 July 1947.

Several small projects were completed during the month including signs on all the office doors, a building directory, and a world situation map which is maintained on a day-to-day basis.

The Historical Section of S-2 has been seriously handicapped by the removal of the regular stenographer with the reduction in force.

Due to the fact that the quality of the department reports has in general been so inadequate, lectures are being prepared to be given early in August to properly train the liaison representatives of each department.

The Office of Public Information was kept quite busy during the month answering inquiries on the "flying disc," which was reported to be in the possession of the 509th Bomb Group. The object turned out to be a radar tracking balloon.

The main project of the month was making all arrangements for a successful Air Force Day. Lt. Colonel Oliver LaFarge, Air Reserve Corps, at Santa Fe, made arrangements for Colonel Blanchard to visit the Governor of New Mexico and ask him to declare Air Force Day in New Mexico on 7 August. RESTRICTED

# Table 1: Locations Visited and Records Reviewed

| Locations Visited | Records Reviewed |
| --- | --- |
| National Archives, Washington, D.C. 1947–49 | Air Force papers on unidentified flying objects. Army Counterintelligence Corps historical files. |
| National Archives II, College Park, MD | Project Blue Book Special Report No. 14. National Security Council meeting minutes, 1947–48. |
| National Archives, National Record Center, Suitland, MD | Army Inspector General reports, 1947–59. Army staff intelligence correspondence, 1947–56. Headquarters Army Air Force message traffic, 1947–54. Army Air Force and Air Materiel Command (Wright Field research and development titles, 1947–50. |
| National Personnel Records Center, St. Louis, MO | Morning reports for RAAF units, July 1947. Eighth Air Force messages, 1947–50. Eighth Air Force correspondence, 1947–51. Eighth Air Force weekly activity summaries, July 1947. Service records of key personnel assigned to RAAF, 1947. Project Sign* investigative reports, 1948. Army Adjutant General correspondence, 1947–49. Missile test firing reports at White Sands, New Mexico, 1947–54. |
| Department of the Air Force, Washington, D.C. | Current and past records management regulations. Report of Air Force Research Regarding the Roswell Incident, July 1994. |
| Department of the Army, Washington, D.C. | Current and past records management regulations. |
| Department of the Air Force Safety Agency, Kirtland Air Force Base, NM | Air accident reports, July 1947 Navy, Washington, D.C. Air accident reports, July 1947 |
| Air Force History Support Office, Boiling Air Force Base, Washington, D.C. | 509th Bomb Group and RAAF monthly histories, July and August 1947. |
| National Security, Fort Meade, MD | FOIA records, Citizens Against UFO Secrecy Agency. |
| Military History Institute, Army War College, Carlisle, PA | Army Counterintelligence Corps reports, 1947. |
| Army Central Facility, Fort Meade, MD | Army Counterintelligence Corps reports, 1947 Security. |
| Central Intelligence Agency, Langley, VA | "Scientific Advisory Panel on Unidentified Flying Objects" (Robertson Panel) report FOIA records, Ground Saucer Watch, Inc. |
| Federal Bureau of Investigation, Washington, D.C. | FOIA records on unidentified flying objects. |
| National Atomic Museum, Kirtland Air Force Base, NM | 509th Bomb Group historical information, 1947. RAAF base newspaper Atomic Blast, July and August 1947. |

* Project Sign was the predecessor to Project Blue Book.

## FBI Teletype Message Dated July 8, 1947

[Note XX indicates area blacked out by marker; spelling is reproduced as is in the original.]

TELETYPE
FBI DALLAS 7-8-47 6-17 PM XX

DIRECTOR AND SAC, CINCINNATI URGENT XX FLYING DISC, INFORMATION CONCERNING XX HEADQUARTERS EIGHTH AIR FORCE, TELEPHONICALLY ADVISED THIS OFFICE THAT AN OBJECT PURPORTING TO BE A FLYING DISC WAS RECOVERED NEAR ROSWELL, NEW MEXICO, THIS DATE. THE DISC IS HEXAGONAL IN SHAPE AND WAS SUSPENDED FROM A BALLOON BY CABLE, WHICH BALLOON WAS APPROXIMATELY TWENTY FEET IN DIAMETER. XX FURTHER ADVISED THAT THE OBJECT FOUND RESEMBLES A HIGH ALTITUDE WEATHER BALLOON WITH A RADAR REFLECTOR, BUT THAT TELEPHONIC CONVERSATION BETWEEN THEIR OFFICE AND WRIGHT FIELD HAD NOT XX BORNE OUT THIS BELIEF. DISC AND BALLOON BEING TRANSPORTED TO WRIGHT FIELD BY SPECIAL PLANE FOR EXAMINATION INFORMATION PROVIDED THIS OFFICE BECAUSE OF NATIONAL INTEREST IN CASE. XX AND FACT THAT NATIONAL BROADCASTING COMPANY, ASSOCIATED PRESS, AND OTHERS ATTEMPTING TO BREAK STORY OF LOCATION OF DISC TODAY. XX ADVISED WOULD REQUEST WRIGHT FIELD TO ADVISE CINCINNATI OFFICE RESULTS OF EXAMINATION, NO FURTHER INVESTIGATION BEING CONDUCTED.

WYLY

RECORDED
END
CXXXX ACK IN ORDER
UA 92 FBI CI MJW
BPI H8
8-38 PM O
6-22 PM OK FBI WASH DC
OK FBI CI

## Comments from the National Security Council

[Letter follows on "National Security Council" letterhead]

National Security Council
Washington, D.C. 20506
April 28, 1995

Memorandum for Mr. Joseph E. Kelley
Director-in-Charge, International Affairs Issues
General Accounting Office

Subject: Request for NSC Records

I am responding to your April 12, 1995, request for information or NSC records related to the crash of an airborne object near Roswell, New Mexico in July 1947. The NSC has no records or information related to the incident at Roswell.

For information about any government records that may document the crash at Roswell, we suggest you contact the National Archives, Textual Reference Division, 8601 Adelphi Road, College Park, Maryland 20740.

/s/ Andrew D. Sens
Executive Secretary

## Comments from the Office of Science and Technology Policy, Executive Office of the President

[Letter follows on "Executive Office of the President, Office of Science and Technology Policy" letterhead]

Executive Office of the President
Office of Science and Technology Policy
Washington D.C. 20500

April 26, 1995

Dear Mr Hunt:

In response to your recent inquiry of April 12, 1995. The Office of Science and Technology Policy reviewed its records regarding the Roswell Incident. OSTP has no direct knowledge of what occurred at Roswell and no records, except for the information I received from the Air Force.

I look forward to receiving the GAO report.

Sincerely,

/s/ John H. Gibbons
Director
Enclosures: As stated

Mr. William Hunt Director, Federal Management Issues United States Government Accounting Office Washington, DC 20548

## Comments from the Department of Energy

[Letter follows on "Department of Energy" letterhead]

Department of Energy
Washington, DC 20585

June 5. 1995

Richard Davis
Director, National Security Analysis
General Accounting Office
Washington, D.C. 20538

Dear Mr. Davis:

This is in response to your request for records related to the crash of an airborne object near Roswell, New Mexico, in July 1947. We conducted an in-depth search for documents related to the crash and have found no such documents.

If you have any questions regarding this matter, please do not hesitate to contact Barry Uhlig of my staff.

Sincerely,

/s/ Joseph F. Vivona
Chief Financial Officer

## Comments from the Federal Bureau of Investigation

[Letter follows on "U.S. Department of Justice, Federal Bureau of Investigation" letterhead]

U.S. Department of Justice
Federal Bureau of Investigation
Washington, D.C. 20535
April 24, 1995

Mr. Richard Davis
Director
Attn: Gary K. Weeter
National Security Analysis
General Accounting Office
Washington, D.C.

Dear Mr. Davis:

This is in response to a letter dated April 7, 1995, from Norman J. Rabkin, Director, Administration of Justice Issues, General Accounting Office, to John E. Collingwood, Inspector in Charge, of Office of Public and Congressional Affairs, FBI, regarding government records concerning the crash of an airborne object near Roswell, New Mexico, in July 1947 (code 701034)

A search of FBI indices for information relating to the crash of an airborne object near Roswell, New Mexico, in 1947, determined that all FBI data concerning the incident has been processed under the provisions of the Freedom of Information Act (FOIA) and is available for review in our FOIA Reading Room. A copy of the document forwarded to me by Gary Weeter is among the documents in the Reading Room. If your staff wishes to review the material, please call Margaret Tremblay, a member of my staff, at least 48 hours in advance of the desired appointment.

Sincerely yours,

/s/ Swanson D. Carter

Supervisory Special Agent
Office of Public and Congressional Affairs

## Comments from the Department of Defense

[Letter follows on "Inspector General, Department of Defense" letterhead]

Inspector General
Department of Defense
400 Army Navy Drive
Arlington, Virginia 22202-2884

May 4, 1995
Mr. Richard Davis
Director, National Security Analysis
U.S. General Accounting Office
441 G Street N.W.
Room 5025
Washington, D.C. 20548

Dear Mr. Davis:

The Department of the Air Force July 1994 report is the DoD response to questions posed in your April 12 letter related to

GAO Code 701034. If you have any questions, please contact my action officer, Pattie Cirino. If she is not available, please contact Ms. Merlene L. Scales.

/s/ Rathryn M. Truex
Deputy Assistant Inspector General for GAO Report
 Analysis
Enclosure

## Comments from the Central Intelligence Agency

[Letter follows on "Central Intelligence Agency" letterhead]

Central Intelligence Agency
Washington, D.C. 20585

Mr. Richard Davis
Director, National Security Analysis
US General Accounting Office
Washington, D.C. 20548

Dear Mr. Davis,

In a letter dated 30 March 1995, this Agency advised you that it would conduct a comprehensive record search to aid in the completion of your investigation of the crash of an airborne object near Roswell, New Mexico, in July 1947. In accordance with your request, we have searched all of our data bases against the terms "Project Mogul" and "Roswell, New Mexico."

The search did not yield any documents related to either of these terms. Therefore, this Agency has no information, beyond those records already reviewed by Mr. Gary Weeter of your staff, relevant to your investigation.

Sincerely, /s/ Nora Slatkin
Executive Director

## Extra Report/Letter from the GAO to Congressman Schiff: Regarding Records Having to Do with "Majestic 12"

GAO
United States
General Accounting Office
Washington, D.C. 20548

National Security and International Affairs Division

94-0692
July 28, 1995

The Honorable Steven H. Schiff
House of Representatives

Dear Mr. Schiff:

In response to your request, we asked several agencies for their views on the authenticity of the publicly circulated written material referred to as Majestic 12. The origin of this material is unknown, but it is purported to represent highly classified government records explaining unidentified flying object recovery procedures and the crash of a disc-shaped aircraft near Roswell, New Mexico, in July 1947.

Since the late 1980s, several federal agencies have been contacted by nongovernmental persons and asked to comment on the authenticity of the Majestic 12 material. The agencies contacted include the Information Security Oversight Office (responsible for overseeing the information security programs of all executive branch agencies that create or handle classified national security information), the Office of the Secretary of the Air Force, Deputy for Security and Investigative Programs, and the National Archives.

These agencies responded to the inquiries by stating that their knowledge of Majestic 12 was limited to the written material submitted to them by nongovernmental persons.

These agencies added that they found no records in their files relating to Majestic 12. Moreover, the agencies' overall conclusion concerning the authenticity of the Majestic 12 written material was the same—there is no evidence that the Majestic 12 written material constitutes actual documents originally created in the executive branch. According to the Information Security Oversight Office and the Air Force, the Majestic 12 material should not be treated as if it had ever been actually classified by an executive branch agency or government official. We found nothing in our work that contradicts the conclusions reached by these agencies.

We also asked the archivists at the Harry S. Truman and Dwight D. Eisenhower libraries for their views on the authenticity of the Majestic 12 material. The archivists said that over the years they have received several inquiries from the public concerning this material. In their search for related records, including classified intelligence and National Security Council documents, they found nothing that appeared to fit the description of the Majestic 12 material or any references to this particular designation.

Lastly, during our review of material received from the public by the Information Security Oversight Office in connection with past Freedom of Information Act requests, we came across a message dated November 17, 1980. The message, which appeared to have been originated by the Operations Division of the Air Force Office of Special Investigations (AFOSI), contained the words "MJ Twelve."

We contacted AFOSI to determine the authenticity of the November 1980 message. In a letter dated February 28, 1995, the Commander, AFOSI, Investigative Operations Center, advised us that a search of AFOSI files failed to disclose any official record copy of the message. The commander also advised us that in connection with an earlier Freedom of Information Act request, AFOSI had been asked to determine the authenticity of the message. At that time, AFOSI concluded that the message was a forgery.

Sincerely yours,

/s/Richard Davis
Director, National Security
Analysis

## Press Release from Congressman Schiff

News Release
U.S. Congressman Steve Schiff, First Congressional District New Mexico
Washington Office: 2404 Rayburn Building
Washington, D.C. 20515
(202) 225-6316
FAX: (202) 225-4975v

District Office: 625 Silver Ave., SW
Suite 140
Albuquerque, NM 87102
(505) 766-2538
FAX (505) 766-1674

Immediate Release
J. Barry Bitzer
July 28th, 1995

*Schiff Receives, Releases Roswell Report (missing documents leave unanswered questions)*

Washington: Congressman Steve Schiff today released the General Accounting Office (GAO) report detailing results of a records audit related to events surrounding a crash in 1947, near Roswell, New Mexico, and the military response.

The 20 page report is the result of constituent information requests to Congressman Schiff and the difficulty he had getting answers from the Department of Defense in the now 48-year-old controversy.

Schiff said important documents, which may have shed more light on what happened at Roswell, are missing. "The GAO report states that the outgoing messages from Roswell Army Air Field (RAAF) for this period of time were destroyed without proper authority. Schiff pointed out that these messages would have shown how military officials in Roswell were explaining to their superiors exactly what happened.

"It is my understanding that these outgoing messages were permanent records, which should never have been destroyed. The GAO could not identify who destroyed the messages, or why." But Schiff pointed out that the GAO estimates that the messages were destroyed over 40 years ago, making further inquiry about their destruction impractical.

Documents revealed by the report include an FBI teletype and reference in a newsletter style internal forum at RAAF that refer to a "radar tracking device"—a reference to a weather balloon. Even though the weather balloon story has since been discredited by the US Air Force, Schiff suggested that the authors of those communications may have been repeating what they were told, rather than consciously adding to what some believe is a "cover up."

"At least this effort caused the Air Force to acknowledge that the crashed vehicle was no weather balloon," Schiff said. "That explanation never fit the fact of high military security used at the time." The Air Force in September, 1994 claimed that the crashed vehicle was a then-classified device to detect evidence of possible Soviet nuclear testing.

Schiff also praised the efforts of the GAO, describing their work as "professional, conscientious and thorough."

A two page letter discussing a related investigation into "Majestic 12" was also delivered.

Schiff will be available to the media Saturday, July 29th, from 10:00 AM to 2:00 PM (Eastern) at 2404 Rayburn MOB in Washington, DC and by telephone: (202) 225-6316.

A copy of the report may be obtained by calling (202) 512-6000 and referencing Document number GAO/NSIAD-95-187.

# PART 6: UFO ORGANIZATIONS

*This is a detailed list of the many organizations that study UFOs or extraterrestrials. Information subject to change.*

Aerial Phenomenon Research: The Indiana Group
18 Davis Drive
Mt. Vernon, Indiana 47620
Francis L. Ridge (Director)
812-838-3120 / 812-838-9843
Publishers of *Indiana UFO Newsletter*
Founded in 1986

A statewide organization which attempts to immediately respond to UFO sightings

The Aetherius Society
6202 Afton Place
Hollywood, California 90028-8298
Detroit Branch
17670 West 12 Mile Road
Southfield, Michigan 48076
313-552-9153 / 313-552-9159
Reverend Lesley Young
Publishers of *The Aetherius Society Journal* and *Cosmic Voice*
Founded in 1960

The Hollywood, California office is the American headquarters for The Society which was founded in England in 1955. In the US, the Society was incorporated in 1960 as a non-profit religious, scientific, and educational organization. The Society is a metaphysical, channeling organization whose founder/president, Sir George King, is a Western Master of Yoga and who has been in contact with Extraterrestrial Intelligences for over 35 years. He acts as a channel for the dissemination of Higher Wisdom from These Sources.

Ancient Astronaut Society
1921 St. Johns Avenue
Highland Park, Illinois 60035-3105
Gene M. Phillips (Founder): 708-295-8899
Publication is *Ancient Skies*
Founded in 1973

Non-profit, tax-exempt organization operated for scientific, literary, and educational purposes. The primary objectives of the Society are to search for evidence of whether Earth was visited in the remote past by intelligent beings from outer space and to determine whether a highly developed, technological civilization existed on Earth before our recorded history. The Society also provides complete study courses in: "Metaphysical and Occult Sciences" and "Cosmic Revelations" to explain the cosmic significance of messages received from Advanced Beings.

Ancient Truth Research Foundation
6146 Eleanor Avenue #205
Los Angeles, California 90036
Albert Rainey
213-464-5948
Publication is *Cosmic Current News*

Interested in many New Age topics, including UFOs.

The Awareness Research Foundation, Inc.
DeSoto Square
No. 29, 35 Ritter Road
Hayesville, North Carolina 28904
Helen I. Hoag (Executive Director)
704-389-8672

New Age organization with many interests, including UFOs; investigates various metaphysical activities and issues findings through publication of various books.

Borderland Sciences Research Foundation (BSRF)
P.O. Box 429
Garberville, California 95429
Contact: Tom Brown
Telephone Number: 707-986-7211
Publication is *Journal of Borderland Research*
Founded in 1945

Functions as clearinghouse, specializing in rare and unusual information. BSRF is an alternative scientific movement which deals with a variety of borderland subjects, including UFOs; a non-profit organization; its members are people who take an active interest in observing the physical, mental, and spiritual environment. In addition BSRF studies: Light

& Color affects on people, Radionics, Dowsing, Free Energy, Orgone Energy, Hollow Earth Mysteries, Anomalies, Fortean Phenomena, Hypnosis, Photography of the Invisible, etc. and offers a catalog of available books, reports, and tapes.

British UFO Research Association (BUFORA)
BM BUFORA
London, WC1N 3XX
Stephen Gamble (Director of Research)
John Spencer (Chairman)
Approximate membership: 500.

Commonly called BUFORA. It was formed in 1962 as a federation of eight regional UK UFO groups. These included the London UFO Research Organization (LUFORO, founded in 1959) the largest UK group at the time and the British Flying Saucer Bureau (BFSB, founded in 1952) which was the oldest UK group.

BUFORA publishes six issues per year of the A4 magazine *UFO Times*. Current annual membership subscription is 18 pounds sterling.

California UFO
1800 South Robertson Blvd.
Box 355
Los Angeles, California 90035
Vicki Cooper (Editor); Don Ecker (Researcher)
Telephone Numbers: 213-273-9409 /818-951-1250
Publication *UFO*

Publishes the bi-monthly *UFO* magazine. Additionally, this organization sponsors annual conferences which concentrate on a variety of UFO-related subjects.

Citizens Against UFO Secrecy (CAUS)
c/o Mr. Lawrence Fawcett
P.O. Box 218
Coventry, Connecticut 06238
*or*
471 Goose Lane
Coventry, Connecticut 06238
Peter Gersten (Director)

Lawrence Fawcett (Asst Director & Publisher)
Barry Greenwood (Research Director & Editor)
Publication is *Just Cause*
Founded in 1978

A non-profit organization to uncover all existing documentation relating to government involvement in UFO investigations and research. To accomplish this, CAUS files numerous Freedom of Information Act (FOIA) lawsuits in an attempt to get the government to release relevant documents. Their *Just Cause* quarterly newsletter carries events and provides updated UFO news from around the world. They published a book too—*Clear Intent*.

Committee for the Scientific Investigation of Claims of the Paranormal (CSICOP)
Refer to. The Skeptical Inquirer
P.O. Box 229
Buffalo, New York 14215
Paul Kurtz (Chairman—Skeptical Inquirer)
Philip J. Klass (UFO Subcommittee)
Lynda Harwood (Public Relations)
716-834-3222
716-834-0841

"The Skeptical Inquirer" is a non-profit, tax-exempt organization. CSICOP is headed by Paul Kurtz and investigates claims of the Paranormal, including UFOs and UFO-related activity. The committee's investigations, findings, commentaries, etc. are published in *The Skeptical Inquirer*.

Contactee
P.O. Box 12
New Milford, New Jersey 07646
Ellen Crystall (Director)

Studies UFOs by direct observation; quarterly newsletter, *Contactee* details activities. The primary goal of Contactee is to educate about world-wide contacts being made with UFOs and to disseminate information to all interested parties.

Contactee also sells books and sponsors various conferences. Regular Member (those who claim to have had alien contact) and Auxiliary Member (those who do not claim UFO contact) membership fee is $20.00 per year and includes the newsletter. Contactee accepts articles for its newsletter.

Cosmic Awareness Communications
P.O. Box 115
Olympia, Washington 98507
Vikki T. (Correspondence Secretary)
Publication is *Revelations of Awareness*

A tax-exempt organization. Studies New Age subjects, including UFOs. This group is centered around the "channelings" of a "Force" which refers to itself as "Cosmic Awareness." CA believes that this "Force" has expressed itself through selected people in history including Jesus, the Buddha, Krishna, Mohammed, and Edgar Cayce, among others. Publication, *Revelations of Awareness*, has published over 300 editions and details various New Age subjects. Subscribers receive a catalog listing all available back issues and subjects covered. Membership is $30.00 per year. Will accept memberships for three month periods ($3.00 per month), prepaid. Individual/Family $3.00/month or $30.00/year New Age-related (including UFOs) books and tapes available.

Delval UFO, Inc.
948 Almshouse Road
Ivyland, Pennsylvania 18974
Anthony Volpe (President)
215-357-2909

Publication is the *Awakening;* the group was founded in 1973. A channeling, contactee UFO organization, founded in 1973. Their publication *Awakening*, is offered 9 times a year; they sell UFO-related books and tapes.

The Fair Witness Project, Inc.
Parent Organization: William L. Moore Publications & Research
4219 West Olive Avenue Suite #247
Burbank, California 91505
213-463-0542
Publication is *Focus*

A non-profit corporation whose income is used to fund the research efforts of qualified persons selected by the Directors of the Fair Witness Project. They accept donations and will send an acknowledgment of that donation for tax purposes.

The Federation
c/o Lady Rhavyn
P.O. Box 231772
Anchorage, Alaska 99523-1772

The Federation is a group of people who feel it is high time we got off this rock and started exploring the great unknown of space. The Federation has drawn out in blue print form a drive system that is a super semi conducting crystalline structure. To get more information on the Federation send a 3.5 floppy and they will place an information packet on it and send it back to you. You must have a Mac that has 5.0 Microsoft Word or better. Send to the above address.

Flying Saucer Information Center
7803 Ruanne Court
Pasadena, Maryland 21122
James H. Wales
Founded in 1954

Acts as a clearing house for the distribution of UFO information to the general public. Laura Mundo began this organization in 1954. Group feels the Earth is in danger due to upcoming radical changes in the atmosphere (sunspot activity) and Space Beings are here to help. They will be able to either solve the problem or take selected Earth people to safe locations (inside their insulated spaceships) until the atmospheric activity calms down. When humans return to Earth after surviving the atmospheric instability, they will begin the Universal Way of Life, which is a standard way of life on other planets. Also believe Space People living on Earth today are to here to monitor us and help.

FORTEAN RESEARCH CENTER (FRC)
P.O. Box 94627
Lincoln, Nebraska 68509
The center runs a Bulletin Board on 402-488-2587.

This was founded in 1982 by Ray Boeche and deals with all aspects of Fortean Phenomena. The current Director is Scott Colbourn.

The Fund for UFO Research, Inc.
P.O. Box 277
Mt. Rainier, Maryland 20712
Bruce Maccabee, Ph.D. (Chairman)
Publication is *Quarterly Report*
Founded in 1979
2000 Members

A non-profit, tax-exempt organization based in Washington, D.C. whose mission is to provide grants for scientific research and public education projects dealing with the UFO phenomenon. Since 1979 has raised more than $150,000.00 from more than 2000 contributors. Also sponsors and awards the annual "Donald E. Keyhoe Journalism Award." The Fund sponsors such projects as the release of U.S. Government documents concerning UFOs under the Freedom of Information Act, computer-aided analysis of UFO photographs, research into major UFO sightings around the world, research into "Operation Majestic 12," psychological testing of people who reported being abducted by apparent aliens, international symposiums and conducts interviews and lectures. The Fund takes the position that many reported UFOs cannot be identified as conventional aerial vehicles or phenomena. Thus, UFO reports are potentially of enormous significance and merit serious scientific research.

Gulf Breeze Skywatch
904-433-2737 (Bruce and Ann Morrison)

Inner-Peace Prosperity Network (IPPN)
12628 Black Saddle Lane
Germantown, Maryland 20874-5001
Patrick O'Connell
301-972-1980

IPPN believes that extraterrestrials have already landed and established underground bases, mainly in the western and southwestern United States. *Trends & Predictions Analyst*, is a compilation of UFO-related theories, news, and current events; newsletter (printed twice a year) also details available books, papers, and tapes for sale by IPPN.

Intercontinental UF Galactic Spacecraft-Research and Analytic Network (ICUFON)
35-40 75th Street Suite 4G
Jackson Heights, New York 11372
Colman S. VonKeviczky (Director)

A non-profit organization whose goal is to persuade the United Nations (and the world's governments) to establish an official World Authority for UFO Affairs (the WASA Project), to seek and establish contact with extraterrestrial galactic powers; maintains that the world's governments have known about UFOs for several decades and that they are conducting covert warfare in an attempt to try to stop any invasion from outer space. ICUFON wants to open full dialogue with any and all extraterrestrial forces.

ICUFON maintains an Archives Department which contains UFO cases, photographs, movie films, declassified military and governmental documentation from all over the world.

INTERNATIONAL COMMITTEE FOR UFO RESEARCH (ICUR)
P.O. Box 314
Penn, High Wycombe, Buckinghamshire
HP10 8DH Great Britain
Chairman: Robert Digby (BUFORA, UK)
Vice-Chairman: Walter Andrus (MUFON, USA);
Secretary: Stephen Gamble (BUFORA, UK)
Treasurer: John Spencer (BUFORA, UK)

Formed in 1979 as a UFOlogical 'United Nations.' The membership consists of representative organizations for various countries. Commonly called ICUR. Members include BUFORA (UK); Center for UFO Studies (USA); CISU (Italy); MUFON (USA); SUFOI (Denmark); Project UNICAT (USA); Project URD (Sweden); VUFORS (Australia). ICUR's objectives are to promote data exchange between groups and to help establish common standards and terminology.

International Fortean Organization (INFO)
P.O. Box 367
Arlington, VA 22210-0367
Raymond Manners (President & Journal Editor)
Publication is INFO Journal
Founded in 1965

A non-profit corporation established for the educational and scientific study of Fortean phenomena. INFO investigates the strange and unreasonable events that happen in this world, including UFOs, lost civilizations, physical anomalies, Atlantis, Bigfoot, vanished civilizations, etc. Today, INFO continues the work of Charles Fort to collect, record, and publish reports of strange occurrences. Their findings are published in the INFO Journal. INFO holds an annual convention, called FortFest, in the Washington D.C. area. Annual membership fee includes the INFO Journal. INFO maintains files on all of its investigations, cases, etc. Slides, books, and tapes are for sale and back issues of INFO Journal are also available. The INFO Research Service performs funded research for the media while the INFO Research Library is open to scholars.

Intruders Foundation
PO Box 30233
New York, New York 10011
212-645-5278

Organization formed by abduction researcher Budd Hopkins to provide support and a forum for abductees to discuss their experiences.

Island Skywatch
164-22 77th Road
Flushing, New York 11366
Bill Knell (Director)
718-591-1854 (24-Hour Hotline)
Publications are Skywatch Journal and New York UFO Report

A tax-exempt organization whose goal is the scientific and objective study of the UFO phenomenon. Membership includes one year subscription to the New York UFO Report and the Island Skywatch Journal, one copy of Hidden Truth: The UFO Story (a two-hour video history about UFOs written by Bill Knell), the opportunity to attend free local meetings, free training as a UFO investigator, and the opportunity to investigate Island Skywatch cases. They offer a wide variety of books, audiotapes, video tapes, for sale. Bill Knell has cable TV UFO show UFOs Over Long Island on the Brookhaven Cable TV system every Thursday at 6:30 p.m. (channel 35). UFO Abductee Support Group offered as well.

J. Allen Hynek Center for UFO Studies (CUFOS)
2457 West Peterson Avenue
Chicago, Illinois 60659
Contacts
Mark Rodeghier (President)
George Eberhart (Librarian & Archivist)
312-271-3611
Publications are The Journal of UFO Studies and International UFO Reporter (IUR)
Founded in 1973

A non-profit organization whose goal is to promote serious research into the UFO phenomena through the expertise of an international group of scientists, academicians, and volunteers. This organization has a worldwide network of field investigators that interview witnesses, examine physical evidence and gather any other relevant information. The major purpose of CUFOS is to act as a clearinghouse—a place where UFO experiences can be reported and researched. Dr. J. Allen Hynek, who was considered one of the world's pre-eminent authorities on the UFO phenomenon, first became involved with UFOs as Scientific Consultant to the U.S. Air Force from 1948 to 1968, and was Scientific Director of CUFOS until his death in 1986. He coined the phrase "close encounters of the third kind" and acted as technical advisor to director Steven Spielberg on the movie of the same name.

CUFOS maintains the world's largest repository of data about UFO phenomena, second only to the US Government! This material includes more than 50,000 cases of UFO sightings and a library of more than 5,000 books and magazines, which cover all aspects of the UFO phenomena. CUFOS promotes various activities, projects, publications, symposiums, conferences, seminars and field trips to various UFO-related locations and sells journals, books, audiocassette tapes, and other publications. The *International UFO Reporter (IUR)*, published bi-monthly, reports on current sightings, news and articles on current UFO topics. CUFOS also publishes the annual *Journal of UFO Studies* which presents a collection of scholarly papers on the UFO phenomenon.

The Massachusetts Center for the study of Aerial
    Phenomena
43 Harrison Street
Reading, Massachusetts 01867
Contact: Jim Melesciuc
617-944-0686

A loose-knit organization comprised of researchers who wish to remain unaffiliated with any specific UFO group and concentrate efforts in individual fields of interest; many members do belong to other UFO groups, such as CAUS, MUFON, CUFOS, etc.

Mutual UFO Network, Inc. (MUFON)
103 Oldtowne Road
Seguin, Texas 78155
Contact: Walter H. Andrus, Jr
Other MUFON Branches:
New Zealand Director for MUFON: Murray Bott
PO Box 27117

Mt Roskill, Auckland 1030
New Zealand
Phone: 64-9-6315825
murrayb@kiwi.gen.nz
Publications are *MUFON UFO Journal, MUFON*, and
    *Field Investigator's Manual*

Founded on May 31, 1969 with a membership of 2500. Originally based in Illinois, it was called the Mid-west UFO Network, changing its name around 1972 to Mutual to represent its growing role as a national and international group.

MUFON has local groups in each state within the USA and has representatives in many countries outside the USA. MUFON runs a bulletin board.

MUFON is a non-profit, international, scientific organization devoted to studying and researching the UFO phenomenon. MUFON sponsors and conducts worldwide conferences, seminars and symposiums. MUFON members believe that a concentrated scientific study by dedicated investigators and researchers will provide the ultimate answer to the UFO enigma. State Director oversees the activities of Field Investigators through State Section Directors. An International Coordinator and seven Continental Coordinators work with Foreign Representatives in each country to investigate UFO activity. MUFON is the "parent organization" for numerous, smaller UFO research groups across the United States and around the world. Since 1970 has sponsored an Annual International UFO Symposium where scientists, engineers, university professors, and authors lecture on their particular specialization to solving the UFO enigma. The copyrighted symposium proceedings are published annually for worldwide distribution. Back issues of symposium proceedings are available. Anyone interested is invited to join MUFON by submitting a membership application and dues for approval.

Mutual UFO Network of North Carolina, Inc.
    (MUFON-NC)
602 Battleground Road
Lincolnton, North Carolina 28092

George D. Fawcett (State Director)
Granville Angell (Treasurer)
Robert H. Hair
704-735-5725
Founded in 1990

Non-profit corporation whose goal is to investigate and research the UFO enigma. MUFON-NC accepts reports of sightings, visitations, etc. and will investigate those cases with the most merit.

MUFON-NC holds quarterly meetings in North Carolina on the first Sunday of February, May, August and November on a rotating basis in different cities; meetings generally run from l pm until 6 pm.

National Investigations Committee on UFOs (NICUFO)
14617 Victory Blvd. Suite 4
P.O. Box 5
Van Nuys, California 91411
Dr. Frank E. Stranges, Ph.D. (President)
818-989-5942
Publications are *UFO Journal* and *Inter-Space-Link-Confidential NL*
Founded in 1967

Maintains one of the world's largest collections of UFO slides, books and tapes. For more information materials write: I.E.C. Book Department, P.O. Box 73, Van Nuys, California 91408.

A non-profit organization whose aim is to conduct research into, and provide education about, the fields of UFOs, Space, and Science phenomena. Members are available to provide lectures throughout the world. Monthly meetings, as well as two UFO seminars per year, are held at NICUFO headquarters in Van Nuys, California.

Based upon their experience, members may serve in one of the following positions: Consultant, State or Provincial Director, State Section Director, Foreign Representative, Field Investigator, Research Specialist, Amateur Radio Operator, Astronomer, Field Investigator Trainee, Translator, UFO News

Clipping Service, Contributing Subscriber or Associate Member (under 18 years of age). MUFON trains its Field Investigators and provides them with the *MUFON Field Investigator's Manual*. Amateur Radio Networks are used to receive and disseminate UFO sighting reports and current UFO information. The time and frequencies of these broadcasts are published in the *MUFON UFO Journal*.

The National Sighting Research Center (NSRC)
P.O. Box 76
Emerson, New Jersey 07630
Bob Sylvester (Co-Director)
Publishes the *National Sighting Yearbook*
Founded in 1988

A non-profit organization composed of 6 part-time research specialists with expertise in microcomputer-based data base management systems (DBMS), statistical analysis, micro telecommunications, and trend analysis. The NSRC acts as an information-gathering organization which compiles massive amounts of data and disseminates it in the form of computerized reports, including information in statistical and graphical form. The goals of NSRC are to provide the professional UFO investigator or researcher with a computerized, highly graphical database summary of all reported sightings of anomalous aerial phenomena within the United States and a clearinghouse for UFO sighting report data; periodically release other publications, in-depth reports requested by other researchers and organizations.

Nevada Aerial Research Group (NARG)
P.O. Box 81407
Las Vegas, Nevada 89180-1407
Contact: Val Valerian
Publishes *The Leading Edge* and *NARG Manual Journal*

A worldwide, New Age organization with researchers and investigators in 12 countries and 37 states. The primary goals of NARG are to provide information on developments in our civilization which affect all of this planet and to investigate all processes that impede evolution.

Pennsylvania Association for the Study of the
  Unexplained (PASU)
6 Oakhill Avenue
Greensburg, Pennsylvania 15601
Stan Gordon (Director)
412-838-7768
PASU Data Exchange
Founded in 1981

A volunteer, non-profit scientific research unit conducts investigations of strange or unusual occurrences, with emphasis on UFOs and UFO-related activity. PASU members donate their time and equipment. PASU is a statewide clearinghouse for reports of UFO sightings and is comprised of individuals with training or experience in the fields of science, engineering, technology or medicine who act as field investigators. Monthly meetings are held to share information. PASU has on file thousands of cases from Pennsylvania that include UFO sightings, creature reports, unusual animal killings, unexplained photographs and other anomalies. PASU attempts to send field investigators directly to the scene of an occurrence to gather information and interview witnesses. The *PASU Data Exchange* newsletter contains information regarding investigations conducted into unusual incidents that have occurred in Pennsylvania.

The Portland UFO Group (PUFOG)
P.O. Box 998
Wilsonville, OR 97070
Jennifer Brown-Jacobs (Director)
503-538-0836
Publications is *PUFOG Newsletter*
Founded in 1989

Currently has 500 Members. A non-profit UFO organization whose monthly seminars are open to the general public; maintain no membership and are unaffiliated with any other UFO organi-

zation. PUFOG is an information group that conducts seminars on the 3rd Sunday of each month at Mt. Hood Community College, Gresham, OR. These seminars present knowledgeable speakers on UFOs and related subjects. Those who attend their seminars pay an admission fee and receive the *PUFOG Newsletter.*

Royal Priest Research
P.O. Box 10546
Sedona, Arizona 86336
Lyssa Royal
602-282-3208
Publication is *The Prism*
Founded in 1975

An independent research group with no members. Lyssa Royal mixes generally accepted research techniques skills with less provable methods, such as channeling. Thus far, their research has produced two books, *The Prism of Lyra—An Exploration of Human Galactic Heritage* (130 pages) and *Visitors From Within* (171 pages). Lyssa Royal organizes and conducts weekly sessions, private consultations, and special events. She offers tapes of her numerous channeling sessions which discuss various topics and extraterrestrial beings both physical and nonphysical. *The Prism* is a periodic newsletter which details news, lists of recent channeling tapes, books, etc.

The Search for Extraterrestrial Intelligence (SETI)
NASA Headquarters:
Office of Space Science and Applications, Washington, D.C.
Michael Braukus
(Phone: 202-358-1547)
Ames Research Center, Mountain View, Calif.
Michael Mewhinney
(Phone: 415-604-9000)
Jet Propulsion Laboratory, Pasadena, Calif.
Mary Hardin
(Phone: 818-354-5011)

Sirian Rainbow Lodge
P.O. Box 2108
St. Petersburg, Florida 33731

Liah Goldenhawk (Cofounder)
L. Baird (Bookkeeper)
813-822-8154
Publication is *Solar Trek*
Founded in 1990

Primarily an extraterrestrial outpost program, provides information from the alien point of view. The Sirian Rainbow Lodge is the StarSystem Sirian Outpost; interested in sharing all types of positive ET Alien knowledge. ET & UFO Network where Contactees and others may share experiences, contacts and opinions. Focuses on believing and possibilities, rather than proving any theories; focuses mainly on occupants of UFOs and alien knowledge.

The Lodge is led by the Bennu who is an alien of the Nordic type from StarSystem Sirius. To raise money, the Lodge sells books and booklets by the Bennu and *Solar Trek*, the ET Alien Quarterly Journal.

## SKYNET

257 Sycamore Glen
Pasadena, California 91105
Ann Druffel (Project Co-Ordinator)
213-256-8655
Publication is *Skynet Guides*
Founded in 1965
Currently 100 members.

Established to serve as a tracking system for UFO reports in the Los Angeles, California area. Its original purpose was to receive UFO reports at the time that witnesses were viewing the objects, thus centering their efforts on real-time viewing, photographing, monitoring, rather than relying on after-the-fact analysis.

Upon joining, members agree to contact other SKYNET members whenever an unusual sighting is occurring for members to view, photograph and monitor the object in real-time while not having to wait for an after-the-fact presentation. This contacting of other SKYNET members that a sighting is occurring is the only obligation of members. All calls from the public receive an in-depth

phone interview by an assigned SKYNET official and if warranted, further field investigations are conducted.

## SOCIETE' BELGE d'ETUDE des PHENOMENES SPATIAUX (SOBEPS)

74 Avenue Paul Janson, B-1070
Bruxelles, Belgium
President: Michel Bougard
Secretary: Lucien Clerebaut

Commonly called SOBEPS and the leading group in Belgium.

Society for Scientific Exploration (SSE)
Office of the Secretary
P.O. Box 3818
University Station
Charlottesville, Virginia 22903-0818
Laurence W. Fredrick (Secretary)
804-924-4905; 804-924-3104
Publishes the *Journal of Scientific Exploration*
Founded in 1982

A tax-exempt group that investigates various anomalies, including UFOs. Although its president is Professor Peter Sturrock of Stanford University, all contact with SSE should be made through Laurence W. Fredrick. The goal of the SSE is to gain further understanding of anomalous phenomena (including UFOs) and to share this knowledge with the public. The Society considers anomalous phenomena to be incidents that appear to contradict existing scientific knowledge; regarded by the scientific community as being outside their established fields of inquiry. They use the *Journal of Scientific Exploration* as an avenue to discuss anomalous phenomena and present research results to the scientific and scholarly community; its members are drawn from practitioners of science who have acquired a first-hand knowledge and understanding of the scientific process. The Society holds annual international meetings and periodically scheduled regional meetings.

To promote cooperation, and to accommodate other levels of activity and interest, the Society has created the categories of

"Corresponding Member" and "Associate." "Associates" receive the *Journal of Scientific Exploration* (two issues a year) and *The Explorer* (two issues a year). An Associate may submit letters and other items for publication in the Newsletter, may submit articles for publication in the Journal (each article must be sponsored by a "Full Member"), and may attend Society meetings by arrangement with a "Full Member." A person wishing to become an "Associate" may do so by completing an Application Form and sending it with a check for the annual dues to the Secretary.

"Full Membership" is reserved for those associated with major universities, government entities or corporate research institutions who have an established reputation in a traditional branch of science. "Emeritus Membership" provides the privileges of Full Membership to similarly qualified retirees at a lower annual rate. "Student Membership" is limited to graduate students enrolled in academic institutions. "Corresponding Membership" is open to members of designated organizations. A "Corresponding Member" receives, and is entitled to submit articles to the *Journal of Scientific Exploration*.

The Society for the Investigation of the Unexplained (SITU)
P.O. Box 265
Little Silver, New Jersey 07739
Nancy Warth (Membership Secretary)
201-842-5229
Publication is *Pursuit*
Founded in 1965

A non-profit, tax-exempt organization; collects data on unexplained events, promotes proper investigation of both individual reports and general subjects, and reports significant data to its members. SITU studies unexplained events that orthodox science does not (or will not) investigate.

SITU maintains reference files which include original reports, newspaper and other clipping correspondence, audio tapes, films,

photographs, drawings, maps, etc. Copies of these items are available to members only. Membership fees include the magazine *Pursuit*, which is published regularly.

System Ready
7154 North University Drive Suite 116
Tarnarac, Florida 33321

Concentrates on building devices which can be used to detect UFOs. Their book, *Detecting UFOs*, details these devices.

Transcendental Communications A Division of LAMAT Research
444 North Amelia #9C
San Dimas, California 91773
Don Grantharn (Director & Systems Operator)
714-599-6769
714-599-6270 (Operates at 300/1200/2400 BPS)
714-599-5045
Publication is *Transcendental Communications Newsletter*

A scientific, investigative organization interested in UFOs and related phenomena. Transcendental Communications is the largest UFO-related computer network bulletin board system (BBS) on the west coast. The aim of Transcendental Communications is to get the word out to those interested in current UFO information; a clearinghouse for books, documents, publications, audio and video tape interviews, seminars, documentaries and UFO films and footage.

The main focus of Transcendental Communications is the operation of a BBS through which interested parties can participate in on-line conversation, read various reports, news items or articles, or leave messages for other members.

Transcendental Communications publishes the *Transcendental Communications Newsletter* which outlines topics that have been discussed on the BBS and provides current UFO-related articles. FAX number available so that interested parties can send them copies of reports, information, etc.

UFO Contact Center International (UFOCCI)
3001 South 288th Street #304
Federal Way, Washington 98003
Aileen Bringle (Director)
206-946-2248
Publication is *The Missing Link*
Founded in 1981

A non-profit organization dedicated to helping people who have had traumatic, bizarre experiences or sightings of UFOs. A secondary goal of UFOCCI is to promote public awareness of the UFO contactee phenomenon. UFOCCI works with each contactee to help them understand their experiences via hypnosis, group meetings and open seminars. Each year, over the Labor Day weekend, UFOCCI conducts a conference called "Jorpah" (which means 'Cosmic Gathering') in which the past year's activities are summed up and discussed. These gatherings are held at different places throughout the country. The date and time of these conferences are announced in *The Missing Link* newsletter. UFOCCI holds monthly meetings the fourth Saturday of each month.

UFO Information Retrieval Center (UFOIRC)
3131 West Cochise Drive #158
Phoenix, Arizona 85051-9501
Thomas M. Olsen (President)
602-997-1523
602-870-3178
Publication is *Reference for Outstanding UFO Sighting Reports*
Founded in 1966

A non-membership organization which collects, analyzes, publishes and disseminates information about UFOs. UFOIRC also compiles statistics, conducts research programs, sponsors photo exhibits, maintains a 200-volume Library, and provides special educational services geared to children and students.

UFOIRC publishes books, symposium proceedings, reprints of magazine articles, and a bibliography of currently available information on the UFO phenomenon.

UFO Investigators League
Box 753
New Brunswick, New Jersey 08903
Timothy Green Beckley
Publishes *UFO Spotters Newsletter*
Founded in 1990

A new organization under the auspices of Timothy Green Beckley who is striving to expand his international network of investigators who wish to investigate UFO cases in their areas.

Members receive membership card, investigators certificate, field manual, and a subscription to the *UFO Spotters Newsletter*. Membership is $20.00 per year.

UFO Study Group of Greater St. Louis
P.O. Box 31544
St. Louis, Missouri 63131
John Schroeder (President)
Helen Hanke (Secretary)
314-352-3058
Publication is *The UFO Enigma*

A non-profit organization formed in 1968 to investigate UFOs and to collect and disseminate information germane to the UFO phenomena. They hold meetings at the Farm and Home building, 110 West Lockwood (at Gore), Webster Groves, Missouri at 2:00 p.m. on the second Sunday of the months September through May.

This group operates in close cooperation with MUFON, CUFOS, and with numerous organizations around the world in order to coordinate UFO research and information.

Ufology Research of Manitoba (UFOROM)
Box 1918
Winnipeg, Manitoba
Canada R3C 3R2
Founded in 1975

UFOROM is a private, non-profit and volunteer organization which is involved in rational discourse, investigation and research on UFOs and related phenomena. All types of UFO-related phenomena have been studied by UFOROM, including traces, crash-retrievals, abductions and cattle mutilations. In addition, some UFOROM associates also study Fortean and psychic phenomena. UFOROM publishes an annual survey of UFO activity in Canada, comparable to the Ferrughelli reports on American cases. Case data is provided by cooperative Canadian researchers across Canada.

UFOROM is not open to general public membership. However, independent investigators and researchers throughout North America and particularly in Canada are associated with UFOROM by way of their contributions of case information and data from their own areas. Such contributions are welcomed and readily acknowledged by UFOROM.

Although UFOROM does not publish a journal or newsletter for general distribution, associates frequently exchange information on an informal basis. This information is made available through articles and reports published in UFO magazines or books, written or edited by UFOROM associates. UFOROM is associated with an irregular ufozine titled the *Swamp Gas Journal.*

UFOROM associates are involved with the J. Allen Hynek Center for UFO Studies (CUFOS), the Mutual UFO Network (MUFON) and various other organizations. UFOROM functions independently, but operates with an understanding of complete cooperation and information exchange with interested and serious researchers in their specialized areas of interest.

UFOROM is devoted to the rational and objective study of UFOs and related phenomena, as well as other controversial phenomena such as crop circles. All views on these phenomena, including both proponent and contrary standpoints, are considered. In this regard, UFOROM associates tend to engage in dialogue with both "believers" and "debunkers." It is hoped that such attempts to "bridge the gap" between the two sides of the debate will encourage more constructive discourse.

United Aerial Phenomena Agency (UAPA)
P.O. Box 347032
Cleveland, Ohio 44134-7032
Allan J. Manak (Chairman)
Rick R. Hilberg (Vice Chairman)
Publications are *Flying Saucer Digest* (quarterly) and *Weirdology* (bi-monthly).
Founded in 1966

A non-profit organization dedicated to the investigation and study of UFOs and related subjects. UAPA sells a wide variety of books, maps, back issues, rare items, etc. A catalog is available.

Universal Articulate Interdimensional Understanding of Science
UNARIUS Academy of Sciences
145 South Magnolia Avenue
El Cajon, California 92020-4522
Dr. Ernest L. Norman (Co-Founder)
Ruth E. Norman (Co-Founder)
Charles Spaegel (Vice President)
619-447-4170
Publication is *UNARIUS Light Magazine*
Founded in 1954.

A non-profit, New Age organization which has pioneered the teaching of Past Life Therapy since 1954. This teaching is given to the student through a curriculum that attunes the truth seeker to the high frequency energy maintained by the authors, who are Advanced Spiritual Beings living on the Inner Planes. UNARIUS receives most of its information and instructions through channeling with the Higher Beings (Space Brothers). UNARIUS writes, publishes, and distributes a complete course of study describing the New Sciences of Life. This course material is covered over 100-plus texts of the UNARIUS Academy of Sciences; augmented by over 100 video programs. The course material covers missing pieces of man's prehistory, the enigma surrounding the dilemma of unresolved problems in science, politics and religion, and the future for mankind in the 21st century. Class sessions are held at the UNARIUS Center on Wednesdays & Sundays at 7:00 p.m. Some courses are also available on TV stations throughout California. All of the materials are directly related to the UNARIUS goal of achieving Higher Awareness. One of this group's main tenets is that there are superior extraterrestrial forces which control the Earth's destiny and which know the fate of mankind. With the teachings provided by UNARIUS, they feel that each person can become cosmically attuned to higher spiritual forces and can become aware of Reality and what is in store for humans. UNARIUS teaches that the Interplanetary Confederation, a coalition of 33 existing planets, is building 33 spacecraft that will form a giant city and will descend to Earth in the year 2001. This "building" or "city" will descend on land purchased for this purpose in the southern California area and will be a gathering spot for people to come and learn about Cosmic Awareness.

Victorian UFO Research Society Inc. (VUFORS)
P.O. Box 43
Moorabbin, Victoria
AUSTRALIA 3189
phone: +61-3-6076849
fax : +61-3-6076198
email: TCook@cmutual.com.au
Founded in 1957
Publication is *The Australian UFO Bulletin*

The "Australian Flying Saucer Research Society (Victorian Branch)" was formed on the 17th of February, 1957 as a branch of the "Australian Flying Saucer Research Society" and later that year was reorganized as the "Victorian Flying Saucer Research Society" with Mr. Peter E. Norris L.L.B. as President. In 1968 the name was again altered—this time to the "Victorian UFO Research Society." The current executive has been in place since 1978. The Society has held a dispassionate attitude on UFOs claiming it is a scientific problem deserving closer attention. Membership of this Society—which maintains the largest membership of any UFO organization in the Southern Hemisphere—is open to all who are genuinely interested in the subject.

# FOR FURTHER SLEUTHING

## CONSPIRACY

### The Central Intelligence Agency: General

Blum, William. *The CIA, A Forgotten History: U.S. Global Interventions Since World War 2*. Zed Press, 1987. A thorough review of the record of CIA involvement when the Cold War turns hot.

Emerson, Steven. *Secret Warriors: Inside the Covert Military Operations of the Reagan Era*. Putnam and Sons, 1986. The best comprehensive account of covert operations during the Reagan years.

Gage, Kit. *At War With Peace: U.S. Covert Operations*. NCARL, First Amendment Foundation, 1990. An indispensable pamphlet chronicling the history of CIA covert actions, its human costs, laws regulating it, and restrictions to information about it. Send $2.50 to NCARL, 1313 West 8th Street, Suite 313, Los Angeles, CA 90017. 213-484-6661.

Garwood, Darrell. *Under Cover: Thirty-Five Years of CIA Deception*. Grove Press, 1985. Fully documented history of covert operations by a former UPI Pentagon correspondent. Includes an extensive chronology.

Powers, Thomas. *The Man Who Kept Secrets—Richard Helms and the CIA*. Knopf, 1979. A portrait of the CIA director who launched nefarious and deadly CIA activities in Chile, Iran, and Vietnam.

Prados, John. *Presidents' Secret Wars: CIA and Pentagon Covert Operations Since World War II*. Morrow, 1986. Good overview with linkage to problem of foreign policy and secrecy.

Prouty, Fletcher. *The Secret Team: The CIA and its Allies in Control of the World*. 1974. Early critical research on the CIA, but it's marred by a somewhat overreaching analysis.

Ranelagh, John. *The Agency: The Rise and Decline of the CIA*. Touchstone/Simon and Schuster, 1987. A revised edition of the most widely accepted comprehensive history of the CIA, now current through Iran-Contragate and the appointment of William Webster as director.

### The Central Intelligence Agency: Specific Countries and Regions

Agee, Philip, and Louis Wolf. *Dirty Work I—The CIA in Western Europe*. Lyle Stuart, 1978. A compilation of articles including the classic "How to Spot a Spook" and a list of seven hundred alleged agents.

———. *Dirty Work II—The CIA in Africa*. Lyle Stuart, 1979. Articles focusing on Africa. Available from Covert Action Information Bulletin, Box 50272, Washington, D.C. 20004.

Bonner, Raymond. *Weakness and Deceit: U.S. Policy and El Salvador*. New York Times Books, 1984.

*The CIA's Nicaraguan Manual: Psychological Operations in Guerrilla Warfare*. Vintage, 1985. A collection of essays written by the CIA and others.

Dickey, Christopher. *With the Contras: A reporter in the fields of Nicaragua*. Simon and Schuster, 1985.

Eveland, Wilbur Crane. *Ropes of Sand: America's Failure in the Middle East*. W.W. Norton, 1980. The CIA attempted to censor this in-depth examination of U.S. activities in the Middle East.

*The Freedom Fighter's Manual*. Grove Press, 1985. A copy, with translation, of the CIA's manual that targets D'Escoto and others in Nicaragua for disruption and assassination.

Immerman, R. H. *The Foreign Policy of Intervention: The CIA in Guatemala*. University of Texas Press, 1983. From the 1954 overthrow of President Arbenz to the later role of the U.S. in Guatemala, our government has played a key role in that country.

Kinzer, Stephen, and Stephen Schleisinger. *Bitter Fruit—The Untold Story of the American Coup in Guatemala.* Doubleday, 1982.

Kornbluh, Peter. *Nicaragua: The Price of Intervention.* Institute for Policy Studies, 1987. Some sections are useful for reference to counterinsurgency.

Leary, William M. *Perilous Missions: Civil Air Transport and CIA Covert Operations in Asia.* University of Alabama, 1984.

Searle, Chris. *Grenada—The Struggle Against Destabilization.* W.W. Norton, 1983. The coordinated efforts of the CIA and economic and diplomatic agencies to resist changes in Grenada.

Sklar, Holly. *Washington's War on Nicaragua.* South End Press, 1988. The only full review of U.S. foreign policy toward Nicaragua. Makes connections between rightist political ideology and support for covert operations as standard U.S. foreign policy tool.

Snepp, Frank. *Decent Interval.* Vintage Books, 1977. A former CIA officer describes the agency's failure to prepare for the evacuation of Saigon in 1975.

Stockwell, John. *In Search of Enemies.* W.W. Norton, 1978. The former head of the CIA's Angolan Task Force criticizes the agency's role in the country.

## The Central Intelligence Agency: Alliances with Dictators, Fascists, and Nazis

Anderson, Scott, and Jon Lee Anderson. *Inside the League: The Shocking Expose of How Terrorists, Nazis, and Latin American Death Squads Have Infiltrated the World Anti-Communist League.* Dodd, Mead, 1986. This traces the role of anti-Semites and neo-Nazis sheltered by CIA in private covert action and propaganda wars around the world and how they network through WACL.

Bellant, Russ. *Old Nazis, the New Right, and the Reagan Administration: The Role of Domestic Fascist Networks in the Republican Party and their Effect on U.S. Cold War Politics.* Political Research Associates, 1988. What the Blowback crowd did with their spare time after the OSS/CIA recruited them to the U.S. Send $6.50 to Political Research Associates, Suite 205, 678 Mass. Ave, Cambridge, MA 02139.

Chomsky, Noam, and Ed Herman. *The Pentagon-CIA Archipelago: The Washington Connection and Third World Fascism.* South End Press, 1978. U.S.

counter-revolutionary violence and subversion in the Third World.

Goulden, Joseph C. *The Death Merchant.* Bantam, 1984. The story of Edwin Wilson, who used his CIA connections to operate an international arms firm and supplied Quaddafi with tons of explosives and with hit men for political assassinations.

Hauser, Thomas. *Missing: The Execution of Charles Horman.* Harcourt Brace Jovanovich (Touchstone/Simon and Schuster Edition, 1988), 1978. American officials turn their back when the Chilean junta murders a young American.

Herman, Edward S. *The Real Terror Network: Terrorism in Fact and Propaganda.* South End Press, 1982. How the CIA's advisors are actually contributing to terrorism, through training, supplying arms, and so on to foreign governments and rebel groups.

Kruger, Henrik. *The Great Heroin Coup: Drugs, Intelligence and International Fascism.* South End Press, 1980. Drug dealing and other activities in Southeast Asia.

Langguth, A. J. *Hidden Terrors.* Pantheon Books, 1978. How the CIA, the Pentagon, and U.S. police advisors encouraged military takeovers in Latin America.

Lernoux, Penny. *Cry of the People—The Struggle for Human Rights in Latin America.* Doubleday, 1982. The Catholic Church in conflict with U.S. policy.

Loftus, John. *The Belarus Secret: The Nazi Connection in America.* Paragon House, 1982. The first full account of the clandestine operation to bring Nazi collaborators to the U.S. to help wage guerrilla warfare against Eastern Bloc nations.

*The Paperclip Conspiracy: The Hunt for the Nazi Scientists.* How the U.S. covered up the thousands of corpses at Nazi slave labor rocket facilities so we would beat the Russians in launching the first intercontinental ballistic missile.

Simpson, Christopher. *Blowback: The First Full Account of America's Recruitment of Nazis, and its Disastrous Effect on Our Domestic and Foreign Policy.* Weidenfeld and Nicolson, 1988. The title says it all.

## The Central Intelligence Agency: At Home

Branch, Taylor, and Eugene M. Propper. *Labyrinth.* Penguin, 1983. The story of the search for the assassins of Orlando Letelier.

Hougan, Jim. *Secret Agenda, Watergate, Deep Throat and the CIA.* Random House, 1984. One of many books exploring the CIA's role in Watergate.

Lee, Martin, and Bruce Shlain. *Acid Dreams: The CIA, LSD and the Sixties Rebellion.* Grove Press, 1985. The CIA thought LSD would revolutionize the spy trade . . . nobody's perfect.

Marks, John P. *Search for the Manchurian Candidate.* Quadrangle Press, 1979. The history of the CIA's drug and behavior control programs.

Scheflin, Alan W., and Edward M. Opton, Jr. *The Mind Manipulators.* Paddington Press, distributed by Grosset and Dunlap, 1978. Reviews behavior-modification experiments by the CIA and the army.

## The Central Intelligence Agency: Memoirs of Former Directors and Employees

Agee, Philip. *Inside the Company.* Penguin Books, 1978. A diary spanning twelve years of Agee's CIA work, with a special focus on Central and South America and Mexico.

———. *On the Run.* Lyle Stuart, 1987. The CIA takes a dim view of Agee's philosophical turnabout and chases him around the world with an alarming lack of humor.

Cline, Ray S. *The CIA under Reagan, Bush and Casey: The Evolution of the Agency from Roosevelt to Reagan.* Acropolis Books, 1981. Expanded version of the former director's memoirs.

Colby, William, and Peter Forbath. *Honorable Men: My Life in the CIA.* Simon and Schuster, 1978. From the former CIA director during the congressional investigations of the agency.

Liddy, G. Gordon. *Will: The Autobiography of G. Gordon Liddy.* St. Martins Press, 1981. Gives insights into the man who had no qualms about torture or murder to "protect" U.S. national security.

Mcgehee, Ralph. *Deadly Deceits: My 25 Years in the CIA.* Sheridan Square, 1983. Author's growing disillusionment with role of CIA as covert action arm of the presidency. Send $9.95 plus $1.50 shipping and handling to IMA 145 W. 4th St., N.Y., N.Y. 10012.

Phillips, David Atlee. *The Night Watch: My 25 Years of Peculiar Service.* Athenum, 1977. A peculiar yet fascinating unapologetic reminiscence.

Smith, Joseph Burkholder. *Portrait of a Cold Warrior.* G.P. Putnam and Sons, 1976. An insightful look from the view of the agent on the street—in the Philippines, Indonesia, and elsewhere.

## THE POLITICS OF COVERT ACTION

## Intelligence Networks and Policy Makers

Bamford, James. *The Puzzle Palace—A Report on America's Most Secret Agency.* Houghton Mifflin, 1982. Details history, bureaucracy, and scope of activities of the National Security Agency.

Beck, Melvin. *Secret Contenders: The Myth of Cold War Counterintelligence.* Sheriden Square Press, 1984. A devastating critique that details the waste and lunacy of some CIA clandestine operations and concludes that U.S. citizens are ultimately the real target of CIA propaganda campaigns.

Bodenheimer, Thomas, and Robert Gould. *Rollback: Right-wing Power in U.S. Foreign Policy.* South End Press, 1989. A look at the confrontational rightist political agenda that fuels U.S. militarism.

Boettcher, Robert, with Gordon L. Freedman. *Gifts of Deceit: Sun Myung Moon, Tongsun Park and the Korean Scandal.* Holt, Rinehart, and Wilson, 1980. Moon's links to the Korean CIA and other assorted dirty linen is hung out in this documented exposé. Shows Moon as a power-hungry antidemocratic theocrat.

Godson, Roy, ed. *Intelligence Requirements for the 1990's: Collection, Analysis, Counterintelligence, and Covert Action.* Lexington Books/D.C. Heath. Edited by one of the more horrific geeks of the intelligence empire, this collection of essays provides a blueprint for creating the U.S. police state. A shopping list for the guardians of post-Constitutional America. Sequel to the popular *Intelligence Requirements for the 1980's* series of books.

Halperin, Morton, et al. *The Lawless State: The Crimes of the U.S. Intelligence Agencies.* Penguin Books, 1978. Overview of efforts to spy and disrupt by the CIA, FBI, NSA, IRS, and grand juries. Available from the American Civil Liberties Union/Center for National Security Studies, 122 Maryland Ave. NE, Washington, D.C. 20002.

Herman, Edward, and Gerry O'Sullivan. *The Terrorism Industry: The Experts and Institutions That Shape View of Terror.* Pantheon, 1990. A thorough discussion of how the concept and reality of terrorism has been packaged and manipulated to promote authoritarian and rightist political ideology.

Kwitny, Jonathan. *The Crimes of Patriots: A True Tale of Dope, Dirty Money, and the CIA.* W. W. Norton, 1987. *Wall Street Journal* reporter Kwitny unravels the mystery of the Nugan Hand Bank scandal.

Laquer, Walter. *A World of Secrets—the Uses and Limits of Intelligence.* The 20th Century Fund, 1985. How foreign intelligence is used and misused, and what can be done, as seen by mainstream critics.

Marchetti, Victor, and John Marks. *The CIA and the Cult of Intelligence.* Dell Books, 1980. Classic overview of the CIA and intelligence operations; updated to include deletions by the CIA.

McCoy, Alfred W., with Cathleen B. Read and Leonard P. Adams II. *The Politics of Heroin in Southeast Asia.* Harper–Colophon Books, 1972. How the CIA and Air America served as the conduit for the Golden Triangle opium trade in an effort to build an anti-Communist army.

Treverton, Gregory F. *Covert Action: The Limits of Intervention in the Postwar World.* Basic Books. A critical reassessment of covert operations as a tool of U.S. foreign policy.

## Iran-Contragate

Barry, Tom, and Deb Preusch. *The Soft War: The Uses and Abuses of U.S. Economic Aid in Central America.* Grove Press, 1988. These researchers from the Albuquerque-based Resource Center have compiled a well-documented critique of the uses of so-called humanitarian aid in Central America.

Chamorro, Edgar. *Packaging the Contras: A Case of CIA Disinformation.* Institute for Media Analysis, 1987. A former Contra leader reveals how the CIA created the image of the Contras as the "democratic alternative." Send $5 plus $1 shipping and handling to 145 W. 4th St., N.Y., N.Y. 10012.

Chomsky, Noam. *The Culture of Terrorism.* South End Press, 1978. A brilliant polemic that argues that behind Iran-Contragate is a relentless drive for world power by the U.S. government.

Cockburn, Leslie. *Out of Control: The Story of the Reagan Administration's Secret War in Nicaragua, the Illegal Arms Pipeline, and the Contra Drug Connection.* Atlantic Monthly Press, 1987. This account by a CBS News correspondent is currently the best-documented exposé on Iran-Contragate.

Marshall, Jonathan, and Peter Dale Scott and Jane Hunter. *The Iran Contra Connection: Secret Teams and Covert Operations in the Reagan Era.* South End Press, 1987. Hunter's section on the Israeli intelligence connection is compelling, but some of the other material drifts into conspiracy-minded conclusions not entirely supported with facts. Still, a good overview of Iran-Contragate covert action as not an isolated incident but a logical outcome of institutionalized U.S. covert action policy.

## The Federal Bureau of Investigation and Cointelpro

Blackstock, Nelson. *COINTELPRO: The FBI's Secret War on Political Freedom.* Vintage Books, 1976. The FBI's campaign to infiltrate and disrupt the Socialist Workers Party; good overview of the other bureau investigations of additional left organizations.

Churchill, Ward, and Jim Vander Wall. *COINTELPRO Papers: Documents from the FBI's Secret Wars Against Dissent in the United States.* South End Press, 1989. Actual FBI documents and commentary make a strong case for convincing skeptics. Replaces the "Counter-intelligence" book previously issued by the NLG.

———. *Agents of Repression: The FBI's Secret Wars Against the Black Panther Party and the American Indian Movement.* South End Press, 1988. A chilling account of the murderous tactics used against non-white political activists.

Criley, Richard. *The FBI v. The First Amendment.* First Amendment Foundation, 1990. The story of how the FBI attempted to "neutralize" the National Committee Against Repressive Legislation (NCARL), which was founded in 1960 as the National Committee to Abolish the House Committee on Un-American Activities (HUAC/HCUA). Send $7.50 to First Amendment Foundation, 1313 W. 8th St., Suite 313, Los Angeles, CA 90017.

Donner, Frank. *The Age of Surveillance: The Aims & Methods of America's Political Intelligence System.* Alfred Knopf, 1980. The classic tome documenting surveillance and harassment in the United States from World War I to 1980.

Garrow, David J. *The FBI and Martin Luther King, Jr.* Norton, 1981. Documents the extensive investigation undertaken by the bureau to find ways to discredit and disrupt his quest for freedom.

Glick, Brian. *War at Home: Covert Action Against U.S. Activists and What We Can Do About It.* South End Press, 1989. Must reading for all serious political activists. Provides a comprehensive and common-sense approach for those who must engage in political activity while facing governmental and right-wing attacks. Includes a cogent analysis of the relationship between U.S. political economy and domestic covert action.

Keller, William W. *The Liberals and J. Edgar Hoover.* Princeton University Press, 1989. How liberal congresspersons squirm and look away when they are supposed to oversee agencies of police power and thus allow their more reactionary colleagues to craft agencies such as the FBI into tools of repression.

Kimball, Penn. *The File.* Avon, 1985. How an innocent man became the subject of an FBI investigation.

Matthiessen, Peter. *In the Spirit of Crazy Horse.* Viking Press, 1983. The story of how the FBI targeted the American Indian Movement.

O'Reilly, Kenneth. *Hoover and the Un-Americans: The FBI, HUAC, and the Red Menace.* Temple University Press, 1983. Documents the role of the FBI in engineering the rise of McCarthyism.

———. *Racial Matters: The FBI's Secret File on Black America, 1960–1972.* Free Press, 1988. How the FBI attacked the civil rights movement while posing as its defender against violent attacks. Useful to expose the film *Mississippi Burning* as a dangerous lie.

Rashke, Richard. *The Killing of Karen Silkwood.* Houghton Mifflin, 1981. The FBI's role in the life and investigation after the death of the Oklahoma atomic worker.

Theoharis, Athan. *Beyond the Hiss Case: The FBI, Congress and the Cold War.* Temple University Press, 1982.

Unger, Sanford. *FBI.* Little Brown and Co., 1976. An in-depth study, with background on many officials;

glossary of acronyms for COINTELPRO investigations.

*Voices from Wounded Knee.* Told by the participants and residents of Wounded Knee. *Akwesasne Notes* (a Native American newspaper published from the Mohawk Nation, Rooseveltown, New York 13683), 1976. An account of the occupation at Wounded Knee, with some details on FBI presence on the Pine Ridge Reservation.

## OTHER ASPECTS OF POLITICAL REPRESSION

Caute, David. *The Great Fear.* Simon and Schuster, 1978. Anti-Communist purge under Truman and Eisenhower.

Feldman, Jonathan. *Universities in the Business of Repression: The Academic-Military-Industrial Complex and Central America.* South End Press, 1989. How campus-based research programs are influenced by a militarist mentality.

Goldstein, Robert J. *Political Repression in Modern America, 1870 to Present, 2nd Edition.* Schenkman Books, Inc, 1978. Government, corporate, and other pressures brought to bear on political groups through the years.

Hougan, Jim. *Spooks: The Haunting of America—The Private Use of Secret Agents.* William Morrow and Co., 1977. How private agents, often former FBI or CIA employees, now provide security services for multinational corporations.

Karp, Walter. *Liberty Under Siege: American Politics 1976-1988.* Henry Holt and Co., 1988. Reviewing this book, Bill Moyers quipped it was "like a cold shower on the morning after. Here, finally, is a reveille for reality, a call to stop this long intoxication with illusion and look at what has been happening to our republic."

Levin, Murray B. *Political Hysteria in America—The Democratic Capacity for Repression.* Basic Books, 1971. Underlying forces that create repressive periods such as the Red Scare of the 1920's and the McCarthy era.

Marx, Gary T. *Under Cover: Police Surveillance in America.* Twentieth Century Fund/University of California Press, 1988. The most thoughtful critical analysis of undercover police techniques currently available.

Morgan, Richard E. *Domestic Intelligence: Monitoring Dissent in America.* University of Texas, 1980. Considers the tension between privacy and the need for government to protect the community, from the perspective of the government.

Mowat, Farley. *My Discovery of America.* Atlantic Monthly Press, 1985. A Canadian naturalist writer details how he was denied entry to the U.S. under the 1950 McCarren-Walters Immigration Act and how the American people came to his support.

Nelson, Anne. *Murder Under Two Flags: The U.S., Puerto Rico, and the Cerro Maravilla Cover-up.* Ticknor and Fields, 1986. How Puerto Rican police officials murdered young "Independenistas" as part of an illegal intelligence operation and then enlisted U.S. government agencies in the cover-up.

O'Toole, George. *The Private Sector: Rent-a-cops, Private Spies and the Police Industrial Complex.* W.W. Norton, 1978. Very hard to find but worth it.

Schultz, Bud, and Ruth Schultz. *It Did Happen Here: Recollections of Political Repression in America.* University of California Press, 1989. With their own words, victims of political repression in the U.S. discuss their lives and their battles. A powerful indictment of the myth of equal justice under law in the U.S.

## MAGAZINES, NEWSLETTERS, AND PERIODICALS

*Covert Action Information Bulletin.* Following in the footsteps of the original 1970's *Counterspy* magazine, this periodical chronicles CIA activities around the world. Also looks at surveillance and disinformation campaigns in the U.S. Write: PO Box 50272, Washington D.C. 20004.

*First Principles: National Security and Civil Liberties.* Newsletter that focuses on intelligence operations that undermine fundamental political rights. Special emphasis on the problems of reform. Write: Center for National Security Studies, 122 Maryland Ave. NE, Washington D.C. 20002.

*Guild Notes.* Newspaper that covers current surveillance and harassment litigation. Write: National Lawyers Guild, 55 Avenue of the Americas, New York, NY 10013.

*Lies of Our Times: A Journal to Correct the Record.* Devoted to the analysis of misinformation, disinformation, and propaganda. Write: Institute for Media Analysis, Inc., Sheriden Square Press, Inc., 145 West 4th Street, New York, N.Y. 10012.

*Movement Support Network News.* This newsletter provides information about current harassment of the sanctuary and Central American movement supporters in the U.S. A recent chronology shows extensive harassment, including visits to activists, IRS audits, and activities at the U.S. border. Costs $7.50 per year ($6 limited income). Write: Center for Constitutional Rights, 666 Broadway, New York, NY 10012.

*The Right to Know & the Freedom to Act.* Newsletter of the National Committee Against Repressive Legislation. A First Amendment monitoring service. Costs $15 annually. Write: NCARL, 1313 West 8th Street, Suite 313, Los Angeles, CA 90017.

## WHAT TO DO

### Freedom of Information Act

"Are You Now or Have You Ever Been in the FBI Files?" Ann Mari Buitrago and Leon Andrew Immerman, 1981, Grove Press. Overview of the FOIA—how to use it, how the FBI will respond, and glossary of terms to help read documents when they arrive.

"FOIA-Kit" Available from the Center for Constitutional Rights, 666 Broadway, New York, NY 10012.

"Using the FOIA—A Step by Step Guide." Center for National Security Studies. Detailed instructions, sample letters, and what to expect from a range of agencies. Send $2 to CNSS, 122 Maryland Ave. N.E., Washington DC 20002.

### Education and Organizing Guides

"Computer Accessed Information Systems (BBS's)." Persons with a computer and modem can read and download information on covert action and repression from the following local computer Bulletin Board Systems: AMNET (617) 221-5815, (3,12,24bps-24hr-8N1); NYONLINE (718) 852-2662, (3,12,24bps-24hr-8N1); Beyond War,

(718) 442-1056; NOWAR, (312) 939-4411 (3,12,24bps-24hr-8N1). For information on the international PEACENET, call (415) 923-0900 [voice], or write PEACENET, 3228 Sacramento St., San Francisco, CA 94115.

"If An Agent Knocks: Federal Investigators and Your Rights." Center for Constitutional Rights (CCR). Explains why it is important to have an attorney with you when you talk to the FBI, regardless of how innocuous the agents' questions may be. English and Spanish editions available. Send $1 plus postage to CCR, 666 Broadway, New York, NY 10012.

"NameBASE (formerly SPYBASE)." A computerized database with search features comprising an index of date and page citations to appearances of the names of more than twenty thousand individuals and organizations in hundreds of books and thousands of newspaper and magazine clippings, all dealing with the CIA, FBI, and U.S. government repression in general. Available for MS-DOS and CP/M machines. Write for pricing for your computer. Available from Public Information Research, P.O. Box 5199, Arlington, VA 22205. 703-241-5437.

"Radical Re-entry (And Departure): Coming through Customs." Center for Constitutional Rights. Because customs agents are stopping political activists at the borders in search of information, such as contacts in Nicaragua, this booklet is helpful for the political traveler. Send $1 plus postage to CCR, 666 Broadway, New York, NY 10012.

"Reports on The Secret Team" Publications and organizing guides on Iran-Contragate and intelligence abuse are available from the Christic Institute. The Christic Institute stresses the role of individual bad actors rather than systemic or institutional problems, and sometimes their allegations stretch beyond their ability to provide documentation, still they have been in the forefront of organizing grassroots opposition to U.S. covert action. Christic Institute, 1324 North Capitol Street, N.W., Washington, D.C. 20002-3337.

## Litigation

"Civil Rights Litigation and Attorneys Fees Annual Handbook." National Lawyers Guild Civil Liberties Committee. A more issue-oriented and broadly-targeted collection of essays. Issued annually. Write: Clark Boardman (see below).

"The Law of Electronic Surveillance." Major update 1984, supplemented annually. James C. Carr. Write: Clark Boardman, 435 Hudson Street, New York, NY 10014.

"Litigation Under the Federal Freedom of Information Act and Privacy Act." Editions updated regularly. Allan Adler, Ed. Important reference book for attorneys using the FOIA; covers many federal agencies. Write: Center for National Security Studies, 122 Maryland Ave. N.E., Washington, D.C. 20002.

"Police Misconduct and Civil Rights Law Report." National Lawyers Guild Civil Liberties Committee, Bi-monthly litigation newsletter and companion to above manual. Write: Clark Boardman (see above).

"Police Misconduct Law and Litigation Manual." Michael Avery and David Rudovsky, National Lawyers Guild Civil Liberties Committee, Updated annually. Write: Clark Boardman (see above).

"Representation of Witnesses Before Federal Grand Juries." The Grand Jury Project. Major update 1984, supplemented annually. Write: Clark Boardman (see above).

## UNUSUAL SCIENCE

Barry, James D. *Ball Lightning and Bead Lightning: Extreme Forms of Atmospheric Electricity.* New York: Plenum Press, 1980. Various theories on known physical aspects and experimental production of ball lightning. Serious research with a large bibliography.

The Manual of Free Energy Devices And Systems, Vol II by D.A.Kelly. Overview and history of "free" energy.

Milton, Richard. *Forbidden Science.* London: Fourth Estate Ltd, 1995. Also published in U.S. as *Alternative Science.* Examines the psychology of scientific censorship that leads to "taboo" fields of research and invention, including historical and contemporary examples, such as the Wright Brothers, cold fusion, parapsychology, Velikovski, N-rays, and others. Milton points out that modern science needs repair. Heavily referenced with a large bibliography.

*Scientific Literacy and the Myth of the Scientific Method* by Henry H. Bauer, (c)1994 U. of Illinois Press. Exposes commonly held myths regarding science researchers.

Sheldrake, Rupert. *Seven Experiments That Could Change the World*. New York: Riverhead Books, 1995. This books asks key questions, including: Why not continuously measure physical constants rather than assume they are constant? Have scientists applied seriously biased expectations to basic physics experiments? Are amputee's "phantom limbs" real? A disturbing look at fundamental assumptions behind modern science.

Stein, G. Harry. *Mind Machines You Can Build*. Top of the Mountain Publishing Co., 1992. Experiments include testing psychotronics and PK ability, building a "wishing" machine and a Hieronymous machine, plus work with pyramids and pendula. Send $13.95 to P.O. Box 2244 Pinelas Park FL 34665-2244. Phone 813-530-0110, fax 813-536-3681.

## ON-LINE

Warning: Sites and pages, particularly those maintained by fans, often disappear or change their addresses without notice. Do a little hunting, and those you do find will lead you to others. Just as some disappear and die, others are born to replace them and expand X-Philes fandom.

### "Official" or Main Sites

The Official X-Files WWW Site
(www.TheX-Files.com/)
The Official X-Files Sites

FOX Online
(www.foxnetwork.com/home.html)
Home page for the FOX Television Network

Welcome to *The X-Files*
(www.foxhome.com/trustno1/)
The 20th Century Fox Home Entertainment X-Files Site

Sky One's X-Files Home Page
(www.sky.co.uk/one/xfiles/)
The U.K. Home of *The X-Files*

*The X-Files* at Rutgers University
(www.rutgers.edu/x-files.html)
The Original X-Files WWW Site!

Falchion's Home Page: X-Files
(www.cs.mu.oz.au/~simc/xfiles.html)
One of the best designed and biggest of all X-Files sites! (U.S. Mirror Site)

Frantik Produktions' *The X-Files:* 1013
(www.winternet.com/~dbrekke/xf.html)
New site determined to become one of the best.

Purity Controlled Webpage
(www.halcyon.com/mulder/xfiles.html)
Great variety and many items. Macintosh Talker, episode guide, FAQ, Sound of the Week, pictures, links, trivia, downloads, Deep Throat Shrine...more!

Internet Movie Database—Gillian Anderson
(us.imdb.com/cache/person-exact/b1321)
Gillian Anderson Filmography and Biography

Internet Movie Database—David Duchovny
(us.imdb.com/cache/person-exact/a30101)
David Duchovny Filmography and Biography

Internet Movie Datbase—Mitch Pileggi
(us.imdb.com/cache/person-exact/a85938)
Mitch Pileggi Filmography

Internet Movie Database—Nicholas Lea
(us.imdb.com/cache/person-exact/a62233)
Nicholas Lea Filmography

Yahoo's X-Files Links
(www.yahoo.com/Entertainment/Television/Shows/Science_Fiction/X_Files__The/)

Yahoo's Gillian Anderson Links
(www.yahoo.com/Entertainment/Movies_and_Films/Actors_and_Actresses/Anderson__Gillian/)

Yahoo's David Duchovny Links Links
(www.yahoo.com/Entertainment/Movies_and_Films/
Actors_and_Actresses/Duchovny__David/)

Federal Bureau of Investigation
(www.fbi.gov/)
Home Page of the FBI

alt.tv.x-files
Usenet Newsgroup for X-Files discussion

## Fan Pages

Gillian Anderson/X-Files
(192.203.249.66/~leejb/scully.html)

Malone's X-Files Homepage
(200.252.252.252/pages/marcello/)

The Netpicker's Guide to *The X-Files*
(aea16.k12.ia.us/ricke/netpickhome.html)

I'm not who I am/I Want To Believe
(amati.cremona.polimi.it/~s057/)

Beth's X-Page
(annie.wellesley.edu/students/sundheim/x-files.html)
Many links to other pages

The Cancer Man Fan Club/Nicotine Brigade
(ariel.ucs.unimelb.edu.au:80/~cthulhu/cm_faq.html)

John's X-files links
(box.argonet.co.uk/users/jmb/xf.html)

*The X-Files*
(cfn.cs.dal.ca/~ae387/X-Files.html)

Xfiles Links
(challenge.tiac.net/users/bpaq/1.2/xfiles.html)

John's X-Files Homepage
(chat.carleton.ca/~jmaitlan/x-files/xfiles.html)

X-Files
(chs-web.umdl.umich.edu/people/students/sdweber/x-files.html)

The J. Edgar Hoover Building Basement
(cs1.un.umist.ac.uk/personal/mulder/)

Mulder, it's me...
(cygnus.rsabbs.com/~kwitzig/gillian.html)
Gillian Anderson links

*THE X-FILES* on the Internet
(cygnus.rsabbs.com/~kwitzig/xf-signal.html)

X-Files Pages
(daniel.drew.edu/~tmancuso/xf.html)

X-Files
(drycas.club.cc.cmu.edu/~julie/xfiles.html)

Re-Vamped X-Files UK Home Page
(dspace.dial.pipex.com/town/square/be39/)

Jenifer's Home Page
(duggy.extern.uscd.edu/~linny/)

David Duchovny Home Page
(duggy.extern.ucsd.edu/~linny/David.html)

Gillian Anderson Home Page
(duggy.extern.ucsd.edu/~linny/Gill.html)

The V-Files (Vancouver)
(dxhral.desy.de/~cborys/tv/xf.html)

World's Largest X-Files Archive
(dynamics.rug.ac.be:81/http://einstein.rug.ac.be:80/~roeland/xfiles/index.html)

The Truth Is Out There
(effie.osir.hihm.no/~tomes/ebilder.html)

Great Sci-Fi Series: *The X-Files*
(exo.com/~zeus/xfiles.html)

*The X-Files*
(flamestrike.hacks.arizona.edu/~andersen/xfiles.htm)

Western's X-Files Club
(gaul.csd.uwo.ca:8080/~walden/WXFC/)
*The X-Files* Fan Club at The University of Western
Ontario, Canada

X-Files: Trust No One
(gnn.com/gnn/wic/sf.05.html)

*The X-Files* Creative Archive
(gossamer.eng.ohio-state.edu/x-files/)

The Truth Is Here
(gpu2.srv.ualberta.ca/~vichan/www/x-files.html)

Eclectic X-Phile Home Page
(hamp.hampshire.edu/~clasS95/x-philes.html)
Articles, Pictures, Reviews

Eureka: X-Philes Registry
(hjs.geol.uib.no/xfiles/xfiles.htm)
Pen Pal listings

Melody's World
(home.earthlink.net/~arneil/index.html)

X-Files
(home.sol.no/cwhansen/x-02001.htm)

X-Files Links
(iccu6.ipswich.gil.com.au/~walcar/)

sCuLLy's home page
(ironbark.bendigo.latrobe.edu.au/~i951642/)

*The X-Files* Page
(is.dal.ca/~jfee/xfiles.html)

*The X-Files* Epicenter
(jackson.freenet.org/jfn/swk7099/xfiles1.html)

Michael's X-Files Page
(members.aol.com/bloeder/x.htm)

Welcome to the Basement!
(members.gnn.com/abbebeck/basement.htm)

Eric's Drawer of THE X FILES
(members.gnn.com/BatsEnd/xfiles.htm)

The X Spot
(members.gnn.com/cwdrew/page2.htm)

Linda's Little 'X-Files' Page
(members.gnn.com/lft/xfiles.htm)

The Underground X-Files Sim
(members.gnn.com/the1kid/uxfsim.htm)

*The X-Files:* UK FAQ pision
(metro.turnpike.net/~ptang/index.html)

Accueil X-FILES HOME PAGE France
(miage.unice.fr/~mathery/index.html)

Mike Quigley's Home Page/X-Files Corner
(mindlink.net/a4369/mq.html)

Daniel's X-Files Homepage
(minyos.xx.rmit.edu.au/~s9507836/xfiles/xfiles.html)
Screen savers, pictures, links

The aus.tv.x-files Archive
(modjadji.anu.edu.au/steve/x-files/)

UFO Landing Site
(netaccess.on.ca/~bnelson/FBI-XFD/ufo.html)
X-Files icons

*The X-Files* Drinking Game
(netaccess.on.ca/~bnelson/FBI-XFD/xfls.html)

Scott's X-Files Page
(newriver.ramlink.net/users/zemerick/xfiles.html)

The X Files Alphabet Book
(odyssey.apana.org.au/~simonjw/xfalphbk/title.html)

*The X-Files*
(oege.htsa.hva.nl:19780/xfiles/index.html)

*The X-Files* Audio Visual Vault
(osiris.sunderland.ac.uk/~ca2gke/x-files.html)

foxfile—The World's Smallest X-Files Site
(ourworld.compuserve.com/homepages/foxtucker/)

Forrest's X-Files Homepage
(ourworld.compuserve.com/homepages/Jeanyus/xf.htm)

The X-Files/Akte X-Die unheimlichen Faelle des FBI
(ourworld.compuserve.com/homepages/lbartsch/xf-l-d.htm)

Post Episode Stories
(ourworld.compuserve.com/homepages/Stephanie/post
   epis.htm)
Fan fiction

The X-Files Page
(oz.plymouth.edu/~m_sull/xfiles.html)

The X-Files News and Pics
(pages.prodigy.com/entertainment/x-files.htm)

The X-Files Computer Art Imagemap
(pages.prodigy.com/NJ/krusty/xfiles.html)

X-Files Institution for Relationshippers
(pages.prodigy.com/KYOUSE/xf-love.htm)

X-philes Home Page
(pages.prodigy.com/xfiles/x-file.htm)

The David Duchovny Estrogen Brigade 2 (DDEB2)
(pdsmacii.as.utexas.edu/lara/ddeb.html)

The X-Files Page
(perso.magic.fr/b/bernier/x-files.htm)

Another X-Files Sound Page
(pilot.msu.edu/~thomp169/sound.htm)

X-Files Links
(pilot.msu.edu/user/potters2/xfiles.htm)

The X-Files
(rschp2.anu.edu.au:8080/XFiles.html)
Australian X-Files Fan Club

Sam's X-Files Home Page
(server.cs.jhu.edu/~ziegler/xfiles.html)

Ben's X-File Page
(server.iadfw.net/~brk/x-files/)

GO GA
(shoga.wwa.com/~phlash/goga.html)
High school and college friends of Gillian Anderson

The X-Files Web Site List
(shrike.depaul.edu/~ajue/xf_sites.html)

John M. Shaw's X-Files Home Page
(sleepy.usu.edu/~slq7z/xfiles.html)

Nina's X-File Page
(student.uq.edu.au/~s315571/x_files.html)

Jens' The X-Files becomes truth
   (studserv.rzpool.tu-cottbus.de/~gehrje/x-files.htm)

K.C.'s X-Files Zone
(temasek.teleview.com.sg/~kimkcw/)

Exposure is Addiction!
(transcend.resnet.cornell.edu/gallery/gallery.html)
Photos

Jason's X-Files Page: Main
(trend1.com/~kraffert/xfiles/)

Red Wolf's X-Files Cast, Quotes And Summaries
(triode.apana.org.au:8080/~redwolf/xfiles.html)

TV Net Posting Board: The X-Files
(tvnet.com/cgi-bin/TVpost/thread/tv/66)
Usenet-like posting board for discussion

The X-Files Resource
(upanet.uleth.ca/~FULARSKI/xf000.html)

DSTEXMEX's X-Files Sound Clips Page
(user.aol.com/dsctexmex/web/x-files.htm)

James' X-Files Homepage
(user.itl.net/~beuzeval/x-files/)

The XXY-Files
(users.aol.com/hytritium/xxy.html)
Parody

Melissa's X-Files Page
(users.aol.com/msrxfiles/x-files.html)

The GAGA
(users.feldspar.com/~jonmg/GA/GAGA.html)
Unofficial Gillian Anderson fan page

Nomis X-Files Page
(users.homenet.ie/~nomis/xfiles.html)

X-Files MegaLinks
(vicnet.net.au/~orgjaw/dan/x-files/X-File.htm)

Kate's X-Files Page
(visi.com/~tvwood/kate.htm)

Cupcake's X-Files collection
(vivanet.com/~ferrellm/xfiles.html)

Fox Mulder or an Alien?
(web.city.ac.uk/~be143/morph_fox.html)

The X-Files in Norway
(web.hibo.no/~Larsen/x-files.html)

Steve's Web
(web.syr.edu/~swoo/start.htm)
Icons for Windows 95.

Unofficial Home Page of Alex Krycek
(weber.u.washington.edu/~kmrobrts/rat.html)

The Sci-Fi Site—The X-Files Main Page
(www.abacus.ghj.com/sci_fi/xfiles/xfiles.htm)

The MulderExploratorium
(www.acy.digex.net/~susanjn/david.html)

X-Files Resource Page
(www.aequalis.com/xfiles/xfiles.html)

The Superdeformed X-Files Page
(www.afn.org/~afn04314/xfiles.htm)

The X-Files U.K. Episode Guide
(www.aladdin.co.uk/u/tim/xfiles.html)

X-Files Mania
(www.albany.edu/~st2072/xfiles/xfiles.html)

Where the X-Philes Hang Out!
(www.algonet.se/~tjomme/x-files/index.html)

Christopher's X-Files Page
(www.aloha.com/~fmulder/xfiles.html)

X-Files Episode Ratings
(www.amaroq.com/x-files/)

The uk.media.tv.sf.x-files Home Page
(www.aston.ac.uk/~tangphy/index.html)
U.K. episode guides, FAQs, links

The Gillian Anderson Testosterone Brigade (GATB)
(www.bchs.uh.edu/~ecantu/GATB/gatb.html)

Enrico's X-Files Page
(www.bchs.uh.edu/~ecantu/xf.html)

X-Files Fan Club Information
(www.bcit.bc.ca/~mevans/xfanclub.html)

GABA Home Page
(www.bioch.ox.ac.uk/~mattrowe/gaba/gaba.html)
Gillian Anderson British Association

Miri's X-Files Page
(www.blarg.net/~miri/xf/)

The X-Files Website
(www.bns.com.au/alee/xfiles.html)
Pictures, sounds, fan fiction, articles.

The Fourth Dimension: X-Files SIG Home Page
(National Capital Freenet)
(www.capitalnet.com/~msa/X-Files.html)

Odyssey X
(www.capitalnet.com/~odyssey/x-files.html)

Actor Lists for The X-Files
(www.castle.net/~tina/xfeps.html)

Hsiawen's X-Files Home Page
(www.centcon.com/~hgh911/)

X-Files Resource Page
(www.clark.net/pub/boscomel/xfiles.html)

Laura's Fan Fiction
(www.clark.net/pub/lcooksey/fanfic.html)

Unofficial X-Files Homepage
(www.compart.fi/~wcone/xfiles/xfiles.html)

Andy's_X-Files_Page
(www.connectnet.net.au/~abutt/xfiles.html)

Rene Weber's X-Files Page
(www.cosc.brocku.ca/~rw94an/x-files/)

X Files
(www.cs.man.ac.uk/~clayd/xfiles.html) mirror site

Berny's *The X-Files* Home-Page
 (www.cs.uni-magdeburg.de/~markgraf/xfiles/xf.html)

*The X-Files* Italian Home Page
(www.cs.unibo.it/~cobianch/index.html)

Ned's Ultimate X-Files List
(www.cusd.claremont.edu/~nkalanta/xfiles.html)

Warwick Trek—The X Files
(www.csv.warwick.ac.uk/~suaap/xfiles.htm)

The Smart Young X-Philes (SYX)
(www.cyberus.ca/~phillips/main.html)

Svenska X-Files Fvreningen pe Internet!
(www.dataphone.se/~doodles/x-files/)

Stephen Day's X-Files World Wide Web Site
(www.demon.co.uk/elpasso/steve/x-files.htm)

X-Files—Deny Everything
(www.dlc.fi/~elorayi/xfiles/)

"X" BBS's Home Page
(www.earthlink.net.net/~kasparov/index.htm)

*The X-Files* Creative
(www.eclipse.co.uk/~dj6523/creative.html)

The David Duchovny Estrogen Brigade 3 (DDEB3)
(www.eden.com/~miri/ddeb3.html)

Strange Things DCU—*The X-Files*
(www.eeng.dcu.ie/~stdcu/x-files/)

Aux frontieres d'URL—French Xphiles
(www.eerie.fr/~alquier/xfiles.html)

The David Duchovny Estrogen Brigade (DDEB)
(www.egr.uh.edu/~escco/DDEB.html)

Purity Control—An X-Files Newsletter
(www.electropub.com/~rzman/pc2.html)

X-Phile Extraordinaire
(www.employee.potsdam.edu/psyc/stillwam/x-files.html)

Hot Rod's X-File Page!
(www.enterprise.ca/~tiger/xfiles.html)
Quicktime and MPEG video clips, pictures, episode
    guides, links, X-TEST, character info

X-files:the Offical Mulder's "I want to believe" Poster Site
(www.epsilon.nl/~rvdnoord/xfiles1.htm)

X-Files Role Playing Game
(www.c3kimo.com/~sherman/xfrpg.htm)

The X Summary
(www.exit109.com/~rdionisio/)

The Gillian And Dave X-Files Page
 (www.feldspar.com/~jonmg/X-Files.html)

The NDS X-Files Page
(www.fl.net.au/~nds/xf.html)
Links, FAQs, pictures, video previews

Unofficial Channels: About Walter Skinner and Mitch
    Pileggi
(www.gatech.edu/lcc/idt/Students/Penberthy/X-
    Files/UnofficialChannels.html)

The Truth Is In Here
(www.geocities.com/athens/3401/0xfiles.html)

Malaysia's X-Files Page
(www.geocities.com/Hollywood/3318/)

Andreas X-Files Page
(www.geocities.com/Hollywood/3451/x-files.html)

X-Files Quotes (Season 1 Index)
 (www.geocities.com/RodeoDrive/1720/q1-index.html)

Peter Tran and Elizabeth Boyd's Home Page
(www.geocities.com/paris/2275/)

Cyberia:Beyond Reality
(www.geopages.com/paris/1879/)

Jon's X-Files Home Page
(www.geocities.com/timessquare/2981/xfiles.html)

Select Dimension—*The X-Files* Quiz
(www.guernsey.net/~spaceman/page11.html)

*The X-Files*
(www.hobart.tased.edu.au/students/kathrynb/)

X-Files Page
(www.hom.net/~red5dot/xfilpage.htm)
Chat Page

Ramone's X-Files Home Page
(www.hookup.net/~ramone/trustno1.html)

X-Files Page
(www.hom.net/~red5dot/xfilpage.htm)

Yet Another X-files Site
(www.HZeeland.nl/~sross/yaxs.html)

*The X-Files*
(www.iguide.com/tv/x-files/)

X-Rate
(www.iinet.net.au/~brianp/xfiles/)
Australian Episode Ratings Survey

Craig: *The X-Files*
(www.iinet.net.au/~craigjp/xfiles.html)

The XTreme X-Page
(www.iinet.net.au/~cwinley/xfiles/xfiles.html)
Images, video, sounds, links, and screen savers.

Paul's X-Files Page
(www.iinet.net.au/~groves/xfiles.html)

*The X-Files*
(www.infinet.com/~rkidder/x-files/top.html)

Gillian Anderson, Class of '86
(www.interbridge.com/gillian/gillery.html)
High school pictures of Gillian.

Rant!—TV—*The X-Files*
(www.interlog.com/~robin/rant/tv/xfiles.html)
Reviews of the latest episode

The Gillian Anderson NeuroTransmitter Association
   (GANTA)
(www.interlog.com/~tigger/ganta.html)

J's X-Files Home Page—The Truth Is Here
(www.interpath.net/~cybervox/x.html)

X-Files World Wide Web Sites
(www.interport.net/~darcom/x-files.html)

KRyan's X-File Sim Home Page
(www.inxpress.net/~paisans/Kenedy'sHomePage/)

Dazed—X-Files Sights & Sounds
(www.io.org/~dazed/xfiles/xfiles.html)

Webchat Broadcasting System: X Files
(www.irsociety.com/cgi-
   bin/webchat_doorway.cgi?Room=X_Files)
Online discussion forum

The Singapore X-Files Home Page
(www.iscs.nus.sg/~chengmin/SXF)

X-Files Singapore!
(www.iscs.nus.sg/~limyeech/xfiles.html)

X-Files su Italway.
(www.italway.it/xfiles/index.html)

Jason's X-Files Page
(www.jersey.net/~jasonch/xfile.htm)

*The X-Files:* MancheXter '96
(www.keele.ac.uk/socs/ks12/drama/graildir/xfconv.
   html)

X-Files: The X-Philes Romantic Association
(www.kersur.net/~leut99/Welcome.html)

The Unofficial X-Files Drinking Game
(www.ksu.edu/~madmat/xfiles.html)

Olcay's World
(www.libtech.com/olo.html)

X-Files (Take 1)
(www.lookup.com/Homepages/93006/x-files.html)

Alf's X-Files
(www.loom.com.au/home/alf/cult_tv/x-
    files/index.html)

Dinan's—*The X-Files*—Web Page
(www.ltm.com/dinan/X-files/html/X-files.html)

Ola Mertenssons X-Files page
(www.ludat.lth.se/~dat92oma/x-files.html)

*The X-Files* Interactive Web Site
(www.magicnet.net/~dpb/x/)

Sue Bannion's X-File Sim Page
(www.mainelink.net/~pbreshe/Sue'sPage.html)

Mulder's X-Files Page
(www.maths.tcd.ie/~sj/tv/xfiles.html)

Gillian Anderson Fan Nation
(www.mcs.net/~romp/gafn.html)

Fwiffo's X-Files
(www.mind.net/fwiffo/xphile.html)

The Truth Is Out There
(www.mindspring.com/~torgo/xfiles.html)

I Want To Believe
(www.msms.doe.k12.ms.us/~kreynold/x-files.html)
The History of *The X-Files*, Ten Signs That You May
    Be An X-Phile

JYW's Domian—*The X-Files*
(www.naples.net/~nfn04195/x-files.html)

X file Title page
(www.nbn.com/people/eddieb/believe.html)

John's X-Files Word Search Puzzle
(www.Neosoft.com/~jrpotter/xfiles.html)

Terminal X
(www.NeoSoft.com/sbanks/xfiles/xfiles.html)

X-Files Video Preview Page
(www.netaxs.com/~hager/x-files.html)
QuickTime Movie Previews

Stuart Johnston's X-Files Homepage
(www.netlink.co.uk/users/smj/x-files/welcome.html)

3 Use your Imagination: The Exfiles
(www.netwit.net.au/~juz/exfiles/)
Pictures and icons

MorningStar's X-Files Links
(www.ny.frontiercomm.net/~freeprny/xfiles.html)

*The X-Files* and UFO related homepage
(www.osir.hihm.no/~tomes/)

Stephen Whitfield's Home Page
(www.ozemail.aust.com/~stphw/)

tSOMi:X Files
(www.ozemail.com.au/~tsomi/)

*The X-Files* Episode Guide
(www.pacificnet.net/~fidodido/xfiles-ep-guide.html)

X-Files Sites
(www.pacifier.com/~bcornel/xfiles.html)

Mitch Pileggi Estrogen Brigade Home Page (MPEB)
(www.pe.net/~mpeb/mpeb.html)

The IDDG X-Files Page
(www.perspective.com/ziggyb/www/x-files.html)

Trust No One!
(www.pipex.net/people/chuck/sf/x-files/)
UK info, mailing lists, fan club addresses

Stephen's Home Page
(www.pipex.net/people/stephene/xfiles/)

*The X-Files:* Operation Paperclip -
(www.powerup.com.au/~tcook/xfiles.html)

I Want To Believe (Gavin Suntop's X-Files Home Page)
(www.prairienet.org/~phyber/files.html)

Moira's X-Files Page
(www.presence.co.uk/moira/)

X-Files Feedback
(www.printnet.com/xRecipes/RecipeMenu.html)

*The X-Files* Sound Page
(www.prograde.com/xfiles/)

Shannon Carver's X-FILES Page
(www.psinet.net.au/~geochem/xfiles.html)

X-Files
(www.public.iastate.edu/~sbwright/xfiles.html)

X-Files Tag Lines
(www.publiccom.com/x/)

Vikram's X-Files Page—Trust No One
(www.radix.net/~pant/xfiles/)

WSFA X-Files home page
(www.rahul.net/dalvenja/wsfa/index.html)

Zig's GATB Home Page
(www.rahul.net/ziggyb/gatb.html)
The Gillian Anderson Testosterone Brigade

Maroubra Beach: X-Files
(www.real.net.au/magazines/tharunka/X-Files.html)

SALON Reviews: Making of a half-minute master-
  piece
(www.salon1999.com/06/reviews/titles.html)
How they made the opening theme to *The X-Files.*

The Kewlest X-Files Page!!!
(www.safari.net/~inigo/Kewl.htm)

Authorized Personnel Only (SciFi Web)
(www.scifiweb.com/XFiles/)

*The X-Files:* the truth is out there...
 (www.servtech.com/public/ptnmring/nate/x-files.html)

x
(www.slip.net/~ridia/x/soon.html)
Requires Macromedia's Shockwave plug-in for
  Netscape 2.0.

X-Files
(www.snafu.de/~murray/xf/index.html)

Duchovnik's Home Page
(www.squidge.org/duchovniks/index.shtml)

X-Files Links
(www.srv.net/people/vandal/xfiles.html)

Bureau of Federal Investigation—X-Files Division
(www.ssc.com/~roland/x-files/x-files.html)

Danny's X-Files Home Page
(www.stack.urc.tue.nl/~danny/x-files.html)

*The X-Files*
(www.studentaccess.com/hp/bigdave/x-files.htm)

Mel's X-Files Homepage
(www.students.uiuc.edu/~boysen/xfiles.html)

X-Files Photo Gallery
(www.syix.com/danafoxx/xfiles.html)

*The X-Files* Episode Guide (UK)
(www.tardis.ed.ac.uk/~dave/guides/X-Files/index.html)

*The X-Files* Resource Page At Port's Place
(www.tasis.com/tasis/students/Portman/x-files.htm)

Xfiles Links
(www.tiac.net/users/bpaq/1.2/xfiles.html)

My X-Files Page
(www.tiac.net/users/gbpeter/indexx.html)

Office of the Assistant Director (a.k.a. The Mitch
  Pileggi Home Page)
(www.tpoint.net/~rmayhall/main.html)

X-Files@Rudy's
(www.transport.com/~rudeman/filex.html)

Jason's X-Files Page
(www.trend1.com/~kraffert/xfiles/)

RobotMan Meets *The X-Files*
(www.tripleg.com.au:80/staff/scott/robotman/)
A cartoon strip parody.

The Unofficial X Files Page
(www.tripod.com/~KBlake/XFiles/)

X-Files Unite!
(www.ualberta.ca/~gpadlows/xfiles.html)

RYYT's X-Files Page
(www.ualberta.ca/~wtsang/xf/xf.html)

The Popcorn Stopover. X-Files Resource Center
(www.ucalgary.ca/~chwchang/xfilespg.htm)

Welcome to My Garden
(www.ultranet.com/~krs/newpage.htm)

The RAT Files
(www.ultranet.com/~mrlou/FBI.html)
Parody

The alt.tv.x-files World Wide Web Home Page
(www.uml.edu/~ccashman/x-files/x-files.html)
FAQ's

Paul Go's Homepage
(www.undergrad.math.uwaterloo.ca:80/~pgo/)

Akte_X
(www.uni-karlsruhe.de/~ukeq/xfiles.html)
German...

*The X-Files*
(www.unix-ag.uni-kl.de/~kleinhen/xfiles/x-files.html)

Vancouver Village—X Marks The Spot
(www.vanmag.com/9408/XMarks.html)
Vancouver Locales

Adam's X-Files Headquarters
(www.voicenet.com/~jkraynak/ak/x-files/)
Images and sounds

X-Files: The Truth Is Here!
(www.wam.umd.edu/~kris/)

Whispers of Truth
(www.wam.umd.edu/~magister/X-Files.html)

The X Files
(www.wco.com/~trustno1/xfiles.html)

Duchovniks Homepage
(www.webcom.com/~walterh/)

The Unofficial X-Files Resource Guide
(www.webcom.com/rybock/xfiles.html)

Ground Zero—The Ultimate X-Files Page
(www.webcom.com/writer/outworld/xfiles.html)

The Artist formerly known as Cybervox's X-Files Page
(www.webpress.net/~ferrell/x/index.html)

Kabrina's X-Files Pages
(www.westol.com/~grady12/xfiles.htm)

Cause Cult Activities—X-Files
(www.world.net/~gcause/xfiles.html)

Josh's X-Files Webpage
(www.wpi.edu/~joshb/x-files.html)

*The X-Files*
(www.yournet.com/~cthomaso/x-files.htm)

*The X-Files* UK
(www.zynet.co.uk:8001/simon/x-files/)

Strongheart's Unofficial X-Files Archive
(www-sc.ucssc.indiana.edu/~ewacker/index.html)
Sounds, pictures, links

*The X-Files* Top Ten Lists
(www2.netdoor.com/~lainh/XFtopten.html)

Scott's X-Files Page
(www2.newriver.net/zemerick/xfiles.html)
Links, pictures, sounds

The X-Files Fan Fiction Home Page
(www2.utep.edu/~trevizo/xff.html)

WWW Publications/Interviews

The Lone Gunman
(www.sky.co.uk/one/xfiles/)
"The Weekly Newsletter of Paranormal Phenomena
 and Conspiracy Theory"

Lone GunMen Conspiracy Brigade Homepage
 (www.geocities.com/Heartland/1121/)
"The Journal of Conspiracy and Paranoia"

The X' Chronicles
(vaxxine.com/xchronicles)
North America's only monthly parapsychology newspaper.

Science Fiction Weekly
(www.scifiweekly.com/sfw/)
Online magazine about all things Science Fiction

XFiC
(www.speakeasy.org/~xfic/)
"The First X-Files Publication on the Web"

## WWW Merchandise

The Official X-Files WWW Site
(www.TheX-Files.com/)
Official X-Files Site, includes merchandise for sale

arT-Vision apparel: X-files
(www.art-vision.com/thexfile.shtml)
X-Files apparel

Braggers Apparel
(pie.vancouver.bc.ca/x-files/main.htm)
Merchandise from The X-Files, Friends, Melrose Place,
 The Simpsons, ER

Conspiracy X
(www.wizvax.net/nmegames/conspiracyx/X.html)
A role playing game based loosely on The X-Files

Fantasy Emporium
(www.atw.fullfeed.com/~fantasy/index.html)
Sci-Fi and fantasy TV and movie merchandise

The Internet Book Shop—X-Files
(www.bookshop.co.uk/XFILES/)
X-Files books and assorted literature

HyperLight Enmterprises X-Files Catalog
(www.iceonline.com/home/roxanneb/www/xfl.html)
X-Files merchandise, including T-shirts, hats, books,
 and more!

Image Entertainment—The X-Files LaserDiscs
(www.image-
 entertainment.com/preview/feb96/0893685.htm)
Information about the release of The X-Files episodes
 on laserdisc.

Movie Madness Merchandise
(www.moviemadness.com)
Merchandise for movies and TV shows such as: Star
 Trek, Babylon 5, Batman, Lion King, Pocahontas,
 James Bond, Friends, Seinfeld, Frasier, E.R., Mad
 About You, and, of course, The X-Files.

Sky One X-Gear
(www.sky.co.uk/shop/xshop/index.html)
X-Files merchandise from the U.K.

"Songs In The Key of X"
(www.wbr.com/x-files)
The tracklisting and music samples from the album
 containing music inspired by The X-Files.

Starland—The Science Fiction Superstore
(www.dash.com/netro/sho/starland.html)
Lots of sci-fi merchandise, including, of course, The X-
 Files.

Starland Australia: X-Files Merchandise
(enterprise.powerup.com.au/~starland/xfiles.htm)
X-Files merchandise from down under.

The X-Store
(www.ishops.com/xstore/)
"The Largest Selection of X-Files Merchandise on the
    Net!"

## Usenet Newsgroups

The availability of these newsgroups depends on your
news server.

alt.tv.x-files
This is the biggie.

alt.tv.x-files.creative
Stories written by the fans for the fans.

alt.binaries.x-files
Postings of graphics, sound files, and video clips for
    downloading

uk.media.tv.sf.x-files
Devoted to X-Philes in the U.K.

aus.tv.x-files
Devoted to X-Philes in Australia.

## Mailing Lists

Primary mailing list:
majordomo@chaos.taylored.com
"subscribe X-FILES" in the message body

Discussion List:
LISTPROC@lists.pipex.com
"SUBSCRIBE X-FILES [YOUR NAME]" in the mes-
    sage body

U.K. mailing list:
listproc@uel.ac.uk
"subscribe X-FILES [YOUR NAME]" in the message
    body

Australian mailing list:
majordomo@blender.digital.com.au
"SUBSCRIBE X FILES [YOUR NAME]" in the mes-
    sage body

German mailing list:
listserv@stargate.pfalz.de
"subscribe xf-de" in the message body

# ADDRESSES

E-mail can be sent to comment on the show at: the_xfiles@delphi.com. If you wish to write in appreciation/support of the show, the addresses are:

Chris Carter
Executive Producer
"The X-Files"
Fox Broadcasting Company
10201 W. Pico Blvd.
Los Angeles, CA 90064
USA

Jonathan Littman
Vice President of Current Programming
Fox Broadcasting Company
P.O. Box 900
Beverly Hills, CA 90123
USA

Note: The different addresses for Fox are more or less interchangable. Regardless of the one you use, your correspondence should reach its destination.

Also, Charles Kennedy, the Vice President of Programming Research at Fox has obtained an Internet address where you can send e-mail to comment on their shows, please include "X-Files" in your subject to help them sort the mail. His address is: foxnet@delphi.com.

Fan mail for either David or Gillian can be sent to:

David/Gillian
c/o X-Files Production Office
Building 10
110-555 Brooks Bank Blvd.
North Vancouver, B.C.
Canada V7J 3S5

Creation Entertainment has established the Official X-Files Fan Club with cooperation from Fox. They can be contacted at the following address:

The Official X-Files Fan Club
411 North Central Ave
Suite 300
Glendale, CA 91203

## INTERVIEWS

Anderson, Gillian. Interview by David Letterman. "The Late Show with David Letterman." CBS, 19 February 1996.

———. "Breakfast Time, fX," 19 May 1995.

———. CBC, 13 April 1995.

———. Interview by Regis Philbin and Kathie Lee Gifford. "The Regis and Kathy Lee Show." 18 May 1995.

———. IRC Chat, 16 September 1995.

———. "Midday."

———. "The Screen Actors Guild Awards Ceremony." February 1996.

———. "The Steve Wright People's Show" in the UK, 3 June 1995.

Carter, Chris. "Live on Delphi." 23 September 1993.

———. America Online, 7 March 1995.

———. C|net, 12 August 1995.

———. Compuserve, late 1995.

———. "The Gabereau Show." CBC Radio, 5 May 1995.

———. KROQ radio show.

———. "The Martin-Molloy Show." 22 November 1995.

Carter, Chris, David Duchovny, and Gillian Anderson. "Sci Fi Buzz." Sci Fi Channel, 19 February 1995.

Duchovny, David. Interview by Jay Leno. "The Tonight Show." NBC, June 1995 and 26 February 1996.

———. Interview by David Letterman. "The Late Show with David Letterman." CBS, July 1996.

———. Interview by Dian Anderson. "The Truth: The Audio Files: An Audio Interview with David Duchovny."

———. Interview by Lisa Canning. "Entertainment Tonight." March 1996.

———. Interview by Rosie O'Donnell. "The Rosie O'Donnell Show." July 1996.

———. Interview by Tom Snyder. "The Late Late Show with Tom Snyder." CBS, 7 July 1995.

———. "Q&A: David Duchovny." E! Online, August 1996.

Duchovny, David, and Gillian Anderson. "Live on Delphi," 14 January 1995.

Morgan, Glen. IRC, 14 December 1994.

———. "AOL Chat." America Online, Spring 1994.

Rabwin, Paul. "AOL Chat," America Online, February 1995.

Interview with X-Files fans. CBC Radio, 20 March 1995.

## NEWSPAPERS

"Busy 'X-Files' Star Juggles Marriage, Baby, Job." *San Luis Obispo Telegram Tribune*, 9 November 1994.

*Constitution*, 24 December 1995.

"Convention Too Weird for All but Fans." *San Diego Union-Tribune*, 12 June 1995.

"File This Sci-Fi Thriller's Magic Formula Under 'X.'" *Los Angeles Times*, 1 December 1994.

"File Under Cerebral: Duchovny." *Boston Globe*, 1 January 1995.

"The Fox and the Skeptic." *Sun Telegraph TV Extra*, 17 September 1995.

*Gannet News Service*, 21 June 1994.

"Inside The X-Files." *Seattle Times*, 13 May 1996.

"Its Originality Marks 'X-Files' as a Cult Above." *San Jose Mercury News*, 22 July 1995.

*Los Angeles Times*, 28 October 1994.

"The Private Side of The X-files Quiet Star." *Washington Post*, 16 June 1996.

"Q & A: Online and On Record with 'X-Files' Mastermind." *The Atlanta Journal & Sacramento Bee*, 9 October 1994.

*San Francisco Chronicle*, 5 September 1993.

"Scully Appeals to Actress: Gillian Anderson Gained Respect for TV, *Philadelphia Inquirer*.

"Secret of X-Files' Success Is Its Secrets." *Vancouver Sun*, 25 July 1996.

*Sydney Morning Herald*, January 1996.

"The Secret's Out." *Sun-Herald Now*, 17 September 1995.

*Washington Times*, 6 January 1994.

"X-Files: The New Generation," *Sacramento Bee*, 21 July 1995.

"The X-Files Continues Plots of the Paranormal." *Orlando Sentinel*, 16 July 1995.

"'X-Files' Creator Treasures Cult Label." *Houston Chronicle*, July 1995.

"X-Files' New Mom Anderson Has No Time for X-haustion." *USA Today*.

"X Marks the File." *Brisbane Sunday Mail*, April/May 1995.

## MAGAZINES

"After a Season in the Sun, The X-Files Returns to Its Roots." *Cinescape*, August 1995.

"Agent of Fortune." *Movieline*, June 1995.

"An Appointment with Dr. Scully." *Wrapped in Plastic*, 12 October 1994.

"Big Time." *Cinescape*, April 1995.

"Closing The X-Files." *Saturday Night*, December 1995.

"A Conversation with The X-Files' Creator Chris Carter." *Sci Fi Entertainment*, December 1994.

"Creepshow." *Details*, February 1995.

"David Duchovny of the X-Files." *Yearling: UK TV Listings Guide*.

"David Hughes Investigates Chris Carter." *The Xfiles*, 1 June 1995.

"Devil's Advocate." *Starlog*, 20 May 1994.

*Extra*, April 14 1995.

"FBI Judas." *Cinefantastique*, October 1995.

"For the Next Generation, It's 'X-Files.'" *EE Times*, 4 March 1996.

"The File on The X-Files." *The Oregonian*, 3 February 1995.

"From Punk Rock to the Paranormal, This 'X-Files' Co-Star Lives on the Edge." *US*, March 1996.

"Gillian Anderson: Future Fantastic" *Yearling: UK TV Listings Guide*.

"I Miss My Aussie Love Letters." *Woman's Day*, 9 October 1995.

"An Interview with Tooms." *Purity Control 3*.

"Making Contact with David Duchovny." *Playgirl*, April 1995.

"Occult Leader." *Who*, March 1995.

*Omni*, December 1994.

*Prydonian Renegade*, June 1994.

"Secret Agent Man." *US*, May 1995.

"Seventeen Questions David Duchovny." *Seventeen*, December 1995.

"Sneak a Peek in The Unanswered X-Files." *The West*, 25 November 1995.

"Sounds of Silence." *Starlog Explorer*, 7 June 1995.

"Supernatural SuXXess." *B.C. Woman*, October 1995.

"Truth Decays: Sleuths After Reagan." *Millennium Pop*, Summer 1994.

"The Truth is Out There." *Sci Fi Channel*.

"WIP Conspires to Re-Examine The X-Files" *Wrapped in Plastic*, 12 October 1994.

"X-Appeal." *The Observer*, 9 July 1995.

"The X-Files Christmas Commercials." *Wrapped in Plastic*, 12 October 1994.

"The X-Files Exposed." *Who*, 19 June 1995.

"X-FILES TRAVAG*illian Anderson*NZA." *TV Hits*, March 1996.

"X-Files Uncovered." *Rolling Stone*, 16 May 1996.

"X-Files Uncovered." *Rolling Stone* (Australian Edition), 1995.

"X-Files Star's X-Rated Role." *New Weekly*, 30 October 1995.

"X-Heroine." *Starlog*, April 1995.

"The X-Man." *Details*, October 1995.

"XPloring the Paranormal." *Producer*, December 1994.

"X Symbol." *Starlog*, June 1995.

"X Symbol." *VanMag*.

"The Unfrozen North." *Time*, 7 November 1994.

"Vision Quest." *Reel West*.

*Who*, October 1995

*Woman's Day*, 15 July 1996.

### Entertainment Weekly

"Alien Nation." 8 October 1993.

"EW Fall TV Preview—The X-Files." 13 September 1996.

"Fall TV Preview." 17 September 1993.

"A Genuine Eccentric." 12 December 1994.

"A Gillian to One." 9 February 1996.
"No Wonder He's Called Fox." 29 September 1995.
"Sci Fi Invades Hollywood." 2 December 1994.
"Veneration X." No. 355, 29 November 1996: 24-58.
"X-Appeal." 18 March 1994.
"The X-Files Exposed." 10 March 1995.
"X Marks What's Hot." 21 January 1994.
"X-Tra Credits: A Guide to The X-Files Supporting
    Players." 9 February 1996.

## TV Guide

"Gillian & Dave's Xcellent Adventure." 11 March 1995.
"20 Things You Need to Know About The X-Files" 6-12
    April 1996.
"X-Files 101." 6 May 1995.

## People

Chris Carter article.
"People's 50 Most Beautiful of 1996." 1996.

"Senior G-Man." 6 May 1996.
"X-Ellence." 9 October 1995.

## People Online

"Cut to the Chase and See Who Came in FIFTH, THIRD,
    and FIRST!" 1996.
9 October 1995.
People Online Profiles: David Duchovny
"People Online's 10 Most Beautiful."

## TV Week

"Deep Throat Talks." 4 November 1995.
"Gillian's Alien Past." 7 October 1995.
"Gillian in Alien Territory." 25 May 1996.
"Gillian's X-Generation Baby." 13 May 1995.
"Just Your Average Paranormal Guy." 2 September
    1995.
"No Rest for the Eerie." 3 June 1995.
"The X-Factor." 11 February 1995.

# INDEX

## A

*Abduction: Human Encounters with Aliens*, effect on Carter's
    writings, 5
Abortion clinic violence investigations, 150–151
Academy Group, as consultant to *Millennium*, 42
Actors, in *X-Files*, 12–14
Alien abductions, 36
Alien conspiracies, 123–125
Alien spacecraft, 45
Alien visitors, 158–197
    federal regulations and, 174–175
Ambrose, Willa, 103–104
Ames, Aldrich, investigation, 150
"Anasazi," 26, 34, 108
"Anasazi" episode, 106–107
Anderson, Gillian, 6, 13–14, 20–21, 23–24, 26–27, 29–33,
    35–36
    critical reviews, 57
    evolution of Scully role, 57–58
    favorite three episodes, 117
    first casting as Scully, 54–56
    Golden Globe Award, 57
    life as an actress, 55–59
    Pileggi and, 76
    pregnancy, 30–32, 98
    profile, 53–54
    relationship to Duchovny, 56, 58
Anderson, Piper, 56, 115
"Apocrypha" episode, 115–116
"Ascension" episode, 97–97
"Aubrey" episode, 100
Australia, reaction in, 22
"Avatar" episode, 118

## B

Bach, Frank, 45
Bartley, John, 10
*Baywatch Nights*, 36
Beghe, Jason, 64, 93
"Beyond the Sea" episode, 90
Black, Catherine, 41–42
Black, Frank, 41–42
"The Blessing Way" episode, 108
Bletcher, Bob, 43
"Blood" episode, 96–97
Books, *X-Files*-based, 133–138
"Born Again" episode, 93
Bounty Hunter, 34, 102
Bowman, Rob, 10
Braidwood, Tom, profile, 82
*The Brothers Karamazov*, 119

*The Burning Zone*, 36
Byers, 81

## C

"The Calusari" episode, 104–105
Carter, Christopher
    address, 217
    casting of Anderson, 54–55
    Cigarette-Smoking Man and, 79–80
    conspiracies, 123–125
    critical reviews and, 7
    David Duchovny and, 67
    Dori Pearson and, 4, 6
    fans and, 131
    favorite three episodes, 117
    first season, 20–25
    fourth season, 39–40
    inspiration from earlier shows, 47–50
    *Millennium* and, 41–43
    *Night Stalker* and, 3–4, 6, 12, 23
    personal background, 3–7
    second season, 26–33
    surfing, 3–4, 7
    third season and, 35–38
    third series possibility, 43
Casting, *X-Files*, 53–82
CBS, *X-Files* clone, 44
CD-ROM, *X-Files*, 138–139
The Centre, 44
Chernobyl, 27
Chung, Jose, 117
Cigarette-Smoking Man, 20, 26, 34–35, 78–80, 119, 121, 125
    Carter and, 79–80
    Krycek and, 76
    Mulder and, 73
Close, Eric, 45–46
"Clyde Bruckman's Final Repose" episode, 110
cockroaches, 113–114
Cointelpro, 201–202
"Colony" episode, 102
Comic books, *X-Files*, 134–138
"Conduit" episode, 86
Conspiracies. *See also* Covert actions, Political repression
    alien and government, 123–125
    government and political, related books, 198–200
    magazines and newsletters, 203
Conventions, for fans, 130–131

Covert actions
    books about, 200–202
    magazines and newsletters, 203
Criminal Justice Information Services, 155
Critical reviews
    Carter and, 7
    first season, 21–22, 87
    second season, 28–30, 96
    third season, 35–36, 111

## D

*Danger Man* series, 49
"Darkness Falls" episode, 92–93
*Dark Skies*, 36, 45–46
Davis, William B., 20
    profile, 78–80
"Deep Throat," 20–21, 125
    first episode, 85
    first season, 85, 87
    profile, 80–81
Deprenyl, 99–100
"Die Hand Die Verletzt" episode, 100–101
Director's Guild award nomination, 111
DNA technology, FBI, 153
"Dod Kalm" episode, 104
"D.P.O." episode, 109
Drug crime index, FBI, 153–154
Drug intelligence squads, FBI, 153
"Duane Barry" episode, 97
Duchovny, David, 6, 13–14, 20–21, 23–24, 30, 36, 54, 62–71
    early acting, 64
    favorite three episodes, 117
    Lea and, 78
    movies, 65–66
    and newfound success, 67–69
    other shows, 70
    Pileggi and, 76
    profile, 62–64, 70–71
    relationship to Anderson, 56, 58
    role as Mulder, 66–69
    *Twin Peaks*, 65
Dupree, Warren James, 90–91

## E

"E.B.E." episode, 21, 91–92
Emmy awards and nominations, 7, 22, 36, 87, 96, 111
"End Game" episode, 102
Episode guide, 16–17

Episode locations, 103
"The Erlenmeyer Flask," 21, 94
Eurisko computer, 87
"Eve" episode, 89
Eve 6,7,8, 89
"Excelsius Dei" episode, 99–100
Extraterrestrials, federal regulations and, 174–175
*EZ Streets*, 44

## F

"Fallen Angel" episode, 88–89
Fans of *X-Files*, 35–36, 129–132
    address of official club, 217
    conventions, 130–131
    female, 130
    online, 129–130
    Web sites, 206–215
FBI
    abortion clinic violence, 150–151
    Aldrich Ames investigation, 150
    brief history, 145–146
    criminal justice information services, 155
    Critical Incident Response Group, 156
    current hiring activity, 147–148
    Disaster Squad, 153
    DNA technology, 153
    drug records index, 153–154
    El Paso Intelligence Center, 154
    equal employment opportunity, 148
    fact sheet, 149
    frequently asked questions, 151
    gang violence investigations, 152
    headquarters, offices at, 146–147
    Integrated Automated Fingerprint Identification System, 153
    international activities, 154
    investigative responsibilities and programs, 148–150
    laboratory division, 154–155
    major recent investigations, 150–152
    mission statement, 145
    National Center for the Analysis of Violent Crime, 156–157
    National Crime Information Center, 153
    National Drug Intelligence Center, 154
    operational assistance, 156–157
    Operation Disconnect, 150
    Operation Horsecollar, 152
    organizational structure, 146
    personnel and employment, 147

Polar Cap investigation, 150
    Project Forge, 152
    Rapid Start Team, 152
    recruitment, 152
    Regional Drug Intelligence Squads, 153
    Rodney King investigation, 151–152
    Safe Streets Program, 152
    training programs, 155–156
    Uniform Crime Reports, 153
"Fearful Symmetry" episode, 103
"F. Emasculata" episode, 105
Fenig, Max, 88–89
"The Field Where I Died" episode, 121
Film, *X-Files* as potential, 40
Film locations, all episodes, 103
Fingerprint Identification System, FBI, 153
"Fire" episode, 89–90
"Firewalker" episode, 99
First season
    episode summaries, 85–94
    rankings and awards, 87
Fourth Season
    episode summaries, 120–122
Fox, and fourth season, 39
Fox executives, 30
Freedman, Jerrold, 10–11
"Fresh Bones" episode, 101–102
Frohike, 82
*The Fugitive*, 47–48

## G

Gallagher, Megan, 42
Gang violence, FBI, 152
Gauthier, Dave, 18
"Genderbender" episode, 90
Gerard, Lieutenant, 47
"Ghost in the Machine" episode, 86–87
*Goblins*, 133
Golden Globe Awards, 7, 28–29, 36, 96, 111
    to Gillian Anderson, 57
Goodwin, R.W., 9–10, 15
Gordon, Howard, 9–11, 37
Government conspiracies, 26–27, 35, 37, 123–125
Government information, access to, 203–204
Grays, UFOs, 158–159
"The Grid," 17
"Grotesque" episode, 114
*Ground Zero*, 133

## H

Haglund, Dean, 82
Haiti, 101–102
Hardin, Jerry, 20–21
    profile, 80–81
Harwood, Bruce, profile, 81
"Hell Money" episode, 117
Henriksen, Lance, 41–42
"Herrenvolk" episode, 120
Hispanic Man, 34
Hodge, 87
Holvey, Charlie, 104–105
"Home" episode, 120
"The Host" episode, 95–96
"Humbug" episode, 104

## I

"Ice" episode, 87–88
Internet, 21–22, 29–30, 35
The Invaders, 47–48
Iran-Contragate, 201
"Irresistible" episode, 100

## J

Jack of All Trades, 44–45
Janssen, David, 47
"The Jersey Devil" episode, 86
Jokebook, X-Files, 140–142
"Jose Chung's 'From Outer Space'" episode, 117–118
Julia Has Two Lovers, 66

## K

Kalifornia, 66
Kendrick, Sally, 89
Kennedy, John F., 45
Kennedy, Mario Mark, In Memoriam, 109
Kimble, Richard, 47
Klotz, Clyde, 56
Kolchak: The Night Stalker. See Night Stalker
Kousakis, 42
Krycek, Alex, 26, 34, 97, 115–116, 125
    profile, 76–78

## L

Langly, 82
Languages, non-English, spoken in X-Files, 115

"Lazarus" episode, 90–91
Lea, Nicholas, profile, 76–78
"The List" episode, 110
"Little Green Men" episode, 95
Locations, episode, 103
Loengard, John, 45–46
Lone Gunmen, 21, 81–82, 106, 125

## M

Mack, John, effect on X-Files, 5, 36
Mackey, Paula, 129
Magazine, X-Files, 138
Mark, Stephen, 42
Martin, Quinn, 47–48
McGavin, Darren, 28
McGoohan, Patrick, 48–50
Millennium, 39, 41–46
    reviews, 41–43
Millennium Group, 41–42
"Miracle Man" episode, 92
Morgan, Darin, 11, 37
Morgan, Glen, 37, 97
Morgan, James, 30
Morrow, B.J., 100
Movie, X-Files as potential, 40
Mulder, Fox, 5–6, 13–14, 20–21, 23–24, 26–27, 31–35, 40
    agent profile, 73–74
    FBI career history, 72–73
    first-season episode summaries, 85–94
    fourth-season episode summaries, 120–122
    second-season episode summaries, 95–107
    third-season episode summaries, 108–119
Mulder, Samantha, 102
Mulderisms, 33
Murdoch, Rupert, 20
Murray, Graeme, 10, 18
Music, 12, 139
"Musings of a Cigarette-Smoking Man" episode, 121

## N

National Center for Analysis of Violent Crime, 156–157
National Crime Information Center 2000, 153
Native Americans, 92
Navajos, 26, 106–108
NBC, X-Files clone, 44–46
Newton, Kim, 11
Nielsen ratings, 28, 35, 87, 96
Night Stalker, 3–4, 6, 12, 23, 28, 47

1993–1994 episodes, 85–94
1994–1995 episodes, 95–107
1995–1996 episodes, 108–119
1996–1997 episodes, 120–122
"Nisei" episode, 112
Nonfiction books, *X-Files*-based, 134
Norway, 104
Novels, *X-Files*, 133–134
Number Six, *Secret Agent* series, 49
Nutter, David, 10, 42

**O**

"One Breath" episode, 98–99
Online fans, 129–130
Operation Disconnect, FBI, 150
Operation Horsecollar, FBI, 152
"Oubliette" episode, 112
"Our Town" episode, 106

**P**

Paddock, Phyllis, H. 101
"Paper Clip" episode, 109
"Paper Hearts" episode, 122
Pearson, Dori, 4, 6
Pfaster, Donny, 100
Pileggi, Mitch, 21
    profile, 75–76
"Piper Maru" episode, 115
Pittson, Todd, 16–17
*Playing God*, 70
Polar Cap, FBI investigation, 150
Political repression, books and magazines, 202–203
Powers, Francis Gary, 45
*The Pretender*, 44
*The Prisoner*, 47–50
Producer's Guild, 36
    award nomination, 111
Production, of X-Files, 14–18
*Profiler*, 44–45
The Project, 123–124
Project Forge, FBI, 152
"Pusher" episode, 116
Pythons, 101

**Q**

Quality Awards, 36, 96, 111
"Quagmire" episode, 118

**R**

Rabwin, Paul, 12, 15
*The Rapture*, Duchovny and, 65–66
"Red Museum" episode, 99
Reeves, Perrey, 65, 70
"Revelations" episode, 113
Rodney King investigation, 151–152
"Roland" episode, 94
Roswell incident, report on, 175–184
    CIA data, 178
    FBI data, 178
Roth, Peter, 43
*Ruins*, 133–134
Russell, Jarod, 44

**S**

Samantha, 26
"Sanguinarium" episode, 121
Sayers, Kimberly, 45–46
Science fiction, Carter and, 3
Screen Actor's Guild, 36
    award, 111
Scully, Dana, 5–6, 13–14, 20–21, 23–24, 29–35, 40
    FBI career history, 60
    first-season episode summaries, 85–94
    fourth-season episode summaries, 120–122
    parents of, 20
    profile, 60–61
    second-season episode summaries, 95–107
    third-season episode summaries, 108–119
Season Four
    episode summaries, 120–122
Season One
    episode summaries, 85–94
    rankings and awards, 87
Season Three
    episode summaries, 108–119
    rankings and awards, 111
Season Two
    episode summaries, 95–107
    rankings and awards, 96
*Secret Agent* series, 49
"The Secrets of the *X-Files*" retrospective, 106, 118
"731" episode, 112–113
"Shadows" episode, 86
"Shapes" episode, 92
Shibian, John, 11
"Shy" episode, 110–111

*Sighting*, UFO documentary series, 8–9
Skinner, Sharon, 118
Skinner, Walter S., 21, 75–76, 115, 125
"Sleepless" episode, 97
Smith, Jeremiah, 34, 119
Smitrovich, Bill, 43
Snow, Mark, 12, 42
"Soft Light" episode, 105–106
"Space" episode, 88
Special effects, 18–19
Spinney, Doug, 92–93
Spotnitz, Frank, 11–12
"Squeeze" episode, 85–86
Surfing, Carter and, 3–4, 7
SWAT teams, FBI, 156
"Syzygy" episode, 114

**T**

"Talitha Cumi" episode, 119
Tarantino, Quentin, 39–40
"Teliko" episode, 120–121
"Terma" episode, 122
"Teso Dos Bichos" episode, 116
Thinnes, Roy, appearance in *X-Files*, 48
Third Season
    episode summaries, 108–119
    rankings and awards, 111
"3" episode, 98
"Tooms" episode, 93
"Tunguska" episode, 122
*Twilight Zone*, 47
*Twin Peaks*, Duchovny and, 65

**U**

UFOs, 8–9, 21–22, 85–86, 88–89, 91, 117
    Air Force definition, 166–167
    federal regulations and, 174–175
    global evidence, 167–169
    glossary of investigative organizations and studies,
        159–166
    Grays, 158–159
    historical evidence, 167–169
    human fear and hostility, 171–172
    investigations into, 158–197
    organizations, detailed list, 185–197
    scientific hypotheses, 172–173
    sightings, cataloging of, 167
    theories behind, 169–171

United Kingdom, reaction in, 22
"Unruhe" episode, 121
Usenet newsgroups, 216

**V**

Vincent, David, 48
Vlaming, Jeff, 11–12

**W**

"The Walk" episode, 111–112
Walker, Ally, 44
Walsh, J.T., 45
Walters, Sam, 44–45
Ward, Megan, 45–46
"War of the Coprophages" episode, 113–114
The Web, 131–132
    fan sites, 206–216
    mailing lists, 217
    *X-File* merchandise, 215–216
    *X-File* sites, 206–215
Weiss, Michael T., 44
Well-Manicured Man, 34
Wells, Larry, In Memoriam, 108
"Wetwired" episode, 118–119
*Whirlwind*, 133
Williams, Steven, 26
    profile, 81
Willis, Jack, agent, 90–91
Wissner, Gary, 42
Wong, James, 30, 37
Writer's Guild Awards, 96
Wunstorf, Peter, 42

**X**

"X," 26, 81
*X-Files*
    actors in, 12–14
    addresses, 217
    birth of, 4–9
    books, 133–138
    casting, 53–82
    CD-ROM, 138–139
    comic books, 134–138
    conventions for fans, 130–131
    creative team behind, 9–12
    critical reviews, 21–22, 28–30
    early problems behind show, 23–24

*X-Files*, continued

    episode guide, 16–17

    fans, 129–132, 217

    fan Web sites, 206–215

    first season, 20–25

    first-season episode summaries, 85–94

    first-season rankings and awards, 87

    fourth season, 39–40

    fourth-season episode summaries, 120–122

    Friday time-slot change, 39

    guns used in, 98

    jokebook, 140–142

    locations of all episodes, 103

    magazine, 138

    movie possibilities, 40

    music, 139

    network disagreements and, 24

    novels inspired by, 133–134

    precursors, 47–50

    pilot, 85

    production of, 14–18

    special effects, 18–19

    second-season, 26–33

    second-season episode summaries, 95–107

    second-season rankings and awards, 96

    third season, 34–38

    third-season changes, 37–38

    third-season episode summaries, 108–119

    third-season rankings and awards, 111

    third-season problems, 36–37

    third-series possibilities, 43

    top ten lines never heard on, 141–142

    Web, 131–132, 206–215

    Web merchandise, 215–216

X-Philes. *See* Fans


**Y**

"Young at Heart" episode, 91


**Z**

Zabel, Bryce, 45–46